Public Administration, Governance and Globalization

Volume 22

Series Editor

Ali Farazmand, School of Public Administration, Florida Atlantic University, Fort Lauderdale, FL, USA

The aim of Public Administration, Governance and Globalization (PAGG) is to publish primary research and theoretical contributions as well as practical reports on fieldwork to help advance the knowledge and understanding about public, nonprofit, private, and nongovernmental organizations and institutions. The governance, administration, and management of these organizations at local, national, regional, and international levels will be discussed in the context of this age of rapid change and globalization. This series on public management offers original materials that contribute to our better understanding of the critical issues as well as routine processes of governance and public administration, now more than ever because of the intricate forces of globalization that affect almost every nation-states and their policy choices at all jurisdictions across the world. The series covers a wide range of topics that address the key issues of interest to scholars, educators, practitioners, and policymakers in public administration capacities around the globe. Books in the series could be research monographs, edited volumes, textbooks, reference volumes or handbooks.

More information about this series at http://www.springer.com/series/8656

Frank Bezzina • Emanuel Camilleri
Vincent Marmarà

Public Service Reforms in a Small Island State

The Case of Malta

 Springer

Frank Bezzina
Faculty of Economics, Management
and Accountancy
University of Malta
Msida, Malta

Emanuel Camilleri
Faculty of Economics, Management
and Accountancy
University of Malta
Msida, Malta

Vincent Marmarà
Faculty of Economics, Management
and Accountancy
University of Malta
Msida, Malta

A publication of the Institute for the Public Services Research Arm, Malta.

ISSN 2512-2347   ISSN 2512-2363   (electronic)
Public Administration, Governance and Globalization
ISBN 978-3-030-74359-8   ISBN 978-3-030-74357-4   (eBook)
https://doi.org/10.1007/978-3-030-74357-4

This Springer imprint is published by the registered company Springer Nature Switzerland AG
The registered company address is: Gewerbestrasse 11, 6330 Cham, Switzerland

*This book is dedicated to all Maltese
Public Servants, past, present and future.*

Foreword

The compendium of analysis in this volume is both a stock take of what the Malta Public Service has achieved during the past 7 years of renewal and a case study of change within the public service of a small island state. Last year, 2020, was promised as the year during which we would evaluate all the measures put in place in the preceding seven years to improve the public service, consolidate what we had achieved and devise the next phase of renewal for the five years starting in 2022. In the following pages, the renewal process is not viewed in isolation but put in context of both the revamp of the islands' economy and its effect on society, and the historical aspect of a public service which traces its roots back to the rule of the Knights of St John and, subsequently, the period of British rule during which we acquired its administrative model.

In 2013, the Public Service was a political issue in Malta as the burden of bureaucracy was a heavy one for both individuals and businesses. This had not been the intention of the reforms which the Public Service underwent in the eighties and nineties. After the 1987 change in government, a reform of the Public Service had been initiated with the aim of making it perform better and be more accountable. This reform followed on from the equally massive 1974 grades restructuring exercise. A report commissioned to analyse what went amiss in the 1987 reform ended up highlighting the same issues which were meant to have been solved. I believe that the latter reform dealt almost entirely with structures and accountability issues of the Public Service believing, perhaps, that these would result in a better delivery of services.

The years following the 1987 general election were dominated by an endeavour in various sectors to reinvigorate the public sector, touching on salary structures and career paths of the various specialisations, which ultimately led to a myriad of sectoral agreements which took a good 5 years to conclude. During that time, as the employees' representative, I was heavily involved in the reform. Weeks upon end were characterised by meetings and negotiations which led to tens of industrial agreements, the vast majority of which bear my signature for the employees' side. Indeed, these agreements still provide the framework of the current grades within the Public Service. That was also the time which brought about the first code of ethics and the first Public Administration Act. Investment in technology gathered momentum. This reform was propelled from the very top through a Cabinet Committee, chaired by the Prime Minister himself, which kept itself abreast and sanctioned or otherwise every move, each measure and every industrial agreement. Yet in 2013, 25 years later, the Public Service ended up on the agenda of that election year, which brought about a change in government.

The new administration in 2013 signalled a new beginning in the very first few days in office with the appointment of new permanent secretaries. There was strong criticism of this bold move, which still surfaces from time to time, but it was the right decision to stir the water, enforce the message that change was urgently needed, show the will to bring about change, and ensure ultimately, as promised, that the public service would no longer weigh down on peoples' lives. There was no other way. Unlike the previous reform, the much-needed changes and renewals were not going to be managed by the Cabinet or any politicians. The public service itself had to map out its vision, its objectives and the accompanying plans to make that vision come true. I am convinced that the new credence which emerged within the Public Service was widely diffused within the ranks and their clients. The analysis and statistics give a clear indication of the sense of belonging of employees and of the appreciation of the general public – 64% of respondents being aware of the renewal undertaken and the endeavours made to provide a better and deeper service for its clients.

When I was appointed Head of the Public Service, I wanted a clear picture of the state of affairs within the Service. I did not want to rely solely on the knowledge and experiences gained from the previous reform and restructuring exercise. Neither did I rest only on the experience gained through my many years in various government departments, the wider public sector or my brief stint within the private sector (also in close liaison with the Public Service). More than being dependent on my assessments or on solutions which, in my opinion, were there waiting to be taken on board, I wanted a clear picture of the then state of affairs. What emerged were a lack of leadership skills and an inverted delegation of authority, with much-needed decisions overstaying their time window in in-trays. The Public Service was aloof of its clients' needs and operating in silos. During my first meeting with heads of departments, I spelt out these deficiencies and, above all, highlighted that there was a veritable void from the position the Public Service was in and its ultimate destination, and how this void would be bridged. Back then, some had a field day pointing fingers, saying that I had no faith in the top echelons. Actually, it was the other way round: I was convinced that we would set a new course and I mapped out what laid ahead of us.

The same problems I listed were also singled out in a comprehensive 2011 report, submitted to the previous administration, which went through the 1987 reform and what it had led to 25 years later. Regretfully, the report sat idle; it was left languishing under wraps. I got to know about the report by chance, but it displayed the fact that, although commissioned, it was never given its due, indicating that by then the will to change the public service had fizzled out.

At the time, only a handful of us believed that this inertia could be overcome but we did manage change and in a relatively short period of time, when one takes into consideration the huge amount of work which needed to be put in and the measures that had to be introduced. Change did happen and the public mood towards the Service has changed. Today the number of believers has increased dramatically.

The client was to be our focus without exception. It was to be the *raison d'être* of any renewal - a Public Service designed to meet our clients' expectations. It follows that the concept of providing a service had to be radicalised in a way as to put our clients in the front seat of the renewal process. This meant a thorough change in the delivery of services. Instead of our client having to hop from one department or desk to another, services were designed for easy access. Our heavily advertised vision was for a public service available to anyone from anywhere 24/7 all year round. This became a reality thanks to the unprecedented investment made in technology and hundreds of online services and the one-stop shops which sprouted up all over Malta, providing hundreds of services under one roof.

Service quality was to stop being subjective rhetoric interpreted according to one's whim. Instead, we gave service quality a measurable definition. By implication, if it can be measured, it can be managed and therefore improved. Our credo was and still is that the client should always and without exception be the focus of renewal in the public service. To achieve this, we had to also invest in our employees.

We embarked on two major projects: the Institute for the Public Services (IPS), which was set up to link training and development with the aims and vision, and servizz.gov, a government agency which came into being 5 years ago to manage and provide, through all means of communication, almost all our public services. Hence, we embarked on one unitary strategy having clear objectives aimed at achieving one vision.

Both IPS and servizz.gov were set up with strategic partners. The need and urgency for a change in limited time led us to join up with those who already had the experience and capacity to help us attain our goals. The IPS was set up with the full partnership of both the country's leading tertiary institutions: the University of Malta and the Malta College of Arts, Science and Technology. The Public Service embraced an opportunity to work hand in hand with these institutions to develop courses, both fruitful and needed, while, at the same time, opening new career opportunities for those students who enrolled. Subsequently, the Public Service enhanced itself to provide its workforce with the necessary skills. Together with these academic institutions, IPS draws up and provides courses which open wider opportunities to hundreds of public officers. Thousands of others are offered the means to progress in their career through personal development and training. The IPS objectives are crystal clear and couple up with other objectives set to attain the Public Service's vision. Prior to IPS coming into being, there were two other attempts to diffuse training among public officers. Both functioned independently of any holistic strategy, hence delivering limited benefits for the Service. The IPS seeks to enhance the leadership skills within the Service and deal with the lack of graduates in the various structures of the Public Service. Above all, we established the need for employees to persist with their personal development to keep themselves up to speed and provide a better service to clients. IPS has also established its research arm which aims to analyse, monitor and absorb information and make recommendations as to how we could continue to enhance the Public Service and where we had gone amiss. The analysis in this study came forth thanks to this IPS function which I consider as crucial.

The same goes for servizz.gov. We did not work in isolation; rather, we required a strategic partner with experience in service delivery. After a transparent public process, a strategic partner was selected and, with the experience of the latter, and management input from our part, we elevated servizz.gov to become the main channel through which all public services were delivered, in one stop shops in the various regions, its online equivalent via mServices, freephone and social media. Statistics show that the service delivery and its quality is very much appreciated by end users, with the freephone facility being probably the most used in the country with calls nearly reaching the one million mark in 2020. Moreover the servizz.gov's online portal has contributed in placing Malta's eGovernment in the top position in the European Union, ranking with a score of 97% for the year 2020 (eGovernment Benchmark Report, 2020). Through servizz.gov, we moved beyond past practices where a client had, by necessity, to rely on multiple government departments – probably even multiple desks within the same department – to receive the service they needed. An online search is what is now required. If one still prefers a more traditional approach, a visit to a one-stop shop is all that is needed.

One appreciates the fact that all this would not have been possible were it not for unprecedented investment in technology, which in the past 5 years exceeded €150 million. For a country such as ours, this investment is indeed substantial: an investment that is ongoing, and which proved its worth during the Covid-19 pandemic; an investment by means of which databases can be synchronised, information dissemination streamlined, work facilitated, and bureaucratic tangles and processes reduced; an investment that has been tailored in such a way that we obtain the best that technology offers.

We defined service quality, which relies on four pillars for guidance. These are: the voice of the clients – the clients' expectations – and therefore continuous contact with them, through whichever means, to truly listen to their needs and, indeed, exceed their expectations. From this, the second pillar emerges, which is service design and policy design. From this follows the delivery of the service itself –the marketing aspect. The fourth pillar, equally important, is accountability. In every action that was carried out, every measure taken, every process that was streamlined – accountability could never be bargained with. Accountability has been a priority insofar as the client is at the centre of the entire renewal processes. Emphasis was put on quality that is measurable. Thus, the mystery shopping systems that are independently carried out serve as an invaluable tool to measure quality, and even accountability. Permanent internal structures were also set up to monitor quality, since these provide a sense of permanence to ensure that whatever is achieved is maintained, managed, and improved.

We wanted accountability to become routine through a number of measures which we launched and which were intended to convey the message that accountability has to be at the forefront of all that we do. I believe that, through this, people who need to access services, trust us and will do so in confidence. This is where statistics indicate that we need to strive more. Although trust in our public administration has soared and stands 12 percentage points higher than the median in the European Union (Euro barometer, August 2020), people are still not entirely convinced that we are accountable enough.

Four annual publications, that now form part of the Public Service's calendar, are a solid step in this direction. Simplification measures that we enacted under this renewal process are now fully laid out, literally, in print. The same was done when it comes to measures announced in the government's annual Budget. We continuously plan for every year, monitor the implementation of every measure, and provide an account of its state of implementation. We can therefore proudly state that, since the origination of these publications, we implemented in excess of 900 simplification measures, and more than 1600 Budget measures.

At the very outset of my appointment, I requested to be provided with the recommendations that had been made in the preceding 5 years – both those emanating from the Auditor General's annual report, and other recommendations that were the result of commissions set up ad hoc or investigations. Hundreds of recommendations had been made, but few had been implemented. Year in, year out the National Audit Office lamented in its reports that its recommendations had gone unheeded and had to be repeated in each yearly succeeding report. We have changed course. The Public Service is now reacting to the National Audit Office's annual report and other reports. We have recently been doing the same with regards to the annual report and recommendations put forward by the Ombudsman. The implementation of recommendations is planned and monitored during the whole process, at the end of which internal auditing is carried out to ensure implementation. We have progressed to a point where the Auditor General expresses satisfaction that 80% of his recommendations are now being implemented. Moreover we now have entities being labelled as a good example by the Auditor himself and whereby no recommendations are proposed. This is exactly where we envisaged to arrive. We are now at a stage where 98% of cases brought before the Ombudsman end positively. Structures were put in place to cater for these publications but, above all, to provide permanence to the changes introduced through planning processes which are also used to implement Key Performance Indicators.

People are at the heart of the Public Service. Covid-19 provided the best evidence to this statement. The Malta Public Service has always found itself at the core of all that has been enacted in our country in recent history, and this is a sure sign of its flexibility. The pandemic has further shown that part of the culture embedded within the Public Service is the will to provide service even in dire circumstances. Government employees, similar to what other countries witnessed, had to vacate offices to continue their work from home, in what was an overnight transition that nonetheless did not adversely impact the services rendered. Circumstances were such that they could have seriously presented a threat to the smooth running of the Public Service, but we managed to transform them into an opportunity to investigate and come up with solutions to strengthen the role of technology, means of communication, and experiences of government employees in all grades. We were already working on a pilot project to further strengthen and make remote working as widely available as possible some 6 months before Covid-19 struck. The pandemic spurred us to quicken the pace and enter a transition period that will enable us to implement systems that will aid us towards reaching this goal. It has also strengthened our resolve to make do with far less paper. By means of remote working, we will not only have achieved a novel, and better, work-life balance, but also have addressed issues of workspace and environmental concerns while delivering even more communication and flexibility in the way in which we operate.

I believe that the investment in people made in the past 7 years has laid the groundwork for us to build further on what we have already implemented. This enabled us to modulate centralised structures to create the People and Standards Division (P&SD) to encapsulate a sole strategy that incorporates both the persons who deliver the service and the quality of the service rendered. We are talking about a strategy that addresses a multitude of factors – be they the necessary personnel training and development (through IPS), managing regulations and industrial relations, to coming up with initiatives tuned to bringing out the best elements within public officers. Schemes such as IDEA provide an opportunity for employees and the public to suggest improvements/innovations to the services rendered, above all when accounting for the fact that, oftentimes, the best ideas are born on the ground. Any strategy, not least this broad one, needs to be principles-based.

This principles-based approach is evident in the recruitment processes, which, without the need of gender quotas, have yielded the highest percentage of women in decision-making positions within the public service ever. (This stands at 46%, which compares favourably with the percentage in several European States and exceeds a number of them too. In 2013, the number of women in decision-making positions in the Public Service was only 21%). This was accompanied by greater flexibility between the grade structures and enhancing the well-being of employees. Moreover, P&SD took under its wing the structures that safeguard and guarantee high quality public services. The concept is one that amalgamates all the elements that make up people management, development, services rendered, and the quality of that same service. It is only thus that a synergetic cycle between people, their training and development, and the quality of their services, can be achieved. One element thus fits in, and is dependent upon the other, for a service of excellence to be delivered. In the context of these structures, then, mystery shopping, the safeguarding of service quality, and the smooth running of initiatives such as the quality label which recognises the efforts of departments and entities, and the officials who strive towards the highest-level of public service they render, can truly be enacted successfully.

The present socio-economic and wider geopolitical contexts which our country finds itself in, allow very little headroom for shortcomings on our part. The analysis which is being presented is the promise that 2020 was the year in which we would take a careful look back and analyse all actions without letting a quarter of a century slip by before taking stock. Only thus can we assure ourselves of still being in time to rectify our shortcomings, whilst further amplifying the effect of our achievements. We are, essentially, self-evaluating after just 7 years and, by the looks of it, we have not fared badly at all. There is, undoubtedly, the capability, and I must say the willingness, to proceed to the second phase of renewal.

The trust shown by government in the Public Service to update and renew itself has had positive results. It also renewed the sense of trust in public officers themselves. It resulted in a new Public Administration Act, which was put forth by the Public Service itself, along with a new appointment process for Permanent Secretaries to involve only the Principal Permanent Secretary and the Public Service Commission with appointments being made by the President of Malta. Moreover, we are doing more with less: in 2012, public sector employees accounted for 27% of the country's workforce; this has now gone down to 21% (May 2020).

The strategy for the coming 5 years starting in 2022 needs to incorporate all elements: people – how to identify the best elements within the Public Service and how we are to continue providing the optimal environments so that people contribute further; service provision – the quest for excellence that truly streamlines and provides a better quality of life to citizens whilst being the engine that spurs a more resilient economy that really and truly distributes the wealth that is created; technology –an invaluable resource, not least through artificial intelligence, which is not without its ethical and accountability concerns. All these disparate factors must in turn lead to higher levels of trust in the public administration.

We must keep building trust in the Public Service. This compendium of analysis has amply demonstrated that the latter has the capacity to renew and update itself to meet users' needs and expectations. This trust should then be returned in the form of a service of excellence that breeds a better living for all those who reside in our country.

Mario Cutajar
Head of the Maltese Public Service

Valletta, Malta

Preface

This book presented a tremendous challenge for the authors and editorial team to document the various Public Service reforms that have occurred in Malta over the centuries. Never in the history of the Maltese Public Service has anyone had the courage, vision and foresight to undertake the task of documenting in detail the diverse Public Service reforms that have been implemented over such a long period of time, particularly in the last 7 years. This book is important because there is a tendency to undervalue and take for granted the work that is conducted by public servants.

The book starts with the era of the Knights of St John in 1530 and examines the Public Service reforms that took place leading to Malta's Independence in 1964, which shall be referred to as 'The beginning'. It then explores the developments that took place to modernise the Maltese public service administration and management in the post independence period, which shall be referred to as 'The turning point'. The book then specifically focuses on the last 7 years. The reason this approach has been adopted is to ensure that the legacy inherited from the Maltese Public Service since 1530 to the modern era is sufficiently documented to give cognisance to the work conducted by our Public Service predecessors. For this reason, documenting this Public Service reforms legacy is viewed as being important since it has not been undertaken previously to such an extent. As it was stated previously, the book then focuses on the last 7 years based on considerable research in the form of official documented evidence and primary research in the form of surveys. These surveys were administered amongst government employees in the Maltese Public Service and the general public as customers and recipients of the various government services. This allowed the researchers to determine the impact of the various reforms on the Public Service's internal environment by linking psychological contract breach to attitudinal outcomes and also to ascertain the societal influence of the various Public Service reforms by conducting cross-sectional surveys and the examination of certain aspects of the mass media. Hence, the extensive secondary and primary research methods adopted are an important feature of this book.

The research indicates that the Maltese Public Service is best described as being in state of continuous transition. This is not to say that the road along the achievement of Public Service reforms has been easy. It must be recognised that there is an in-bred resistance to change in most organisations and the Maltese Public Service is not an exception. However, an important aspect that the research has revealed is that the Maltese Public Service has always, throughout various eras, faced up to the various challenges and succeeded in making Malta a better place for its citizens. Equally important is that Public Service reforms are highly dependent on the leadership attitude of those leading the Public Service at any particular point in time. Here, reference is being made to the vision of the Maltese Prime Minister and the Cabinet, and the vision and driving force of the Head of the Public Service and his management team. This management team is not just restricted to Permanent Secretaries, since the Public Service consists of many layers of management. However, having a visionary leadership at the top ensures a cascading effect on the various levels of management. Moreover, vision determines whether the reforms are merely incremental or transformational. The research shows that many of the documented Maltese Public Service reforms, particularly those of the last 7 years have been transformational.

The above provides the basic reason why it was considered important for this book to be written. It is imperative for this book to be seen as a starting point in documenting the legacy of the Maltese Public Service reforms that have been implemented to this point in time. It is hoped that the documentation of the Maltese Public Service reforms does not stop with this book but will continue with further publications in the future, so that the legacy of the work being conducted by public servants is not lost.

Msida, Malta   Frank Bezzina
                                                                           Emanuel Camilleri
                                                                            Vincent Marmarà

About This Book

The hallmark of this book is the extensive amount of research into the Maltese Public Service reforms. Thus, this book makes fundamental reading for University students undertaking courses in Public Policy, and Public Administration and Management.

The book consists of four parts. The *first part* is titled: Public Service Reform Historical Background and consists of two chapters. The titles of these two chapters are 'Historical Background of the Maltese Public Service Administration and Management "The Beginning"' and 'Historical Background of the Maltese Public Service Administration and Management "The Turning Point"', respectively. The first chapter specifically addresses the Maltese Public Service reforms in the distant past by examining the various reforms during three primary eras, namely: (a) The Knights (1530–1798); (b) The French occupation (1798–1800); and (c) British rule (1800–1964). The second chapter considers the Maltese Public Service reforms in the recent past that includes: (a) The post-Independence era (1964–1971); (b) The 1970s social reform era until 1979; (c) The reforms of the 1980s; and (d) The road to EU membership and its immediate aftermath (1990-March 2013).The research methodology varies with the period under study. Hence, the Maltese Public Service reforms in the distant past are based on secondary data using available historical documents and diverse literature; whereas the Public Service reforms in the recent past are also based on secondary data using mainly official government documents, particularly the Government Financial Estimates for the years spanning 1964 to 2008.

The *second part* of the book is titled: Public Service Reform: "The Best of Times" and consists of five chapters that examine in detail the various Maltese Public Service reforms that were implemented these past 7 years, since March 2013. These Public Service reforms have been segmented into five categories, with each reform category representing an individual chapter. Hence, the five chapters within the second part are the following:

(a) Chapter 3: Transparency and Accountability Public Service Reforms
(b) Chapter 4: Civil Service Systems and HRM Public Service Reforms

(c) Chapter 5: Service Delivery and Digitalisation Reforms
(d) Chapter 6: Organisation and Management Government Reforms
(e) Chapter 7: Policy Making, Coordination and Implementation Government Reforms

The research methodology for the second part of the book was based upon secondary research using official government publications and legislative initiatives undertaken during this period. The research has identified and documented 93 particular Maltese Public Service reforms, and if the recent reforms related to the Venice Commission were to be included, the reforms would number over 100. As stated previously, the Public Service reforms were classified into five categories. The first four categories (Chaps. 3, 4, 5, and 6) accounted for about 16% of the reforms each and the fifth category (Chap. 7) accounted for about 36% of the reforms. The research also revealed that most of the Public Service reforms were implemented in 2014, 2016 and 2017 (18–19% each). These three particular years (2014, 2016 and 2017) account for about 55% of all the implemented Maltese Public Service reforms.

The *third part* of the book is titled: Public Service Reform: The Research and consists of four chapters, namely:

(a) Chapter 8: Organisational Impact of Public Service Reforms: Assessing the Internal Impact
(b) Chapter 9: Societal Impact of Public Service Reforms
(c) Chapter 10: Fair Deals in the Maltese Public Service: Linking Psychological Contract Breach to Attitudinal Outcomes
(d) Chapter 11: Societal Impact of Public Service Reforms: Cross-Sectional Surveys and the Media

These chapters address two specific aspects, namely, Maltese Public Service reforms in the '*Present*' by focusing on the reforms of the past 7 years (starting March 2013), and Maltese Public Service reforms in the '*Immediate Present*' that deal with the current organisational internal and external impact of Public Service reforms (i.e. the now status). The research methodology for these chapters is mainly based upon primary research through cross-sectional surveys of government employees and the general public to ascertain their perceptions regarding the various Maltese Public Service reform measures. This provided a snapshot of the Public Service today in terms of various variables in relation to a range of implement reforms. The objective of Chap. 8 is to describe the institutional reforms through the neo-institutional theory that provides a theoretical perspective of organisational behaviour that is influenced by other organisations, the key stakeholders, and the wider economic and social force. This chapter illustrates that Public Service strategies, structures and managerial actions are intimately related with each other to produce a broad and complex picture of a continuous Public Service reform process.

On the other hand, Chap. 9 critically reviews the literature concerning a number of ideas, methodologies and instruments that have been used to understand the societal impact of public services and Public Service reform; or that can be associated with related potential. These are namely the Net Promoter Score (NPS), Service Quality (SERVQUAL), Customer Satisfaction (CSAT) and trust in Public Services.

Chapter 10 is based upon a study that was conducted in a double wave of change, related to the internal and external environment of the Maltese Public Service. The research examined the psychological contract aspect that is defined as the perceived exchange relationship between employer and employee. This provided the researchers with a strong index of the quality and state of the employment relationship. People in an employment relationship construe an exchange process whereby they expect specific returns for service provisions. Indeed, the basis of the employment relationship is often captured in a social exchange relationship and the employment relationship is best seen through the lens of social exchange theory. This study did not demonstrate the expected negative reactions and pessimistic ratings by employees. More precisely, the research findings suggest that the Maltese Public Service is coping and managing well the various changes being implemented as it becomes more people-oriented and embraces a new corporate identity. Furthermore, the study demonstrates how specific factors are associated to others and hence require leadership skills and abilities to steer people management in ways that ensure the maintenance of effective working relationships and therefore positive attitudes at work.

Chapter 11 concluded the third part of the book with a very detailed study of the societal impact of the Maltese Public Service reforms, using cross-sectional surveys and examining the material, such as the letters to Editors related to mass media (i.e. newspapers) over a lengthy period of years. Thus, the chapter provides a deeper understanding of the success and the degree of impact attained by the introduction and implementation of a variety of public services. It also contributed towards suggesting improvements that may be made to enhance the user-oriented relationship by focusing on the particular needs of each demographic sector. Chapter 11 is based upon original research and is organised into two major segments. The first segment evaluates the methodology and other demographic considerations; and the second segment analyses and discusses the research findings. On the whole, respondents confirm the government's success in introducing, facilitating and implementing various measures and initiatives. This had a positive resulting effect on community level service provision and, consequently, quality of life on all fronts.

The *fourth part* of the book and is titled: Public Service Reform: The Future and consists of one chapter, namely: 'Public Service Reform: The Future (A New Beginning)'. Hence, this chapter is about the future and is based upon extensive literature research regarding the future developing trends related to worldwide Public Service reforms. In this regard, information technology plays a critical part as an essential change agent. It provides opportunities for governments to initiate Public Service reforms, with the intention of improving the living standards of its citizens, in a variety of sectors. This chapter illustrates that Public Service reforms and the systems they generate as a platform for service delivery are full of challenges and require sustained commitment from all levels of the Public Service. It also demonstrated that Public Service employees need to look for new ways of implementing change by taking advantage of the opportunities that technology provides in the day-to-day operations of government and its decision-making process. However, the most important factor for change to occur is to have strong, capable and, above all, visionary leadership. Visionary leaders see things and make sense of them and are not afraid to take the plunge.

Contents

Contributors

Chapter Contributors

Dr Emanuel Camilleri   Visiting Senior Lecturer, Faculty of Economics, Management & Accountancy, University of Malta – Chapters 1, 2 and 12

Dr Vincent Marmarà Lecturer, Faculty of Economics, Management & Accountancy, University of Malta – Chapters 3, 5, 7 and 11

Dr Colin Borg Academic Registrar, Office of the Registrar and Lecturer, Faculty of Economics, Management & Accountancy, University of Malta – Chapters 3, 4, 5, 6 and 8

Professor Frank Bezzina Pro-Rector for International Development and Quality Assurance and Dean of the Faculty of Economics, Management & Accountancy, University of Malta – Chapters 4, 6, 7 and 10

Dr Maria Brown Lecturer, Faculty of Education, University of Malta – Chapter 9

Professor Vincent Cassar Faculty of Economics, Management & Accountancy, University of Malta – Chapter 10

Book Review
Professor Godfrey Pirotta, Professor of Government and Policy Studies, University of Malta

Editorial Board
Professor Frank Bezzina; Dr Emanuel Camilleri; and Dr Vincent Marmarà

List of Figures

List of Tables

Part I
Public Service Reform Historical Background

The focus of this book is on the Maltese public service reforms under the new Labour administration commencing in 2013 to the 2020 that has seen the advancement of public service administration and management that can only be described as transformational or revolutionary. Never, in the history of the Maltese public service, have so many changes taken place in such a short period of time, which have had considerable positive impact on the lives of so many citizens in Malta, particularly minority groups. However, before focusing on the fundamental objective of the book, it is appropriate to provide a historical background of the way the Maltese public service administration and management has developed over the years prior to 2013. The intention of the first two chapters is to set the broad scene by: (a) providing a general and brief description of the historical environment of public service administration and management in Malta covering the period from the sovereignty of the Knights of St John to Malta's Independence in 1964, which shall be referred to as "The beginning"; and (b) the developments that took place to modernise public service administration and management in the post-independence period, which shall be referred to as "The turning point."

Moreover, the author of Part I of this book does not claim to be a historian but is a public service management practitioner whose career extends for over half a century in various senior public service posts in Malta and abroad. The research method that shall be used, particularly for the first chapter, due to the scarcity of literature about specific public service administration and management during the period of influence of the Knights of St John (1530–1798), will be similar to the scientific method of interpolation and extrapolation, namely to use known facts as the starting point from which to draw inferences or conclusions about something that may be unknown or unclear. Our ancestors or occupiers, depending on the view one takes, have left behind them an abounding legacy that can be seen and, in most cases, still enjoyed today. By examining this rich legacy, one may appreciate and contemplate the plausible public service administration and management organisational environment in place at the time this legacy was created, in projects such as the construction of the bastions and fortifications, amongst many others.

Chapter 1
Historical Background of the Maltese Public Service Administration and Management (The Beginning)

"Every new beginning comes from some other beginning's end."

Seneca, Roman Stoic philosopher (c. 4 BC–AD 65)

The Maltese Public Service has a long and honourable history. Hence, it is appropriate to commence this text with a historical background of this praiseworthy organisation. The Maltese islands in some form or other always had a public service organisation as its administrative basis. However, a new and illustrious era resulted under the rule of the Knights of the Order of Saint John (1530–1798). During this period, we find evidence of various administrative policies that are normally associated with modern society, such as defence, fiscal, monetary, urban planning, health, and education and culture. The French ousted the Knights in 1798. The French turned out to be very poor administrators, and in fact were unable to feed themselves, let alone the Maltese population of about 100,000 inhabitants at that time. This triggered a public uprising in 1798. By January 1799, evidence of starvation and its consequences were manifest as a way of life, with the number of deaths amounting to 20% of the population. Hence, French rule lasted a mere 2 years until 1800. British rule in Malta commenced in 1800, initially as a British Protectorate, until Malta gained its independence in 1964. Thus, every governing administration that ruled the Maltese Islands had an institution, such as the public service to support it in formulating and implementing its policies. For centuries, Malta's foreign rulers assigned the islands a fortress role on the strength of its highly strategic location in the Mediterranean. Thus, Maltese public administration and management was highly geared towards supporting the established naval and military bases. Maltese public administration and management was in continuous transition under different foreign rulers with their consequent diverse national and management cultures.

F. Bezzina et al., *Public Service Reforms in a Small Island State*,
Public Administration, Governance and Globalization 22,
https://doi.org/10.1007/978-3-030-74357-4_1

1.1   Introduction

It is best to describe Maltese public administration and management as being in state of continuous transition. Having said this, it is also recognised that there is an in-bred resistance to change in most organisations, but such organisations are expected to face up to new and sometimes demanding challenges. These challenges, in the case of public administration and management organisations, include responding to recessions, moving towards independence, act in response to pressures for economic diversification, international diplomacy, pandemics and even war. Public administration is a characteristic that is applicable to all nations, no matter what their respective system of government. However, nations differ from each other in the way they may apply public administration at various levels, namely, central, intermediate, and local. It is this relationship between the different levels of government within a nation, which creates a major concern for public administration. According to Rabin et al. (1989), public administration is viewed as a distinct profession that consists of exceedingly trained administrative, executive, or directive categories of public employees, often referred to as public servants or civil servants. Moreover, the civil service makes use of a wide range of employees that perform various types of services, such as general administrative support; technical and professional services support; and other services such as the military, the judiciary, and the police. Public administration is often viewed as consisting of members who have the responsibility for formulating (or drafting) the policies and programs of governments, specifically in such areas as planning, organising, directing, coordinating, and controlling of government operations. Hence, a civil servant is an individual directly employed in the administration of the internal affairs of the state, and whose role and status is not political, ministerial, military, or involved with law enforcement.

The Maltese Public Service consists of ministries and departments of Government and provides the core of the Government's administrative machinery, but this machinery has other components. These include statutory authorities and agencies, Government foundations, and companies with a Government majority shareholding. These entities are part of the so-called public sector but not the Public Service. Public Service employees are referred to as public officers and as Government employees. The latter term reflects the fact that Public Service employees work in ministries and departments, which are integral components of the Government of Malta. By contrast, entities in the wider public sector have their own legal personality that is separate from that of the Government. This means that, while such entities belong to the Government, they are not part of the Government. Accordingly, their employees are not Government employees. Having said this, certain attributes are common to all civil services. For instance, senior civil servants are considered as the professional advisers to those that formulate state policy. Civil servants in every country are expected to assist, advice, and alert those responsible for formulating state policy and once the policy has been approved, to provide the support and organisation for implementing it. Hence, the political members of the executive, that is, the members who have been elected or appointed to give political direction to government, are ultimately responsible for the policy decisions. However, public administration is somewhat different from public management. As explained above, the focus of public administration is on formulating public policies and coordinating their implementation. On the other hand, public management involves conducting managerial activities in public organisations. Administration involves carrying out one's assigned duties with ultimate responsibility resting on the executive. By contrast, management involves having one's own sphere of responsibility and carrying responsibility for decisions taken within that sphere. Therefore, public managers carry out the managerial operations of public organisations. In other words, public management has the objective of improving the quality and efficiency of the services delivered by public organisations. Hence, it is management's responsibility to ensure that the framework for policy success is both efficiently and effectively conducted. Therefore, public management is mainly related to planning and taking action, whilst public administration is concerned with the application of policies that prescribe how management employees should act.

1.1.1 Incremental and Transformational Change

Additionally, the impact that public service policies may have once implemented is what many refer to as incremental or transformational affect. Incremental change is sometimes referred to as first order change that does not modify the organisation's core activities in a drastic way. Hence, incremental change is a process that modifies, adjusts, or refines what is currently taking place, with no major disruption to the organisation's normal activities. Incremental change may be characterised by the following aspects: (a) change mainly occurs through a series of small steps; (b) change may occur over a long period of time, but no particular phase in the process uses an excessive quantity of time; and (c) the change process and associated phases are often (but not always) planned beforehand. At times, incremental changes happen as part of a natural process to resolve concerns as they occur without too much disruption and do not provoke resistance to the change. An example of incremental change is implementing a new information application process to improve the organisation's efficiency. By using an incremental method, Public Service administration can reduce the risk and is able to concentrate on trying to enhance the processes that are already in place, rather than going back to the drawing board. Incremental change is a satisfactory approach when the concerns are related to the functionality within a government. Thus, incremental change is a more stable approach to resolving concerns that do not require an erratic change and facilitate sustainable and continuous improvement.

On the other hand, transformational change (also known as radical change) refers to a significant modification of the organisation's fundamental practices, services, products, culture, and values. Transformational change happens when: (a) there is a large difference between what is currently taking place and what is planned to take place in the future; (b) there is a revolutionary variation of the organisation's underlying processes; and (c) there is a shift toward a totally innovative organisational position (Gass, 2010). Transformational change demands that government administration halts a current practice and creates a completely new and better way of undertaking various functions, thus radically improving government management. Hence, depending on the status and exigency of a concern, transformational change can be an acceptable policy to foster immediate change. However, transformational change can provoke resistance to change due to the uncertainty created and may even impair how citizens view their government's actions. Transformational change in the public service is risky but it may also provide great benefits (Gaille, 2018). It is risky because there may be obstacles to speedy change due to disagreements between various stakeholders who have different agendas when involved in decision-making. For instance, reforms related to social issues, such as IVF treatment, divorce, and LGBT rights, particularly where minority groups are involved. For significant issues such as climate change, citizens are insistent that politicians recognise the urgency and take radical action by introducing innovative policies that protects the human destruction of the environment.

Hence, the state of transition of the Maltese public administration and management that was previously referred to at the beginning of the introductory paragraph varies from incremental to transformational change. In the sections that follow, the reader will be able to discern the type of changes that have occurred in Malta in the various periods by the different public service administrators, starting with the Knights of the Order of Saint John in 1530; followed by the French occupation under Napoleon in 1798; to be succeeded by Malta being placed under the protection of the British Crown in 1800 and under British Rule in 1814; and finally the gaining of independence from the United Kingdom as a Constitutional Monarchy in 1964.

1.2 Public Administration and Management Under the Knights of the Order of St John (1530–1798)

Literature about public administration and management during the period when the Knights of the Order of St John were in Malta are not readily available. However, their legacy is well documented and is everywhere to be seen. The wide range of physical and non-physical achievements of the Knights of the Order of St John had an impact on the Maltese society during their period and is even felt to this very day. The magnitude of their efforts implies that the Knights were supported in their undertakings by a well-structured organisation. It is argued that this well-structured organisation is comparable or equivalent to what today is known as the Public Service. It is also maintained that this public service organisation was managed by Heads of Departments that were indigenous Maltese. This is a unique characteristic of the development of the Maltese Public Service, even under British rule. The knights of Malta had established an extensive system of administration which survived not only well into the British period but some of its institutions, like the Monte di Pietà, a health system and the University of Malta, remain with us today. We also find the remnants of their terminology within state institutions, such as the Almoner, still present.

When the Knights of the Order of St John of Jerusalem were offered Malta as their new headquarters by Charles V of Spain in 1524, they sent a Commission to investigate. They concluded that "Malta was little more than a rock inadequately covered with soil, its main products being cotton, honey and cumin, which were exchanged for corn" (Pirotta, 1996, p.29–31). Hence, at first, they were disappointed because they viewed Malta as little more than a rock in the middle of the Mediterranean. However, this turned out to be the Island's major strength! They soon realized that Malta was at the centre of the Mediterranean shipping lanes, and thus they began to appreciate its strategic value. Before the Knights arrived, the Maltese Islands were under the influence of the feudal laws. The Maltese needed a change, as they were being robbed of their few belongings and taxed on the few crops they produced by the foreign lords.

The Knights established a form of government that was heavily dependent on customs duties, income from privateering and huge sums of money earned from properties scattered all over Europe. The Knights brought with them administrative order and embarked on a massive infrastructural investment programme that required an efficient public administration and management. It is likely that the public services at that time focused on defensive fortifications and supporting infrastructure, such as roads, water supply, sewage and agriculture (food supply). One of the first steps that the Knights took upon taking control of the Maltese Islands was to conduct the first census in 1530 that showed a population of circa 15,000 people in Malta and 4659 in Gozo (Vassallo, 1997). The Maltese public administration and management evolved around the militaristic strategic value of the Islands. This development appears to have been the birth of contemporary public administration and management in Malta. The discussion below will be based on historical records for various societal sectors, to illustrate how the Maltese public administration and management developed within each sector, many of which are regarded as transformational developments.

1.2.1 Defence Policy

In 1531 AD, the Knights staged their first attacks from their new naval base in Malta, forming part of a Christian fleet under the command of Admiral Andrea Doria in attacks on the Turks at Modone, on the Ottoman fort at Coronna and, in 1535, on Tunis (Ware Allen, 2006, p.1). Between 1530–1798 the Knights built Fort Chambray; Fort Manoel; Fort Ricasoli; Fort St Angelo; Fort St Elmo; Fort St Michael; Fort San Salvator; and Fort Tigne. Furthermore, between 1605 and 1720 the Knights built 31 watch towers on the coastal parameter of the Maltese Islands.

As well as these activities, for centuries, the Order of Malta's fleet took part in the most important manoeuvres in the Mediterranean against the Ottoman fleet and against North African pirates (SMHO, 2020). It is argued that the massive structures related to the fortification of Malta would have required the support of a well-disciplined public service having robust project management and procurement procedures to be in place. It is also reasonable to assume that the building structure of the magnitude undertaken by the Knights also required the support of strict building regulations.

1.2.2   Fiscal Policy: Customs

When the Knights took over in 1530, Malta was a country with a clear comparative disadvantage in agriculture and was heavily dependent on imports from abroad. Nevertheless, the knights continued a system whereby the government was heavily dependent on a tax on imported grains and established a grain monopoly, which bought wheat and sold it at a fixed price (Sharp, 2009). According to Persson (1999) it was common in preindustrial times, for the government of Malta to be heavily involved in the regulation of the supply of grain, and under the Knights the Grandmaster really was the "baker of last resort". According to Sharp (2009), the importation of wheat was governed by a state monopoly, the Università of Valletta, which took over from the Università of Mdina with the granting of Malta to the Knights of St John of Jerusalem in perpetual fief in 1530. The Università was originally a form of local government, first established in 1397, but under the knights it became almost exclusively involved with the management of the grain trade and administration of the massafrumentaria, or grain fund. Sharp (2009) contends that the Università of Valletta had a monopoly on the importation of wheat, but it also imported other goods, such as oil, cattle and tobacco. Moreover, it controlled the markets by fixing the price of wheat, as well as by administering the system of weights and measures and controlling quality. The Università also became a form of public bank, receiving private capital to finance its operations (Sharp, 2009). According to Mea (2005), although wheat was exempt from direct duty, the difference between the purchase and selling prices amounted to an indirect tax on consumers, since part of the revenue raised went to pay interest on loans raised by the Università from private sources.

Hence, the Università sold the wheat at a fixed price to the mill operators to guarantee that the price of bread was stable in the long-term. Thus, the fluctuation of the world wheat prices meant that losses and gains were absorbed by the Università and the Maltese population was protected from the adverse effects of the fluctuating prices. Sharp (2009) argues that this system was a product of unstable times, when the Knights were concerned with ensuring adequate supplies for the population at a time of piracy, famine and frequent international conflicts. He contends that this policy was successful, but on the other hand it also inflated the price of wheat, due to the institutional demands of the grain monopoly, which had to both purchase wheat and distribute it locally. Sharp (2009) argues that the Knights exercised almost complete control over the Università. They understood the important benefits of doing so, since they controlled all the grain supplies that kept the people well fed and avoided political agitation provoked by the nobility they had displaced (Pirotta, 1996).

William Thornton, who was sent to Malta to conduct a rear audit of the finances of the island since the blockade by the British, contends that the Università was insolvent even before the arrival of the French, with a deficiency of capital equal to 1,230,098 scudi. Thornton (1836) argues that this meant that more loans were needed: 233,047 scudi at 6 per cent interest, and 997,051 scudi at 3 per cent interest, thus giving an annual charge of 43,894 scudi. He contends that despite the assistance from the Grandmaster in the form of an excise on wine, which brought in 28,500 scudi, this still amounted to a considerable indirect tax through the price of bread. Hence, the Knights seemed to be adopting a deficit fiscal policy regarding this matter. The current Customs administration that operates from Custom House was purposely built by the Knights of St John in 1774 (Aquilina, 2011).

1.2.3 Fiscal Policy: Monetary

The Knights soon began to mint its own coins as it settled in Malta (Central Bank of Malta (CBM), 2014). The Knights initially adopted the monetary system of Sicily when arriving in Malta. Moreover, in 1609, the Council of the Order appointed a Commission to study the new regulations issued for the Sicilian Mint at Messina to ensure that coins struck in Malta would in future conform in weight and fineness to those of Sicily (Restelli and Sammut, 1977). It is also known that from time to time foreign coins, including Spanish Doubloons and Piastres, Venetian Zecchini, Livournine, Genovine and Louis d'Or were allowed to circulate with the local coinage. According to Restelli and Sammut (1977), the Master of the Mint at Messina strongly disapproved the freedom for the Knights to mint its own coins and introduce its own currency. However, with the intervention of Pope Clement VII, the Knights were permitted to strike its own coins in Malta. The first coins that seem to have been minted in Malta by the Knights were struck during the brief reign of the second Grand Master, Pietro del Ponte (1534–35). During its 268-year rule in Malta, the Knights minted coins in various denominations and metals, namely in gold, silver and copper. Restelli and Sammut (1977) argue that the Knights in 1565 encountered critical financial difficulties following Malta's Great Siege by the Turks but required the necessary funds to support its building programme for the new city of Valletta, where several thousand of labourers needed to be paid. Hence, they found it expedient to strike fiduciary copper coins to support the local monetary system. The reverse side of these coins depicted clasped hands surrounded by the legend "NON-AES SED FIDES", (Not Money but Trust). According to Giacomo Bosio, historian of the Order, Grand Master Jean de La Valette (1557–1568) promised to redeem these copper coins in "noble metal" and also fixed their rate of exchange at par not only with Maltese silver coins but also with Sicilian silver pieces CBM (2014).

The fiduciary copper coins, struck by other Grand Masters continued to pass current in Malta at par with Sicilian silver and to maintain their value with local silver coins, until the death of Grand Master Antoine de Paule in 1636, as the amount put in circulation had remained more or less proportionate to the internal needs of the Island (Restelli and Sammut, 1977). However, according to Restelli and Sammut (1977) when Grand Master Jean-Paul Lascaris Castellar (1636–1657) continued to mint these fiduciary pieces in excessive quantities, the rate of exchange between copper and silver was completely unbalanced and increased rapidly from year to year to such an extent that in 1764 local copper was reported to be losing the amount of 107% in exchange for silver. This illustrates that the Knight's public administration and management policies related to fiscal monetary management was not always successful. According to CBM (2014), the office of Grand Master Antonio Manoel de Vilhena (1722–1736) was the first to strike the 12 zecchini gold piece, the highest denomination of the Order's coinage and he also introduced the silver 2 scudi and the 8 and 12 tari pieces. Thus, the Knights' minting art reached its peak in the minting of gold and silver coins during the office of Grand Master de Vilhena. Additionally, according to Restelli and Sammut (1977), the highest value silver coin struck by the Knights was the Maltese dollar, known as the "pezza", "onciad'argento" or "uqija" that was first issued during the long reign of Grand Master Emmanuel Pinto (1741–1773).

1.2.4   Urban Planning Policy

SMHO (2020) contends that following the victory of the Great Siege of the Ottomans, the Grand Master Fra' Jean de la Vallette decided to build the city and port of La Valletta (Valletta). The location was chosen at the extreme end of the peninsula known as Xebbir-Ras (Sheb point), of which the name originates from the lighthouse. The site is also known as Mount Sciberras (or Sciberras Peninsula), probably named after the family that owned the land. The site was specifically chosen to help fortify the Order's position in Malta and provide the Knights with a stronger foothold on the island (SMHO, 2020).

According to SMHO (2020), the design of Valletta was unique and differed from earlier medieval Maltese city planning that had mostly consisted of irregular winding streets and alleys that were easier to defend in the event of a siege by foreign powers. Valletta was designed by Francesco Laparelli who was a military engineer and provided his services on request of Pope Pius V, who (together with King Philip II of Spain) supported the project with financial aid. Valletta's design was based on rectangular grids of streets that were wide and straight, with the grid commencing at the City Gate and ending on the other side of Valletta, at Fort St Elmo that overlooks both sea ports near Valletta: The Grand Harbour on the East side and Marsamxett on the West side (SMHO, 2020). To fortify the city against attacks from outside, the city was surrounded by bastions, some of which were built up to 47 m (or 153 feet) high. Lansink (2018) argues that the design and planning of Valletta is truly unique with the city's defence in mind, with some of its streets falling steeply as you get closer towards the back of the city, making it difficult for enemy troops to manoeuvre. These streets have stairs that were built in such a way that knights in heavy armour would be able to climb the steps. At the turn of the seventeenth century, Valletta had grown into a sizeable city for the standards of those days and became a popular place to settle among the local population, considering its safe fortification, while former capital Mdina had lost much of its allure after the Great Siege (Lansink, 2018).

Apart from having an urban planning policy, the Knights had also in place a water and drainage policy. According to Ellul (2007), Grand Master Fra Alof de Wignacourt built the Wignacourt Aqueduct between 1610 and 1614 to carry a constant supply of good drinking water from Dingli and Rabat to the capital Valletta. Over 15 km long, the aqueduct mostly ran underground, but was carried on a series of stone arches where depressions were encountered along the route. The aqueduct remained in use until the early twentieth century, and some of its arches still survive until this day.

1.2.5 Health Policy

The first hospital operating in Malta was in 1372, while in Gozo the first hospital was established in 1454. However, the arrival of the Knights in 1530 saw the expansion of health services as part of a state-organized social services system (Savona-Ventura, 1999). In fact, the island was given a large new hospital, considered to be one of the best organised and most effective in the world (SMHO, 2020). According to Savona-Ventura (1999), towards the end of the eighteenth century (1798), the hospitals in use during the time of the Knights included the celebrated Sacra Infermeria (Holy Infirmary) for men and the Casetta for females, which were both located at Valletta to service the south-eastern harbour region. Moreover, the medieval Santo Spirito Hospital located at Rabat provided health services to the rural central region, which catered for underprivileged patients of both sexes (Savona-Ventura, 1999). Additionally, these hospitals were complemented by other health centres, such as a number of hospices for the elderly and infirm that included the 280-bed hospice for both sexes at Floriana, the 80-bed hospice for both sexes at Saura Hospital at Rabat, and the 15-bed hospice for females at Żebbuġ (Savona-Ventura, 1999).

Being an Island, Malta to a certain extent was protected from infectious diseases. However, it was exposed to these infectious diseases, due to numerous shipping, mariners and associated passengers from mainland Europe and other surrounding countries. Hence, the Knight's health policy included the establishment of a quarantine hospital on Manoel Island (Savona-Ventura, 1999). Gozo was also served by two hospitals, one for males and one for females, both situated at Victoria. An interesting development during this time was having Caterina Vitale (1566–1619) as the first female pharmacist and chemist in Malta, and the first female pharmacist of the Knights Hospitaller (Malta Independent, 2007). Caterina Vitale who was originally from Greece, provided pharmacies to the Sacra Infermeria and was described as a successful businessperson who became very rich and was a benefactor of the Carmelites (Malta Independent, 2007; Hoe, 2015).

1.2.6   Education and Culture Policy

The Maltese education policy under the Knights was particularly transformational, with the foundation in 1530 of the Collegium Melitensæ, through the intercession of Pope Clement VIII. In 1592, the Jesuits opened a College in Valletta and in 1769 Grand Master Emmanuel Pinto established it into a University, which was the predecessor to today's University of Malta. As a result, the University of Malta is one of the oldest existing universities in Europe, and the oldest Commonwealth University outside of the United Kingdom. The School of Anatomy and Surgery was founded by Grand Master Fra Nicolas Cotoner at the Sacra Infermeria in Valletta, in 1676, and the faculty of medicine followed. In particular, the Order contributed to the development of ophthalmology and pharmacology (SMHO, 2020). The Sacra Infermeria itself was known as one of the finest and most advanced hospitals in Europe (SMHO, 2020). Spiteri (2013a, b) argues that difficulties in the running of the Sacra Infermeria commenced in the late eighteenth century due to the critical financial position of the Knights. He maintains that cost cutting measures were introduced in the 1780s and the Knights managed to restore the finances and maintain the Hospital for some years. However, the difficulties resulting from the French Revolution made the maintenance and operation of the Hospital impossible and during the 1790s the Knights had to reduce the number of staff and some of the services given at the Hospital, with the silver ware having to be melted to mint coins (Spiteri, 2013a, b). A Diocesan Seminary was also instituted, with several other colleges being set up by various Religious Orders. Significant studies in the Maltese language, up till then a spoken language only, were embarked upon by two scholars, the Gozitan Canon Agius Sultana (1712–1770) known as De Soldanins and Mikiel Anton Vassalli (1764–1829).

Culture was also an important aspect of public service administration and management under the Knights. According to SMHO (2020), the knights transformed Malta, undertaking urban construction projects: palaces and churches were built, as well as formidable new defence bastions and gardens. Architecture flourished as well as artistic patronage. For instance, throughout the eighteenth century, Baroque architecture became popular in Malta, which was mainly associated with the Grandmasters António Manoel de Vilhena and Manuel Pinto da Fonseca, both of whom were Portuguese (Spiteri, 2013a, b). According to Spiteri (2013a, b), during de Vilhena's reign, the city of Mdina was significantly remodelled in the Baroque style. Other noteworthy Baroque structures built during de Vilhena's reign include

Fort Manoel and the Manoel Theatre. The town of Floriana also flourished around this era between the Floriana Lines and Valletta, and it was given the title of Borgo Vilhena by the Grandmaster. The Baroque style was still going strong during Pinto's tenure that continued from 1741 to 1773. Other major buildings during this period include Auberge de Castille and the Valletta Waterfront (POM, 2008).

Carnival was introduced by Grand Master Piero de Ponte with the first celebration date in Malta being 1535 (Cassar Pullicino, 1949). Cassar Pullicino (1949) argues that although the Maltese carnival was likely to have been celebrated before the Knights arrived in Malta, the general rejuvenation for the carnival tradition was by Grand Master Piero de Ponte with the first celebration date in Malta being 1535. It started taking place officially in Birgu where a number of knights played games and displayed their skills in various pageants and tournaments. During the Knight's tenure the population of the Maltese Islands increased significantly from approximately 25,000 in 1530 to 91,273 in the late 1700s. A great number of churches were built in the towns and villages on the specific designs of Maltese architects such as Gerolamo Cassar and his son Vittorio, Tommaso Dingli and Lorenzo Gafà. These churches were embroidered with works of art, the product of foreign and Maltese artists, such as Mattia Preti, Stefano and Alessio Erardi and Francesco Zahra. This is likely to have caused the increase in the popularity for celebrating the local village patron Saint feast as it is known today.

The Knights also had an impressive environment and recreation policy. They established an impressive number of gardens, including Boschetto woodlands (Buskett Gardens); San Anton Gardens; Floriana gardens – the first garden city in Europe, with the Mall; St Philip's; Argotti; Sa Maison; Upper Barrakka Gardens; and Lower Barrakka Gardens, a total of 14 gardens in all, with two Gardens planned in Gozo. These gardens illustrating the Knights' long-term vision are still being enjoyed at the present time. Surprisingly, the Knights also had a foreign policy that saw them take part in the colonization of the Americas. On 21 May 1651, they acquired four islands in the Caribbean: Saint Barthélemy, Saint Christopher, Saint Croix and Saint Martin. These were purchased from the French Compagnie des Îles de l'Amérique, which had just been dissolved. The Order controlled the islands under the governorship of Phillippe de Longvilliers de Poincy until his death, and in 1665 the four islands were sold to the French West India Company. In fact, this marked the end of the Knight's influence outside the Mediterranean (Allen, 1990). As illustrated in the above brief notes, the impact of the Knight's contribution to public administration and management can only be described as extraordinary. They had every conceivable policy that you would find in any established government at that time and to a great extent today. Their policies could not have been put into practice unless they had in place a public service organisation that was capable of implementing these various public administration policies and had great public management capabilities.

1.3   Public Administration and Management During the French Occupation Under Napoleon (1530–1798)

The ousting of the Knights by Napoleon Bonaparte in 1798 brought to a close their rule. It must be noted that the Knights brought with them substantial income from property, particularly from France. Hence, the Order was in decline for several years due to the French Revolution and by the extension of French influence over much of Europe (Cohen, 1920, Chapter V, The Fall 1789–1798). These factors resulted in diminishing the Order's income with the consequence that the defences and its system of paternal government in Malta became unsustainable. The French public administration and management era only lasted about 2 years. Napoleon appointed Bosredom de Ransijat as President of the Civil Commission of Government in Malta (Hardman, 1909, p.77). Bosredom de Ransijat had served as Secretary of the Treasury under the Knights and is credited with having introduced new accounting reforms, such as the practice of periodical publishing of a printed balance sheet (Hardman, 1909, p.3). Maltese public administration and management under the French occupation is characterised by the evolution of the bureaucratic process. Typically, the term bureaucracy combines organizational structure, procedures, protocols, and a set of regulations in place to manage activity, usually in large organizations, such as governments. However, 2 years of internal hostilities had a disastrous effect on the Maltese economy and public administration, with most of the governmental institutions being bankrupt.

The ousting of the Knights in 1798 required the reorganization of the health services, with the segregation of civil and military patients in hospitals. Hence, the Sacra Infermeria was taken over by the French to be used as a Military Hospital being named the Grand Hôpital. A new Hôpital Civil for male civilians was established in Valletta (Savona-Ventura, 1999). According to Zerafa (2019), the French occupiers did not demonstrate many competencies to administer and manage Malta, and in fact were unable to feed themselves, let alone the Maltese population of about 100,000 inhabitants at that time. In fact, this triggered a public uprising (demonstrations) at Rabat in 1798. By January 1799, evidence of starvation and its consequences were manifest as a way of life, with the number of deaths amounting to 20% of the population (20,000) (Zerafa, 2019). Thus, the French turned out to be very poor administrators. Napoleon spent only a few days in Malta, from 12 to 19 June. His headquarters was located at Palazzo Parisio, which is currently the Ministry for Foreign Affairs building next to Auberge de Castile in Valletta. Napoleon issued several decrees, grouped in four categories, namely, social, administrative, educational, and Church-State relations (Hardman, 1909, p.84–88). These reforms were based on the principles of the French Revolution.

1.3.1   Social Policy

Under Napoleon's decree, the people of Malta were granted equality before the law, and they were recognised as French citizens; the Maltese nobility was abolished, and slaves were freed; a government was established ruled by five Maltese people; freedom of speech and the press were instituted, even though the only newspaper was Journal de Malta, which was published by the government; political prisoners including Mikiel Anton Vassalli and those who took part in the Rising of the Priests were freed, while the Jewish population was given permission to build a synagogue (Lyceum, 2013).

1.3.2   Public Administration Policy and Management

All of the Knight's property was taken over by the French authorities. A Commission of Government was established to govern the islands consisting of a Military Governor, Commissioner, President of the Civil Commission, Secretary to the Commissioner, and ten members (Di Marco, 2013). Furthermore, according to Di Marco (2013), Malta and Gozo were divided into 12 cantons, 10 for Malta and two for Gozo, with each canton being managed by a president, secretary and four members. This is considered to be the first time that Malta and Gozo had a central and local government public administration and management structure to take the overall governance of Malta and Gozo. Additionally, a national guard was established with 900 men (Hardman, 1909, p.83).

1.3.3   Education Policy

The education policy was based on three major components: (a) the French established Primary schools in the main towns and villages; (b) sixty students were to be allowed to study in France; and (c) the University of Malta was to be renamed Polytechnique, and scientific subjects were to be taught there (Scicluna, 1936; Calleja, 1994; Xerri, 2016). As stated previously, the Sacra Infermeria, which is viewed as Malta's first medical school, was taken over by the French to be used as a Military Hospital being named the Grand Hôpital, with a new Hôpital Civil for male civilians being established in Valletta (Savona-Ventura, 1999).

1.3.4   Church-State Relations Policy

The Church-State Relations policy was based on four fundamental principles: (a) the appropriation of the Church's wide-ranging property on Malta by the Government; (b) religious orders were allowed to keep only one convent each; (c) the inquisition was abolished, and the last inquisitor was expelled from the islands; and (d) the Court of appeals to the Roman Curia were disallowed (Hardman, 1909, p.93). The looting of church property by French troops was one of the reasons for the Maltese uprising (apart from starvation), which brought French rule to a short end (Hardman, 1909, p.110). Many of the above public administration and management policies were viewed as being highly innovative and transformational. However, the French did not have enough time to put most of these reforms to practice, because less than 3 months after Napoleon had left Malta, the Maltese rose up in revolt against their new masters.

When Napoleon returned to France from Egypt, the relief of Malta was given top priority. But the ships that left Toulon for Malta were captured by the British (Hardman, 1909, p.271). From then onwards no relief forces or supplies were sent from France and Governor Vaubois had to introduce food rationing. In the summer of 1800 life for the French garrison became desperate. Bosredon de Ransijat wrote in his diary: '*Apart from the donkeys, mules and horses which continued to be slaughtered and eaten as before, the greater part of the dogs and cats as well as a quantity of rats followed their fate. The latest hunt, made quite recently, for those animals in the military bakery netted 55 of those frightful rodents. It was solely in this locality that one could hope to find them, being bigger than those found in other places*' (Bosredon de Ransijat and Scicluna, 2013). Hence, by 5th October 1800, the French capitulated to the British commanders. However, the Maltese leaders were left out from the negotiations about the conditions of the surrender of Malta.

1.4   Public Administration and Management Under British Rule (1800–1964)

The successful uprising against the French brought with it a great deal of uncertainty, since the Maltese leaders recognised that they required the help from a powerful ally to absolutely expel the French. The British, long-standing adversaries of the French were viewed as the only practical choice. Hence, British rule in Malta commenced in 1800 initially as a British Protectorate and with public administration and management being entrusted to Captain Alexander Ball who was appointed President of the National Congress made up of representatives from the principal towns and villages (Hardman, 1909, p.513). In 1801, Captain Alexander Ball was replaced as Civil Commissioner by Sir Charles Cameron. The National Congress formally requested King Ferdinand IV of Naples to assign his sovereign rights over the Maltese Islands to King George III of Great Britain. King George accepted and instituted the Maltese 'nation' full protection of all their privileges under the British Crown (Hardman, 1909, p.358).

The period 1801 to 1803 was particularly critical, because Article 10 of the Peace Treaty of Amiens (March 1802) between Britain and France, stipulated that Britain had to evacuate the islands within a few months and relinquish the islands to the Knights; the Great Powers were to guarantee the neutrality of the Order of St John; Maltese nobles were to be accepted as Knights of St John; and the Maltese were to have a share in governing the islands with the Knights. Although the Maltese were to be given a share in the administration, something which they had never enjoyed before, and could now for the first time be elevated as Knights, they rejected the Treaty as they did not wish for the return of the Order. In June 1802, assembled in Congress, Maltese leaders drafted the Declaration of rights of the Maltese Islands and its Dependencies, which reiterated their primordial rights and the manner they wanted to be governed by the British (Frendo, 2004, p.26). This declaration was submitted to Sir Charles Cameron, Civil Commissioner for presentation to the King.

The conditions under Article 10 (and the drafted Declaration) were mostly discarded when the war between Britain and France resumed in May 1803. Lord Liverpool, British Prime Minister, recognised, similar to Admiral Nelson, the strategic position of Malta as a naval base for the British fleet in the Mediterranean. Thus, Malta was ruled by Britain by the appointment of Civil Commissioners (Hardman, 1909, p.474). This period is also characterized by numerous political uncertainties since sovereignty over Malta was contested by several powers (Hardman, 1909, p.454). However, in 1812 Britain and Russia signed a secret treaty, where Russia renounced all its claims to Malta, which meant that the principal barrier for permanent British rule over Malta was thus removed (Hardman, 1909, p.525). In 1812, a Royal Commission was tasked to report on Malta and to make recommendations about its future governance. But, by May 1813, with Britain and its allies closing on victory over Napoleon, Malta was declared a British Crown Colony with Sir Thomas Maitland as its first military governor. The Commission of 1812 had 'suggested the formation of an advisory Council of four English and four Maltese in order to temper the absolute rule' of governors (Cremona, 1994, p.2). Bathurst, at the time Secretary of State for War and the Colonies left the formation of such a Council in the hands of the Governor, which was never established. Governors were appointed by the Secretary of State for the Colonies. Malta's status as a British Crown Colony was confirmed by the Treaty of Paris of 1814, and reaffirmed by the Congress of Vienna of 1815 (Hardman, 1909, p.533–534).

This transformational change of British policy was of enormous concern to the Maltese patriots, who although pro-British, had aspired that Malta would have British Protectorate status. A protectorate status was seen as a way for Britain to look after the defence of the islands in case of attack, however, leaving the local government in the hands of a Maltese elected assembly. The Maltese felt resentful when the British ignored their request for a protectorate status and were helpless to resist this superpower of their time. Ball noted the Maltese had grasped the basic fact that Britain was the only power that could either relieve them or starve them (Pirotta, 1996, p.50). Moreover, the Congress of Vienna had accepted Britain's possession of Malta. Malta's income became mainly dependent on custom dues and a new sliding tax on grain. British funds were conspicuous by their absence at this time. Thus, the Maltese Islands remained a part of the British Empire until 1964 when they obtained Independence.

1.4.1   Public Administration and Public Management Policy: Captain Alexander Ball

In 1802, Captain Alexander Ball was reappointed as Civil Commissioner instead of Sir Charles Cameron due to his popularity with the Maltese (Pirotta, 1996, p.60). Captain Ball made the following key public administration and public management policy decisions (Pirotta, 1996, p.62; Lyceum, 2008, p.2):

(a) Halted the departure of the British troops as agreed at the Treaty of Amiens.
(b) Mitigated resistance by adopting an incremental change approach. For instance, very minor changes were made to the laws. The Code of Grand Master de Rohan and the administration of justice, the old Universitas (local councils) of Valletta, Mdina and Gozo remained as they had been under the Knights.
(c) Maintained the currency of the Knights, such as the scudo, tari and grano. This currency was not fully replaced until 1854 even though the pound Sterling was introduced in 1825.
(d) Defence was strengthened due to the war with France and four British Infantry Regiments were stationed in Malta. The Maltese militia regiments instituted by Grand Master de Rohan were maintained by establishing the Royal Malta Fencible Regiment to guard the coastal forts.
(e) The Civil Commissioner had firm control of the government with unlimited power and was not answerable to authority in Malta.
(f) Re-established the government departments that were left in great confusion by the French. Heads of Department were appointed from suitable Maltese Public Servants. These appointments were unique, since no other British Colony had indigenous citizens appointed as Heads of Public Service Departments.
(g) Took direct control for financial matters to mitigate corruption and increase efficiency. It is noted that Ball's financial administration was far from efficient and this is evidenced by William Thornton's rare Audit under Maitland and the fact that years after his replacement, he was still being chased by the British Treasury because of his administration's confusion. Ball defended himself by saying that those he had trusted had let him down.
(h) Halted persons carry arms without a licence.
(i) Piracy (corsairing) was declared illegal in 1807 because it was viewed as damaging British trade interests in the Mediterranean and was punishable by the death penalty. But privateering against enemy ships continued.
(j) Diversified agriculture by introducing the cultivation of the potato crop that became very popular with the lower classes. Cotton remained a primary export

item for some time, although cotton was in decline due to cheaper and better-quality cotton from Egypt and the United States.

The era of 1800 to 1813 was characterised as a period of confusion, and corruption was ripe at every level of government, but it was also a period of economic boom (Pirotta, 1996, p.81). Napoleon imposed a blockade against British goods, which triggered retaliation from Britain whereby neutral states were prevented from trading with France and its allies. This Continental Blockade after 1806 and during Captain Ball's tenure resulted in an economic boom. Malta became the centre for contraband trade of British goods smuggled into Europe, thus earning it the title of the 'emporium (supermarket) of the Mediterranean' (Hardman, 1909, p.537). During this period, the traffic of cargo ships using the Grand Harbour grew considerably. Malta became a maritime hub, with insurance companies and businessmen from the United Kingdom establishing their headquarters in Malta (Hardman, 1909, p.537). Malta became a logistics and transhipment centre, whereby goods were ordered directly from Britain, stored in Maltese warehouses and then transhipped into Europe. This required the Government to initiate an extensive building programme of warehouses on the harbour front. Hence, there was a substantial growth in employment and an expansion of foreign trade with ports in the Mediterranean. This attracted the establishment of commercial banks, namely the Anglo-Maltese Bank and the Banco di Malta in 1809 and 1812 respectively (MacGill, 1839, p.65). Additionally, there was the build-up of British troops stationed in Malta numbering into the thousands resulting in merchants, tradesmen, shopkeepers, innkeepers, stevedores, sailors, boatman and farmers all increasing their profits. The Grand Harbour became a cosmopolitan centre resulting in a sharp increase in the value of housing and price of rents in the vicinity of the Grand Harbour. However, this economic boom was short lived with the end of the Continental Blockade in 1812 that resulted in a decline in commerce and an increase in unemployment and poverty, since most Mediterranean countries started trading directly with Britain. The outcome of this was a general decline of merchant shipping in the Grand Harbour resulting in an increase in unemployment and a decrease in wages.

1.4.2   Public Administration and Public Management Policy: Sir Hildebrand Oakes

In 1810, Sir Hildebrand Oakes succeeded Captain Alexander Ball as Civil Commissioner at a time when economic conditions in Malta were favourable. According to Hardman (1909, p.510), Sir Oakes was presented with a petition by Marquis Nicolo Testaferrata representing the Maltese, suggesting the following changes: (a) government posts should be occupied by Maltese; (b) rent on government property to be reduced; and (c) a Consiglio Popolare as a representative council of government to be set up. This petition was sent to Lord Liverpool, Foreign Secretary (who became Prime Minister in 1812) that resulted in the setting-up of a

Royal Commission. Deficiencies in Malta's public accounts were so common that the 1812 Royal Commission was also required to investigate all matters related to revenues and expenditure (Pirotta, 1996, p.80). The Royal Commission of Inquiry to Malta had the following tasks: (a) to determine the civil liberties that may be given to the Maltese without endangering the security of fortress Malta; and (b) to investigate the structure of Maltese institutions and society that included, the administration, law courts, taxation, commerce and education, and recommend specific reforms that had the aim of enhancing efficiency and progress. The findings of the Royal Commission of Inquiry were to be submitted in a report to the British Government, who would then decide which recommendations were to be accepted. The Report of the Commission of Inquiry of 1812 was never fully published, so the Maltese at that time could only speculate as to its full contents and proposals (Pirotta, 1996, p.97).

Unfortunately, the Royal Commission consisted of conservative members and its chairman was Sir Oakes himself. Sir Oakes had a direct conflict of interest in that he was thus appointed to be judge of his own administration with the authority to interview people who were supposed to criticise his own administration. The Royal Commission of 1811–1812 concluded that: (a) Malta was to have a military governor; (b) the Governor was to establish an advisory council consisting of eight members, equally distributed among the British and Maltese; (c) the administration of justice was to be reformed according to the English model; (d) the English Language together with Italian were to become the official language of the government; and (e) the Maltese desired to become part to the British Empire (Gebruiker, 2012, p.14). When appointed in 1813, Governor Maitland insisted in having free and unencumbered power in Malta (Pirotta, 1996, p.96). Thus, Maitland refused to appoint an advisory council even when the British in this council were to be four out of seven members, not as proposed by the Royal Commission of eight members, equally distributed among the British and Maltese (Gebruiker, 2012, p.14). Furthermore, the Advisory Council only discussed the agenda items put forward by him. Hence, Maitland simply kept the entire government and chose all government officials (mostly British) himself. Due to his autocratic attitude, the Maltese nicknamed him King Tom, because he pretended to govern like a king. During his tenure, public administration and management was strictly to the Governor's direct intervention because he had held all civil and military powers in his hands.

The Government's health policy came under pressure when in March 1813 the plague broke out in Malta, although it was not until May 1813 that the sickness was diagnosed as the plague (Angefry, 2014). This brought about a steep decrease in agricultural produce, and local and foreign trade, since many foreign countries closed their ports to Maltese ships. Preventive measures adopted by the sanitary authorities to stem the spread of the pestilence were based on the assumption that the plague was a contagious disease conveyed from a sick to a healthy person by touching the patient's body, belongings or clothes (Angefry, 2014). Thus, food was immersed in water and coins were plunged in vinegar before being exchanged. On 5th May 1813, the Board of Health officially declared the plague epidemic and published a set of rules in an attempt to restrain the disease from spreading further

(Angefry, 2014). Sir Hildebrand Oakes in June 1813 ordered strict quarantine between the Harbour towns and the villages, but people became careless and there was little enforcement of the rules.

1.4.3   Public Administration and Public Management Policy: Sir Thomas Maitland

When Governor Maitland arrived in October 1813, stricter quarantine measures were enforced by building walls around Qormi (where the last cases were reported) manned by armed guards. By April 1814, Qormi had no further cases. Despite these measures, the plague was reported in Gozo in January 1814, killing 200 people. By September 1814, Maitland requested foreign countries to open their harbours to Maltese ships. However, Sicily opened its harbours to Maltese ships in 1815, but other countries removed quarantine restrictions against Malta in the 1820s. Moreover, peace in Europe in 1815 meant that the number of British troops required in Malta decreased resulting in less domestic trade. The risk of another outbreak of plague remained for years. In fact, between 1819 and 1841, twelve ships entered the harbour with the infection on board. In all these cases the plague was stopped from spreading outside the Lazzaretto, the quarantine facility and hospital on Manoel Island in Gżira. Generally, there was a re-emergence of the segregation of health services under the British with hospital services being organized for civilians, military and naval personnel (Savona-Ventura, 1999).

The moment Maitland got rid of the plague he set about reorganizing the Maltese judicial system on the suggestions of the Royal Commission. According to Pirotta (1996, p.101), in 1814, the new Constitutions of the Courts were proclaimed and put into force. The most important changes were the following: (a) the Consolato del Mare of 1697 was turned into a Commercial Court; and (b) the Corte della Castellania was divided into two halls: The Criminal Court and the Civil Court. All judges were appointed until retirement by the Governor and confirmed by the King and they were prohibited from working privately as lawyers (Pirotta, 1996, p.100; Hardman, 1909, p.532). Cases were to be considered in an open court that was open to the public. The Court of Appeal consisted of two halls, one for commercial and one for civil cases. However, there was no appeal from the Criminal Court. The Governor and two judges made up the Supreme Court of Justice to deal with exceptional cases. Italian was made the language of the Courts. One main criticism to these reforms was that, except for commercial cases, few changes were made to the Criminal Code of Grand Master Rohan (1784). One positive note was that the laws that permitted privateering, torture and slavery were abolished.

Governor Maitland also introduced important public administration and public management reforms by reorganizing the Government Departments, but only Englishmen were appointed to the higher posts of the Civil Service (Pirotta, 1996, p.98). The most important Government posts were the Chief Secretary, Treasurer,

Auditor, Crown Advocate, Superintendent of Quarantine, Collector of Customs, Superintendent of Marine Police, Officer of Port Duties and a Collector of Land Revenue. He established Gozo as a separate directorate with its own Commandant, Collector of Land Revenue, Magistrates and Police. For instance, an important development in Maltese public administration and management was the establishment of the Audit Department in 1814 to address lax accounting practices, corruption, poor financial information, competence of officials and inadequate remuneration (Sant, 2014). Every department or governing body was subjected to strict audit. Additionally, a police corps was established in 1814, organised on the English model and headed by an Inspector-General directly responsible to Maitland as Governor (Police, 2020). The Maltese were appointed to the lowest offices of the administration. British government officials received high salaries, with Maitland having a salary of £10,000 a year. Thus, the Government Treasury was under constant strain and had difficulty sustaining this payroll policy. Maitland did not have a high opinion of the Maltese. He viewed the Maltese as too ignorant and irresponsible to be given greater responsibility in public administration and management. A number of Maltese liberals objected about the poor state of education and the high illiteracy of the common people. A voluntary association was instituted to establish primary schools in the larger towns and villages. For example, the Normal School at Valletta had 200 pupils, mostly boys in 1821. Children were admitted at the age of six for an entry fee of five scudi. This undertaking began to fail because the Government was not committed to this reform and therefore did not provide financial backing. The British Government was of the opinion that the Islands had limited resources and viewed education for the Maltese as an additional cost.

The government's fiscal and monetary policy was viewed as being important by Governor Maitland, who made certain that strict control on finances was maintained. He instructed that payment orders were issued from the Treasury only on his authorisation (Pirotta, 1996, p.102). This was required due to his payroll policy where top public servants (all Englishmen), including himself were paid extraordinarily high salaries. The Government revenue at that time came from three sources: (a) rent on government property; (b) quarantine dues on ships entering harbour; and (c) custom duties on all imported goods (Pirotta, 1996, p.104). Maltese commerce was increased by the fostering of exports of Maltese produce and by introducing a Maltese transhipment hub policy (a centre for entrepôt trade) between Europe and the Levant. Thus, Maitland reduced custom duties to encourage further foreign trade. By 1819, he abolished export duty and fixed import duties at 1% on British imported goods and 2% on all other foreign goods. Furthermore, in 1820 he reduced quarantine charges and the transit duty was abolished. In 1818, Maitland appointed a Board of Grain Supply under his supervision and abolished the Maltese Università dei Grani that had been in operation since the time of the Knights (Pirotta, 1996, p.112). Hence, the Government kept a monopoly on the importation of grain, providing it with about one third of its total annual revenue. He argued that government monopoly on grain would result in lower grain prices, since grain was the staple food of the lower classes. However, the monopoly on grain was abolished in 1822 against his wishes (Pirotta, 1996, p.104).

Maitland remained Governor until his death on 17 January 1824. By 1829, Malta had to compete with Greece, when Greece became an independent country and the Levant trade was dominated by the large Greek merchant navy. In 1825, the Maltese scudo and the other circulating currencies at the time were officially replaced by the pound sterling, with the lowest-valued coin being a one-third farthing coin minted at irregular intervals, the last such issue occurring in 1913, keeping alive the tradition of the Maltese "grano," equal to one-twelfth of a penny. Despite this, scudi and other foreign coinage continued to circulate in limited amounts, and the last scudi were withdrawn over 60 years later in October and November 1886 (CBM, 2014). The final quarter of the 1800s provided further technical and financial progress in line with the Belle Epoque (between the Franco-Prussian War to the outbreak of World War I), with the following years resulting in the foundation of the Anglo-Egyptian Bank in 1864 (HSBC, 2020). Progress was also registered in other aspects, such as the beginning of operation of the Malta Railway in 1883 (Pirotta, 1996, p.404) and the commencement of the tram services in 1904; the issuing of the first definitive postage stamps in 1885; the discovery in 1886 by Surgeon Major David Bruce of the microbe that caused the Maltese Fever; and with Themistocles Zammit discovering the fever's sources in 1905.

1.4.4 Public Administration and Public Management Policy: Governor More O'Ferall

Maltese public administration and management continued to evolve but always under British direct rule. During the Greek War of Independence, Malta became an important base for British, French and Russian naval forces, particularly after the Battle of Navarino of 1827. The Maltese economy boomed during this period; however, the end of the war in 1832 brought with it an economic decline (Pirotta, 1996, p.131). Hence, it appears that Malta's economic prosperity was very closely related to military activity in Europe, particularly in the Mediterranean. In 1839, press censorship was abolished; however, there was only one newspaper at the time that was owned by the government (Pirotta, 1996, p.2). Freedom of the press was granted on the recommendation of the Commission of 1836–38. It was this Commission that won, in practice not merely in words, for the Maltese the right of being appointed to the highest office of the civil service. In fact, this recommendation was put immediately into practice and, from this period onwards, Maltese officers began to replace British officials as head of departments. It was here, in 1838 that the service started becoming truly Maltese. Furthermore, this Commission, known as the Austin and Lewis Commission made several changes to the administration that were considered notable.

Following the 1846 Carnival riots, a Council of Government with elected members was established in 1849 (Pirotta, 1996, p.197), with Governor More O'Ferall, being Malta's first civilian Governor. The 1849 Council of Government consisted of

18 persons. However, only eight members were to be Maltese through elections, the rest were British nominated by the Governor. According to Gebruiker (2012), to qualify to vote a person was to be between the ages of 21 and 60 years, be a land-owner or/and a person of means, and competently versed in the English or Italian language. More important than who could vote was the creation of the Official Majority. This majority was made up of Maltese Heads of Departments, who were obliged to vote under the direction of the Governor. This meant that these Heads were really like Ministers and this was to bring them into constant conflict with the elected minority. The British government, under the so-called Cardwell Rule, sought to curb abuse of the official majority by giving power to the elected minority over financial votes. He argued that these restrictions meant that the number of eligible voters was very small and purged not only the illiterate but many professional men, cultured persons and ecclesiastics due to the property qualification. 1849 constitution was viewed as being important because it incorporated the elective principle that represents a preliminary stage in the advance towards representative Government (Gebruiker, 2012). In 1883, due to the diminishing number of voters, the franchise was extended by lowering the property qualification of landowners from 100 scudi (or £8) to 75 scudi (or £6) and by removing the language (English or Italian) barrier (Gebruiker, 2012). Gebruiker (2012) contends that, while this helped to increase the number of eligible voters, it did not resolve the claims for voting rights of the educated and professional persons who did not own or pay rent for property of the required value. This was resolved with further amendments in 1887 where the Council of Government was entrusted with 'dual control' always under British rule.

Whilst the above has focused on political reforms, it is now appropriate to focus on the many reforms introduced by More O'Ferrall related to public institutions. Governor More O'Ferall displayed enormous foresight in tackling the social, economic and political-administrative problems of Malta (Pirotta, 1991, p.201). More O'Ferall first focused on infrastructure improvements to ensure economic growth, by developing Malta as a transhipment hub. He achieved this by escalating the development of the mercantile port; reduced the quarantine period for shipping originating from the Eastern Mediterranean; expanded the shipbuilding and ship repair facilities; enhanced the logistics facilities with more warehouses and bonded stores, particularly for the storage of grain; and managed to unite merchants in one officially recognised Chamber of Commerce (Pirotta, 1991, p.202).

His second focus was the administrative reforms related to the administration of Crown property, the Charitable Institutions and education. He was convinced that government property was undervalued with a resulting loss of revenue. He therefore undertook measures to revalue government property to reflect a realistic value. This reform was delayed for 2 years due to its unpopularity and was implemented in 1851. With regard to charities, the Governor was of the view that government charities should be strictly limited to those most in need and that those housed in charitable institutions must, if capable of so doing, contribute through their labour towards the expense of their upkeep (Pirotta, 1991, p.203). According to Pirotta (1991, p.203), the governor offered those who chose to leave the asylum, specifically the House of Industry for girls at Floriana, the same sum they cost in the house; placing those who refused in a separate building, obliging them to wash and work for all the public establishments without pay. The House of Industry at Floriana was later established as a public hospital by the governor, but he was not happy with the administration of the health services (Pirotta, 1991, p.203). According to Pirotta (1991, p.203), after appointing an Inspector of Hospitals, the medical service improved, particularly with the extension of the hospitals at Floriana, Mdina and Gozo; the opening of 21 dispensaries throughout Malta and Gozo; and further medical assistance and vaccination to the poor in the rural areas. Governor More O'Ferrall was also eager to improve education because, in his view, although the number of elementary schools had increased to 18, the labouring poor failed to send their children in adequate numbers; and he attempted through the promotion of a young priest, Canon Pullicino to study the education system at Dublin, to remove the mistrust that had arisen due to the Protestant form of religious prayers at particular schools (Pirotta, 1991, p.204).

Governor More O'Ferrall believed that the public service administration needed more direction and that measures were required to increase its morale by engaging public servants with proven ability Pirotta (1991, p.204). According to Pirotta (1991, p.204), two measures were implemented, firstly More O'Ferrall established the Office of Comptroller of Civil Contracts so that departments were no longer permitted to make their own contracts, but instead all government contracts were concluded through this office; and secondly, he strengthened the effectiveness of the Chief Secretary and the Auditor-General by centralising government offices into one premise, and establishing a central records repository that archived all records under the supervision of a notary. Employing public servants with proven ability was a tough issue to resolve because in most instances Governors were at liberty to employ anyone who in their opinion was best able to conduct the allocated tasks. Although some safeguards against abuse existed, such as, the requirement that most appointments had to be confirmed by the Secretary of State and that Governors in their annual reports had to inform the Colonial Office of persons who in their opinion were suited by character and ability for future employment in the civil service of the colony, More O'Ferrall held that these safeguards were not enough (Pirotta, 1991, p.205). According to Pirotta (1991, p.204), More O'Ferrall believed that the low morale in the service, particularly in the lower grades was due to the system that promoted older persons who were unsuccessful in previous quests, at the determent of diligent career public servants.

More O'Ferrall recognised that entry to the public service was largely unregulated and therefore proposed that a fixed age limit (between 20 and 30 years old) be established for those entering the public service, and that promotions were to be made on the basis of seniority, subject to the candidate being qualified (Pirotta, 1991, p.205). According to Pirotta (1991, p.206–207), despite known abuses, there was opposition to this proposal from Earl Grey at the Colonial Office, not so much about the age limitation, but he did not approve that seniority should be established as the main criteria for promotion. In the face of this disagreement, the Governor proposed that those wishing to enter the service be subject to an examination

(Pirotta, 1991, p.207). According to Pirotta (1991, p.207), this proposal came a full 6 years before the same proposal was made in the Northcote-Trevelyan Report, which had also encountered resistance. Pirotta (1991, p.208) observes that Merivale, the Under-Secretary and Grey the Colonial Secretary, did not venture an opinion or comment on O'Ferrall's proposal to introduce a system of competitive examinations; and O'Ferrall himself did not press the issue further during his tenure nor did he try to implement it, although the reasons for this remain obscure. In Britain, the pressure to reform the British civil service and ensure that those admitted fully merited their position was increasing; with the solution proposed by reformers was that of entry after a competitive examination. Pirotta argues that British ministers were reluctant to lose their patronage of appointments and it was agreed that only those nominated by ministers could sit for the exam.

1.4.5   Public Administration and Public Management Policy: Governor Sir William Reid

According to Pirotta (1991, p.208), in Malta the system of competitive examinations was introduced for the first time in 1857 by Governor Reid. Pirotta observes that Reid did not follow the British system of nomination and examination, but opened the exams to any male person that was ready to qualify himself to sit for the examination, with the only restriction being that candidates must be under 22 years of age when sitting for the examination. The first examination for clerkships in the public service was announced in the Government Gazette of February 1857 and held in March, with two more examinations being held in May and November 1857 (Pirotta, 1991, p.209–210). Furthermore, Governor Reid also established a Civil Service Commission to oversee the process with the examinations being held under the control of a Board appointed by the Governor, which included the Rector of the University as President, the Inspector of charitable Institutions, the Public Librarian, the Director of Primary Schools, and the Assistant Superintendent of the Ports (Pirotta, 1991, p.210). Pirotta (1991, p.210), argues that Malta provided the first example of a Government to introduce open competition for entry into the civil service throughout the whole of the Empire, including Britain.

1.4.6   Public Administration and Public Management Policy: Rowsell-Julyan-Keenan Royal Commission

Another important reform development was in 1878 when a Royal Commission (Rowsell-Julyan-Keenan Commission) was established to examine various aspects of public service administration and make appropriate recommendations. According to Pirotta (1991, p.275), Rowsell was assigned with investigating the system of taxation in Malta and to recommend ways to improve it; Julyan, was charged with inquiring into every aspect of Maltese public administration; and Keenan was to inquire into the education system and to advise how best to advance the study of English. Rowsell conducted a comprehensive study of the taxation system and recommended the total abolishment of the grain tax and to replace it with other revenue sources, which he specified as being items consumed mainly by the middle classes (Pirotta, 1991, p.296). According to Pirotta (1991, p.297), Sir Michael Hicks-Beach, who had replaced Lord Carnarvon as Secretary of State for the Colonies, taking into consideration the peculiar circumstances of Malta, viewed the wheat tax as being too important as a source of revenue for the local government to agree to its total abolition. However, he recognised that the grain tax was open in principle to some very grave objections and he proposed to reduce it by one-half, with the loss in revenue to be recouped by new taxes on beer, wine and spirits, tonnage dues, store rent on bonded goods, licences and education fees (Pirotta, 1991, p.297). Pirotta notes that the grain tax that had much to do with the poverty of the Maltese and the resultant 1921 riots was finally removed by the 1947 Labour government with the introduction of income tax.

Commissioner Julyan was assigned four objectives, namely to examine every department of government with the aim of determining whether it would be possible to downsize them in terms of numbers and cost; to report on the possibility of promoting English as the official language of the colony; to investigate Maltese demands to reduce the remuneration of the Governor from local sources; and to examine the subject of the drawback of customs' duties allowed to the imperial Government on account of corn and cattle consumed by the Garrison and Fleet (Pirotta, 1991, p.299).

Julyan admitted that there appeared to be limited room for downsizing of the public service, and that the salary of the governor was to continue to be contributed from imperial funds (i.e. two-fifths of the Governor's salary), since Malta was considered to be a military and naval station of great importance (Pirotta, 1991, p.299–301). He also recommended that the Governor should come from the civil rank and not be a military Governor, because the civil affairs of the island required the undivided attention of a competent administrator; a military career did not afford the kind of training calculated to produce such an administrator; and that it was not possible for a military officer of high rank and advanced age, to perform efficiently the combined duties of Commander of the Forces and of civil administrator (Pirotta, 1991, p.299–301). However, Julyan in the end recommended that the Governor should have military duties as well as civil administration. He proposed the formation of an Executive Council to assist and advise the Governor on all matters connected with the civil administration, which would also serve to lighten the responsibilities of the Governor and Chief Secretary, even though these officers would be included in its membership (Pirotta, 1991, p.302–303).

Regarding the collection of land revenue, Julyan insisted that the responsibility for expenditure and government contracts should not be under the control of departmental officials (Pirotta, 1991, p.304). Hence, he recommended the establishment of a Contracts Committee that would be responsible for the Land Revenue and

Public Works departments as separate entities. The Contracts Committee would thus be responsible for the sale or letting of public property, public works and for the acquisition of supplies (Pirotta, 1991, p.304). According to Pirotta (1991, p.305) the Contracts Committee would be composed of the Auditor-General (as *ex-officio* Director of contracts), and two other Heads of Department, namely the Collector of customs, and the Collector of Land Revenue (later to be known as Receiver-General). However, when a matter before the Contracts Committee involved Charitable Institutions, or ports, or public works, the head of these departments respectively would sit on the Contracts Committee as a substitute for one of the normal members. Hence, Land Revenue became a financial department under the responsibility of a Receiver-General, who also took over the issuing of all licences for which a fee was charged, and thus the Treasury ceased its operations (Pirotta, 1991, p.305).

Julyan advocated the desirability of an independent audit of public accounts but he was also aware that Malta lacked professional accountants or auditors to conduct such audits (Pirotta, 1991, p.321). According to Pirotta (1991, p.321), to overcome this difficulty, Julyan suggested that: (a) the Auditor-General was also to be appointed Director of Contracts and Chairman of the Contracts Committee responsible for preparing all the details prior to the approval of tenders, and for the formal completion of the documents; (b) the Auditor-General would also be responsible for preparing the Annual and Supplementary Estimates, instead of the Chief Secretary's Office; (c) a Finance Committee was to be established consisting of the Chief Secretary as Chairman, the Auditor-General, the Receiver-General and the Collector of Customs. The Auditor-General would submit the Annual and Supplementary Estimates to this Committee after explaining their details so that the Estimates may be submitted to the Council of Government for approval; and (d) the Auditor-General was to be responsible for collecting all materials necessary for the publication of the Government Gazette and the Annual Blue Book instead of the Chief Secretary's Office. Pirotta (1991, p.321) argues that these recommendations indicate Julyan's strategy to strengthen the role of the Audit-Office from one of nominal financial policeman to one with extensive opportunity for overview. He contends that the Contracts Committee and the Finance Committee, in which the Audit-Office was to have the leading role, were to become regulatory bodies to ensure that no measure involving the expenditure of public funds was adopted without either the knowledge or consent of the Auditor-General (Pirotta, 1991, p.321).

Julyan also addressed the issue of the desirability to promote English as the official language of the colony. He argued that there was no real justification for continuing with the policy of preferring Italian as the official language of the colony because the Census of 1861 showed that only around 10% of the population could speak and write Italian, and that ignorance of the English language was depriving the local population from participating in the opportunities offered by the British Empire, particularly emigration (Pirotta, 1991, p.326). Julyan viewed emigration as the solution to the growing poverty. Hence, Julyan recommended English should become the sole language of administration; no communication with the public was to be made in Italian; no demand for payment or other claim upon the Government be accepted unless it was prepared in English; the number of marks for English language in competitive examinations be appreciably higher than for Italian; and no clerk be eligible for promotion from one class to another and no Head of Department or professional officer be appointed, unless they had acquired and retained a thorough knowledge of English (Pirotta, 1991, p.328). However, according to Pirotta (1991, p.328), Julyan declared that he was opposed to forcibly preventing the educated classes from using Italian or that the Maltese language should be eradicated. Julyan in his report declared that the success of these recommendations depended upon the support of the Chief Secretary and Crown Advocate, who were both opponents to these reforms; hence he suggested obtaining approval of the Secretary of State, since no legislative amendments were necessary, and that the recommendations could be implemented through instructions from the Colonial Office (Pirotta, 1991, p.328–329). Keenan's Report was submitted in June 1879, 3 months after Julyan's report and focused on the education system, particularly to advise how to best advance the study of English. Hence, the report was not directly related to public service administration reform. He also recommended the Anglicisation of the educational and judicial systems (Pirotta, 1991, p.329–330) the reaction to this came in 1903 when the 1849 form of Council of Government under British rule was re-established (Pirotta, 1996, p.344).

1.4.7 Public Administration and Public Management Policy: Mowatt-Rea-Chalmers Royal Commission

However, the first decades of the twentieth century were not dominated by the language issue but by the severe financial and economic conditions. According to Pirotta (1991, p.402), the government between 1906 and 1911 recorded a series of successive annual deficits that swiftly pushed Malta towards insolvency. This crisis had a severe impact on the growing population that degenerated further by the rapid rise in inflation that came with the Great War of 1914–18 (Pirotta, 1991, p.402). To address this economic crisis, Viscount Harcourt, Crewe's successor as Secretary of State for the Colonies, established a Royal Commission in November 1911, composed of three members, namely Francis Mowatt as Chairman, Russell Rea, and MacKenzie Chalmers as members, with the mandate to examine the finances and economy of the Islands; review every aspect of the public service; and look into the existing judicial practices and procedures that prejudiced individual rights and caused loss of trade and custom to the colony (Pirotta, 1991, p.411–412). According to Pirotta (1991, p.412), the Report of the Royal Commission on the Finances, Economic Position and Judicial Procedure of Malta of 1911, is viewed as providing, to this day, the best account of the economic implications for Malta arising from its strategic geographic location and its centuries old role as a fortress. However, Pirotta (1991, p.413) argues that the recommendations proposed by the Commissioners were neither new nor to have any significant impact.

According to Pirotta (1991, p.413–414), the Commissioners proposed a number of recommendations, namely, (a) mass emigration to resolve the acute unemployment concern; (b) contribution by the Imperial Government for the maintenance of all public works that were linked to the health and comfort of the armed forces; (c) Malta was to cease paying a contribution for its defence to the Imperial Government or for the Imperial Government to pay an equitable rent for all facilities used by H.M.'s Forces in Malta for purposes other than fortifications; (d) reduce the bread tax by half, and substitute the reduced tax by imposing duties on other items, such as imported tobacco, beer and sugar, and possibly, from an imposition of a succession duty and a tax on houses; (e) simplify the judicial process, phase the reduction of the number of courts, judges and supporting employees, and increase Court fees to make the judicial institution self-sustaining; (f) use of Maltese not Italian in the oral proceedings of the inferior courts, and giving Maltese citizens the option to have their case tried in native Maltese in the superior court; and (g) curtail the ambitious scale of administration and associated expenditure, implying significant downsizing that the local government had continuously opposed during this period, when the colony was rapidly on the road to bankruptcy.

The commissioners were not able to propose any areas where significant savings may be made in the public service because they were not in a position to undertake a comprehensive study of the various departments (Pirotta, 1991, p.414). However, apart from suggesting that a separate Royal Commission be established to specifically examine the Public Service departments to identify where savings may be made, they proposed a number of recommendations regarding this issue: (a) clerical staff to be divided into two classes (instead of 4) as in Britain, with the First Division performing intellectual work and the Second Division performing routine duties; (b) raise the entrance admission age and have a more advanced examination for the upper class, with an elementary test for the lower level; and (c) occasional promotions to the upper class based on exceptional merit and judicious remuneration for the lower class (Pirotta, 1991, p.415).

1.4.8   Public Administration and Public Management Policy: The Clauson Committee

The recommendation to specifically examine the Public Service departments was supported by the appointment of the Clauson Committee, which had the mandate to investigate the expenditure of the Government of Malta and the organization of the Government Departments. It is this committee that steered Malta towards a more stable financial position (Pirotta, 1991, p.415). According to Pirotta (1991, p.416), the success of the Clauson Committee was due to a number of factors: (a) it was prepared to risk unpopularity by specifically identifying the offices that could be safely eliminated; (b) advocated drastic reduction in public expenditure; and (c) was able to take advantage of the stand, taken by the elected members of Council before the Royal Commission, in favour of such measures. The Clauson Committee considered that its primary task was to indicate economies sufficiently great enough to enable the Government to continue without an increase of taxation (Pirotta, 1991, p.417).

It is not the intention of this chapter to describe in detail the various measures proposed by the Clauson Committee; however, it is noted that the proposals and arguments in support of these proposals generally maintained the spirit of the recommendations made by the Royal Commission of 1911. The Clauson Committee advocated the complete separation between the Receiver-General and the Auditor-General, thus proposing a redefinition of their duties. They promoted the notion that the Receiver-General's duties be defined by Colonial Regulations and therefore his designation should be that of Treasurer and that the Auditor-General should not hold a seat on any of the existing Councils in Malta, since his responsibility was to ensure that each department, and the government as a body, was conducting its affairs according to the financial regulations and to call attention to irregularities when they failed to do so; therefore he could not be expected to examine decisions in which he had previously shared and agreed to as a member of the Executive and Legislative Council (Pirotta, 1991, p.418). The Clauson Committee strongly suggested the appointment of staff Auditor under the supervision of the Colonial Audit Department that would permit an independent audit to be conducted free from the pressures and internal politics of a small community, but this had to be supplemented by the improvement of the mechanisms in place for controlling expenditure within individual departments (Pirotta, 1991, p.419).

Despite the various recommendations that were made during this period, financial difficulties persisted, and unemployment continued to increase. According to Pirotta (1991, p.402–403) the economic crisis had a number of repercussions for the Maltese public service, namely: (a) the economic predicament and its resolution was viewed as being the responsibility of senior administrators and that the downsizing of the public service and reduction in public service expenditure was viewed as a likely solution to the economic crisis; (b) the growth of working class militancy, especially in the harbour, the dockyards and the public service itself; and (c) the grant, in 1921, of a modified form of responsible government to Malta. Because Malta had to import most of its food supplies, the prices of goods increased substantially during the war, making things very difficult for the population. Despite the subsidies given by government and the establishment of price control systems, these measures did not alleviate the difficulties encountered by those employed on a fixed wage, such as public servants (Pirotta, 1991, p.425). In May 1918, the clerical class submitted a complaint with the Governor regarding their existing condition, with the aim of securing long term reform, particularly the anomalies created by the Clauson Committee.

The Secretary of State for the Colonies authorised the grant of a rebate in the price of bread for members of the clerical establishments, whose salary was below £150 a year, and of war bonuses to nearly all categories of clerks (Pirotta, 1991, p.426). However, this was rejected and a meeting for all the government clerks was summoned for September 1918 to decide on a plan of action; claiming that their salaries should, at least, be sufficient to enable them to meet their primary needs (Pirotta, 1991, p.426). The result of the meeting was a Memorandum that expressed the view of those present, which was presented to the Governor by a delegation representing the clerks. This Memorandum attracted a forceful reaction from the Secretary of State in which further bonuses were offered subject to the Governor's approval, but no major concession was made (Pirotta, 1991, p.427). As a result, a second Memorandum was compiled that contested the views of Secretary of State and also reaffirmed the Clerical Class' claim that their difficulties had arisen from the adoption of the recommendations of the Clauson Committee, which had resulted in smaller annual increments, amongst other points (Pirotta, 1991, p.427–428). The tone of the memorandum was indicative of the mood prevailing among members of the clerical class and of the many difficulties facing the government in 1918, some of which were of an economic and financial nature (Pirotta, 1991, p.428).

1.4.9   Public Administration and Public Management Policy: Sette Giugno Public Riots

According to Pirotta (1991, p.428), as early as January 1918 the Governor had informed the Secretary of State that the mass of the population had hardly anything to eat and if paraffin could not be obtained, no means to cook the food. Furthermore, petitions for self-government became more frequent and insistent. To make matters worse and despite the grave financial condition of government, in January 1919 the Governor proposed a salary increase for Heads of Departments serving on the Councils that he justified on the basis that they were confidential advisers of the Governor (Pirotta, 1991, p.429). The outcome of this was that in May 1919, after street demonstrations and some violent incidents, the clerks initiated the first association within the public service, known as the Civil Service Association, which demanded the improvement of temporary war bonuses and the readjustment of salaries (Pirotta, 1991, p.430). This was followed in November 1919 with the formation of the Malta Union of Teachers (Pirotta, 1991, p.430). By the middle of July 1919, the Civil Service Association was recognised by the Governor; however by then the crisis in the Island had already reached its climax, since on June 7th, 1919 after considerable retrenchments and the expectation of other dismissals from the armed services and the dockyard, violent riots broke out in Valletta (Pirotta, 1991, p.431).

Hence, as a result of the social distress prevailing in Malta and the serious Sette Giugno public riots of 7th June 1919 in Valletta (Pirotta, 1991, p.402), the British authorities gave Malta a modified form of responsible government with greater autonomy for the locals during 1920s (Pirotta, 1996, p.341). This provided the opportunity for Maltese public administration to take on a distinct and prominent role. However, despite this, home rule was refused to the Maltese until 1921 (Pirotta, 1996, p.438). In 1921, self-government was granted under British rule, with Filippo Sciberras convening the first National Assembly in 1921. During this period the locals at times experienced considerable poverty (Attard, 1988). This was mainly due to overpopulation and the high dependency on British military expenditure that fluctuated with the demands of war. During the twentieth century, the British administration introduced a number of liberal constitutional reforms that were generally opposed by the Church and the privileged Maltese who preferred to hold on to their feudal privileges (Luke, 1949; Attard, 1988).

Malta obtained a bicameral parliament with a Senate and an elected Legislative Assembly (with Joseph Howard as Prime Minister) between 1921 and 1933. The 1930s is viewed as a period of instability regarding the relations between the Maltese political elite, the Maltese church, and the British rulers with the 1921 Constitution being suspended twice: (i) in 1930–32, following a conflict between the governing Constitutional Party and Church and the latter's subsequent imposition of mortal sin on voters of the party and its allies, thus making a free and fair election impossible; and (ii) in 1933, following the Government's budgetary vote for the teaching of Italian in elementary schools (Ardizzone, 1996). Hence, during the suspension of the 1921 Constitution, Malta return to its former state as a Crown Colony with the status it held in 1813. Before the arrival of the British, Italian had been the official language for hundreds of years and the language for the educated privileged. However, Italian was reduced in importance by the upsurge in the use of English. In 1934, English and Maltese were declared the sole official languages. That year only about 15% of the population could speak Italian fluently (Luke, 1949). This meant that out of 58,000 males qualified by age to be jurors, only 767 could qualify by language, as only Italian had until then been used in the courts (Luke, 1949).

1.4.10   Public Administration and Public Management Policy: Revising the Constitution

The Constitution was revised in 1936 to permit the nomination of members to the Executive Council under British rule. It was revised once more in 1939 to allow again an elected Council of Government under British rule. However, this period is viewed as being dominated by the defence policy of the British rulers and public service administration and management was geared towards the defence of Malta, as a British military base. Before World War II, the Royal Navy's Mediterranean Fleet's headquarters was in Valletta harbour. However, the headquarters of the Royal Navy's Mediterranean Fleet was moved to Alexandria, Egypt, in April 1937 despite Winston Churchill's objections (Bierman and Smith, 2002, p.36). According to Titterton (2002, p.xiii) there was a serious concern that Malta was susceptible to air attacks from Europe. When Italy declared war on 10th June 1940, Malta had a mere garrison of less than 4000 soldiers with about 5 weeks of food supplies for the population of about three hundred thousand. Furthermore, Malta's air defences were limited to about 42 anti-aircraft guns (34 'heavy' and eight 'light') and four Gloster Gladiators with only three pilots being available. Moreover, the Luqa Airfield was still under construction. This illustrates that Malta during the years preceding World War II was not viewed as a major military base. During World War I, Malta became known as the Nurse of the Mediterranean due to the number of wounded soldiers who came to be treated. During World War II, Malta became once again a fortress island reminiscent of the 1565 Great Siege.

Since, Malta was a British colony that was located close to Sicily and the Axis shipping lanes, Malta was continuously bombarded by the Italian and German air forces. Malta also attracted continuous bombing because it was a staging post for launching attacks by the British on the Italian navy and submarine base; and was also a listening post for monitoring German radio messages including Enigma traffic (Calvocoressi, 1981, p.42, 44). By the end of August 1940, the Gladiators were reinforced by 12 Hawker Hurricanes. During the first 5 months of combat, the island's aircraft destroyed or damaged about 37 Italian aircraft. Hence, Malta became a serious problem for the enemy forces and in January 1941, the German X. Fliegerkorps arrived in Sicily as the Afrika Korps arrived in Libya. The death toll on the Maltese population escalated to over 1150 persons killed in the first year or so of the commencement of hostilities. On 15th April 1942, King George VI awarded the George Cross 'to the island fortress of Malta – its people and defenders' and on 8th December 1943, Franklin D. Roosevelt arrived in Malta and awarded a United States Presidential Citation to the people of Malta on behalf of the people of the United States (Rudolf and Berg, 2010, p.106, 197–198). The Allies launched their invasion of Sicily from Malta in 1943. After the Cassibile armistice in the same year, the Italian Fleet surrendered to the Allies in Malta. In 1945, Churchill and Roosevelt met in Malta prior to the Yalta Conference with Joseph Stalin.

1.4.11   Public Administration and Public Management Policy: Road to Self-Government

After the Second World War, the 1946 National Assembly resulted in the 1947 constitution, with the Maltese islands attaining self-government, and Dr. Paul Boffa became the fifth Prime Minister of Malta. Zammit Marmara (2010) argues that Sir Paul Boffa was instrumental in obtaining recognition for the Maltese Language in the law courts, and the introduction of compulsory primary education and old-age pensions. He contends that the Labour Party had included compulsory education in its manifesto since the first general election of 1921. Furthermore, the Labour parliamentary group urged the British Administration to improve education, the outcome being the Compulsory Education Ordinance of 1946, which made it compulsory for children, aged 6–14, to attend school (Zammit Marmara, 2010). Cocks (2012) observes that an important milestone for Sir Paul Boffa was when his party granted the right for women over 21 to vote, which resulted in an overwhelming electoral victory in 1947. During the 1947 legislature, Sir Paul Boffa introduced the Old Age Pensions Act of 1948 and the Income Tax Act of the same year (Cocks,

2012). In 1949, following the Labour Party's ultimatum to Britain concerning financial help, the Labour Party split up and Dom Mintoff became leader of the Malta Labour Party (MLP).

In 1950, the MLP insisted on either full integration with the UK or else self-determination (independence). On the other hand, the Partit Nazzjonalista (PN) of Giorgio Borġ Olivier favoured independence, with the same 'dominion status' of Canada, Australia and New Zealand. In 1949, the Maltese Senate (Upper House of Parliament) was abolished. In December 1955, a Round Table Conference was held in London to discuss the future of Malta that was attended by the new Prime Minister, Dom Mintoff; Opposition Leader, Borġ Olivier; and other Maltese politicians, along with the British Colonial Secretary, Alan Lennox-Boyd. The British government decided to offer Malta three seats in the British House of Commons (The Spectator, 1956, p.3) with the condition that the Home Office would have responsibility for Maltese affairs through the Colonial Office (Smith, 2006, p.133). The British also proposed that: (a) the Maltese Parliament would retain responsibility over all affairs except defence, foreign policy, and taxation; and (b) the Maltese were to have social and economic parity with the UK. A referendum regarding the UK integration was held on the 11th and 12th February 1956, with just over 77 percent of those that voted being in favour of the proposal. However, because the Nationalist Party boycotted the referendum, only 59.1 per cent of the electorate voted, thus the parliamentary opposition claimed that the result was inconclusive (Zarb Dimech, 2011). During the years 1955–58, administration experts were engaged to advice on a reform of the public service. This gave rise to new approaches to the training of civil servants with economics becoming so important that scholarships were offered to civil servants to study in Britain. Also, during this period, several social reforms took place, which extended the role of the civil service, such as the introduction of National Insurance, attempts to establish a National Health Service and extension of education at technical level amongst many others.

Circumstances were also changing during this period in that the strategic importance of Malta to the Royal Navy was decreasing resulting in the reluctance of the British government to maintain the naval dockyards, which were the main employer of skilled labour in Malta. Things came to a head when the Admiralty decided to dismiss 40 workers at the dockyard. Time (1958) reported the Maltese Prime Minister declaring that '*representatives of the Maltese people in Parliament declare that they are no longer bound by agreements and obligations toward the British government...*' (The 1958 Caravaggio incident). The Colonial Secretary reacted by sending a cable to the Prime Minister, stating that he had '*recklessly hazarded*' the whole integration process (Time, 1958). The Prime Minister resigned as a sign of protest, while the Leader of the Opposition refused to form an alternative government. This resulted in the Maltese islands reverting back to direct colonial administration from London, with the Malta Labour Party abandoning support for integration and advocating independence. In 1959, an Interim Constitution was instituted that granted the establishment of an Executive Council under British rule.

1.4.12   Public Administration and Public Management Policy: Blood Commission and the Attainment of Independence

In 1961, the Blood Commission recommended a new constitution allowing partial self-government, where broadcasting; defence and foreign policy; police; and other strategic aspects were excluded under what was known as 'Reserved Matters'. In March 1962, Giorgio Borġ Olivier became Prime Minister when the Stolper report was delivered. According to Grech (2015), the United Nations had conducted a study of the Maltese economy during the years preceding independence (Stolper et al., 1964) that had recommended mass emigration as the only feasible solution in the long run. This was similar to the recommendation dating back to over half a century of the Royal Commission Report on the Finances, Economic Position and Judicial Procedure of Malta of 1911, that proposed mass emigration to resolve the acute unemployment concern (Pirotta, 1991, p.412). However, Grech (2015) observes that there was a divergence of opinion regarding mass emigration. He cites Balogh and Seers (1955) who had argued that in a small country like Malta, emigration would have a negative impact due to the limited pool of skilled workforce. On 21st September 1964, Malta gained its (partial) independence. Grech (2015) argues that contrary to the dire predictions of the experts contributing to the Stolper Report, there was instead considerable success in developing alternative sources of employment to reliance on the British naval base, which before its dismantling had accounted for over a quarter of total employment (Findlay and Wellisz, 1993).

According to Warrington (2008), the creation of the State of Malta in March 1962 displaced the Administrative Class of the Malta Civil Service from its commanding position in the constitutional order. It is noted that the public service is the oldest governing institution in Malta and was established considerably before the creation of parliament and political parties. Thus, every governing administration that ruled the Maltese Islands had an institution, such as the public service to support it in formulating and implementing its policies. Warrington (2008) contends that as Malta attained statehood, the fate of the administrative elite, which he views as falling from grace, signified a transition from the conventional administrative foundation that was based upon three pillars: British overlordship, the civil service, and the Catholic hierarchy. Warrington (2008) argues that Malta's administrative traditions stemmed from four centuries of well-organised, generally benevolent, but alien and authoritarian government, first under the Knights of St John (1530–1798), later under British rule (1800–1964), where the civil administration serviced, supported and secured a large military establishment projecting power overseas.

It must be recognised that Malta was viewed as having great strategic importance and thus developed into an important military and naval base. Hence, the economic policies during the years under different rulers were dominated by this aspect. Under the British Rule, the major industry that was the main employer on the Island was the Royal Naval Dockyard and the associated military presence. The expansion and growth of various industries, such as tourism, textile and manufacturing experienced a boost mainly after the Maltese independence was granted from Britain in

1964. The chapters that follow will provide details of the transition that has taken place in public administration and management in Malta over the years. A transition, where 'Fortress Malta' and the military connotation that the term projects, is no longer part of the Maltese vocabulary.

1.5 Conclusion

For centuries, Malta's foreign rulers assigned the islands a fortress role on the strength of its highly strategic location in the Mediterranean. In fact, the livelihood of the Maltese people became dependent to a very large extent on employment in naval and military establishments and maritime trade related activities. Thus, Maltese public administration and management was highly geared towards supporting the established naval and military bases. In 1955, for instance, 36% of the Maltese workforce was employed directly with British defence departments; 25% with Government; and 39% in private industry that had a major input in supporting the British defence departments and government. Maltese public administration and management was in continuous transition under different foreign rulers with their consequent diverse national and management cultures.

References

Allen, D. F. (1990). *The social and religious world of a knight of Malta in the Caribbean, c. 1632-1660.* Available from: http://maltahistory.eu5.net/cc/CC08.html. Accessed on: 31 Jan 2020.

Angefry. (2014). *The rise and fall of the callus fortunes – Plague of Malta 1813.* Available from: https://lancstolevant.wordpress.com/2014/12/31/the-rise-and-fall-of-the-callus-fortunes-plague-of-malta-1813/. Accessed on: 11 Feb 2020.

Aquilina, J. (2011). *The Malta Customs Department.* WIPO inter-regional symposium on enforcement of intellectual property rights (IPRs), Belgrade.

Ardizzone, P. (1996). *Italian cultural initiatives in the 1930s for Malta and for the Maltese communities abroad.* Available from: http://www.intratext.com/IXT/ITA2413/_P6.HTM. Accessed on: 6 Feb 2020.

Attard, J. (1988). *Britain and Malta.* Publishers Enterprises Group (PEG) Ltd.

Balogh, T., & Seers, D. (1955). *The economic problems of Malta: An interim report.* Government Printing Office (Malta).

Bierman, J., & Smith, C. (2002). *The Battle of Alamein: Turning Point, World War II.* Viking Adult. Available from:https://archive.org/details/battleofalameint00bier/page/36. Accessed on: 7 Feb 2020.

Bosredon de Ransijat, J., & Scicluna, J. (2013). *Blockade: Malta 1798–1800 : the diary and memoirs of a French knight during the occupation of Malta.* Malta University Press.

Calleja, J. (1994). The evolution of education in Malta. A philosophy in the making. *Revue des mondes musulmans et de la Méditerranée, 71,* 185–197.

Calvocoressi, P. (1981). *Top secret ultra – Volume 10 of Ballantine espionage intelligence library* (reprint ed.). Ballantine Books.

Cassar Pullicino, J. (1949). *The order of St. John in Maltese folk memory.* Available from: https://web.archive.org/web/20160417173522/http://melitensiawth.com/incoming/Index/ Scientia%20%28Malta%29/Scientia.%2015%281949%294%28Oct.-Dec.%29/01.pdf. Accessed on: 31 Jan 2020.

Central Bank of Malta (CBM). (2014). *Coinage of the Knights in Malta. Central Bank of Malta. Archived from the original.* Available from: http://www.centralbankmalta.org/site/currency1b. html. Accessed on: 30 Jan 2020.

Cocks, J. (2012). *Sir Paul Boffa: The doctor and politician.* The Times, 6 July 2012. Available from: https://timesofmalta.com/articles/view/Sir-Paul-Boffa-The-doctor-and-politician.427390. Accessed on: 4 Aug 2020.

Cohen, R. (1920). *Knights of Malta, 1523–1798.* Available from: http://www.phoenixmasonry.org/ knights_of_malta.htm. Accessed on: 6 Feb 2020.

Cremona, J.J. (1994). *The Maltese constitution and constitutional history since 1813.* PEG Publications.

Di Marco, E. (2013). The state of the Maltese economy at the end of the eighteenth century. Considerations based on the deeds of a local notary Stefano Farrugia. *Journal of Maltese History, 3*(2), 91–100.

Ellul, M. (2007). Wignacourt aqueduct. *Times of Malta 3rd February 2007.* Available from: http:// www.timesofmalta.com/articles/view/20070203/local/wignacourt-aqueduct.27666. Accessed on: 30 Jan 2020.

Findlay, R., & Wellisz, S. (1993). *The political economy of poverty, equity and growth: Five small open economies.* World Bank.

Frendo, H. (2004). *Storja Ta' Malta (Vol.3).* Klabb Kotba Maltin.

Gass, R. (2010). *What is transformational change?* Co-founder of the Rockwood Leadership Institute, Social Transformation Project.

Gaille, B. (2018). *Advantages and disadvantages of transformational leadership.* BrandonGaille. Available   from: https://brandongaille.com/22-advantages-and-disadvantages-of-transformational-leadership/. Accessed on: 31 Jan 2020.

Gebruiker (2012). *A brief history of the Franchise in Malta under British Rule.* Available from: http://melitensiawth.com/incoming/Index/Scientia%20(Malta)/Scientia.%2028(1962)1(Jan.-Mar.)/02.pdf. Accessed on: 11 Feb 2020.

Grech, A. G. (2015). *The evolution of the Maltese economy since independence.* Munich personal RePEc archive. Available from: https://mpra.ub.uni-muenchen.de/68392/. Accessed on: 5/82020.

Hardman, W. (1909). *A history of Malta during the period of the French and British occupations, 1798-1815.* Longmans, Green, and Co. Available from: https://archive.org/stream/ historyofmaltadu00hard#page/272/mode/2up/search/Ball. Accessed on: 5 Feb 2020.

Hoe, S. (2015). *Malta: Women, history, books and places.* Holo Books /The Arbitration Press.

HSBC. (2020). *The HSBC Group in Malta – Fact Sheet.* HSBC Bank Malta p.l.c. Available from: https://www.about.hsbc.com.mt/hsbc-in-malta. Accessed on: 11 Feb 2020.

Lansink, E. (2018). *Malta Uncovered.* Available from: https://www.maltauncovered.com/valletta-capital-city/history/. Accessed on: 30 Jan 2020.

Luke, S. H. (1949). *Malta – An account and an appreciation.* George G. Harrap & Ltd..

Lyceum. (2008). *Maltese History: The first years of British Rule 1800–1824.* Available at: https:// storjaweb.files.wordpress.com/2016/10/unit_g_early_british_rule_in_malta_to_1824_13p. pdf. Accessed on: 5 Feb 2020.

Lyceum. (2013). *Malta under the French: 1798–1800.* Available at: https://storjaweb.files.word-press.com/2016/10/unit_f_-malta_under_the_french_occupation_13p.pdf. Accessed on: 31 Jan 2020.

MacGill, T. (1839). *A hand book, or guide, for strangers visiting Malta.* Available from: https:// books.google.com.mt/books?id=bJ8NAAAAYAAJ&pg=PA65#v=onepage&q&f=false. Accessed on: 6 Feb 2020.

Malta Independent (2007). *'Sex in the City' tour: The knights and their ladies of the night*. Malta Independent, 27th March 2007. Available from: https://web.archive.org/web/20161206180216/ http://www.independent.com.mt/articles/2007-03-25/news/sex-in-the-city-tour-the-knights-and-their-ladies-of-the-night-171028/. Accessed on: 31 Jan 2020.

Mea, J. (2005). Customs tariff in Malta since 1530. *Journal of the Maltese Historical Society,* 2(2), 88–94.

Office of the Prime Minister (OPM). (2008). *Auberge de Castille. Office of the Prime Minister.* Available from: https://web.archive.org/web/20080705182935/http://www.opm.gov.mt/ auberge.de.castille.htm. Accessed on: 31 Jan 2020.

Persson, K. G. (1999). *Grain Markets in Europe 1500–1900: Integration and deregulation (Cambridge studies in modern economic history)*. Cambridge University Press.

Pirotta, G. (1991). *The administrative politics of a micro-state: The Maltese Public Service, 1800-1940*. Submitted by Godfrey A. Pirotta for the degree of PhD of the University of Bath 1991.

Pirotta, G. (1996). *The Maltese public service 1800–1940: The administrative politics of a micro-state, Malta*. Mireva Publications.

Police. (2020). *History of the Malta Police*. Available from: https://pulizija.gov.mt/en/police-force/ Pages/History-of-the-Malta-Police.aspx. Accessed on: 11 Feb 2020.

Rabin, J., Hildreth, W.B., & Miller, G. J. (1989). *Handbook of public administration*. J. Rabin, W. Bartley Hildreth, & G. J. Miller (Eds): Marcel Dekker

Restilli, F. & Sammut, J. C. (1977). The Coinage of the Knights in Malta (2 Volumes). Available from: https://bdlbooks.com/product/the-coinage-of-the-knights-in-malta/. Accessed on: 30 Jan 2020.

Rudolf, U. J., & Berg, W. G. (2010). *Historical dictionary of Malta*. The Scarecrow Press.

Sant, M. (2014). Celebrating two centuries of public auditing in Malta. *The Times of Malta, 12 October 2014*. Available from: https://timesofmalta.com/articles/view/Celebrating-two-centuries-of-public-auditing-in-Malta.539451. Accessed on: 11 Feb 2020.

Savona-Ventura, C. (1999). Civil hospitals in Malta in the last two hundred years. *HistoriaHospitalium, 21*, 45–63. Michael Triltsch Verlag: Available from: https://www.um.edu. mt/library/oar//handle/123456789/23708. Accessed on: 30 Jan 2020.

Scicluna, S. H. (1936). *The French occupation of Malta*. Empire Press.

Sharp, P. R. (2009). Malta and the nineteenth century grain trade: British free trade in a microcosm of empire? *Journal of Maltese History, 1*(2), 20–34.

SMHO. (2020). Sovereign Military Hospitaller Order of St John of Jerusalem of Rhodes and of Malta. Available from: https://www.orderofmalta.int/history/1048-to-the-present/. Accessed on: 30 Jan 2020.

Smith, S. C. (2006). *British documents on the end of the empire (series B volume 11): Malta*. The Stationery Office.

Spiteri, R. (2013a). *Maltese history: C. Some of the order's projects in Malta*. Available from: https:// storjaweb.files.wordpress.com/2016/10/unit_c_case_studies_of_hospitaller_projects_14p.pdf. Accessed on: 31 Jan 2020.

Spiteri, R. (2013b). *Relations between Church & State in British Malta 1800 to 1975*. Available from: https://storjaweb.files.wordpress.com/2016/10/unit_m_relations_between_church__ state_under_the_british_1800_to_1984_14p.pdf. Accessed on: 11 Feb 2020.

Stolper, W.F., Hellberg, R.E.R., & Callander, S.O. (1964). *Economic adaptation and development in Malta*. Report prepared for the Government of Malta under the United Nations Programme of Technical and Assistance of the Department of Economic and Social Affairs.

The Spectator. (1956). *Dangerous game*. The Spectator, 10 February 1956. Available from: http://archive.spectator.co.uk/article/10th-february-1956/3/dangerous-game). Accessed on: 7 Feb 2020.

Thornton, W.H. (1836). *Memoir of the finances of Malta, under the government of the order of St John of Jerusalem, during the last years of its dominion, and as compared with those of the present time, Malta, 1836*. Printed at the Government Press, Malta, 1836.

Time. (1958). *Penny-Wise. Time Magazine, 13 January 1958*. Available from: http://content.time. com/time/magazine/article/0,9171,862830,00.html. Accessed on: 7 Feb 2020.

Titterton, G. A. (2002). *The Royal Navy and the Mediterranean* (Vol. 2). Routledge, Taylor and Francis Group.

Ware Allen, B. (2006). *Emperor Vs. Pirate: Tunis 1535*. Available from: https://www.historynet. com/emperor-vs-pirate-tunis-1535.htm. Accessed on: 8 Feb 2020.

Warrington, E. (2008). The fall from grace of an administrative elite: The administrative class of the Malta civil service and the transfer of power – April 1958 to September 1964. *Journal of Maltese History, 1*(1), 48–66.

Vassallo, V. G. (1997). *Notable dates in Malta's history*. Available from: http://www.vassallomalta. com/notabledates.htm. Accessed on: 8 Feb 2020.

Xerri, J. A. (2016). *L-Iżvilupp tal-Edukazzjoni f'Malta: 1430–1924*. Sensiela Kotba Socjalisti.

Zarb Dimech, A. (2011). *Maltese Referenda past and present*. The Malta Independent. Available from: (http://www.independent.com.mt/articles/2011-05-29/news/maltese-referenda-past-and-present-293274/). Accessed on: 7 Feb 2020.

Zammit Marmara, D. (2010). *Pawlu Boffa*. Sensiela Kotba Soċjalisti.

Zerafa, T. (2019). *The French occupation*. Times of Malta, 25 January 2019. Available from: https:// timesofmalta.com/articles/view/the-french-occupation.700140. Accessed on: 31 Jan 2020.

Chapter 2
Historical Background of the Maltese Public Service Administration and Management (The Turning Point)

"In the modern era, it isn't enough to write, you must also be the Writer, with a capital 'W,' and play your part as the protagonist in the cautionary narrative in which you will fail or triumph, be in or out, hot or cold, ride the wheel of fortune."

Tony Kushner, American dramatist (Born: July 1956)

Malta gained independence from the United Kingdom on 21st September 1964. However, Malta still relied on its military strategic position in the Mediterranean for its economic survival. It was not until 31st March 1979 that Malta ceased being a fortress island, when all military and naval facilities closed down. The Government declared 31st March 1979 as "Freedom Day." This day marks the historical event when the last British troops and the Royal Navy left Malta after their presence that date back to 1800. On taking power in 1971, the Labour Government signified that it wanted to re-negotiate the military and naval lease agreement with the United Kingdom. Following prolonged and at times apprehensive talks, a new agreement was signed, whereby the lease was extended till the end of March 1979 at a greatly increased rent. On 31 March 1979, the last British Forces left Malta. For the first time in a millennium, Malta was no longer a military base of a foreign power and it became in effect independent (de facto) and independent as a legal right (de jure). Thus, the Maltese public administration faced its first major challenge in the post-independence era. The challenge was the transformation from administering an economy based on foreign defence activities to a free market economy. The 1970s and 1980's were characterised by an upsurge in economic growth and the introduction of a host of social benefits and services in a radical effort to curb poverty. In fact, successive government administrations over the decades have focused on economic growth and improving the social welfare of the Maltese citizen. Public Service employees have always risen to the challenge under various governments with different ideological philosophies, with the specific aim of serving the Maltese citizen.

© The Author(s), under exclusive license to Springer Nature Switzerland AG 2021
F. Bezzina et al., *Public Service Reforms in a Small Island State*,
Public Administration, Governance and Globalization 22,
https://doi.org/10.1007/978-3-030-74357-4_2

2.1   Introduction

Malta gained independence from the United Kingdom on 21st September 1964. Under its 1964 constitution, Malta became a liberal parliamentary democracy within the Commonwealth, with Queen Elizabeth II as sovereign of Malta, and a Governor-General exercising executive authority on her behalf. The direction and control of the government and the nation's affairs were vested in the cabinet under the leadership of a Maltese Prime Minister. However, it was not until December 1974 that Malta became a Republic with executive authority being vested in a Maltese president, and it was not until Freedom Day of March 1979 that all foreign defence bases ceased operations in Malta.

The Maltese public administration faced its first major contemporary challenge in this post-independence era. The challenge was the transformation from administering an economy based on foreign defence activities to a free market economy. This development required a complete overhaul of government organization, particularly the creation of new government ministries and numerous other governing authorities. Clearly, the role of public administration and management was highly dependent on the Government philosophy and strategic direction in a particular period. Hence, the transition period of the 1960s and 1970s is characterised by new industrial legislation; the creation of industrial estates and industrial incentives; tourism and port development; revised customs structure; a regime of tax and duty concessions to industry; the conversion of the Royal Naval Dockyard to commercial ship repairing; and a programme of infrastructural works and state aid to stimulate private sector intervention. Furthermore, a new dimension was added to Maltese public administration and management. The Government in the 1970s launched major social reforms in housing, health, education and welfare benefits that enabled the development of a welfare state. This presented a major challenge and required new competencies for Maltese public administration and management employees. These industrial and social reforms fully shifted the focus of public administration and management away from a bureaucratic driven mindset towards becoming citizen centric.

This chapter will trace Public Service administration and management over an approximate period of half a century. The chapter commences with the post-1964 independence period, leading into the social reforms of the 1970s, through the technological and somewhat turbulent developments of the 1980s, the continuing technological developments and preparedness for European Union (EU) Membership of the 1990s, and the eventual achievement of EU Membership and monetary union of the 2000s up to March 2013.

2.2   Public Administration and Management in the Post-Independence Era

The immediate post-independence years of the 1960s were critical for Malta's development and, to a great extent, established the foundation for the Public Service administration and management of the modern era. The mid to late 1960s was described as the Great Society at the time when President Lyndon B. Johnson launched a set of domestic programs in the United States in 1964–65 (Woods, 2016). Woods (2016) argued that the Great Society marked the culmination of the effort by liberals to use the concept of positive rights (the right to a decent education, a good job, adequate health care) as opposed to negative rights (freedom of religion, freedom of speech, the right to vote) to achieve social and economic justice. According to Woods (2016), President Johnson contended that '*poverty, ignorance, and ill health were not the fault of a class or group — they were boils on the body politic. These things were not the result of evil intent or greed on the part of groups or individuals, but seemingly free radicals that everyone hoped to see eliminated from the environment.*'

Moreover, the 1960s can also be generally characterised as an era of nationalism and anti-colonialism across the globe. This, coupled with the decline of the British navy, saw the influence of a major colonial power dwindling to its lowest level. At independence in September 1964, Malta entered a very turbulent period. Hence, on attaining Independence in 1964, the Maltese became masters of their own home in the Cold War era and a world in turmoil. The old empires were crumbling, and new rivalries became discernible by the ever-growing impact of globalisation and the resultant international trade. Malta had become independent and had to earn its keep through its own strategies and initiatives. It also had to undertake new responsibilities at the United Nations, the International Monetary Fund amongst many others, placing much greater responsibility on the Public Service administrators and managers, who often found themselves in uncharted waters.

2.2.1   Maltese State of Affairs Leading Up to the Independence of September 1964

According to IBRD (1963), the per capita income of the Maltese people in 1963 (about $390) exceeded those of some other southern European countries, such as Spain, Greece and Cyprus, but was lower than Italy. Furthermore, it was reported that the high standard of living had been made possible mainly by British military expenditure, which had been equivalent to about half of Malta's national income and accounted for about two-thirds of its foreign exchange earnings. The British military services, excluding a large Admiralty Dockyard, directly employed about 16,000 workers, or some 17% of the total labour force. A small part of the Government's current expenditure and almost all its capital expenditure were financed from the United Kingdom's grants and loans. Savings in 1963 were high, representing about 19% of the national income and were largely invested abroad. IBRD (1963) contended that, as a result of Malta's reduced importance as a strategic base, British military expenditure declined. This placed a large part of the Admiralty Dockyard, which was leased to a private firm and was the largest single employer (5600 workers) in the private sector, in a very precarious financial position. Moreover, IBRD (1963) confirmed that an investigation into this company's financial affairs, led the Malta Government to appoint a provisional Council of Administration that took over the management of the Dockyard.

IBRD (1963) also contended that alternative sources of income and employment were being sought for the Maltese labour force by government, particularly as a result of encouraging the establishment of new industries, amongst them tourism. Under the government's 5-year Development Plan of 1959/60–1964/65, high priority had been given to establishing new industries, particularly tourism. However, progress during the first 3 years of the plan had been reported as being rather slow (IBRD, 1963). IBRD (1963) concluded that Malta was facing a major problem of reorientation and diversification. The Maltese had a long tradition of hard work and industrial skills, but they were experiencing difficulties in shifting from assured work for the military service, to the competitive world of producing for export. They also reported that Malta's external public debt was small ($3.4 million equivalent), but the Government at that time had planned to borrow abroad an additional $18.1 million under the Development Plan. The service payment on this debt (including the loan repayment) was expected to average about $1.9 million per annum, which was estimated to account for about 20% of the domestic exports in 1964. IBRD (1963) argued that in carrying out its reconstruction program, Malta required substantial assistance from abroad. They concluded that in view of the magnitude of the adjustments being faced by Malta and Malta's continued financial dependence on the United Kingdom at the time, the envisaged Bank loan relied on a United Kingdom guarantee. IBRD (1963) reported the following trends regarding Malta during this period:

(a) Emigration ranged from a high of 10,000 to a low of 2000 persons a year, with a declining trend.
(b) Unemployment had risen and by December 1962 exceeded 6% of the labour force.
(c) Employment of the labour force numbering about 94,000 was utilised in primary production (8%); manufacturing and construction (26%); government (18%); military services (17%); commerce (12%); and other services (19%).
(d) A low ratio of labour force to population of working age (about 54%) was experienced due to the small number of women in the labour force (18% in 1960). However, there was evidence that more women were entering employment, mainly due to the new industries.
(e) An advanced social security system, where the National Insurance Act provided benefits for sickness, old age, injury, amongst others.

(f) The minimum wage for industrial workers in government or the military services (equivalent to U.S. $0.38 per hour) was considerably less than in most industrialized countries of Europe, but more than that of Spain and Southern Italy. In the private industry, minimum wages were somewhat lower.

(g) Illiteracy rate was relatively high at about 30%.

(h) There was little poverty. Living standards in Malta were among the highest in southern Europe and were evenly spread. Despite the concentration of people in townships, there were no serious problems of housing, but water was very limited and a major concern at that time.

IBRD (1963) argued that the Development Plan (1959/60–1964/65) gave high priority to manufacturing industries in order to provide alternative income and employment to workers that were to be released from Military Services. The incentives provided by government included the following:

(a) Income tax holidays of up to 10 years;

(b) Exemption from import duties on capital goods and, in some cases, raw materials;

(c) Imposing anti-dumping duties;

(d) Providing grants and loans for fixed capital expenditure ranging from one-third to one-half;

(e) Providing fully serviced sites and ready-built factories at the government's Industrial Estate at a nominal rent.

These measures were specifically applied to new or expanding enterprises that were likely to create employment or increase the national product. Basically, the above describes the situation of Malta in 1963, leading to Independence in September 1964. It also provides an indication of the work that was being undertaken by the Public Service in preparation for Malta's Independence to establish a robust Public Service administration and management institution, to ensure Malta's success in the future.

2.2.2 Public Administration and Management in the Post-Independence Era until 1971

Public service administration and management under the leadership of Prime Minister Dr George Borg Olivier (1962–1971) can only be characterised as 'Laissez-Faire', where the introduction of the public administration and management reforms were incremental in nature and reactive to the economic circumstances of that time. Laissez-faire leadership, also known as 'delegative' leadership, is where a group of elite members in the Public Service are given the authority to make the decisions, and the executive members (the Prime Minister and Ministers) in most instances are hands-off. This leadership style has several possible drawbacks, but it also has benefits in certain circumstances. Laissez-faire leadership does not necessarily mean that leaders abdicate their responsibilities. On the contrary, Laissez-faire leaders give authority to their administrators but still take full responsibility for the decisions and actions taken by their delegates. For example, according to Lashinsky (2011), Steve Jobs at Apple would give directives to his team about what he desired, but then left it up to their own devices to figure out how to fulfil his wishes. Laissez-faire leadership proves beneficial when the top public servants have the skills to succeed and are motivated and capable of working on their own. Thus, they can work independently and can achieve the tasks with very little guidance. Obviously, this type of leadership requires a great deal of trust and the leader needs to have full confidence in his management team, in terms of skills, knowledge, and follow through, to complete their undertakings without being micromanaged.

In the 1960s, the Nationalist government lead by Dr Borg Oliver was perceived as a 'conservative administration' (Dowdall, 1972). This conservative attitude was also mirrored by the Public Service elite. This conservative outlook may have resulted from the paternal relationship that existed with the British Government, and the fact that historically Public Service officers were mainly subject to the authority of British officials, without being given the opportunity to initiate any major undertaking without their approval. Consequently, in general, the Maltese public servants of the 1960s tended to lack expertise, were risk averse and held a very conservative mind-set, with all its implications. Under these circumstances, laissez-faire leadership may not have been the best approach, particularly where group members lacked the knowledge or experience, they needed to complete tasks and make decisions on a national level. This point is significant because Dr Borg Oliver's opponent, Dom Mintoff, who became Prime Minister in 1971, had a diametrically opposite management leadership style to that of Dr Borg Oliver, which tended to lead to transformational change, as opposed to the incremental adjustment that a conservative standpoint encourages. Having said this, it is not excluded that a laissez-faire approach to leadership may have brought out certain qualities from exceptional and gifted Public Service leaders at that time. After the 1964 independence, senior public servants were required to be creative, particularly under the laissez-faire mode of leadership. They also needed to be highly motivated, skilled, and dedicated to their work that were conducive to obtaining good results during the creation of an independent nation.

The challenge that was encountered by the Public Service in the post-independence 1960s was its capacity to implement government policies regarding economic development, external trade and foreign relations (Alshinawi, 2014, p.16). According to Alshinawi (2014, p.17), Dr Borg Oliver's Nationalist Party was committed to further Malta's Western European values and interests, 'emphasised' the continuity of Malta's links with Britain and pursued 'a closer relationship with the European Economic Community'. Whilst, according to Findlay and Wellisz (1993, p.271), Dom Mintoff's Labour opposition pursued an electoral campaign based on a 'platform of non-alignment, government leadership in the economy, and social reform'. As it will be shown later in this chapter, the view expressed by Alshinawi (2014), and Findlay and Wellisz (1993) above will be confirmed by the research conducted using the Financial Estimates (Ordinary Budget) for the relevant years, namely the periods 1964 to 1971 and 1971 to 1987.

In the immediate post-independence period, public administration and management was confronted with a major challenge related to an extremely rigid economic structure, in a scenario in which very few alternative activities existed to offset the effects of British defence spending fluctuations, which resulted from a long history of dependence on the colonial military and defence sector (Alshinawi, 2014, p.19). In fact, according to Dowdall (1972, p.467), Malta was described as an excellent example where a weak and penetrated state was able to exploit a larger dependent and developed nation. Thus, the key obstacle the government and its Public Service administration and management organisation had to overcome was to adopt a turnaround strategy, whereby Malta embraced industrialization to provide employment to a large proportion of a wage-earning labouring class. Events at the time suggest that this turnaround strategy was continued by both the Nationalist and Labour administrations in preparation for the complete closure of the naval base, when the Royal Navy finally withdrew in 1979.

Like other developing and aspiring nations, the government in Malta had a number of important objectives that were aligned with the economic theories of that period, namely, a higher degree of production ownership; protection of domestic industries and markets; and setting of trade barriers (Alshinawi, 2014, p.20). Tanzi (1997, pp. 1–2) argued that these objectives from a historical viewpoint were typical from the early twentieth century. He maintained that all countries experienced a significant growth in the role of the government in the economy, including a considerable escalation in public spending in industrial countries. Hence, the state through its public administration and management organisation was expected to define and plan economic strategy, and to bring together the required resources for the building of the social and physical infrastructure needed. Thus, Alshinawi (2014, p.20–21) contends that the public administration and management organisation on behalf of government needed to take the lead in initiating political reforms; formulating fundamental national economic development plans; and taking an active role in dealing with foreign capital. Moreover, to increase the much-needed international trade and secure foreign investment, the Malta government initiated diplomatic relations with several countries in mid to late 1960s, including Italy, Australia, Libya, USA and USSR, amongst others.

An insight into the role of public administration and management in Malta may be explored by examining in some detail the Malta Government Estimates for the financial years 1963–1964 to 1970–1971. Table 2.1 illustrates that Public Service activities focused five sectors, namely Customs and Excise (45%); Licences and Other Indirect Taxes (8%); Income Tax (10%); Fees of Office and Reimbursements (8%); and revenue related to currency (8%).

Table 2.1 suggests that Customs and Excise consistently dominated the Public Service activities during this period. This is not surprising, since this activity had always been the focus of successive governments since the time of the Knights. Moreover, Income Tax had an increasing trend over the years, reflecting government's endeavours through its public administration and management organisation

Table 2.1 Government estimates by financial years – revenue expressed as %

Ordinary revenue	1963–64	1964–65	1965–66	1966–67	1967–68	1968–69	1969–70	1970–71	Ave.
Customs & excise	47%	43%	43%	43%	45%	45%	47%	42%	**45%**
Harbour & quarantine	0%	0%	0%	0%	0%	0%	0%	0%	0%
Licences, Taxes etc.	6%	6%	6%	7%	8%	8%	10%	9%	**8%**
Income Tax	9%	10%	8%	10%	11%	10%	11%	14%	**10%**
Succession & donation	2%	2%	2%	3%	2%	2%	3%	3%	2%
Fees of Court	0%	0%	0%	0%	0%	0%	0%	0%	0%
Fees of office & reimbursements	6%	8%	9%	9%	7%	8%	7%	7%	**8%**
Posts	2%	3%	3%	3%	4%	3%	3%	2%	3%
Telephones	2%	2%	2%	2%	2%	2%	2%	2%	2%
Water	2%	2%	2%	2%	2%	2%	2%	1%	2%
Rents	1%	1%	1%	1%	1%	1%	1%	1%	1%
Interest	2%	3%	2%	0%	1%	1%	1%	1%	1%
Pensions Contributions	0.34%	0.32%	0.32%	0.29%	0.29%	0.26%	0.24%	0.22%	0.28%
Lotteries	4%	4%	3%	3%	4%	4%	4%	3%	4%
Note Security Fund	10%	8%	8%	12%	9%	2%	0%	0%	**6%**
Central Bank of Malta	0%	0%	0%	0%	0%	5%	6%	9%	**2%**
Miscellaneous Receipts	1%	1%	1%	1%	1%	1%	1%	2%	1%
Land Sales	0%	0%	0%	0%	0%	0%	0%	0%	0%
Civil Aviation	2%	2%	2%	2%	2%	2%	2%	2%	2%
Electricity	3%	0%	0%	0%	0%	0%	0%	0%	0%
Civil Defence	0%	0%	0%	0%	0%	0%	0%	0%	0%
Total Ordinary Revenue:	*100%*	*95%*	*92%*	*99%*	*98%*	*98%*	*100%*	*100%*	*98%*
Contribution by British government towards Technical Education	0%	1%	1%	1%	2%	2%	0%	0%	1%
Contribution by British government towards Ordinary Services	0%	4%	7%	0%	0%	0%	0%	0%	1%
Total Revenue:	**100%**	**100%**	**100%**	**100%**	**100%**	**100%**	**100%**	**100%**	**100%**

Source: Malta Government Estimates for the financial years 1963–1964 to 1970–1971

to expand economic growth and resultant employment levels. Furthermore, the increased trend in Income Tax was relatively gradual reflecting an incremental approach (rather than transformational) to economic development. This public administration and management activity were supported by the Public Service employment levels, where Customs and Ports had employed 4.5% of public servants; Inland Revenue, 2.0%; and Treasury 1.3% (see Table 2.4). It is also noted that even though a National Insurance Act was in place in 1963 (IBRD, 1963), the pension contributions were very low and limited to certain categories of government employees. In fact, the revenue nomenclature 'Pension Contributions' was amended over the years, it commenced with the nomenclature of 'Pensions and Retiring Allowances Contributions', in 1963–1964 it was amended to 'Widows and Orphans Pension Scheme', and in 1965–1966 it was modified to 'Pension Contributions'. This change in title may be indicative of government's future intension to widen the national insurance scheme at that time to a more inclusive one. However, the financial figures suggest that this did not happen in the 1962–1971 period. Moreover, Table 2.1 indicates an important public administration and management reform related to the establishment of the Central Bank of Malta in 1968. This is significant because the Central Bank of Malta was the key advisor regarding the government's monetary policy. Thus, the Ministry of Finance, Customs and Ports defined the fiscal policy, while the Central Bank of Malta focused on the monetary policy.

Table 2.2 provides details of the Ordinary Expenditure for years 1963–1964 to 1970–1971 expressed as a percentage of the total ordinary expenditure for various cost components within the public administration and management organisation. Table 2.2 reveals a number of important aspects related to public administration and management activities and related possible reforms at that time. For instance, most of the ordinary expenditure was consumed by the following public administration and management entities and associated activities, namely, Ministry of Finance, Customs and Ports (23.5%); Ministry of Trade, Industry, and Agriculture (17.5%); and Ministry of Education, Culture and Tourism (16%). Hence, these ministries on average spent about 57% of the total recurrent expenditure, indicating the main thrust of government's fiscal policy during this period. Table 2.2 also suggests certain sectors that attracted government reforms. For instance, the Malta Land Force, which is equivalent to today's Malta Armed Forces, was not established until 1968, with the first budget allocation being provided in the 1969–1970 budget. However, a major public administration and management reform at this time was related to foreign affairs. Table 2.2 suggests that before independence Malta's foreign affairs were limited to the Commissioner for Malta in London and Commissioner for Malta in Australia. However, Table 2.2 suggests that in the 1965–1966 budget allocation, two key Departments were established, namely the Commonwealth and Foreign Affairs and Representation at the United Nations. This was followed in 1968 by establishing embassies in USA, Italy, and Libya, and representation at Geneva. The year after (1969), a representative office was established with the European Communities. Hence, this public administration and management reform appeared to be targeting foreign trade and building foreign relationships.

Other public administration and management reforms are also revealed by Tables 2.3 and 2.4. Table 2.3 presents the Capital Expenditure for various capital categories related to the years 1963–1964 to 1970–1971 as a percentage of total expenditure. On the other hand, Table 2.4 shows the staff compliment for the various ministries and related departments related to the years 1963–1964 to 1970–1971 as a

Table 2.2 Government estimates by financial years – ordinary expenditure expressed in %

Ordinary expenditure	1963–64	1964–65	1965–66	1966–67	1967–68	1968–69	1969–70	1970–71	Ave.
Governor General	0.2%	0.3%	0.2%	0.2%	0.2%	0.2%	0.2%	0.1%	0.2%
House of Representatives	0.3%	0.3%	0.3%	0.3%	0.3%	0.3%	0.3%	0.2%	0.3%
Prime Minister	*9.7%*	*9.7%*	*9.3%*	*8.7%*	*7.5%*	*9.2%*	*8.9%*	*7.4%*	*8.8%*
Office of the Prime Minister	0.5%	0.5%	0.4%	0.5%	0.5%	0.6%	0.5%	0.4%	0.5%
Malta Land Force	0.0%	0.0%	0.0%	0.0%	0.0%	0.0%	0.6%	1.0%	0.2%
Police	5.5%	5.3%	5.3%	5.0%	4.2%	5.5%	5.0%	3.9%	5.0%
Civil Aviation	2.2%	2.3%	1.7%	1.8%	1.5%	1.7%	1.5%	0.9%	1.7%
Civil Defence	0.5%	0.4%	0.4%	0.4%	0.3%	0.3%	0.4%	0.3%	0.3%
Commissioner for Gozo	0.1%	0.1%	0.1%	0.1%	0.1%	0.1%	0.1%	0.0%	0.1%
Statistics	0.3%	0.5%	0.7%	0.3%	0.4%	0.3%	0.3%	0.3%	0.4%
Information	0.7%	0.7%	0.7%	0.7%	0.7%	0.8%	0.6%	0.5%	0.7%
Ministry of Commonwealth and Foreign Affairs	*0.3%*	*0.4%*	*1.2%*	*1.5%*	*1.9%*	*2.6%*	*2.3%*	*1.7%*	*1.5%*
Commonwealth and Foreign Affairs	0.0%	0.0%	0.6%	0.8%	0.7%	2.6%	2.3%	1.7%	1.1%
Representation at the United Nations	0.0%	0.0%	0.2%	0.2%	0.3%	0.0%	0.0%	0.0%	0.1%
Commissioner for Malta in London	0.2%	0.2%	0.2%	0.2%	0.2%	0.0%	0.0%	0.0%	0.1%
Commissioner for Malta in Australia	0.2%	0.2%	0.2%	0.2%	0.2%	0.0%	0.0%	0.0%	0.1%
Embassy to the USA	0.0%	0.0%	0.0%	0.0%	0.3%	0.0%	0.0%	0.0%	0.0%
Embassy to the Italy	0.0%	0.0%	0.0%	0.0%	0.2%	0.0%	0.0%	0.0%	0.0%
Embassy to the Libya	0.0%	0.0%	0.0%	0.0%	0.1%	0.0%	0.0%	0.0%	0.0%
European Communities	0.0%	0.0%	0.0%	0.0%	0.0%	0.0%	0.0%	0.0%	0.0%
Representation at Geneva	0.0%	0.0%	0.0%	0.0%	0.0%	0.0%	0.0%	0.0%	0.0%
Ministry of Finance, Customs and Port	*15.9%*	*19.4%*	*19.0%*	*20.1%*	*29.6%*	*19.7%*	*22.7%*	*41.2%*	*23.5%*
Finance	0.2%	0.2%	0.2%	0.2%	0.2%	0.2%	0.2%	0.1%	0.2%
Treasury	0.7%	0.6%	0.6%	0.6%	0.6%	0.6%	0.5%	0.4%	0.6%
Miscellaneous Services	2.3%	4.4%	3.2%	3.3%	14.7%	2.8%	5.0%	11.7%	5.9%
Pensions	4.8%	5.2%	5.7%	6.0%	5.4%	5.9%	5.9%	5.6%	5.6%
Public Debt and Property Charges	3.8%	4.2%	4.4%	4.7%	4.4%	5.4%	6.6%	20.0%	6.7%

(continued)

Table 2.2   (continued)

Ordinary expenditure	1963– 64	1964– 65	1965– 66	1966– 67	1967– 68	1968– 69	1969– 70	1970– 71	Ave.
Inland Revenue	0.8%	0.9%	0.9%	0.9%	0.9%	1.2%	1.2%	0.9%	1.0%
Customs and Port	3.1%	3.7%	3.9%	4.1%	3.2%	3.4%	2.7%	2.0%	3.3%
Port	0.0%	0.0%	0.0%	0.0%	0.0%	0.0%	0.4%	0.3%	0.1%
Audit	0.3%	0.2%	0.3%	0.3%	0.2%	0.3%	0.2%	0.2%	0.2%
Ministry of Trade, Industry and Agriculture	*21.3%*	*19.4%*	*18.2%*	*18.0%*	*15.5%*	*17.7%*	*17.2%*	*12.4%*	*17.5%*
Trade and Industry	0.8%	1.0%	1.8%	1.2%	0.6%	0.7%	0.8%	0.6%	0.9%
Subsidies	8.8%	7.8%	6.0%	6.5%	5.5%	6.1%	6.0%	4.5%	6.4%
Agriculture	2.4%	2.4%	2.4%	2.4%	1.8%	2.1%	2.0%	1.4%	2.1%
Posts and Telephones	3.5%	3.6%	3.6%	3.6%	3.3%	4.1%	3.8%	2.7%	3.5%
Water [and Electricity]	5.1%	3.7%	3.7%	3.5%	3.5%	3.8%	3.8%	2.7%	3.7%
Lighting Streets and Roads	0.6%	0.8%	0.8%	0.8%	0.7%	0.8%	0.7%	0.5%	0.7%
Ministry of Education, Culture and Tourism	*15.7%*	*15.5%*	*16.0%*	*16.3%*	*14.7%*	*17.3%*	*17.6%*	*14.7%*	*16.0%*
Education	15.5%	15.3%	15.7%	16.0%	14.5%	17.1%	17.4%	14.6%	15.8%
Public Libraries	0.1%	0.1%	0.1%	0.1%	0.1%	0.1%	0.1%	0.1%	0.1%
Museum	0.2%	0.1%	0.2%	0.2%	0.1%	0.1%	0.1%	0.1%	0.1%
Ministry of Justice and Parliamentary Affairs	*1.6%*	*1.5%*	*1.5%*	*1.5%*	*1.3%*	*1.5%*	*1.3%*	*1.0%*	*1.4%*
Legal Departments	0.4%	0.4%	0.4%	0.4%	0.3%	0.4%	0.4%	0.3%	0.4%
Judicial	0.7%	0.7%	0.7%	0.7%	0.6%	0.6%	0.6%	0.5%	0.6%
Lands	0.2%	0.2%	0.2%	0.2%	0.2%	0.2%	0.2%	0.2%	0.2%
Prisons	0.2%	0.2%	0.2%	0.2%	0.2%	0.2%	0.2%	0.1%	0.2%
Ministry of Public Building and Works	*7.0%*	*6.6%*	*6.8%*	*6.6%*	*5.9%*	*6.2%*	*6.1%*	*4.4%*	*6.2%*
Public Works	1.7%	1.6%	1.6%	1.6%	1.4%	1.5%	1.4%	1.1%	1.5%
Public Works Annually Recurrent	5.3%	5.0%	5.2%	5.0%	4.5%	4.7%	4.7%	3.3%	4.7%
Ministry of Labour, Employment and Welfare	*13.9%*	*13.3%*	*13.8%*	*13.4%*	*10.7%*	*10.6%*	*9.1%*	*6.3%*	*11.4%*
Emigration, Labour & Social Welfare	13.9%	13.3%	13.8%	13.4%	10.7%	10.6%	9.1%	6.3%	11.4%
Ministry of Health	*14.1%*	*13.6%*	*13.6%*	*13.4%*	*12.3%*	*14.7%*	*14.2%*	*10.5%*	*13.3%*
Health	14.1%	13.6%	13.6%	13.4%	12.3%	14.7%	14.2%	10.5%	13.3%
Total Ordinary Expenditure:	**100%**	**100%**	**100%**	**100%**	**100%**	**100%**	**100%**	**100%**	**100%**

Source: Malta Government Estimates for the financial years 1963–1964 to 1970–1971

Table 2.3 Government estimates by financial years – capital expenditure expressed in %

Capital expenditure	1963–64	1964–65	1965–66	1966–67	1967–68	1968–69	1969–70	1970–71	Ave.
Basic Services	*17.51*	*13.63*	*19.97*	*18.16*	*15.40*	*10.46*	*14.69*	*12.78*	*15.32*
Telephones	2.20	1.54	3.85	4.26	4.73	2.17	5.32	3.52	3.45
Roads	15.31	12.10	16.12	13.90	10.67	8.29	9.37	9.26	11.88
Economic Services	*46.88*	*53.25*	*41.90*	*51.68*	*59.67*	*69.77*	*69.21*	*64.70*	*57.13*
Water	4.00	3.58	6.34	6.84	4.77	17.04	11.64	4.83	7.38
Port Development	1.35	1.05	0.44	2.38	1.41	1.33	1.12	2.31	1.42
Electricity	4.15	6.25	6.48	3.05	2.36	1.43	1.11	1.33	3.27
Industrial Development	14.81	23.72	10.38	9.90	7.86	16.86	19.68	20.99	15.52
Tourism	4.23	6.72	5.40	16.11	16.75	9.75	6.98	5.75	8.96
Agriculture and Fisheries	4.58	3.45	5.44	6.51	5.16	3.97	2.73	2.06	4.24
Milk Marketing Undertaking	0.19	0.43	0.93	1.29	1.55	0.89	0.21	0.59	0.76
Technical Education	13.58	8.05	6.49	5.60	3.05	3.11	1.40	1.02	5.29
Higher Education	0.00	0.00	0.00	0.00	0.00	1.96	1.80	1.08	0.60
Malta Development Corp.	0.00	0.00	0.00	0.00	16.77	1.19	1.02	0.72	2.46
Malta Drydocks Corporation	0.00	0.00	0.00	0.00	0.00	12.22	21.49	24.02	7.22
Civil Aviation	0.00	0.00	0.00	0.00	0.00	0.00	0.03	0.01	0.01
Social Services	*35.61*	*33.12*	*38.13*	*30.16*	*24.93*	*19.78*	*16.10*	*22.52*	*27.54*
Education	8.45	4.21	3.32	3.84	4.02	2.53	1.31	1.84	3.69
Antiquities	1.01	0.56	0.82	1.17	0.90	0.78	0.47	0.28	0.75
Health	2.96	2.12	2.04	1.21	1.00	2.65	2.27	2.74	2.13
Housing	4.80	3.64	5.61	5.41	2.24	1.07	4.31	11.52	4.83
Sewers	5.75	4.79	6.96	6.41	5.44	4.21	2.97	2.63	4.90
Public Buildings & Sundry other works and services	12.63	17.80	19.37	10.50	9.43	7.07	4.09	3.20	10.51
War Damage Compensation	0.00	0.00	0.00	1.63	1.90	1.47	0.68	0.30	0.75
Total:	*100*	*100*	*100*	*100*	*100*	*100*	*100*	*100*	*100*

Source: Malta Government Estimates for the financial years 1963–1964 to 1970–1971

percentage of total staff compliment. Table 2.3 indicates that the bulk of the capital expenditure, with an average of over 57%, was allocated to economic services, and emphasised industrial development (16%), tourism (9%), water production (7%), technical education (5%) and agriculture and fisheries (4%). However, Tables 2.3 and 2.4 also reveal three important developments during that period: (a) the recognition of Higher Education as a separate entity, apart from technical, primary and grammar schools with a capital allocation in the 1968–1969 Budget; (b) the establishment of the Malta Development Corporation and Malta Drydocks Corporation

Table 2.4   Government estimates by financial years – staff compliment expressed as %

Staff compliment	1963–64	1964–65	1965–66	1966–67	1967–68	1968–69	1969–70	1970–71	Ave.
Governor General	0.27	0.25	0.25	0.25	0.25	0.27	0.26	0.22	**0.3**
House of Representatives	0.33	0.33	0.32	0.31	0.30	0.32	0.31	0.28	**0.3**
Prime Minister	*18.01*	*18.52*	*18.06*	*17.32*	*16.95*	*17.33*	*17.36*	*15.81*	*17.4*
Office of the Prime Minister	0.94	0.94	0.77	0.95	1.03	1.11	1.20	1.14	**1.0**
Malta Land Force	0.00	0.00	0.00	0.00	0.00	0.00	0.22	0.21	**0.1**
Police	13.06	13.57	13.39	12.52	12.12	12.42	12.04	11.03	**12.5**
Civil Aviation	0.47	0.47	0.46	0.47	0.48	0.49	0.51	0.44	**0.5**
Civil Defence	0.85	0.82	0.78	0.75	0.69	0.74	0.76	0.65	**0.8**
Statistics	0.94	0.93	0.92	0.93	0.93	0.91	0.99	0.93	**0.9**
Commissioner for Gozo	0.16	0.17	0.16	0.16	0.15	0.15	0.14	0.13	**0.2**
Information	1.58	1.62	1.59	1.54	1.54	1.52	1.50	1.29	**1.5**
Commonwealth & Foreign Affairs	*0.49*	*0.36*	*0.90*	*1.17*	*1.40*	*1.43*	*1.48*	*1.25*	*1.1*
Common. & Foreign Affairs	0.34	0.20	0.59	0.74	0.72	0.67	0.67	0.56	**0.6**
Representation at UN	0.00	0.00	0.07	0.09	0.11	0.11	0.12	0.10	**0.1**
Commissioner for London	0.08	0.08	0.15	0.23	0.23	0.23	0.22	0.19	**0.2**
Commissioner for Australia	0.06	0.07	0.09	0.11	0.10	0.11	0.11	0.08	**0.1**
Embassy to the USA	0.00	0.00	0.00	0.00	0.06	0.06	0.05	0.05	**0.0**
Embassy to the Italy	0.00	0.00	0.00	0.00	0.10	0.10	0.12	0.10	**0.1**
Embassy to the Libya	0.00	0.00	0.00	0.00	0.06	0.07	0.09	0.08	**0.0**
European Communities	0.00	0.00	0.00	0.00	0.00	0.06	0.08	0.07	**0.0**
Representation at Geneva	0.00	0.00	0.00	0.00	0.02	0.02	0.04	0.03	**0.0**
Finance, Customs & Port	*8.66*	*8.70*	*8.61*	*8.60*	*8.75*	*8.45*	*8.98*	*8.01*	*8.6*
Finance	0.36	0.36	0.36	0.30	0.41	0.40	0.45	0.38	**0.4**
Treasury	1.34	1.33	1.28	1.25	1.21	1.22	1.28	1.12	**1.3**
Misc. Services (PSC)	0.10	0.09	0.09	0.09	0.09	0.10	0.10	0.08	**0.1**
Inland Revenue	1.87	1.95	1.91	1.95	1.94	2.01	2.13	1.90	**2.0**
Customs and Port	4.37	4.33	4.33	4.34	4.45	4.71	5.02	4.54	**4.5**
Audit	0.64	0.63	0.63	0.67	0.64	0.62	0.59	0.50	**0.6**
Trade, Industry & Agri.	*15.32*	*13.82*	*13.39*	*13.22*	*13.14*	*12.99*	*13.13*	*11.35*	*13.3*
Trade and Industry	1.18	1.22	1.25	1.24	1.27	1.37	1.38	1.23	**1.3**
Agriculture	2.44	2.41	2.35	2.33	2.26	2.21	2.18	1.90	**2.3**
Co-operatives	0.06	0.06	0.06	0.06	0.06	0.06	0.05	0.05	**0.1**

(continued)

Table 2.4 (continued)

Staff compliment	1963–64	1964–65	1965–66	1966–67	1967–68	1968–69	1969–70	1970–71	Ave.
Pitkali Markets	0.51	0.50	0.49	0.47	0.45	0.44	0.44	0.37	**0.5**
Posts and Telephones	6.82	6.66	6.34	6.24	6.32	6.17	6.41	5.51	**6.3**
Water [Electricity T/f to Electricity Board in 1966–67]	4.32	2.96	2.89	2.88	2.78	2.75	2.67	2.30	**2.9**
Educ., Culture & Tourism	***31.27***	***32.34***	***33.47***	***34.30***	***34.47***	***34.54***	***34.02***	***36.53***	***33.9***
Education	30.69	31.77	32.91	33.73	33.90	33.89	33.35	35.94	**33.3**
Public Libraries	0.24	0.24	0.23	0.23	0.24	0.24	0.25	0.22	**0.2**
Museum	0.34	0.34	0.32	0.33	0.33	0.41	0.43	0.38	**0.4**
Justice and Parliamentary Affairs	***3.54***	***3.54***	***3.48***	***3.38***	***3.34***	***3.34***	***3.26***	***2.90***	***3.3***
Legal Departments	0.88	0.87	0.86	0.84	0.86	0.90	0.88	0.81	**0.9**
Judicial	1.54	1.51	1.50	1.46	1.43	1.42	1.39	1.20	**1.4**
Lands	0.66	0.69	0.68	0.66	0.63	0.62	0.59	0.57	**0.6**
Prisons	0.47	0.46	0.45	0.43	0.42	0.40	0.39	0.33	**0.4**
Public Building & Works	***4.35***	***4.31***	***4.21***	***4.21***	***4.11***	***4.02***	***4.06***	***3.47***	***4.1***
Public Works	4.35	4.31	4.21	4.21	4.11	4.02	4.06	3.47	**4.1**
Labour, Employment & Welfare	***3.66***	***3.87***	***3.76***	***3.70***	***3.63***	***3.57***	***3.57***	***3.12***	***3.6***
Emigration, Labour & Social Welfare	3.66	3.87	3.76	3.70	3.63	3.57	3.57	3.12	**3.6**
Ministry of Health	***14.10***	***13.96***	***13.55***	***13.54***	***13.66***	***13.73***	***13.57***	***17.06***	***14.1***
Medical and Health	14.10	13.96	13.55	13.54	13.66	13.73	13.57	17.06	**14.1**
Total Staff Compliment:	**100**	**100**	**100**	**100**	**100**	**100**	**100**	**100**	**100**

Source: Malta Government Estimates for the financial years 1963–1964 to 1970–1971

in 1968, and 1969 respectively; and (c) the establishment of the Electricity Board in the 1966–1967 Budget as the responsible entity for electricity generation (i.e. the birth of EneMalta).

Table 2.5 shows most of the Ministries and their respective Departments for the period 1963–1964 to 1970–1971. Table 2.5 illustrates that the government in the immediate post-independence period had the restructuring of the public administration and management organisation (Public Service) as a key priority. The analysis of the Financial Estimates for the period 1963–1964 to 1970–1971 reveals that the Ministry of Education; Ministry of Justice; Ministry of Works and Housing; Ministry of Labour and Social Welfare; and Ministry of Health experienced only a name change, with the departments within these Ministries remaining the same throughout the period under examination. For instance, in 1966–1967, the Ministry of Education became known as Ministry of Education, Culture and Tourism; the Ministry of Justice became known as Ministry of Justice and Parliamentary Affairs;

Table 2.5 Government estimates by financial years – ministries and departments

1963–1964	1964–1965	1965–1966	1966–1967	1967–1968
Prime Minister and Minister of Econ. Planning & Finance	*Prime Minister and Minister of Econ. Planning & Finance*	*Prime Minister*	*Prime Minister*	*Prime Minister*
Office of the Prime Minister	Office of the Prime Minister	Office of the Prime Minister	Office of the Prime Minister	Office of the Prime Minister
Police/Civil Aviation/Defence	Police/Civil Aviation/Defence	Police/Civil Aviation/ Defence	Police/Civil Aviation/ Defence	Police/Civil Aviation/ Defence
Commissioner for Gozo	Commissioner for Gozo	Commissioner for Gozo	Commissioner for Gozo	Commissioner for Gozo
Information/Statistics	Information/Statistics	Information	Information/Statistics	Information/Statistics
		Ministry of Commonwealth and Foreign Affairs	*Ministry of Commonwealth and Foreign Affairs*	*Ministry of Commonwealth and Foreign Affairs*
		Common. & Foreign Affairs	*Common. & Foreign Affairs*	*Common. & Foreign Affairs*
		Representation at the UN	Representation at the UN	Representation at the UN
Commissioner for London	Commissioner for London	Commissioner for London	Commissioner for London	Commissioner for London
Commissioner for Australia	Commissioner for Australia	Commissioner for Australia	Commissioner for Australia	Commissioner for Australia
		Ministry of Economic Planning & Finance	*Ministry of Finance, Customs and Port*	*Ministry of Finance, Customs and Port*
Econ. Planning and Finance	Econ. Planning and Finance	Econ. Planning and Finance	Finance	Finance
Treasury	Treasury	Treasury	Treasury	Treasury
Miscellaneous Services	Miscellaneous Services	Miscellaneous Services	Miscellaneous Services	Miscellaneous Services
Pensions/Charges	Pensions/Charges	Pensions/Charges	Pensions/Charges	Pensions/Charges
Public Debt and Property	Public Debt and Property	Public Debt and Property	Public Debt and Property	Public Debt and Property
Inland Revenue/Audit	Inland Revenue/Audit	Inland Revenue/Audit	Inland Revenue/Audit	Inland Revenue/Audit
		Statistics	Customs and Port	Customs and Port

(continued)

Table 2.5 (continued)

1963–1964	1964–1965	1965–1966	1966–1967	1967–1968
Ministry of Industrial Development and Tourism	*Ministry of Industrial Development and Tourism*	*Ministry of Industrial Development and Tourism*	*Ministry of Trade, Industry and Agriculture*	*Ministry of Trade, Industry and Agriculture*
Trade and Industry/Subsidies	Trade and Industry/Subsidies	Trade and Industry/Subsidies	Trade and Industry/Subsidies	Trade and Industry/Subsidies
Customs and Port	Customs and Port	Customs and Port		
Ministry of Agriculture, Power and Communication	*Ministry of Agriculture, Power and Communication*	*Ministry of Agriculture, Power and Communication*		
Posts and Telephones	Posts and Telephones	Posts and Telephones	Posts and Telephones	Posts and Telephones
Agriculture	Agriculture	Agriculture	Agriculture	Agriculture
Water and Electricity	Water [and Electricity]	Water [and Electricity]	Water	Water
Lighting Streets and Roads	Lighting Streets and Roads	Lighting Streets and Roads	Lighting Streets and Roads	Lighting Streets and Roads

1968–1969	1969–1970	1970–1971
Prime Minister	*Prime Minister*	*Prime Minister*
Office of the Prime Minister	Office of the Prime Minister	Office of the Prime Minister
Police/ Civil Aviation/Defence	Police/ Civil Aviation/Defence	Police/ Civil Aviation/Defence
Commissioner for Gozo	Commissioner for Gozo	Commissioner for Gozo
Information/Statistics	Information/Statistics	Information/Statistics
Ministry of Commonwealth and Foreign Affairs	*Ministry of Commonwealth and Foreign Affairs*	*Ministry of Commonwealth and Foreign Affairs*
Common. & Foreign Affairs	*Common. & Foreign Affairs*	*Common. & Foreign Affairs*
Representation at the UN	Representation at the UN	Representation at the UN
Commissioner for London	Commissioner for London	Commissioner for London
Commissioner for Australia	Commissioner for Australia	Commissioner for Australia
Embassy to the USA	Embassy to the USA	Embassy to the USA
Embassy to the Italy	Embassy to the Italy	Embassy to the Italy
Embassy to the Libya	Embassy to the Libya	Embassy to the Libya
Representation at Geneva	Representation at Geneva	European Communities

1968–1969	1969–1970	1970–1971
Ministry of Finance, Customs and Port	**Ministry of Finance, Customs and Port**	**Ministry of Finance, Customs and Port**
Finance	Finance	Finance
Treasury	Treasury	Treasury
Miscellaneous Services	Miscellaneous Services	Miscellaneous Services
Pensions/Charges	Pensions/Charges	Pensions/Charges
Public Debt and Property	Public Debt and Property	Public Debt and Property
Inland Revenue/Audit	Inland Revenue/Audit	Inland Revenue/Audit
Customs and Port	Customs and Port	Customs and Port
Ministry of Trade, Industry and Agriculture	**Ministry of Trade, Industry and Agriculture**	**Ministry of Trade, Industry and Agriculture**
Trade and Industry	Trade and Industry	Trade and Industry
Subsidies	Subsidies	Subsidies
Posts and Telephones	Posts and Telephones	Posts and Telephones
Agriculture	Agriculture	Agriculture
Water	Water	Water
Lighting Streets and Roads	Lighting Streets and Roads	Lighting Streets and Roads

Source: Malta Government Estimates for the financial years 1963–1964 to 1970–1971

the Ministry of Works and Housing became known as Ministry of Public Building and Works; the Ministry of Labour and Social Welfare became known as Ministry of Labour, Employment and Welfare; and the Ministry of Health remind the same. However, there was no change to the departments within the respective Ministries. Hence, these Ministries did not experience a dramatic change to their operational functions during this period.

However, a major change was experienced in the portfolio of the Prime Minister and Minister of Economic Planning and Finance; the Ministry of Industrial Development and Tourism; and the Ministry of Agriculture, Power and Communication. In 1965–1966, the portfolio regarding the Prime Minister and Minister of Economic Planning and Finance was sub-divided into three distinct Ministries, namely Prime Minister; Ministry of Commonwealth and Foreign Affairs; and Ministry of Economic Planning and Finance. This was a key change in the public administration and management organisation, which appeared to shift the government's focus on: (a) establishing a robust relationship with other nations, possibly to boost foreign trade, particularly exports for Maltese goods and attracting foreign investment to Malta; and (b) building a sustainable economic system regarding economic planning and the establishment of revenue generation activities and stringent financial controls on spending. The other key change was the amalgamation in 1966–1967 of the Ministry of Industrial Development and Tourism, and the Ministry of Agriculture, Power and Communication into one ministry, namely, the Ministry of Trade, Industry and Agriculture. However, the Department for Customs and Ports within the Ministry of Industrial Development and Tourism was allocated to the Ministry of Finance, Customs and Ports. Surprisingly, Tourism did not feature in any of the Ministries. However, it is noted that although the word 'Tourism' was included in the title of the Ministry of Industrial Development and Tourism up to 1965–1966, the Financial Estimates for that period do not reveal a department or other entity as being established for this particular function.

Hence, public administration and management in the post-independence era, up to 1971, was focused on giving birth to a nation in a period where the British Empire was at its death throes and could no longer sustain the defence spending at similar levels as its glorious past. This period was a completely new phase for Malta's Public Service. It had to advice government on ways that enabled Malta to fend for itself by defining and implementing a turnaround development strategy, replacing Malta's traditional military base economy dependent on a foreign power, to an open market economy that needed to survive in a harsh competitive world. Some may argue that the government's application to join NATO betrayed a mindset that did not view Malta as ever breaking away from its traditional role as a military facility, attempting merely to exchange Britain for NATO.

2.2.3 Public Administration and Management in the 1970s Social Reform Era Until 1979

Brick (2012, p.1537) argues that the 1970s were viewed as a *'pivot of change'* in world history that particularly gave attention to the economic turmoil, which followed the end of the post-war economic boom (Marglin & Schor, 1991). In the Western world, social progressive values that commenced and flourished in the 1960s, such as escalating political awareness and economic liberty of women, continued to intensify. The 1970s saw global acceptance of concepts that included ever more flexible and varied gender roles for women in industrialized societies. More women entered the work force, but the gender role of men remained as that of a breadwinner. Generally, the public in the 1970s were greatly influenced by the swift pace of societal change and the desire for a more classless and democratic society in cultures that were subjected to prolonged colonisation and had a tradition of hierarchical social structure. On 1st July 1971, the twenty-sixth Amendment to the United States Constitution was ratified, lowering the voting age for all federal and state elections from 21 years to 18 years, resolving the anomaly whereby young men were being drafted to fight in the Vietnam War before they were old enough to vote.

The 1973 oil crises caused by the oil embargoes of the Organization of Arab Petroleum Exporting Countries resulted in an economic recession of industrialized countries (Japan being an exception). The outcome of this crisis was the commencement of stagflation resulting in a period of rising prices and unemployment but little growth in consumer demand and business activity. This initiated a political and economic trend, replacing Keynesian economic theory with neoliberal economic theory. The 1970s also saw a cooling of superpower tensions, with the aggressive US–Soviet conflicts of the 1950s and 1960s giving way to the policy of 'détente', which endorsed the concept that global concerns could be resolved at the negotiating table. Détente was, in some measure, a consequence in opposition to the policies of the previous 25 years, which had brought the world perilously close to nuclear confrontation on quite a few occasions. It was also a response to the weakened position of the US following its withdrawal and defeat in the Vietnam War. However, US–Soviet geopolitical rivalry was unrelenting throughout the 1970s, through more discreet activity as the two superpowers persistently manoeuvred for control of smaller countries.

The gay movement made a gigantic leap forward in the 1970s when Harvey Milk was the first openly gay person to be elected to public office in a major city in the US, serving on the San Francisco Board of Supervisors from 1977–1978. His life and political career embodied the rise of the lesbian, gay, bisexual, and transgender (LGBT) civil rights movement. Various celebrities, including Freddie Mercury and Andy Warhol, also 'came out' during this decade, bringing gay culture further into the limelight. 1978 would become known as the *'Year of Three Popes'*. In August 1978, Paul VI, who had ruled since 1963, died and his successor was Cardinal Albino Luciano, who took the name John Paul. Fatefully, Pope John Paul's tenure lasted only 33 days due to his premature death, and the Catholic Church had to elect another pope. On October 16, 1978, Karol Wojtyła, a Polish cardinal, was elected Pope John Paul II. He was the first non-Italian pope since 1523. In the United Kingdom, the 1979 elections resulted in the victory of its Conservative leader, Margaret Thatcher, the first female British Prime Minister. On being elected Prime Minister, she initiated a neoliberal economic policy of reducing government spending, drastically weakening the power of trade unions, promoting economic and trade liberalization, and instituting New Public Management concepts.

It is in this world scenario that Dom Mintoff's Labour Party was elected to government in June 1971 and remained in power throughout the 1970s and beyond. It must also be noted that Dom Mintoff was a member of the famous Fabian Society. From the first Fabian tract (Why are the Many Poor?) and the original Fabian Essays published in 1889, in the wake of the Match Girls' Strike, the society was (and still is) characterised by a passionate commitment to social justice and a belief in the progressive improvement of society (The Guardian, 2001). The Fabian Society was always in the forefront in promoting the welfare state, free national health, women's rights, and gay rights, amongst many other societal issues. It is contended that this world scenario of the 1970s and the leftist attitude of Fabian thinking, must have had an important influence on Don Mintoff's philosophy and the way public administration and management evolved during the 1970s period. According to Montebello (2012, p.43), Mintoff's public administration policies were very similar to those of the Fabian Society.

Scicluna (2011) notes that Mintoff's government of 1971 had implemented reforms related to the homosexuality and adultery laws in 1972 (until then a criminal offence liable to imprisonment); the declaration of a Republic in 1974; and the Marriage Act in 1975. According to Alshinawi (2014), Maltese public administration and management of 1971–1987 had planning for resource allocation as a priority over and above the market. Dowdall (1972, p.465) argued that public administration and management was dominated by an emphasis on Socialist, Mediterranean and non-aligned policies. He contended that the government promoted national sovereignty with active negotiations, which led to the agreement on the total withdrawal of British forces by 1979, and also forged 'special friendship ties' with China and Libya, which were regarded as anti-West, since they were viewed as being pro-Libyan and pro-Eastern. Ironically Malta's first opening to Communist Europe came in 1968 with diplomatic ties to Czechoslovakia under a Nationalist administration. Moreover, in the 1970s period there was a tendency for the public (incited vested interests) to focus too much on China and Libya and ignoring the huge investment in terms of factories by German and British firms. In the 1970s, Mintoff recognised that foreign aid was essential if Malta was to achieve its economic and social goals, similar to the way EU funds are viewed today. The source of foreign aid in the 1970s was even more critical because high inflation and the 1973 oil crisis meant that not much aid could be obtained from European states. However, the government administration of that time realised that the welfare state would not have been built without such aid and that money could be attracted from oil-rich Arab countries. Furthermore, the government's public administration policy was not in favour of any formal alliance with or opposed to any major power bloc, safeguarding the importance of Malta's neutrality (Pirotta, 1985, p.182–86; Pirotta, 1997, p.107–207).

Alshinawi (2014) contends that although the government during the nineteen seventies (and most of the eighties) acquired additional external finance, economic growth was hindered by the weakness of the local commercial and industrial base, and the scarcity of domestic investment opportunities (Dowdall, 1972, p.466–67). This view is somewhat contested because economic growth did slowdown in the 1980s but not for the 1970s, when Malta experienced one of its biggest economic growth periods (at least in the first part of the 1970s). However, economic growth stalled in the 1980s chiefly due to several unpopular economic policies, such as restrictions on the importation of a variety of goods. Moreover, Alshinawi (2014) argues that public administration and management was required to assume greater responsibility for deciding what should be produced and to direct small low-level enterprises to produce in accordance to the national 'development strategy'. Alshinawi (2014) claims that like many other countries in the early stages of development, Malta's public administration and management was expected to determine the objective of economic independence, exercise control on economic operations and formulate key decisions regarding the production and distribution of wealth, using a fixed price system. This resulted in Malta's public administration and management formulating a series of 5 year 'National Development Plans' that reflected a central planning process. Hence, the role of public administration and management became extremely important as the Maltese economy grew and became more complex as it integrated into the global market. However, the 1970s will be particularly heralded as a decade of major social reforms unprecedented with past Public Service administration and management. Table 2.6 shows key Public Service administration and management reforms that were implemented by the government in the 1970s.

According to Boissevain (2012, p.348), the Labour Government of 1971 was elected on a manifesto that set out a programme of administrative reform, explicitly stressing discipline; the institution of an ombudsman; a renegotiated defence treaty; a 40-hour work week; considerably more help to the underprivileged social categories, including increased pensions, more housing and children allowances; the takeover together with the General Workers' Union of the ex-naval dockyard; and income tax reform. He argues that from 1971 until the 1976 elections, the Labour Government (through its Public Service administration and management organisation) implemented most of the electoral promises, except for the appointment of an ombudsman. Upon being elected in 1971, the Prime Minister's Office (OPM) sent a memorandum to all department heads prohibiting civil servants engaging in private work and for them to make a declaration of their commercial interests, and whether they were engaged in employment outside government service (Boissevain, 2012, p.350). According to Boissevain (2012, p.350) the government set about reducing salary differences between departments and parastatal corporations; it introduced a 5-day week; and reduced the differentials between the highest and lowest grades from one-to-eight to one-to-five. By 1974, pay-as-you-earn income tax was

Table 2.6 Key public service reforms implemented by government in the 1970s

Year	Reform	Source
1971	Malta Dry docks managed by workers committee	Cutajar (2012, p.30)
1971	Death penalty abolished	Cutajar (2012, p.30)
1972	Agreement with UK to close military bases by 1979	Cutajar (2012, p.30)
1972	Annual bonus payment	Cutajar (2012, p.30)
1972	Introduction of Maltese currency	Cutajar (2012, p.30)
1972	Intensive housing building programme	Cutajar (2012, p.30)
1972	Established Air Malta and Sea Malta	Boissevain (2012, p.350)
1972	Established Bank of Valletta	Boissevain (2012, p.350)
1972	Mandatory education age increased to 16 from 14	Boissevain (2012, p.350)
1972	Children allowance	Boissevain (2012, p.350)
1972	Decriminalisation of homosexuality	Scicluna (2011)
1974	Malta becomes a Republic	Boissevain (2012, p.349)
1974	Introduction and recognition of human rights	Cutajar (2012, p.32)
1974	Voting age decreased to 18 years	Cutajar (2012, p.32)
1974	Pension for the disabled	Cutajar (2012, p.32)
1974	Introduction of minimum wage	Cutajar (2012, p.32)
1974	Introduced kindergartens	Cutajar (2012)
1974	Civil marriage (Marriage Act)	Scicluna (2011)
1974	Established Mid-Med Bank	Boissevain (2012, p.350)
1974	Broadcasting controlled by Maltese	Boissevain (2012, p.350)
1974	Equal pay for women for equal work as men	Cutajar (2012, p.32)
1974	Industrial Relations Act	Cutajar (2012, p.32)
1974	Established Enemata and fuel bunkering	Cutajar (2012, p.32)
1974	Established Investment Finance Bank	Cutajar (2012)
1974	Established Lohombus Corporation for housing loans	Cutajar (2012)
1974	Established Faculty of Education at University	Cutajar (2012, p.32)
1976	Established Housing Authority	Mangion (2012, p.378)
1976	Mental Health Act	Mangion (2012, p.378)
1976	Employment Commission (political discrimination)	Mangion (2012, p.378)
1979	Cessation of Military bases in Malta	Cutajar (2012, p.33)
1979	Created two thirds National Pension Scheme	Boissevain (2012, p.350)
1979	Established national health scheme	Cutajar (2012, p.33)
1979	Paid maternity leave	Cutajar (2012, p.33)
1979	Established Junior Lyceums	Cutajar (2012, p.33)
1979	Free education for all	Cutajar (2012, p.33)

introduced and greater control was placed by mitigating smuggling (Boissevain, 2012, p.350).

However, this reform came at a price. According to Boissevain (2012, p.350) the top-heavy, slow-moving civil service had been subjected to a forceful discipline and was considerably reduced, with the consequence that serious tensions were created resulting in a significant number of resignations. Furthermore, in general, all government employees, particularly the higher grades, had their comparative incomes reduced due to a more equitable distribution of income; the elimination of a second job; and a more efficient tax collection system (Boissevain, 2012, p.350). Boissevain (2012, p.351) argues that the government's drive to instil discipline, encourage harder work, stop pilferage and wastage, did not only irritate the fat-cat professionals and government employees, but also affected the government's relationship with trade unions. Members of the professional class, who in the past paid only a token tax for years, were enraged with the government, because income tax was being assessed on the basis of their estimated earnings, thus severely affecting their lifestyles (Boissevain, 2012, p.350). In the later years of the 1970s, the government focused on two important reform areas, namely medical services and higher education. A serious confrontation took place with the medical profession when government endeavoured to reduce the influence of the Malta Association of Medical Practitioners (MAM) by curtailing its authority related to the determination of who had the qualifications to practice medicine in Malta. Furthermore, the government declared that new medical graduates were to serve for a few years as interns in government hospitals before leaving the islands to specialise or work elsewhere, leading to a partial strike as a protest. Consequently, the government locked out striking doctors in its employment at government hospitals and later as the dispute escalated, dismissed them from the service. The remaining Maltese doctors were aided by doctors brought in from other countries, sometimes following agreements with foreign governments.

A similar aggressive dispute developed with the university when government launched a plan to restructure higher education in 1977. The government introduced the student worker scheme, where students would work for 6 months and study for 6 months to ensure that graduates were trained in skills required by the country and would have no difficulty in finding employment upon graduating. It is not the objective of this chapter to delve into the merits of these issues. However, it is noted that the public administration and management organisation had the objective of reforming the various systems and its reform process was being resisted. As so often happens, resistance to change is common when dealing with transformational change. Another important observation is that many influential people who had occupied (or still occupied) high positions, had an axe to grind against the government of that time. This observation is significant because these same persons were also influential in later years when there was a change of government in 1987, particularly the Public Service Reform Commission that was established in the late 1980s.

Moreover, when one examines the various reforms that were instituted during this period it becomes evident that the workload of the employees working in government departments increased tremendously, particularly for those reforms that involved numerous processes, such as pensions, children's allowance, taxation, customs, employment workbooks and education, amongst many others. Table 2.7 illustrates that ordinary revenue, recurrent costs and capital expenditure, including the staff compliment to manage these cost elements, all increased considerably over the years, particularly during the reform implementation years. Hence, Table 2.7 illustrates that the specific reforms required a corresponding number of employees to

Table 2.7 Government financial statistics and staff compliment 1970–1979

Financial Year	Ordinary Revenue	Ordinary Expenditure	Capital Expenditure	Total Expenditure	Staff Compliment
1970–1971*	29,168,858	37,048,589	12,532,944	49,581,533	13,289
1971–1972	35,549,794	39,368,697	12,436,345	51,805,042	12,993
1972–1973	47,801,204	33,318,078	8,318,448	41,636,526	12,826
1973–1974	54,623,236	38,334,000	16,324,168	54,658,168	13,287
1974–1975	71,593,236	47,800,748	14,106,752	61,907,500	14,885
1975–1976*	81,622,539	55,305,126	36,158,813	91,463,939	17,868
1976–1977	97,578,697	61,975,875	31,912,769	93,888,644	18,061
1977–1978	96,742,000	67,290,253	24,800,000	92,090,253	18,309
1978–1979	105,368,078	74,877,130	30,346,001	105,223,131	19,435

Source: Malta Government Estimates financial years 1970–1971 to 1978–1979. * Election year

support them. Additionally, Table 2.8 demonstrates that considerable restructuring of government to operate the Public Service administration and management functions took place during the 1970s. For instance, the number of Ministries increased from nine to twelve up to 1979, with functions related to Sports and the Environment specifically appearing in Ministerial titles.

By 1979, a number of Ministries were given a wider portfolio, such as the Ministry of Finance, Customs and People's Financial Investments; the Ministry of Trade, Industry and Parastatal and People's Industries; and the Ministry of Development, Energy, Port and Telecommunications. Airport and Port development were given a greater significance in the financial estimates, with Airport Development being directly under the responsibility of the Prime Minister. Ship repair, ship building, telecommunications and port development were also given priority in the restructuring that took place during this time. Tourism was given more prominence under the responsibility of a specific Ministry, which was responsible for all tourism related functions, such as the catering school, the Malta Government Tourist Board and the Hotels and Catering Establishments Board. Moreover, a Ministry for Agriculture and Fisheries was also established to explicitly look after the agriculture and fisheries sectors. One must also keep in mind that the use of technology was very restricted in the 1970s. What is taken for granted today was simply not available or had restrictive uses during that time. For instance, the common copying machines as we know them today were chemical based with restrictive copying options; and word processors were non-existent, with letters and documents being normally sent to a typing pool using typewriters. Even the simple calculator that was viewed as a priceless tool had limited options. However, official documents reveal that as early as January 1978, government was considering significant Public Service reforms related to data processing (computerisation) for various administrative systems to support the numerous social reforms that were being implemented.

Discussions to establish an information centre for data processing to feed information to countries bordering the Mediterranean were conducted in 1978 (Ministry

Table 2.8 Government estimates by financial years – ministries and departments

1970–1971	1974–1975	1979–1980
Prime Minister	*Prime Minister*	*Prime Minister*
Office of the Prime Minister	Office of the Prime Minister	Office of the Prime Minister
Malta Land Force	Armed Forces of Malta	Armed Forces of Malta
Police; Civil Aviation; Statistics	Police; Civil Aviation; Statis.	Police; Civil Aviation; Statistics
Information; Civil Defence	Commonwealth & Foreign Aff.	Prisons; Airport Development
Commissioner for Gozo		Pioneer Corps & Others
Ministry of Commonwealth and Foreign Affairs		*Ministry of Foreign Affairs*
Commonwealth & Foreign Aff.		Foreign Affairs
Ministry of Finance, Customs and Port	*Ministry of Finance and Customs*	*Ministry of Finance, Customs and People's Financial Investments*
Finance; Treasury; IRD; Audit	Finance; Treasury; IRD; Audit	Finance; Treasury; IRD; Audit
Miscellaneous Services; Pensions/Charges		Miscellaneous Services; Pensions/Charges
Public Debt and Property		Public Debt and Property
Customs and Port	Customs	Customs
	Public Lotto and Government Lotteries	Public Lotto and Government Lotteries
	Public Service Commission	Sundry Services and Supplies
		Port Development
Ministry of Trade, Industry and Agriculture	*Ministry of Trade, Industry, Agriculture and Tourism*	*Ministry of Trade, Industry and Parastatal and People's Industries*
Trade; Industry	Trade; Industry	Trade; Industry
Agriculture	Agriculture	Parastatal & People's Indus.
Subsidies, Posts, Telephones, Water	Malta Gov. Tourist Board Hotels & Catering Est Board	
	Milk Marketing Undertaking	
Ministry of Education, Culture and Tourism	*Ministry of Education and Culture*	*Ministry of Education*
Education; Public Libraries	Education; Public Libraries	Education; Public Libraries
Museum	Museum	
Ministry of Justice and Parliamentary Affairs	*Ministry of Justice and Parliamentary Affairs*	*Ministry of Justice, Lands, Housing & Parliamentary Aff*
Legal Departments	Crown Advocate General's Chambers	Legal Departments
	Public Registry; Notary to Government	
	Housing	Housing

(continued)

Table 2.8 (continued)

1970–1971	1974–1975	1979–1980
Judicial; Prisons; Lands	Judicial; Prisons; Lands	Judicial; Prisons; Lands
Ministry of Public Building & Works	*Ministry of Public Building & Works*	*Ministry of Works and Sports*
Public Works	Public Works	Public Works
		Water; Sewers; Roads; Lighting Streets
		Sports, Public Buildings and Gardens
Ministry of Labour, Employment and Welfare	*Ministry of Labour, Employment and Welfare*	*Ministry of Labour, Culture and Welfare*
Emigration, Labour & Social Welfare	Labour & Emigration; Social Welfare	Labour, Culture and Welfare NI; Museums and National
		Monuments
Ministry of Health	*Ministry of Health*	*Ministry of Health and Environment*
Health	Health	Health
	Ministry of Development	*Ministry of Development, Energy, Port and Telecommunications*
	Posts; Ports	Posts; Ports
	Telephones; Water	MDC; Development of Industries
		Ship Repair Docks & Shipbuilding Yard
		Telecommunications; Port Development
		Electricity
		Ministry of Agriculture and Fisheries
		Agriculture, Fisheries
		Milk Marketing Undertaking; Subsidies
		Ministry of Tourism
		Tourism; Catering School
		Malta Government Tourist Board
		Hotels & Catering Establishments Board

Source: Malta Government Estimates for the financial years 19701980

of Commonwealth and Foreign Affairs, 1978). Moreover, a report submitted to the Maltese government refers to a submission by government to the European Commission Joint Research Centre (ISPRA) that was established on 18th December 1978. This report also makes reference to the tender specifications issued by the Maltese Government in August 1979, related to the computing and hardware needs of the Maltese Government, particularly related to the Inland Revenue Department

(Camilleri, 1979). The Camilleri (1979) report recommended the establishment of a centralised computer bureau to enable the development and processing of information management systems to take place. This rather silent Public Service reform transformation was initiated without the usual fanfare. However, as it shall be shown, the 1980s saw a tremendous development in information technology and systems development as part of the Public Service reform process, which is viewed as being the foundation for today's technological advancement in government administration and management.

2.2.4 Public Administration and Management in the Turbulent 1980s

In the 1980s, conservative politics and Reaganomics continued to influence the way of life around the world, as the Berlin Wall disintegrated, and new computer technologies materialized. The 1980s emphasised materialism and consumerism and witnessed major socioeconomic change attributable to the development in technology and a universal departure from planned economies and towards laissez-faire capitalism. Laissez-faire capitalism, which was in principal introduced by Margaret Thatcher, British Prime Minister (1979–90) and Ronald Regan 40th President of the United States (1981–1989), is an economic system in which transactions between private parties mitigate government intervention and these parties had complete control over the means of production. In its pure form, laissez-faire capitalism excluded any form of government intervention, such as regulation, taxation, privilege, imperialism, tariffs and subsidies. Margaret Thatcher (nicknamed The Iron Lady) instituted widespread economic reforms, including the privatisation of industries and the de-regulation of stock markets, mirroring similar reforms initiated by Ronald Reagan in the United States. However, industrial relations in the United Kingdom deteriorated to the lowest level possible, particularly that of the miners' strike (1984–85), which severely affected the coal industry. According to Van der Velden, et al. (2007, p.353) at its height, the strike involved 142,000 mineworkers, making it the biggest since the 1926 General Strike. The BBC referred to this strike as 'the most bitter industrial dispute in British history', (BBC, 1984). As the United Kingdom and the United States moved towards supply-side economics strategies, as opposed to Keynesian policies that boosted demand, a trend emerged in the direction of global instability of international trade. Hence, the early 1980s were characterised by a harsh global economic recession that affected much of the developed world, except for Japan and West Germany. Developing countries worldwide encountered economic and social difficulties as they endured the effects from the multiple debt crises of the 1980s, requiring many of them to apply for financial aid from the International Monetary Fund and the World Bank.

Additionally, as economic deconstruction intensified in the developed world, many multinational companies associated with the manufacturing industry relocated into Thailand, Mexico, South Korea, Taiwan, and China, to take advantage of the available cheap labour. According to Friedman (2009, p.4) the 1980s saw, for the first time in world history, transpacific trade (with East Asia, such as China and Latin America, primarily with Mexico) to be identical to that of transatlantic trade (with Western Europe or with neighbouring Canada), consolidating American economic power (Friedman, 2009, p.45). China, under the leadership of Deng Xiaoping, initiated extensive reforms in the 1980s, opening its economy to the West and allowing capitalist enterprises to operate in a market socialist system. However, by 1989, students and workers protested in the Tiananmen Square against government corruption, which was suppressed by the People's Liberation Army. In the Soviet Union, the 11th Five-Year Plan that was launched in 1981 during a period of economic stagnation failed to meet most of the established targets. By 1986, nationalism in the Eastern Bloc reappeared strongly, accompanied by a desire for democracy in communist-led socialist states. This, combined with economic recession resulted in Mikhail Gorbachev (who became leader of the Soviet Union in 1985) to introduce the policy of glasnost and perestroika, which reduced Communist Party power, legalized dissent and sanctioned limited forms of capitalism, such as joint ventures with Western firms. Consequently, the subsequent Soviet Union Five-Year Plan was aimed to speed up the restructuring of the Soviet economy by introducing reforms that decentralized production and distribution systems, rather than having centralised control. Lewis (1988) argued that after mounting tension for almost a decade, relations between the West and East had improved significantly by 1988, thus the Soviet Union became reluctant to defend governments in its satellite states. Gorbachev pursued negotiation with the United States to decrease tensions further, leading to the Malta Summit where a meeting between George Bush and Mikhail Gorbachev took place in early December 1989, just a few weeks after the fall of the Berlin Wall, thus, bringing closer the end the Cold War.

The Solidarity movement that involved workers demanding political liberalization and democracy in Poland commenced in 1980 and was successful in encouraging people in other communist states to demand a similar political reform as attained in Poland. The eventual collapse of communism in Eastern Europe was generally peaceful, such as the Czechoslovak 'Velvet Revolution'. The only exception was Romania, where leader Nicolae Ceauşescu was charged with genocide and shot on Christmas Day of 1989. In Yugoslavia, the death of communist leader Josip Broz Tito in May 1980 brought with it extreme turmoil, with political reform of the communist system shifting towards ethnic nationalism and inter-ethnic hostility, especially in Serbia. The demolition of the Berlin Wall, at the end of the decade, signified a massive shakeup in the geopolitical shift. During this period, the European Union continued to grow with the accession of Greece in 1981, and Spain and Portugal in 1986. In 1983, Bettino Craxi became the first Italian socialist Prime Minister, becoming one of the longest-serving Prime Ministers in the history of Italian Republic (from 1983 to 1987). Major civil discontent and violence took place in the Middle East, including the Bombing of Libya in 1986, and the First Intifada in the Gaza Strip and the West Bank. This growing civil unrest in the Middle East contributed in Islamism becoming a powerful political force in the 1980s and the birth of many terrorist organizations, including Al Qaeda.

However, another vibrant revolution was taking place analogous to the above, related to technology. This momentous revolution may have been overshadowed by the turbulent years described above. Although microcomputers were available during the mid-1970s, it was not until IBM released its first Personal Computer in August 1981 that a significant market uptake resulted. In 1982, 'The Personal Computer' was awarded the famous 'Man of the Year' title by Time magazine (Samueli, 2014). According to Samueli (2014) two years before a machine was awarded this title, Microsoft CEO Bill Gates had predicted 'A computer on every desk and in every home'. Samueli (2014) argues that it was in the 1980s that real progress was made, and companies like Amstrad, IBM, Apple and Microsoft took over manufacturing and programming. He contends that computers began to make sense, prices started falling, actual sizes became smaller and the machines were able to accomplish many complicated things. Microsoft released the operating systems MS-DOS (1981), Windows 1.0 (1985), and Windows 2.0 (1987). The ARPANET project changed its protocol in 1983 to TCP/IP that became the dominant communications protocol, which would be utilised as the basis for the Internet. Moreover, in 1989 the British computer scientist Tim Berners-Lee developed the first successful communication between a Hypertext Transfer Protocol (HTTP) client and server via the internet, which would later, became the foundation of the World Wide Web.

These developments had serious implications for the labour market because while only large companies could afford computers (mainframe and mini computers) due to their high cost, these developments meant that even small firms, which were the vast majority in many countries, particularly in the developing nations, were able to attain a computing capability with a consequent reduction in manpower. Furthermore, the sophistication of the traditional computing power developed throughout the 1960s and 1970s, such as robotics in manufacturing and application software packages for service industries were having an extreme impact on reducing manpower in large corporations in both the manufacturing and service industries, particularly the financial sector. Although, technology was an opportunity to increase productivity, the impact on decreasing employment levels was nevertheless acute, particularly is countries where supply-side economics strategies were being applied and in circumstances were economic recession was being experienced. Hence, the 1980s were very turbulent years indeed in every aspect of life, be it social, political or economic.

It is in the light of the above world scenario and the fact that Malta was still a very young nation trying to survive in a very turbulent and uncertain economic conditions, that the Public Service reforms of the Malta Government of the 1980s must be judged. Moreover, it is noted that the leader of the parliamentary opposition between 1980 and May 1987 presented the opposition's position is a more forceful manner, unlike his predecessor who was viewed as being more reconciliatory is his approach. It is also argued that the labour government of the 1980s was to some extent going against the global economic and socio-political trends of that time. These global trends emphasised supply-side economics strategies that promoted non-government intervention in business dealings. Additionally, the labour government of 1976 was elected on the manifesto that embraced strong socialist ideological principles, whereas in the 1980s socialism, which was (rightly or wrongly) associated with communism, was undesirable. The consequence of this was that the parliamentary opposition took advantage of the East European events that were taking place, particularly in Poland, at a time when Catholics had a Polish Pope. The 1980s (up to May 1987) were marred with numerous violent episodes that in most cases were politically motivated. It is not the intention of this chapter to attribute blame of the violent activities that took place during this period. However, Vassallo (2011) argues that pundits on both sides of the political divide question what appears to be a case of selective memory and in the same article, former Nationalist Minister Michael Falzon and Dr Wenzu Mintoff, former Labour MP and the first chairman of Alternattiva Demokratika, both pinpoint to the anomaly that some of those who were involved in the violence of the 1980s under the Labour government, were later promoted several ranks in the police force to very senior posts under the Nationalist administration. The strategy of tension in the 1980s was also based on the provocation of those who always threw the first stone and were the first to hide their hands (Vassallo, 2011, p.3).

Findlay and Wellisz (1993, p.256–292) argued that from the early 1980s, the Malta government reacted to the prevailing economic trend and public administration and management movement by relaxing somewhat its centralist planning policies, with signs of an opening in the economy. They contended that there was more of a mixed-economic planning, where the price system was not entirely free (under some government control or heavily regulated), combined with state-led planning, which however was not extensive enough to constitute a planned economy. According to Alshinawi (2014, p. 21), when the Nationalist Party took office in 1987, there was an increase in speed towards a more open market economy, with cautious liberalisation and privatisation in the restructuring of the industrial and financial sectors. Hence, by 1987, emphasis was put on the implementation of policy reforms towards market economy, primacy of division of labour, and price system for values set by supply and demand (Alshinawi, 2014, p.17). A detailed examination of the government financial estimates for years 1980 to 1989 yielded the major Public Service administration and management reforms for that period, as shown in Table 2.9. Table 2.9 highlights that the key aspects dominating the public administration and management reform process between 1980 and 1987 were the following:

(a) Strengthening the heavy industrial productive capacity, such as the tranship-ment port at Marsaxlokk; expanding the productive capacity of the dry docks; and establishing the Marsa Ship Building complex.
(b) Initiating and strengthening the financial sector, such as the Accountancy Profession Act and setting-up of the Accountancy Board; and initiating the Insurance Business Act.
(c) Reforming the education sector, such as merging the new university and old university into the University of Malta; freezing Church School fees at 1982

Table 2.9 Key public service reforms implemented by government in the 1980s

Year	Reform	Source financial estimates
1980	Law regarding prevention and control of marine pollution	1980, p.38
1980	Setting-up of Acc. Board (Accountancy Profession Act)	1982, p.72
1980	Bulk buying of essential commodities/industrial materials	1980, p.64
1980	Building of transhipment port at Marsaxlokk	1981, p.97
1980	Disbanding of Malta Pioneer Corps and Dirghajn-il-Maltin	1981, p.97
1980	New 300,000 capacity Dock completed	1981, p.116
1980	Merging New University & Old University	1981, p.167
1980	Inauguration of Ta' Qali National Stadium	1982, p.118
1981	Publication of Development Plan 1981-1985	1982, p.42
1981	Establishment of Government Computer Centre (GCC)	1982, p.71
1981	Insurance Business Act	1982, p.72
1981	Austrian-Maltese Renewable Energy Research Centre	1984, p.183
1982	GCC: IRD; Treasury payroll & pensions; Central Office of Statistics; Pitkali & Farmers payments; and Mid-Med Bank Systems	1983, p.211 1984, p.219
1982	Legal notice freezing Church School fees at 1982 levels	MaltaToday,25Apr2010, p.12
1983	White paper on devolution of Church property	1984, p.83
1983	GCC: Labour Workbooks; Social Service payments for accident & injury benefits, marriage grants; pharmaceutical inventory control; obstetrics; gynaecology systems	1984, p.105
1984	Amendment Education Act: Licensing of private schools	1985, p.65
1984	GCC: Central Supplies Stock Control; Children's Allowances; Law Courts Monitoring; Central Bank Exchange Control; Dispensaries and Prescription of Free Medicines; Price Enforcement; DOI Labelling system; Land Registry system; Air Malta bond register; Civil Aviation Revenue Accounts system; Water and Electricity billing; Electoral Register system; Health Department Patients File Systems	1985, p.101
1984	Malta Shipbuilding Co Ltd operational	1985, p.103
1985	Agreement signed in Rome with Holy See officials.	1986, p.65
1985	GCC: Population Census; Post Office Philately; Public Registry Wills & Deeds; TeleMalta local/overseas billing; National Insurance; Xandir Malta TV Licences Systems	1986, p.101 1986, p.80
1985	Employment Incentive Scheme (combat unemployment)	1987, p.140
1986	GCC: Telephone Directory; Flight Information; Trade Department Licensing; Lands Department rent collection; Wireless Telegraphy Frequency Management; Customs Department Manifest Control; Telex Billing; Passport Issuance; Agriculture/Fisheries Census systems	1987, p.100
1986	Set-up of Federation of Parents Association (education)	1987, p. 217
1986	Computer awareness courses extended to secondary schools	1987, p. 218
1987	Electoral reform: Constitutional and electoral law	1988, p. 61
1987	Auxiliary Workers and Training Scheme	1988, p. 113

(continued)

Table 2.9 (continued)

Year	Reform	Source financial estimates
1987	Dispute between Government and MAM settled	1988, p. 117
1987	GCC: IRD PAYE system; National Insurance contributions system; Public Lotto system.	1988, p. 143
1988	Set-up Commission for Investigation of Injustices	1988, p. 39
1988	Arabic language in schools no longer mandatory	1988, p. 91
1988	Discussions reopened with Vatican re Church Schools	1988, p. 92
1988	White Paper on establishing Public Transport Authority	1989, p. 42
1988	Public Service Reform Commission appointed	1989, p. 44
1988	Operations Review initiated	1989, p. 44
1989	Reinstatement of academic staff and Rector of Old University; incorporation of Faculty of Theology within University	1989, p. 98
1989	GCC: Telemalta payroll and HR system; Wireless Telegraphy Frequency Management; Telemalta maritime radio billing; Social Services Parental system; Xandir Malta Contributors system; OPM regulatory boards registration and control system; Department of Elderly Monitoring; Xandir Malta payroll and HR system; Civil Aviation Eurocontrol system; Trade Department harmonization system; Household budgetary survey; Xandir Malta air time scheduling system	1989, p. 155 1990, p. 167
1989	First report of Operations Review issued	1990, p. 46
1989	First report of Public Service Reform Commission	1990, p. 46

Source: Malta Government Estimates for financial years 1980–1989 Programme of Activities

levels; publishing a white paper on the devolution of Church property; amending the Education Act regarding the licensing of private schools; the agreement signed in Rome with Holy See officials regarding church schools and property; and setting up of the Federation of Parents Association (education).

(d) Public service reforms through the application of technological solutions, such as the setting up of the Government Computer Centre and its software development programme over the 1980s.

(e) Other innovative developments, such as the law regarding prevention and control of marine pollution; bulk buying of essential commodities and industrial materials; inauguration of Ta' Qali National Stadium; and establishing the Austrian-Maltese renewable energy research centre.

Most of the above reforms were related to transformational change and as such attracted extreme levels of resistance, particularly when the change directly impacted certain sections of the general public, the church, employee unions, and influential and conservative institutions. Here reference is particularly being made to the reforms related to the education sector (Church Schools and University). According to DOI (1985, p.3), when the then Prime Minister Dr Karmenu Mifsud Bonniċi was asked about government's official position on the issue of Church Schools, he replied that the principle of free education should be accepted and that the Church in Malta should allocate some of its resources to ensure that Church schools provide free education. Hence, it is argued that this dispute and the resistance it generated was all about elitism, since generally Church schools had a reputation of being better than government schools and were only available to those who could afford paying their fees. It is argued that the likely root cause for the disagreement regarding the establishment of the University of Malta was resistance to change by conservative elements and elitism, since generally the authorities and academic staff at the Old University were extremely conservative in their attitude and considered themselves to be part of an exclusive class. Whilst the social reforms of the 1970s were consolidated during this period (1980 to 1987) and various social benefits were increased, it became evident that these reforms introduced a much heavier workload on Public Service employees. Processes at the various government departments were mostly manual, and only the Inland Revenue Department (IRD) had a very low-level computing facility. The IRD computing facility processed its very own limited systems, payroll for the Treasury Department, and various smaller systems for the National Statistics Office. Moreover, up to 1981 the financial estimates show that there was only one post of 'Programmer' and one post of 'Systems Analyst' in the whole Public Service (Financial Estimates 1981, p.49).

The Government had issued a tender in August 1979 regarding the computing and hardware needs related to IRD (Camilleri, 1979). Two further reports were issued in 1980, namely: 'EDP Policy and Computer Hardware Needs for the Maltese Government and Associated Institutions' and 'Electronic Data Processing Organisation for the Maltese Government and Associated Institutions' (Camilleri, 1980a, b). The recommendations in these reports were accepted by the government and the majority were implemented. In the inauguration speech on the opening of the Government Computer Centre, the Minister of Finance, Customs and People's Financial Investments stated that the Government Computer Centre was to provide processing and software development services to all Government Departments, Parastatal Companies and Banks (Cassar, 1981, p.2). The Times of Malta (and other newspapers) published a dedicated supplement regarding this event, where the Government Computer Centre was described as one of the most modern in Europe (Times of Malta, 1981). Table 2.9 illustrates that the driving force for Public Service administration and management reform was the Ministry of Finance, Customs and People's Financial Investments, that had the direct responsibility for the Government Computer Centre. It should be noted that the systems identified at Table 2.9 through the various Financial Estimates were replacing manual processes, which meant that the employees at the Government Computer Centre had the function of conducting business process reengineering (i.e. simplification of procedures), the development and production of computer software, which at that time was not commercially available, and populating the various databases with the relevant historical and the then current information. The Financial Estimates for 1982 show that the Government Computer Centre had 85 employees, this grew to 115 in 1987 and 126 in 1988 (Financial Estimates, 1982, p.99; 1987, p.114; and 1988, p.154 respectively). The Government Computer Centre applications software inventory records also reveal that between January 1982 and April 1987 a total of 69 systems were fully developed and implemented, while a further 35 systems were developed and implemented between June 1987 and 1991.

The above demonstrates that the notion that Prime Minister, Dom Mintoff was against computer technology was not altogether factual. However, he was extremely cautious of the consequences of computer technology on the labour market. Mintoff understood that, in Malta, employment of individuals, whatever their class, was important for sustaining our type of economy and he feared that technology would replace human resources, thereby creating unemployment. Unemployment in the 1980s was rising, with Malta having 10,000 registered as unemployed by March 1985 (DOI, 1985, p.22; DOI, 1985, p.33). Disbanding of Malta Pioneer Corps and Dirgħajn-il-Maltin in 1980 made matters worse. According to Jones (1982), new technologies that emerged in the 1970s and 1980s had become 'labour-displacing' rather than 'labour-complementing' in their nature. He maintained that, as a result, manufacturing no longer existed as a dominant employer, but that many countries were at that time in the process of 'de-industrialising' and moving to largely service-based economies instead. He cautioned that, in the 1980s, service jobs were also being replaced by computerisation and modern telecommunications technologies. It is a fact that in Malta during the 1980s (up to May 1987) those applying for an import licence related to computer equipment had to declare that no labour redundancies would result. However, this was mainly a tool for monitoring the loss of jobs related to computerisation during this delicate period, because the records indicate that no licence regarding the importation of computer equipment was ever rejected. Table 2.9 also shows that reforms implemented between May 1987 and 1989 (the end of the decade under discussion) had three characteristics:

(a) Some were regressive in an attempt to turn back the clock, such as declaring the Arabic language in schools as no longer mandatory; reopening discussions with the Vatican regarding Church Schools; incorporating the Faculty of Theology within University; and reinstating academic staff and Rector of the Old University. It is interesting to note that it was under the post-May 1987 administration that the Arabic course was reintroduced at the University when it was discovered that the government found that it could not find translators of Arabic among the Maltese. Hence, the exclusion of Arabic as a mandatory subject from schools came at a price;

(b) To correct perceived so-called injustices during the previous government administration, such as establishing a Commission for the Investigation of Injustices; and

(c) To map a way forward for the Public Service, such as the appointment of the Public Service Reform Commission and initiating an Operations Review.

The focus of this chapter is Public Service administration and management reform. Hence, of particular interest is © above. It is noted that two reports were issued in 1989, the Operations Review (undated) and the first report of Public Service Reform Commission (July 1989). These will be considered with other material when discussing the 1990s. However, two observations may be made at this stage: (a) the Chairman of the Public Service Reform Commission (PSRC) was seriously involved in a dispute with the Labour Government in relation to the reforms regarding the University of Malta in the 1970s; and (b) the person conducting the Operations Review was depicted as a management guru by the new administration, but it later emerged in a court case that his qualifications were meagre O-Level standard and had worked for the Canadian Government in the Department of Correctional Services. Moreover, many of the reforms in these reports were copied from similar exercises in Britain and New Zealand with little thought to the Maltese environment. This becomes evident from the fact that the authors of these reports never actually explained the advantages and disadvantages of these reforms. Over the years, some of the reforms that were instituted abroad were overturned, but in Malta no such debate took place, with some of the reforms remaining, even though they were practically irrelevant, while others were politically motivated.

2.2.5   Public Administration and Management: The Road to EU Membership and its Immediate Aftermath (1990 – March 2013)

The 1990s epitomized the systematic social liberalization of most countries, together with an increase in the impact of capitalism that would continue until the Great Recession of the late 2000s/early 2010s. This period is characterised as being dominated by a mixture of issues, including the continued mass mobilization of capital markets through neo-liberalism; the conclusion of the Cold War; the beginning of the widespread dissemination of new communications media, such as the Internet from the middle of the decade onwards; increasing mistrust towards governments; and the end of the Soviet Union. The outcome of this mixture of issues was a recurring process of consolidation and repositioning of economic and political power throughout the globe and within countries. According to Antohi and Tismăneanu (1999, p.85), the 1990s was an era of spreading capitalism, with the former countries of the Warsaw Pact moving from single-party socialist states to multi-party states with private sector economies. Germany was reunified on 3 October 1990 after the fall of the Berlin Wall. This event constrained Germany to focus on transforming the former communist East to a capitalist culture, after the integration of the provincial governments and associated economic structures. Some Eastern European economies struggled after the fall of communism, but Poland, Hungary, Czech Republic, Estonia, Latvia and Lithuania enjoyed healthy economic growth rates in the late 1990s.

Generally, the 1990s was a difficult period for the former Soviet Union, where the GDP declined as the economies were restructured to produce much needed consumer goods, instead of military related produce. Moreover, the Russian financial crisis of the 1990s resulted in hyperinflation, which required economic intervention from the International Monetary Fund and other western countries, to assist the

Russian economy recover. However, many countries, particularly the high-income nations such as those in Western Europe, the United States, Canada, Australia, New Zealand, Japan, Singapore, Hong Kong, Taiwan, and South Korea all experienced sturdy economic growth for most of the 1990s. In 1992, the European Union formulated and adopted the Maastricht Treaty, which resulted in the freedom of movement of EU citizens between member states, followed in 1995 by free trade agreements. These developments coincided with the establishment of the World Trade Organization (WTO) in January 1995 under the Marrakesh Agreement, which was signed by 123 nations on 15th April 1994, making it the largest international economic organization in the world. However, WTO attracted vocal anti-globalization protests as well as increasing hostility towards neo-liberalism. A further development was the adoption of the Euro on 1st January 1999 as the European Union's official currency, thus phasing out national currencies for those EU countries wishing to join the Euro-zone. The 1990s and early 2000s were stained by ethnic tensions and violence in former Yugoslavia and the bombing and destruction of the World Trade Centre in New York on 11th September 2001.

The 1990s and beyond heralded tremendous advances in technology, particularly in the area of communications, with the World Wide Web that come into sight in 1990 being continuously improved and enhanced throughout the decade and beyond. The dot-com bubble of 1997–2000 resulted in the generation of wealth for a number of entrepreneurs, before it burst between 2000 and 2001. According to the Bureau of Labour Statistics (1999), between 1990 and 1997, individual personal computer ownership in the US rose from 15% to 35%. The first web browser went online in 1993 and by 2001, more than 50% of some Western countries had Internet access, and more than 25% had cell phone access. However, the Great Recession of 2009 brought with it economic devastation to most countries. This resulted in a massive global economic downturn that shocked the world financial markets, particularly the banking and real estate sectors. The outcome of this economic catastrophe was a significant increase in home mortgage foreclosures worldwide, causing millions of people to lose their homes and life savings. It is contended that the events during this particular period encouraged and provided an added impetus for the Maltese government to seek European Union membership with urgency. Furthermore, Public Service administration and management activities were dominated by four key factors all having the objective of paving the way for Malta to become a European Union member state:

(a) The recommendations of the Public Service Reform Commission leading to the restructuring of the Public Service;
(b) The establishment of the Management Systems Unit that took over the implementation of Information Communications Technology (ICT) within the Public Service;
(c) The closure of the Government Computer Centre; and
(d) The Public Service administrative and legal reforms necessary for European Membership.

In 1988, the Government established a Public Service Reform Commission (PSRC) to examine the organization of the Public Service and to recommend a means by which the Public Service can efficiently respond to the changing needs for effective government. The PSRC's three public reports in July 1989, January 1990 and February 1990 launched a series of government reforms that were to be implemented over a decade ranging from the delivery of Public Services to the working of the Constitution, including the judiciary and legislature. According to PSRC (1989), recommendations of the PSRC leading to the restructuring of the Public Service had the following goals:

- Win public confidence in the Public Service;
- Create a culture of excellence and integrity;
- Define the role of the Public Service;
- Develop administrative structures and management systems;
- Define and develop employee competence;
- Select and retain the brightest and ablest;
- Improve the quality of management;
- Invest in technology and plant;
- Increase planning and audit capabilities;
- Define and contain executive discretion; and
- Institutionalise change.

There is no doubt that the goals of the PSRC were commendable. However, whether these goals were achieved within the period under examination is very questionable. Some viewed these goals and the proposed reforms as a wish list, while others were more optimistic. It should be noted that the PSRC report of 1989, which constituted the main report, was not unanimously agreed to by all the members of the PSRC, with one member expressing his reservations on at least seven points (PSRC, 1989, p.74). The PSRC report was very critical of Public Service employees, particularly the senior management category. In fact, the harsh criticism of the then Public Service was one of the reserved points. It is argued that the composition of the PSRC was its main weakness, placing doubt on the political motivation of the whole reform process. Hence, it is contended that the PSRC lacked absolute credibility. As stated in a previous section, the events of the 1980's were turbulent and a key reason for this was the general political divisiveness that existed at that time. Moreover, public servants, particularly those occupying the senior management posts (irrespective of their political views), were in most cases viewed as government collaborators, and were therefore looked down upon by those having anti-labour sentiments in the post May 1987 government circles. Additionally, the Chairman of the PSRC had a particularly serious dispute with the labour government in the 1970s, over the reform of the education system related to the transition of the Old University to the New University, apart from the fact that the political sentiments of the other members of the PSRC were well known to be anti-labour. Hence, the PSRC would have been more credible if its composition consisted of persons who had a mixture of moderate political views.

Ironically, the PSRC was very critical of the past extreme political partisan tendencies, yet its composition was far from being politically neutral. According to PSRC (1989, p.58), it was proposed that the posts of Director and above should not be tenured but should be on contractual terms for definite periods. This was noted as a reserved point by the dissenting member of the PSRC, who expressed the opinion that security of tenure provided continuity and a measure of independence in the discharge of their function (PSRC, 1989, p.76). It was argued that having a contractual arrangement for such posts was likely to result in instances where there would be acquiescence to decisions due to fear of not having ones contract renewed; thus providing the means for the politicisation of the Public Service, as former promotion procedures were eliminated giving the political side a freer hand in making appointments. It is interesting to note, that in the early 1990s the then Prime Minister was found responsible for political discrimination by the Employment Commission, related to the exclusion of a senior Public Service employee from the then newly established Management Systems Unit (MSU). This was a historical event because it was the first time that a Prime Minister was found guilty of political discrimination in Malta, which resulted in him tendering his resignation, although the resignation was eventually not accepted by the President. This political discrimination case was followed by at least two other cases, with guilty verdicts being handed down by the Employment Commission against the Prime Ministers at that time. It is noted that the Employment Commission was established in accordance with Chapter XI, Clause 120 of the Constitution of Malta, as amended in 1974 and was an important reform to protect individuals against political discrimination.

The PSRC reports advocated transformational change in many aspects of Public Service administration and management, which required non-conventional and progressive leadership. However, during the period under review (1990–March 2013) Public Service reform was generally headed by conservative thinking. Hence, Public Service reforms tended to be implemented on a selective basis and at a much slower rate than that intended by the PSRC. An Operations Review of Public Service administration and management was undertaken concurrently with the PSRC's work. However, the reform implementation programme did not commence until 1991, leading to a major restructuring of the Maltese public administration, including the formulation of an information systems strategic plan, which defined new modes of service delivery. The Operations Review of the public administration was very critical of the operational capabilities of the various government departments and provided general recommendations for reforming them. As one may expect, this harsh criticism did not go down very well with the incumbents of those managing the various departments, thus a certain amount of animosity was generated, which was later transformed and grow to resistance. A key outcome of the Operations Review was the setting up of the Management Systems Unit (MSU), which took over the implementation of Information Communications Technology (ICT) within the Public Service and provided management consultancy services to government. The MSU was provided with a hefty budget running to about the equivalent of €16 million per annum. This generous budget enabled the MSU to procure the latest ICT equipment and engage a large number (about 50) of expatriate consultants at exorbitant salaries (in many cases tax free) to conduct its programme of works. It should be noted that during the 1990s, a technology revolution was taking place, where multi-user systems (later known as file servers) were attainable at relatively low prices and enabled real-time systems to be readily implemented. Moreover, Telemalta, which was the telecommunications provider for the Maltese islands, heavily invested in its communications network and commenced installing fibre optic cabling between the various telephone exchanges to enhance data communication speed.

This development enabled the MSU to establish a robust government data communications network linking all Ministries and their respective departments. The legacy systems and more importantly, the related databases from the Government Computer Centre enabled the various real-time systems to be implemented at a fairly rapid rate. The MSU tended to focus on the operational aspect (the communications network and processing) of technology and outsourced most of the application software development to external commercial enterprises. However, certain strategic systems, such as those of the Inland Revenue, were still maintained by MSU employees (ex-Government Computer Centre staff). A major criticism of the MSU was the lack of technology transfer to Maltese personnel regarding applications software development. This was due to the applications software outsourcing policy, where packaged application systems were procured with very little technology transfer taking place. Moreover, the expatriate employees were paid far more than their Maltese counterparts, which tended to create internal friction between staff. Additionally, the expatriate employees were not seen as transferring their knowledge and experience to Maltese employees that were working under their direction. The general public perception was that wastage of public funds was taking place at the MSU. On the change of government administration in 1996, the MSU's budget was curtailed by a significant amount (almost half); most of the expatriate staff had their contracts terminated; financial control mechanisms were implemented to mitigate financial abuse; and the MSU was renamed Malta Information Technology and Training Limited (MITTS). Currently, this organisation has again had a name change to Malta Information Technology Agency (MITA).

The closure of the Government Computer Centre (GCC) in late 1991 resulted in a complete shift of emphasis in the technological development strategy of government. GCC had two major operational divisions, namely the Operations and Processing Division and the Applications Systems Development Division. The MSU with the new technology developments related to communications network capabilities of the 1990s, particularly the growth of the use of the Internet and eMail, focused on the Operations and Processing aspects. However, it neglected the applications systems development facet. The applications systems development aspects were mainly outsourced; thus, a robust strategic function was permitted to diminish by the MSU. On the other hand, the MSU was required to strengthening its procurement and contractual function, and to reinforce its project management capability. This was meant to ensure that the outsourced work was delivered on time, to budget and to specification. However, this strategy was not very successful and eventually resulted in the applications systems development function being an unfortunate casualty that has never recovered.

Concurrently, with the various public administration and management reform, a challenging and a most difficult transition in Maltese public administration and management was taking place, namely Malta's accession into the European Union. On 16 July 1990, Malta formally applied for European Community membership receiving a favourable opinion by the European Commission in June 1993. Upon taking the decision to apply for EU membership, the government adopted a phased approach to implementing Public Service administration and management reform. Three organisations referred to as 'Central Agencies for Change' were established within the remit of the Office of the Prime Minister (OPM), these included the Management System Unit (MSU) that has already been discussed; the Management and Personnel Office (MPO); and the Staff Development Organisation (SDO). These three new organisations provided the planning and technical support for reform initiatives during the first phase period of 1990 to 1995. Starting from 1990, the key changes that were undertaken as part of the Public Service administration and management reform included:

- Reorganising the entire classification structure of the Public Service that consisted of some 100 different salary scales, based on a simplified 20-scale salary structure;
- Minimising the worth of seniority as a criterion for promotions and placing greater emphasis on performance;
- Introducing a system of three-year renewable contractual appointments for senior management positions;
- Delegating management powers to line ministries and departments to enable managers to manage without constantly having to refer to central authorities;
- Making improvements in financial management, notably through the introduction of a system of three-year business and financial planning;
- Strengthening the ethical framework of public administration through the publication of a code of ethics, backed up by the establishment or strengthening of institutions such as the Office of the Ombudsman, the Public Accounts Committee of Parliament and the National Audit Office;
- Instituting a massive programme of investment in information technology; and
- Considerably expanding in-service training activities for public officers.

The first phase experienced the birth of a Parliamentary Ombudsman in 1995 and the creation of the Quality Service Charter Programme. The Quality Service Charter Programme had the objective of improving the quality of Public Services by encouraging departments and government offices to maintain specific quality standards, either for the entire array of the services they provide, or for certain sectors. However, despite a great deal of media hype, the Quality Service Charters never really produced the desired results. In concert, with the Public Service administration and management reform process, several additional new initiatives, which were essential for Malta to join the European Union, were also being implemented. Among these initiatives were the introduction of Value Added Tax (VAT) and the establishment of the VAT Department in 1994. The results of the first phase were contentious. Public opinion did not support the efforts of the Government during this first phase. It is difficult to determine whether this unpopularity was due to the introduction of VAT and its associated fiscal cash registers, or the Public Service administration and management reform process, or other measures that were being introduced during this period, or a combination of these various factors. However, the reforms that affected human resource management, technological modernization and the transformation of the Public Service did not particularly help to win public support for the Government. The outcome of all this was the unpopularity of the Government, which eventually lead to the defeat of the Nationalist Party at the electoral polls to the Labour party under the banner of '*New Labour*' in October 1996 with the slogan '*Putting the Citizen First*'. The new government on taking office suspended Malta's application for EU membership.

Hence, the second phase of Public Service reform commenced in October 1996, with the election of the Labour Party to form a Government, with a majority of one electoral parliamentary seat. The point regarding the parliamentary majority is important, because it had an impact on the stability of the Government during this period. At the commencement of the second phase, the MSU was divided into two distinct organisations, namely the Management Efficiency Unit (MEU) and Malta Information Technology and Training Services Ltd (MITTS). Both were the responsibility of the OPM. The MEU was responsible for the consultancy and planning function, whilst MITTS was responsible for the ICT function of Government. Due to internal conflicts within the government, a snap general election was initiated on 5th September 1998 that saw a Nationalist government being elected. The new administration immediately resumed Malta's European Union membership application and its Public Service reform process. The SDO, which was responsible for training, was merged with the MPO, responsible for human resource management strategies. The Head of Public Service, the Principal Permanent Secretary, maintained his responsibility to oversee the Public Service reform process. Moreover, several ministries were delegated with political responsibilities over the Public Service reform process. For instance, the Ministry of Justice was responsible for service quality and eGovernment; the Ministry of Finance had the responsibility for the liberalisation of state owned entities through a privatisation process and implemented government policy on salary negotiations; and the Cabinet as a whole was responsible for internal controls.

An eGovernment initiative was embarked upon in late 2000, with the publication of a white paper on the subject. This initiative was supported with the enactment of the electronic commerce and data protection legislation; the initiation of an electronic payment gateway; and the inauguration of an Internet portal (www.gov.mt) for the delivery of services. Some of the services available via the Internet at that time included the renewal of trade licences; the ordering of birth and other certificates; the payment of government rents; the filing of company income tax returns; a comprehensive database of Maltese laws, regulations and Court judgements; and the display of information on planning applications through a geographic interface. Experimentation with mGovernment (the provision of services via mobile phone) commenced in 2003, with over 8000 students receiving their summer 2003 Matsec examination results via SMS from the Department of Examinations. In 2003, a new phase of Public Service reform commenced. This was referred to as the Public Service Change Programme that comprised of three key objectives, which featured in the White Paper on a Public Service Act, entitled *A Public Service for the 21st Century*. The three objectives were as follows:

(a) To improve the efficiency of Government operations through more flexible and results-oriented management;
(b) To establish safeguards and hold the heads of departments accountable for their use of delegated powers;
(c) To strengthen the leadership of the Public Service so as to ensure that the provisions are put into effect and it is capable of taking co-ordinated action, notwithstanding the devolution of powers to the heads of department.

On December 2002, Malta concluded the negotiations for EU membership after closed all the remaining chapters. In 2003, the Malta government ratified the Accession Treaty in Athens and on 1st May 2004, Malta officially became a member state of the EU. Furthermore, on 1st January 2008 Malta introduced the Euro as its currency. The changes from all of these initiatives have served as the foundation for the launch of a new phase of reform, which aimed at delivering visible results to the public, through the provisions of the Public Administration Service Act of 2009. Additionally, the Maltese public administration had to interact with EU institutions to contribute to the development of EU legislative proposals in specific fields and in so doing highlight Malta's concerns and interests. Moreover, Maltese public administration had also to transpose or directly implement EU Directives into national legislation, while concurrently, continue to fulfil its traditional role of Public Service delivery. The years following Malta accession as an EU Member State has been dominated by an EU assimilation process. An EU Secretariat was established at the OPM with the objective of acting as a central coordinating unit in European affairs, while at the same time permitting each ministry to manage EU affairs within its own sphere of responsibility. From this restructuring emerged two new government departments, namely, the Internal Audit Directorate (IAD) and the Planning and Priorities Coordination Division (PPCD). The IAD came into fruition under the responsibility of the Cabinet Office from the need to have improved financial control across the Public Service, and due to a responsibility originating from the fulfilment of obligations arising as a result of the Maltese Government legislation-screening process. The PPCD was established owing to the reality of EU membership.

Later, the internal audit function was designated as the Internal Audit and Investigations Directorate (IAID). This Directorate was recognized by the Commission's Anti-Fraud Office (OLAF) as the anti-fraud coordinating service of the Maltese Government. Over the years, the IAID was charged with the new responsibilities, mainly in the area of EU funds. The IAID was also assigned as the auditing authority in terms of the Structural and Cohesion funds and the certifying body for the Agricultural funds. In 2010, the SDO, which was the training arm of Government, was transformed into the Centre for Development, Research and

Training (CDRT). This organisation was enhanced to conduct research for Government Ministries related to the formulation of various policies. However, this organisation did not embrace the research function and basically remained a Public Service training centre like its predecessor, SDO. In 2011, the Public Administration Human Resource Organisation (PAHRO) was established to take over the functions of MPO, with an expanded mandate, progressing from the traditional concept of micro HR Management, towards a macro and comprehensive outlook, comprising of: (i) workforce planning; (ii) change management; (iii) guidance and support provision to line Ministries and Departments; (iv) monitoring the implementation of HR Management in line Ministries and Departments; and (v) promoting leadership development. With the establishment of PAHRO in 2011, the Public Service Management Code (PSMC) was also published. The PSMC comprised of 406 pages and upheld the core principles and values of the Public Service, enshrined in the Public Administration Act (PAA), which was enacted in November 2009. In January 2013, a Public Service Reform Review was completed. This resulted in a draft report that contained 54 specific recommendations and initiatives, targeting five major aspects:

(a) Improving Public Service delivery quality;
(b) Improving Public Service delivery through ICT improvements;
(c) Improving Public Service organisational structures;
(d) Reducing Public Service administrative burdens;
(e) Staff Development and Research.

However, this review was overtaken by events due to a change of government in March 2013. March 2013 resulted in the Maltese electorate voting the Malta Labour Party into Government. This Labour Government is characterised by being led by a young and dynamic Prime Minister, with most of the Ministers also coming from the younger generation. This is an important point because the rate of growth and change that took place in Malta during this administration can only be described as extraordinary. On the other hand, the Nationalist Government being in power for nearly 25 years took its toll in terms of its dynamism. The same persons, with some exceptions, remained in Government throughout the 25 years. Thus, it is suggested that the Government ran out of energy when Malta became an EU member state and later joined the Euro zone. The combination of a conservative Headship of the Public Service and a tired Government had severe implications for the Public Administration reform process, specifically at the execution stage, where many paper initiatives were never put to practical use. On the other hand, the change of government in March 2013 also resulted in a change in the headship of the Public Service, which brought with it a more dynamic and enthusiastic attitude. Foremost, several public service reforms were to be initiated by the Public Service itself and not by politicians, since the Public Service was given a certain degree of independence to do this. This and many other developments will be treated in the chapters to follow.

2.2.6   *Conclusion*

This chapter has briefly tracked the history of the Maltese Public Service adminis-tration and management reform process since Malta gained its independence from the United Kingdom on 21st September 1964 to March 2013. It has shown how Public Service employees have always rose to the challenge under various govern-ments with different ideological philosophies. Each decade and period that has been discussed provided unique challenges for the Public Service employees, who can only be described as courageous and innovative under a whole range of economic and social circumstances. The various economic and social circumstances that the Public Service has served under and more importantly, the results that have been achieved in every administrative period is ample proof that the Public Service Reform Commission of 1989 was not justified in its harsh criticism of the employ-ees and the management team that lead the Public Service during the different times.

The EU accession process resulted in a complete review of all Maltese legisla-tion and public administrative and management structures; the establishment of new departments, such as the VAT Department and the Internal Audit and Investigations Directorate; the liberalization and privatization of various state owned entities; and the termination of subsidies and state aid. One may not entirely agree with certain agreements and procedures that were applied, but generally, the work achieved by the Public Service employees was outstanding. The magnitude of the challenge faced by Maltese public administration must also be seen in the context of its size. The size of a Public Service is relative to the population of the country it serves. Hence, the size of the Public Service in Malta is rather small. However, the EU legislative burden on Maltese public administration is equal to that of the larger member countries.

It is noted that the right type of leadership is essential to the Public Service administration and management reform process, because a dynamic and enthusias-tic attitude at the top has the impact of cascading this stance to the lower levels of the Public Service, with more positive results. Finally, it is appropriate to end this section with a quote from Niccolo Machiavelli (The Prince, 1515, Chapter VI): 'There is nothing more difficult to take in hand, more perilous to conduct, or more uncertain in its success, than to take the lead in the introduction of a new order of things'.

References

Alshinawi, A. (2014). Malta's post-independence policy-making: An international political econ-omy perspective. *Journal of Maltese History, 4*(1).

Antohi, S., & Tismăneanu, V. (1999). *"Independence reborn and the demons of the velvet rev-olution" in between past and future: The revolutions of 1989 and their aftermath.* Central European University Press.

BBC. (1984). *1984: The beginning of the end for British coal.* BBC News. Available from: http://news.bbc.co.uk/onthisday/hi/dates/stories/march/12/newsid_3503000/3503346.stm. Accessed on: 21 Mar 2020.

Boissevian, J. (2012). Mintoff and Malta: The autocracy of haste. In M. Cutajar (Ed.), *Mintoff il-bniedem u l-istorja*. Pubblikazzjoni SKS.

Brick, H. (2012). Review: Daniel T. Rodgers. Age of fracture. *American Historical Review, 117*(5).

Bureau of Labor Statistics. (1999). *Computer ownership up sharply in the 1990s.* Issues in labor statistics, summary 99, 4 March 1999. US Department of Labor, Bureau of Labor Statistics.

Camilleri, E. (1979). *Comments on computing and hardware needs of the Maltese hovernment.* .

Camilleri, E. (1980a). EDP policy and computer hardware needs for the Maltese Government and Associated Institutions. In *Ministry of finance, customs and people's financial investments.* Valletta.

Camilleri, E. (1980b). Electronic data processing organisation for the Maltese Government and Associated Institutions. In *Ministry of finance, customs and people's financial investments.* Valletta.

Cassar, J. (1981). *Speech of the minister for finance, customs and people's financial investments on the occasion of the inauguration of the government computer centre.* Department of Information, Wednesday, 18th November 1981.

Cutajar, M. (2012). *Mintoff il-bniedem u l-istorja.* Pubblikazzjoni SKS.

DOI. (1985). *Karmenu: Dialogues with the press.* Information Division.

Dowdall, J. (1972). The political economy of Malta. *The Round Table, 62*(248).

Findlay, R., & Wellisz, S. (1993). *A World Bank comparative study: The political economy of poverty, equity and growth: Five small open economies (section on Malta).* Oxford University Press Inc..

Friedman, G. (2009). *The next 100 years: A forecast for the 21st century.* Anchor Books, Random House.

IBRD. (1963). *The economy of Malta.* International Bank for Reconstruction and Development, August 5, 1963, Department of Operations, Europe. Available from: http://documents.worldbank.org/curated/en/466121468300657154/pdf/multi0page.pdf. Accessed on: 13 Feb 2020.

Jones, B. (1982). *Sleepers, wake! Technology and the future of work.* Oxford University Press.

Lashinsky, A. (2011). *How Apple works: Inside the world's biggest startup.* Available from: https://fortune.com/2011/05/09/inside-apple/. Accessed on: 22 Feb 2020.

Lewis, F. (1988). *Foreign affairs: Cold war recedes.* May 29th 1988 New York Times. Available from: https://www.nytimes.com/1988/05/29/opinion/foreign-affairs-cold-war-recedes.html. Accessed on: 21 Mar 2020.

Machiavelli, N. (1515). *The prince.* Antonio Blado d'Asola. Translated by W. K. Marriott. 1908.

Mangion, R. (2012). Mintoff, Il-Kostituzzjoni u L-Leġiżlazzjoni Maltija. In M. Cutajar (Ed.), *Mintoff il-bniedem u l-istorja.* Pubblikazzjoni SKS.

Marglin, S. A., & Schor, J. B. (1991). *Golden age of capitalism: Reinterpreting the postwar experience.* Clarendon Press.

Ministry of Common wealth and Foreign Affairs. (1978). *Extract from notes on meeting with Mr Debbons, Consul of Malta in Pittsburgh, Pennsylvania, 16th January 1978.* CFA: 241/64/II.

Montebello, M. (2012). *Illuminiżmu u Nazzjonaliżmu.* In M. Cutajar (Ed.), *Mintoff il-bniedem u l-istorja.* Pubblikazzjoni SKS.

Pirotta, G. A. (1985). Malta's foreign policy after Mintoff. *Political Quarterly, 56*(2).

Pirotta, G. A. (1997). Politics and public service reform in small states: Malta. *Public Administration and Development, 17*(1), 1997.

PSRC. (1989). Public Service Reform Commission: A new public service for Malta. A report on the organisation of the Public Service. .

Samueli, M. (2014). *26 December 1982: Personal computer named 'man of the year'.* MoneyWeek, 26 Dec 2014. Available from: https://moneyweek.com/370787/26-december-1982-personal-computer-named-man-of-the-year. Accessed on: 21 Mar 2020.

Scicluna, M. (2011). Divorce and the history of Church-State relations in Malta (II). *Malta Independent, Wednesday, 4 May 2011.*

Tanzi, V. (1997). *The changing role of the state in the economy: A historical perspective.* IMF Working Paper no. 97/114 (September, 1997).

Times of Malta. (1981). Government computer Centre – one of the most modern in Europe. *Times of Malta, Wednesday, 18th November 1981.*

The Guardian. (2001). The Fabian Society: A brief history. *The Guardian, 13 August, 2001.*

Van der Velden, S., Dribbusch, H., Lyddon, D., & Vandaele, K. (2007). *Strikes around the world, 1968–2005: Case-studies of 15 countries.* Amsterdam University Press.

Vassallo, R. (2011). PN remembers the violence of the 1980s... *Malta Today, 30 November 2011.* Available from: https://www.maltatoday.com.mt/news/national/14190/pn-remembers-the-violence-of-the-1980s#.XnciX25FxPY. Accessed on: 22 Mar 2020.

Woods, R. B. (2016). How the great society reforms of the 1960s were different from the new deal. *Time, April 5th 2016.*

Part II
Public Service Reform: "The Best of Times"

*"It was the best of times, it was the worst of times, it was the
age of wisdom, it was the age of foolishness, it was the epoch of
belief, it was the epoch of incredulity, it was the season of light,
it was the season of darkness, it was the spring of hope, it was
the winter of despair."*

(Charles Dickens, author of: A Tale of Two Cities)

As stated in Part I, the focus of this book is on the Maltese Public Service reforms under the new Labour administration commencing in 2013 to the 2020 that has seen the advancement of Public Service administration and management, which can only be described as revolutionary. Never, in the history of the Maltese Public Service, have so many reforms taken place in such a short period of time, which have had considerable positive impact on the lives of so many citizens in Malta, particularly minority groups. It is no wonder that many consider this period as the *Best of Times!*

The previous two chapters have provided a historical background of the way the Maltese Public Service administration and management has developed over the years prior to 2013. The intention of these chapters was to set the broad scene from the time of the sovereignty of the Knights of St John to Malta's Independence in 1964, which I shall refer to as the *"Beginning"*, to the post-Independence period that focused on the developments to modernise Public Service administration and management, which is referred to as *"The turning point."*

The research suggests that it is proper to describe the Maltese Public Service as being in state of continuous transition. Having said this, it is recognised that there is an in-bred resistance to change in most organisations and the Maltese Public Service is not an exception. However, the research findings show that the Maltese Public Service has always, throughout various eras, faced up to the various challenges and succeeded in making Malta a better place for its citizens. Transformational reforms do not just happen from thin air. Transformational reforms are highly dependent on the leadership attitude of those leading the Public Service at any specific point in time, particularly the vision of the Prime Minister and the Cabinet team, and the vision and driving force of the Head of the Public Service. One needs to recognise that vision determines whether the reforms will be merely incremental or transformational.

The public sector in Malta, like most other EU member states, is the largest service provider and thus it impacts the full spectrum of the Maltese population. Furthermore, one must recognise that individuals, while being the largest in volume, are just one class of customers that the Maltese Government, through its Public Service, must satisfy. Hence, the business community and civil society are also important customers that the Public Service must assist to satisfy their particular needs. Moreover, people cannot be viewed and classified under a single heading of individuals because various classes of people require different needs. Therefore, a distinction must also be made between different classes of individuals, such as, children, students, gender, senior citizens, and persons with special needs, amongst many others.

The key dynamics of public administration reforms in Malta are all about bringing together the innovative ideas from various stakeholders in the private, public, and civil sectors to meet customer expectations in every sector. This is an ambitious task, a task that is not easy to achieve, but technology is the greatest facilitator for making this to happen. Malta up to seven years ago, like many other EU Member States, was experiencing several austerity measures, which lead to a more production-oriented approach to providing public services, with the primary objective of reducing costs. However, past and recent investment in ICT has allowed the Malta Public Service providers to review their mode of operations with the aim of providing a more efficient and effective service delivery resulting in the provision of value for money services through improved quality. This has resulted in a customer-oriented approach by permitting customer accessibility to various Maltese public services on seven days, twenty-four hours a week basis from anywhere. The general outcome of this, is that the Malta government through its Public Service organisations is seeking new sustainable models for service delivery that empower their customers to receive a better, efficient and effective service at the same or lower cost.

March 2013 resulted in the Maltese electorate voting the Malta Labour Party into Government. This Labour Government is characterised by being led by a young and dynamic Prime Minister, with most of the Ministers also coming from the younger generation. This is an important observation because the rate of growth and change that has taken place in Malta in these last seven years can only be described as extraordinary. The research has identified and documented ninety-three reforms. Furthermore, if the recent reforms related to the Venice Commission were to be included, the reforms would number over one hundred. These public service reforms have been classified into five categories, namely:

1. Transparency and Accountability Mechanisms;
2. Civil Service Systems and HRM;
3. Service delivery and Digitalization;
4. Organisation and Management of Government;
5. Policy Making, Coordination and Implementation.

A chapter has been dedicated in Part II for each of these five reform categories. These chapters will provide a comprehensive analysis of the various reforms that have been implemented in the past seven years. Furthermore, the reader will find that most of the implement reforms are transformational or rather revolutionary, that reflects the innovative and dynamic vision of the Government leadership at both the executive and administrative levels.

Chapter 3
Transparency and Accountability Public Service Reforms

*"Transparency is for those who carry out public duties and
exercise public power. Privacy is for everyone else."*

Glenn Greenwald
American Journalist, Lawyer and Writer

Transparency and accountability are two basic principles for democratic government. There is a two-way relationship between transparency and accountability. Accountability characterizes the form of transparency that is necessary. In contrast, the quality of the unrestricted information available establishes the type of accountability that is possible. In democracies, principles of accountability and transparency influence not only government, but also on all types of entities that operate under public laws. This Chapter illustrates the type of transparency and accountability reforms that have been implemented at many different governing levels, namely, state agencies reforms in the form of legislation and structures that influence the operations of Malta's Public Service; national policies that have a comprehensive influence in the manner that the Public Services directs its strategy; and structural changes and new procedures within the Public Services that have strengthened the notion of good governance in its totality. This Chapter revealed that issues of good governance can be found in all Public Service administrative processes and is therefore intimately related to all operational aspects in so many different governmental departments and ministries. Such a comprehensive outlook was possible by embracing an inward and an outward perspective of the Public Service in the analysis conducted by the authors.

© The Author(s), under exclusive license to Springer Nature Switzerland AG 2021   91
F. Bezzina et al., *Public Service Reforms in a Small Island State*,
Public Administration, Governance and Globalization 22,
https://doi.org/10.1007/978-3-030-74357-4_3

3.1 Introduction: Transparency and Accountability in Small States

Challenges linked to corruption and maladministration has always been at the forefront for small island states. Malta is no exception to this phenomenon, especially when the public administration is involved. To mitigate the risks of maladministration in a public setting, a system of checks and balances in the form of legislative and institutional framework is essential to provide the necessary platform for a Public Service to function appropriately. Sound public sector management helps the respective governments to deliver services to the citizens efficiently and effectively, which public administrative system ensures value for public money (Shah, 2007).

Therefore, it is no surprise that improving transparency, good governance and accountability within the *modus operandi* of the Public Service have been identified as one of the main priorities of Malta's national Government. The most important reforms that are analysed in this chapter encapsulate the Whistleblower Act, measures against corruption related to public officers, the financing of Political Parties Act and eParticipation.

3.2 State-Oriented Reforms That Influenced the Public Service

States have embarked on several governing reforms that have increasingly influenced the Public Service both in terms of using public money wisely as well as being more competitive and customer focused. The reforms are not directly infused within the operations of the Public Service but influence extensively the conditions surrounding the public administration. The reforms can be classified into two main categories: state-initiated public sector related and purely public-service connected.

3.2.1 State-Initiated Legislative Reforms

The first two kinds of reforms were concentrated in the political arena, the first focused on the political class and the risk associated of having corruption and kickbacks associated with political executives. The second kind of reform is more of an organisational nature; it is linked to the manner that political parties are organised and operationalised.

The removal of prescription on acts of political corruption from politicians and public officials was introduced in 2013, when a bill was presented with the principal objective of removing the applicability of prescription to the offence of corruption when committed by persons elected to political office, and to further implement the provisions of the Criminal Law Convention on Corruption of the Council of Europe.

This entails that elected officials can be prosecuted without recourse to prescription even after an indeterminate number of years after the crime is committed. The bill also includes a consequential amendment to the Civil Code which excludes the plea of prescription in actions for the recovery of damages suffered by the Government, by a Local Council or by other public entities as a result of an act of corruption of an elected holder of political office (Criminal Code, 2013). The scrutiny on the members of Parliament was further strengthened in 2018 when a Commissioner for Standards was appointed to investigate Members of Parliament, including Cabinet members, on breaches of statutory or ethical duties. The Standards Commissioner has the power to consider whether ministers, parliamentary secretaries or other members of Parliament have acted in ways that are against the law; are in breach of any ethical or other duty set out by law; or constitute an abuse of power (Commissioner for Standards in Public Life, 2020).

Turning the attention on the legal framework, the financing of Political Parties Act (Cap. 544, 2016) was introduced and was intended to support transparency and accountability when it comes to political parties. The Act regulates the way that political parties function, the way they are financed and how they participate in elections. It also introduces specific obligations and limits about the financing of political parties; increases the permissible spending on candidates' electoral campaigns; imposes stricter controls on such spending; and introduces more effective sanctions against breaches of these rules. This is a crucial Act given that policy initiatives emerge during political parties' fora and which are later incorporated in the political parties manifestoes. The Act was subsequently strengthened by adding another clause in 2017 regarding the donations received from third parties. Political parties are to present to the Electoral Commission a return showing any donations above €7000 received from individuals, corporate entities or other entities.

The Protection of the Whistleblower Act (Cap. 527, 2013) that came into force on 16th September 2013 has also further strengthened and broadened good governance at a political level. The Act makes provision for procedures for employees in both the private sector and the public administration who may disclose information regarding improper practices by their employers. The Act offers employees the protection from detrimental actions. It gives citizens the right to report an act of abuse, corruption or illegality in a safe manner. The Act was devised with the aim of leading to a change in mentality and culture and facilitated the process of reporting any unlawful activities and providing full protection from any disciplinary action or any retribution. In order to instil the spirit outlined in the Act, every Government Ministry now has a government official appointed at the level of Assistant Director or above to serve as Whistleblowing Officer. The officer's role involves receiving reports. In addition to this measure, a high-ranking Civil Servant working within the Cabinet Office has been entrusted with the role of serving as External Whistleblowing Officer. This officer will receive all reports.

3.2.2   Reform at State Agencies: Judicial Reform

The introduction of new legislation that strengthened good governance was accentuated by the enhancement of the judicial powers and independency. In 2013, a judicial reform introduced new mechanisms in the manner that judges are appointed. Power was not in the hands of the Prime Minister in an absolute manner any longer and judges started to be scrutinised through an independent board. In 2018, the Venice Commission put forward a series of recommendations. The most significant suggestions of the Venice Commission were to amend the role of the attorney general, by separating prosecutorial powers from the advisory role. Two of the laws enforced by the Government in this regard were: a law which strengthened judicial independence by reforming the manner in which judicial appointments and discipline take place; and a law decreasing the powers of the Attorney General in drug and other cases (Government of Malta, 2018).

The justice reform mirrors another fundamental principle of governance, which is the Rule of Law: the need to have working legal frameworks that are fair and which can be enforced impartially in a reasonable time. It is not the remit of this *ex-ante* evaluation to analyse the rule of law from a national and a political perspective. The aim of this report is to assess those state's institutions that influence the operational efficiency of the Public Service. One of the institutions, that is a pillar of the separation of powers, and influences the public administration are the law courts. A major criticism from an operational point-of-view was the excessive time taken to decide on a case. Such a situation meant that cases of public maladministration are decided after a long period of time. It is important that a functioning democracy has efficient law courts that serve as a check and balance on the Public Service. In November 2013, a Justice Reform Commission that was set-up for the purpose to submit its recommendations for a reform in justice proposed a total of 450 recommendations. The annual evaluations of the European Commission, following the gradual implementation of the recommendations by the Justice Reform Commission, have been positive especially in terms of the efficiency of the system.

Efficiency has continued to improve both in terms of the clearance rate, which is the rate at which cases in Court are decided when compared with the number of cases which are filed, in the length of proceedings which, year after year, are becoming shorter, and the number of pending cases which continued to decrease as a result of the reduction in the clearance rate and disposition time. According to the 2017 evaluation and scoreboard, the average number of days for a case in the Civil Court to be decided was reduced by 50%, from 707 days to 447 days. With regards to administrative cases, the average number of days for a case to be decided was reduced from 1457 to 495 days, when compared to the year 2015. There were other positive factors that were highlighted by the EU Commission. Malta classified in first place when it comes to the appointment of women to the judiciary and in second place when it comes to the training of the judiciary in European laws. The Maltese justice system leads when it comes to the use of technology to administer Court cases.

A significant step forward in curbing waste of time was the introduction of sending a message to the involved parties when a court hearing is postponed to another date. The public perception of the Courts' independence and the faith in the Courts and the judiciary is also strong. This is extremely important for a country that is to ascertain an effective redress of maladministration. Negative factors that were highlighted by the Commission was that Malta is in last place when it comes to the relationship between the Courts and the media, and at the bottom of the scoreboard in the number of Judges and Magistrates who serve in the Maltese Courts.

3.2.3   National Policy-Oriented Reforms That Influenced the Operational Capabilities of the Public Services

State's reforms that influenced the governance of the Public Services can also be attributed to the design and implementation of policies. The National Digital Strategy for the period 2014–2020 (Digital Malta, 2014) aided transparency and put forward a suite of guiding principles and actions for ICT to be used for socio-economic development. The strategy was the catalyst to determine how ICT can make a difference in areas such as the economy, employment, industry and small businesses, and how it can be used for national development, to empower citizens and transform government. The Digital Strategy encompassed a suite of benefits that ICT can bring including improvements in the educational sector, stronger businesses, a more efficient Government, sustainable economic growth and much more. Digital Malta also sets out how government can be closer to the citizen using technology and become more efficient in the way public services are delivered.

The National Digital Strategy was a crucial policy development for the country, but its affect was also trickled down within the Maltese Public Service. The Digital Strategy has contributed to the building structures for the implementation of eParticipation and eGovernment. eParticipation comprises of online services to facilitate the provision of information, online public consultations and the involvement of citizens in decision-making processes. eGovernment is a programme whereby public services and information are electronically available to citizens and businesses anytime and anywhere. These services reduce the need for citizens' physical presence to receive over-the-counter service and save time travelling to and between Government offices. Citizens also enjoy the convenience of making electronic payments while receiving notifications via SMS and social media. By November 2017, Malta was classified first among all EU countries in the provision of online services (European Union, 2018).

The ICT related Public Service reforms were also implemented in public procurement. In 2016, the New Regulatory Framework for Public Procurement Concession and Utilities Contracts was implemented. These reforms had two main aims: the increase in transparency and accountability and the reengineered public procurement processes that rendered public procurement more efficient and effective. Therefore, in practice, this regulatory framework had the objective of increasing effectiveness, transparency and accountability in government related to procurement activities, for example the way the Government buys products and services. New practices were introduced, such as the use of the Electronic Public Procurement System for all tender calls. This system saves time and money and is much easier than the manual system used in the past. It has become preferable to issue a call for tenders (rather than just asking for three quotes), irrespective of the service or product. The new regulatory framework aims to wipe out any companies or individuals that engage in precarious employment, corruption, fraud, money laundering, tax evasion, evasion of employees' social security contribution, organised crime, employment of minors and other forms of people trafficking, among others.

The state's direct and indirect influence on the Public Service is not always evident and it stems from the changes that governments introduce which ultimately inspire the political culture to be directed in a particular path. The revised voting age to grant 16-year-olds the right to vote in 2018 has put youths in a much better position to lead at a political level. This political development can have a future effect on both the political class and the Public Service leaders. The Constitution was amended in March 2018, where Malta became the second European Union member state to grant 16-year-olds the right to vote in national elections. This reform saw an increase of 8500 more voters, with the first opportunity to exercise this new right in 2019.

Political culture is influenced at large by the media, the flexibility as well as the freedom of expression to convey the necessary messages. The freedom of the press and the decriminalisation of libel in the form of the Media and Defamation Act (Malta Parliament, 2018) that was enacted in 2018 had a transparency and an accountability dimension. Therefore, this Act has contributed towards a stronger democracy and better governance. The Act allows for journalistic freedom through the decriminalisation of libel. It removes references to offending 'public morals or decency' and prevents plaintiffs from filing garnishee orders against journalists and only allows applicants to file one libel suit per story.

3.3   Public Service Reforms in Transparency and Accountability

The transparency and accountability reforms might have had an impact on the level of trust in the national government as well. The Eurobarometer for the June 2019 survey revealed that 58% of Maltese trust their government. This rate is by far more than EU average that was 34%. Furthermore, the Maltese trust in their government for June 2019 is much higher when compared to the November 2012 Eurobarometer survey, which was recorded at 34%. The trust in the public administration in June 2019 was 65%, which is also higher when compared to the rate of 51% registered amongst EU countries. How did the Public Service achieve such a standard? There are several explanations for this achievement.

3.3.1   State's Reforms That Have Helped to Build a Relationship Between the Central Government and the Public Service

State reforms were not only limited to the state entities themselves, but it has impacted on the Public Service in a manner that it has created a working relationship between the state institutions and the machinery of the Public Service. In fact, the new Public Administration Act was essential. In 2017, the Public Administration Act has been amended to permit the examination by a parliamentary committee to scrutinise the future appointments of ambassadors and the heads of various regulatory entities, and thus would be conferring to parliament more powers that would strengthen the country's democracy. The amendments were applicable not only to the Public Service but also to state's authorities, including the Central Bank, MFSA, Transport Malta, Planning Authority, Malta Tourism Authority, Medicines Authority, Financial Intelligence Unit, among others.

The commitment to stronger governance and improved transparency is manifested through the relationship that exists between the work conducted by the central government and the Public Service. This central Government–Public Service relationship exists in several manners but is mainly evident either through the annual implementation of the budgetary measures, the adoption of measures emanating from the Ombudsman's Annual Reports, as well as the reports written by the National Audit Office (NAO). Currently, the public service gives an account of the measures being implemented due to budgetary measures, simplification measures and electoral manifesto. Moreover, Malta's public administration publishes a report entitled '*Governance – Action on the Parliamentary Ombudsman's Annual Report*' on cases handled by the Parliamentary Ombudsman, the Commissioner for Education, the Commissioner for Environment & Planning and the Commissioner for Health during an annual period. The report provides an outline of each case handled and its status, as well as a presented set of conclusions or recommendations made by the Ombudsman and his Commissioner, and how these have been acted upon by the Public Administration. A similar report is also published related to the recommendations made by the NAO and how these recommendations when practically possible are implemented.

3.3.1.1   The National Audit Office (NAO)

The National Audit Office (NAO) is the first public entity that serves as a check and balance on the Public Services operations. In 2017, 332 interventions and action plans have been drafted in reaction to NAO's recommendations. The NAO is Malta's supreme audit institution, established as an autonomous body by the Constitution in 1997, and regulated by the Auditor General and National Audit Office Act (Cap. 396), to audit the financial accounts and transactions undertaken by the country's governing institutions, Public Service and non-departmental bodies, and to report its findings to the House of Representatives.

The NAO reports to Parliament in an independent, professionally objective and fair manner. The NAO allows for government and other organisations utilising public funds to be held accountable for the stewardship of those funds in providing public services. In fulfilling its constitutional function, the NAO faces the challenge of crafting reports that facilitate improvements in governance and performance as well as securing accountability. The National Audit Office (NAO) conducted several audits to various public sector and Public Service entities. In 2017, 11 Ministries were involved in financial and compliance audits and a total of 169 recommendations were put forward. A reaction on the NAO recommendations started to be published by the Public Service Administration around 2014.

The Director General of the NAO revealed that 80% of the recommendations are being taken on board. This is a very positive rate when compared to other European public administrations. The NAO faces the challenge that it must adapt to the changing governing landscape and must revisit its core audit function to effectively address emerging concerns. The governing and managerial challenges include the new ways of delivering public services are being devised, through partnerships with the private sector for the provision of critical services, the re-establishment of departments as statutory authorities and the extended utilisation of digital technology. The impetus driving such reforms is to improve efficiency, yet this also presents significant risk in terms of accountability and oversight, value for money and service delivery. The successful implementation of these initiatives rest on the government's ability to manage such change.

3.3.1.2   The Auditor General

A parliamentary officer, the Auditor General, could now audit any government entity in the annual report — a publication that was a true evidence of accountability while consolidating transparency. The year 2017 recorded the highest implementation rate ever of the Auditor General's recommendations.

3.3.1.3   The Office of the Ombudsman

Another channel of redress for public administrative decisions and actions is the Office of the Ombudsman. The Ombudsman mediates between aggrieved individuals and public administrators and assumes a role of acting as the conscience of the public administration. The Office of the Ombudsman, which was created in Malta in 1995, reports directly to the Parliament. The Ombudsman has a crucial role to ensure fairness, openness, dedication, commitment, accountability and the promotion of the right in public administration and to investigate maladministration and grievances.

Table 3.1 The number of Ombudsman cases per year between 2012 and 2017

Year	2012	2013	2014	2015	2016	2017
Number of cases	615	493	538	611	557	520

Source: Parliamentary Ombudsman of Malta – Annual Report 2017

Table 3.2 Top five ministries with the greatest number of complaints in 2017

Ministry	Number of cases
Ministry for Home Affairs and National Security	43
Office of the Prime Minister	40
Ministry for Justice, Culture and Local Government	31
Ministry for Education and Employment	30
Ministry for Finance	30

Source: Parliamentary Ombudsman of Malta – Annual Report 2017

Table 3.3 Outcomes of the complaints against the public administration in 2017

Type of outcome	Number of cases
Sustained cases	18 (6%)
Cases not sustained	63 (22%)
Resolved by informal action	114 (40%)
Given advice/assistance	35 (12%)
Outside jurisdiction/declined	49 (16%)
Declined (time-barred, trivial etc.)	12 (4%)

Source: Parliamentary Ombudsman of Malta – Annual Report 2017

In 2010, an amendment to Article 17 A of the Ombudsman Act empowered the Ombudsman to appoint specialised Commissioners for administrative investigations in three policy areas: health, education and planning. These specialised commissioners provide better focus in specific public policy areas. Table 3.1 exhibits the number of Ombudsman cases per year in six consecutive years from 2012 and 2017. The information shows a stable average number of cases of 556 per year. This shows the level of trust that the Ombudsman has among the citizens. The breadth of the nature of investigated cases is considerable given that in 2017 there were 87 different public administrative units that were investigated.

Table 3.2 reveals the top five Ministries that lodged a complaint and Table 3.4 shows the nature of the complaints vis-à-vis maladministration. While the Ministry for Justice and Home Affairs tops the number of cases, the most common complaint is that of lack of fairness or balance. It totals 51% from all cases.

Table 3.3 shows that most cases were either not sustained, resolved by informal action or were deemed by the Ombudsman as outside his legal jurisdiction. Given that a very large percentage were dealt with informal action, the Public Service could investigate more possibilities how cases are solved before they end up being dealt by a formal channel such as the Ombudsman.

Table 3.4 Nature of complaints against the public administration in 2017

Nature	Number of cases
Contrary to law or rigid application of rules	36 (10%)
Improper discrimination	37 (11%)
Failure to provide information	11 (3%)
Undue delay or failure to act	82 (25%)
Lack of fairness or balance	170 (51%)

Source: Parliamentary Ombudsman of Malta – Annual Report 2017

Table 3.5 Calls for applications issued by the Public Service between 2012 and 2016

Year	Number of calls
2012	544
2013	484
2014	641
2015	608
2016	500

Source: Public Service Commission Annual Report – Annual Report 2016

3.3.1.4   The Public Service Commission and the SAAC

The Public Service Commission which was set up in terms of Article 109 of the Constitution of Malta, is another important watchdog of the Public Service functioning and plays a key role in the dynamics of regulatory governance. The role of the Commission is to advice the Prime Minister in the making of appointments to public office, the removal of staff from public office and the exercise of discipline over public officers. The year 2016 brought into effect a decentralisation process which meant that certain functions that were normally conducted by the Commission were now under the responsibility of the Ministries and Line Departments, notably the recruitment function. This resulted in a significantly reduced recruitment process. Nevertheless, the Commission's role of being a watchdog is now more focused from an auditing perspective. The Commission is now expected to ensure the efficiency and effectiveness of the entire decentralised recruitment process.

Table 3.5 reveals the amount of calls that the Public Service publishes per year. In most years the number of calls exceeds 500 and 600. The figures show the voluminous number of calls that were being scrutinised by the Public Service Commission. In 2016, there were a total of 321 petitions that in many of the cases were lodged by the applicants prior to the publication of the selection process result. The petitions were addressed directly to the Commission. 268 were confirmed as ineligible, 47 were found to be eligible, 3 calls for applications were withdrawn and re-issued, and another 3 cases were still being considered by the PSC.

In 2017, the Commission considered a total of 657 written representations addressed directly to the Commission on matters regarding selection processes relating to appointments in the Public Service. Most of the representations received were lodged by applicants prior to the publication of the results, and these mainly involved complaints by applicants who were declared ineligible by selection boards after applying for a vacancy.

The Commission ruled in favour of 178 applicants whom it deemed were eligible. Four hundred and sixteen other representations were not upheld. Sixty three representations were not yet decided upon, as at 31st December 2017. In the same year, the Commission received a total of 216 petitions in respect of the results obtained by individuals who believed that the result of the selection process was not a fair reflection of their merits. Nine of these petitions were not made within the 10 working days allowed for the submission of petitions in respect of appointments and promotions. These petitions were thus not considered by the Commission. Regarding posts or positions in Salary Scale 6 or below, the 10 working days start to count from the day after a notification appears on the website of the respective Ministry, stating that the result has been issued. In the case of vacancies in Scale 5 or higher, where results are sent directly to applicants, the 10 working days start to count from the day after the result is received by the applicants concerned. In nine instances investigations were discontinued. The Commission therefore considered 198 petitions. 30 petitions were upheld, and revised results were drawn up and re-published. In 157 other cases, the appeals were not upheld. Another 11 petitions were still being investigated as at 31st December 2017.

3.3.2   Better Governance by Strengthening the Internal Structural Arrangements and Developing Institutional Capacity within the Public Service

State's reforms that helped the Public Service to function better and to improve in terms of transparency and accountability were subsequently strengthened by reforms within the Public Service itself. The Maltese Public Service must cater for hundreds of thousands of citizens by offering hundreds of services to its customers. From an organisational and institutional perspective, the availability of so many services add to the complexity of the Public Service. Complexity should not be an underestimated variable when assessing the operations of a public administration. To the contrary, it is a central concept that requires careful attention. By considering this scenario, two major governing and managerial variables are of essence that strengthens transparency and accountability: the development of institutional capacity and the simplification of processes.

Institutional capacity can be strengthened through three different courses of action: by consolidating the human resources capacity, by developing the governing structures and streamlining the managerial processes. This section is focused on the development of governing structures. A review of the governing structures was fundamental in order to rejuvenate the Public Service from a governing and a managerial perspective. The Maltese Public Service embarked on a whole-system based approach which entails that the Public Service was and is expected to improve its governance at all levels and stages. Changes were affected not only where it is visible to the general public but throughout the governing and managerial engine. This is a crucial notion since internal restructuring creates a ripple effect on the service delivered by the Public Service in general. Several measures were undertaken in order to strengthen the central capacity of the Public Services through various manners: First, by strengthening the capacity of central units; second, by strengthening the capacity of the ministries; and third, by creating new entities or directorates within the Public Service. Several central Public Service units experienced major structural changes in order to cater for the increasing complexity and rising aspiration of the citizens.

The revisiting of the SAAC (Senior Appointments Advisory Committee) functioning was intended to identify the best people who are the most capable and suitable to fill the senior positions vacancies. The functioning of the SAAC is flexible in a way that it is possible to look beyond the field of applicants if there are officers who are better suited for the position and who have not applied for one reason or another. In some instances, it was found necessary to fill a headship position through a lateral transfer of an officer in another position at the same level. In such cases, the Permanent Secretary must be consulted. Nevertheless, these are not common cases. The usual procedure of the call for applications is followed when engaging a new employee in a headship position. The issue of good governance is given prominence since candidates are expected to demonstrate their proficiency in the Public Administration Act (PAA), Directives under the PAA, the Freedom of Information, Customer Care, Public Service Management Code, Disciplinary Procedures, Data Protection, Public Procurement, Better Regulation, Green Initiatives, Governance and Official Secrets Act. A substantial development was implemented in 2017 by transforming the previous Public Administration HR Office (PAHRO) into a People and Standards Division. The internal structures were organised into six specialised directorates that, through the course of this ex-ante evaluation report, their main functions and contribution towards better governance and managerialism is analysed. The six directorates include: the main office of the permanent secretary, quality and standards, research and personnel systems, people resourcing and compliance, people support and wellbeing and the industrial relations.

The amalgamation of the Inland Revenue Department (IRD) with the Value Added Tax (VAT) Department provided an avenue for consolidated information which will increase the effectiveness of risk management across the tax system. The Office of the Commissioner for Revenue will be integrated into a one organisational set-up as from April 2019. Resources are used more effectively, and flexibility is significantly improved. There has been an increased compliance across the taxation system as well as increased professionalism, uniformity and consistency. The Central Procurement Unit also experienced a restructuring exercise by creating seven Ministerial Procurement Units (MPUs). The MPUs fall under the responsibility of the office of the respective Permanent Secretary or under the responsibility of any other person in an equivalent post, being so delegated by the Minister responsible for that Ministry. Principally, the Ministerial Procurement Unit (MPU) is a unit which administers calls for tenders published under an open procedure, where the estimated value of such calls for tender is above ten thousand euro (€10,000) but does not exceed two hundred and fifty thousand euro (€250,000). This was a structural move that strengthened the central capability in order to keep up with the procurement load and in parallel resulted in devolution of power to the Ministries. The MPUs that were created so far are within the Ministries for Home Affairs and National Security (2016), Education and Employment (2016), Justice, Culture and Local Government (2017), Family, Children's Rights and Social Solidarity (2017), Gozo (2017) and Environment, Sustainable Development and Climate Change (2018).

New structures were created at the community level such as the *servizz.gov* and another new structure consisted of a dedicated unit within the Ministry for Justice, Culture and Local Government which oversees the implementation of the Freedom of Information Act and maintains an electronic system that can be used by applicants to submit their requests for information. This system also allows for processing of such requests by all Government Ministries, Departments and entities. In 2018, a new directorate tasked with Public Sector Performance and Evaluation within the Budget Affairs Division of the Ministry responsible for Finance, has been set up with the remit to establish frameworks that seek to phase out unnecessary expenditure, reduce waste and inefficiencies and ensure a better match between public programmes and policy outcomes. Accountability and transparency reforms were also introduced not only through purely structural reforms but through new governing arrangements in the form of a Code of Ethics and Public Administration Bill. In 2018, the Code of Ethics for Public Employees was reviewed to make public officers more accountable and also to prohibit them from accepting gifts, payments, compensations, privileges or any form of solicitation unless, where gifts are concerned, they are token in nature and are not such as to serve as an inducement or influence the execution of the duties of a public employee or a board member. In 2019, the Public Administration Bill introduced a clause that forbids high-ranking public officials inside regulatory authorities for 2 years from accepting jobs with entities with which they would have had dealings for the last 5 years. Upon implementation of the revolving door employment, a board was established in order to determine the roles subject to this condition. Any public officials breaching this condition would be subject to a penalty equivalent to 3 years' pay.

3.4   Conclusion

This Chapter has demonstrated that transparency and accountability transcends on so many different governing facets: first, state agencies reforms in the form of legislation and structures that influence the operations of Malta's Public Service; second; national policies that have a comprehensive influence in the manner that the Public Services directs its strategy; and third, structural changes and new procedures within the Public Services that have strengthened the notion of good governance in its totality. This Chapter revealed that issues of good governance can be found in all Public Service administrative processes and is therefore intimately related to all operational aspects in so many different governmental departments and ministries. Such a comprehensive outlook was possible by embracing an inward and an outward perspective of the Public Service in the analysis conducted by the authors.

References

Commissioner for Standards in Public Life. (2020). *The role of the standards commissioner.* Available at: https://standardscommissioner.com/the-role-of-the-commissioner/

Criminal Code. (2013). *Amendment to Article 115 of the Criminal Code.* Available at: http://www.justiceservices.gov.mt/DownloadDocument.aspx?app=lp&itemid=24817&l=1

Digital Malta. (2014). *National digital strategy 2014-2020.* Available at: https://digitalmalta.org.mt/en/Documents/Digital%20Malta%202014%20-%202020.pdf

European Union. (2018). *eGovernment Benchmark 2017: Taking stock of user-centric design and delivery of digital public services in Europe,* final background report, Vol. 2. Available at: https://op.europa.eu/en/publication-detail/-/publication/7f1b4ecb-f9a7-11e7-b8f5-01aa75ed71a1/language-en

Financing of Political Parties Act. (2016). *Chapter 544.* Available at: http://www.justiceservices.gov.mt/DownloadDocument.aspx?app=lom&itemid=12345&l=1

Government of Malta. (2018). *Press Release by the Malta Government,* PR182734. Available at: https://www.gov.mt/en/Government/DOI/Press%20Releases/Pages/2018/December/17/pr182734en.aspx

Malta Parliament. (2018). *Act No. XI of 2018 – Media and defamation act.* Available at: https://parlament.mt/13th-leg/acts/act-xi-of-2018/

Public Service Commission. (2013–2016). *Annual reports.*

Parliamentary Ombudsman. (2013–2017). Annual reports, House of the Representatives .

Shah, A. (2007). *Performance accountability and combating corruption.* Public Sector Corruption and Accountability Series, the World Bank.

The Protection of the Whistleblower Act. (2013). Available at: https://justice.gov.mt/en/justice/whistleblower/Pages/Whistleblower's-Act.aspx

Chapter 4
Civil Service Systems and HRM Public Service Reforms

> *"Take the civil service out of government and the country will collapse, take politics out of government and the country will flourish."*
>
> Abhijit Naskar
> Neuroscientist and Bestselling Author

This Chapter illustrates that a variety of reforms have been introduced regarding Civil Service Systems and HRM Public Service Reforms. These have contributed and strengthened the thrust towards enhancing professionalism in HRM practices within the Public Service. However, despite these important reforms, several other reforms are required to strike a balance between the exigencies of the Public Service and the improvement of the wellbeing and performance of public officers through telework, work-life balance, family-friendly measures and training. Government is the largest employer in Malta; thus, this balance is difficult to achieve, particularly when considering the reliance that a small island state has on the Public Service. This challenge is further accentuated with the unanticipated circumstances, significantly the crisis of COVID-19 that has highlighted the need to invest more in human resources management and new ways of conducting normal work practices. Programmes intended to promote and foster motivation in Public Service employees are to be particularly emphasized. Motivational systems vary from the performance management programmes that specifically focus on performance appraisal, to robust flexible work-life balance arrangements. The former has seen a radical improvement in the last 6 years, but the latter needs a more solid framework in an era where teleworking and flexibility is dominating the labour market. The reform related to the Institute for Public Services is to be continued and consolidated, especially about the aspect of instilling the Public Service values and excellence in all training provided by the Institute. The long-term vision of the Institute is to transform itself into an Academy that marks the professional status of a rapidly evolving Public Service.

4.1   Introduction: An Overview of Essential Public Service Reforms

Public administrations around Europe are experiencing a threefold challenge of: first, delivering better with less resources available especially in times of restricted budgets due to COVID-19 crisis; second, adapting Public Service provision to demographic, technological and societal changes; and third, improving the business climate through the simplification of processers by adopting smarter regulations, reducing administrative burden and providing better services to support growth and competitiveness (Heichlinger et al., 2018). When considering these challenges and the scenario of a micro-state such as Malta that does not possess any natural resources, the effective management of the Public Service are of paramount importance and the human resources element is essential. This reality is an integral component of the overarching goal of the Public Service that is to provide the best quality of service to its clients and to make these services more accessible to its users. This aim can only be achieved by ensuring that the employees delivering this service are equipped with the necessary skills, capabilities and knowledge in order to have a developed professional workforce. Public Service reforms entail a comprehensive HR strategy which would support the selection, development and mobility of its employees.

Before analysing the human resources dimension, it is important that an overview of the essential Public Service reforms is provided. The analysis dates as from 2013 and consists of 54 recommendations targeting five major aspects, namely: (1) Strengthening the quality of Public Service leadership, including corporate leadership and organisation by selecting, training, developing and retaining the best; (2) Strengthening the quality of the Public Service management cadre at the disposal of the Public Service by improved career planning, professional development structure (theory and practice based) including mentoring and robust performance appraisal systems; (3) Strengthening the strategic, business and financial planning, budgeting, reporting, monitoring and accountability framework by strengthening the governing regulatory, planning, reporting, monitoring and enforcement systems and capacity; (4) Improving service quality and delivery principally through business process simplification, streamlining and consolidation; strengthening adopted quality systems and improved exploitation of ICT capacity and capabilities; and (5) Improving the Public Service raison d'être, scope, organisation and governance structure by rationalising the core functions of the Public Service as is necessary in context of a more complex Public Service delivery environment (including the wider scope for local government, public sector, private sector and non-government organisation involvement).

The above five aspects that emerged from the Public Service Reform Review have dominated the reform agenda of the current administration. The review was further strengthened through the governance framework for the design, planning, monitoring, review and implementation of government's programme for Public Service Renewal. This framework serves as the basis of the Public Service renewal exercise. It was laid down with the aim of: (1) Improving fiscal performance and return on resource investment; (2) Improving Public Service identity, repute and delivery; (3) Realigning internal Human Resource capacity to ensure improved performance and delivery at all levels; and (4) Strengthening the policy-making capacity of the Public Service to manage and operate in a more complex Public Service delivery environment, including mechanisms that increase transparency, accountability and which contribute to a stronger national democracy. The essence of any Public Service reform is human resources. The maximisation of the output that may be provided by Public Service employees is the key for a successful reform (De Freitas Bradley, 2017).

4.2 Strategic Workforce Planning in the Maltese Public Service

The very first fundamental aspect of human resources management reform is taking stock of the current public administrative workforce so that a strategic plan is devised for the future. The essence of strategic workforce planning is the creation of a process within the Public Service that proactively anticipates current and future human resources needs. Effective human resources planning ensures that the Public Service meets its targets and set key performance indicators (KPIs). The core of the Public Service is its workforce and the Public Service employees make the strategy happen. Strategic workforce planning helps the Public Service to ensure stable staffing levels across every department, with the right skills in the right positions for more successful results and a higher return on investment.

4.2.1 Analysis of Employee Volumes

Analysis at ministerial level is being conducted as part of a holistic headcount review. The analysis is being done in line with the 3-year HR Planning requirement as per Directive 10; the totals of employees received through the plan for each ministry were matched against Payroll data for the same period and for each Ministry. This was to ensure that data was real and correlating exactly to the number of employees being paid from the Government payroll system. As part of the exercise, organigrams have been collated for all ministries and government entities in order to establish working structures and corrective action would need to be taken if there are any organisational defects. The monitoring for all additional headcounts against requests is being approved according to yearly circulars issued by the Ministry for Finance (MFIN) and People and Standards Division (P&SD), as well as ongoing discussions with the coordinating committee and MFIN for any additional *ad hoc* requests. All numbers are updated in the submitted HR Plans. The identified milestones within this initiative strongly indicate an effort of creating a comprehensive headcount planning and talent management strategy.

4.2.2   Evaluating the Current Workforce: The Skills Profiling Exercise

In any headcount planning strategy, it is crucial to evaluate the current workforce. The first element is the collection of data on the current workforce. This exercise would also serve to check whether the Public Service has the right number of employees with the necessary skills in the right roles so that the Public Service can execute on its business strategy. The second element would be to predict future trends by identifying current and predicted future critical roles and identify which job grades are experiencing high turnover rates. By being forward-planning and prioritising of resources exigencies will help the Public Service in workforce forecasting and staff planning. These are at present collated through the HR database and payroll data, and through the Skills Profiling Exercise, and split according to competency levels. These qualifications, in addition to other skills and competences, will shortly be visible on a responsive website entitled *My Personal Kiosk*, where each employee could see and verify such details. The Skills Profiling Exercise originates from the Flexicurity Pathway, one of the main pillars of Malta's National Reform Programme. The Flexicurity Pathway stipulates that a skills audit of the national working population is to be carried out. To this end, Government, as an employer, has conducted a skills audit of its workforce. From a management perspective, Skills Profiling assists in identifying Skills Gaps (the Skills possessed by employees compared to the skills needed by the organisation to carry out its mandate) and to identify measures to bridge identified gaps (through training, redeployments, etc).

From the employees' perspective, they will benefit from better opportunities for their own self-development and higher satisfaction and motivation at their place of work. An individual's Skills Profile is a summary of his/her work experience, skills and abilities. The Skills Profile includes the Present Employment Details, Formal Qualifications, Employment History and Part-Time Employment, Language Skills, Organisational & Social Skills, Computer & IT-related Skills, Technical and Artistic Skills, Work Preferences and Job Mobility. On the first day of employment in the Public Service, new recruits are requested to compile their Skills Profile, so that the relevant database is maintained up to date. As from the last quarter of 2019, *My Personal Kiosk* responsive website started to include the employees Skills & Qualifications. All employees now have the facility to view data held at P&SD of their skills and qualifications, as they had submitted through the Skills Profiling exercise. The last updates to the skills profiling data have been made in 2015, after which employees were requested to contact their HR Sections to update their records accordingly. This enabled HR Sections to make the necessary updates in the Skills and Qualifications Dakar Module. Through this facility, Public Service employees can view their updated skills and qualifications through *My Personal Kiosk*.

The introduction of meetings with HR administrators at Line Ministries allowed managers to identify and mentor employees with potential for progression and who can fill critical gaps with training and identify criteria for benchmarking. A monthly DCS (Directors of Corporate Services) Forum and regular meetings between the Coordinating Committee on Strategic HR Planning and the key players of the People Management/Resourcing processes are held on an ongoing basis. Outreach sessions were also conducted where employees from P&SD would meet DCSs in line Ministries to discuss any items related to HR. In line with compliance checks on systems and corrective measures that are followed upon for implementation, training requirements are identified and delivered for specific areas at line ministries for the key players. In the year 2019, four sessions were held. Topics discussed during each session incorporated the following: Devices and Data Plans for Inspectorates within Ministries; Percentage increase in pensions when employees opt to remain in employment after retiring age; Fringe Benefits interpretation and overview; Raising Awareness about Domestic Violence and Violence at the Workplace; Overview of the new Dakar HR Reports; Overview of the new Dakar Discipline Module. Apart from these main topics, other topics of common interest are also discussed, with the participation of all P&SD Directors, and in some instances, also with the participation of the Permanent Secretary in charge of P&SD.

4.2.3   Establishing HR Key Performance Indicators (KPIs) and HR Systems Assessments

Establishing metrics or Key Performance Indicators (KPIs) including salary data, position requirements, retirement eligibility information, employee skill sets & qualifications, staff turnover rates, would help towards providing a cohesive picture of the current workforce trends. If these metrics could be maintained through a database system by having real-time data, this would allow HR practitioners to respond more effectively to internal and external factors and to have insights on the workforce market. This initiative was later replaced since HR plans have been linked with financial and business plans. Linking HR plans in partnership with financial plans is critical since such an exercise will help in managing headcount within budget and with the projection of costs associated with hiring new staff and developing current employees.

HR systems assessments as well as compliance checks are carried out regularly to ensure adherence to Directives that reflect timeframes and methods following a series of delegated processes to the ministries. An implementation plan is then drawn up with any corrective measures to be addressed and followed upon. Ministries are required to prepare 3-year HR plans, revisable annually, as part of the Business and Financial Planning process under the Fiscal Responsibility Act (Chapter 534 of the Laws of Malta). Having a holistic and forward-planning approach would ensure that there is a direct link between strategic organisational goals, budgets and talent management strategies and that these elements are aligned across the Public Service in order to give the Public Service an edge with private institutions. Naturally, this initiative would prove to be more effective if it is linked with a talent management strategy by being strongly tied in with recruitment, training and development and succession planning.

4.2.3.1 Position Descriptions

An initiative which is strongly tied in with strategic workforce planning and is also strongly linked with the Headcount reviews is reviewing position descriptions. The new job descriptions were, primarily, modified and updated to reflect the new provisions specified in the Addendum regarding the Selection Exercises for General Service Grades signed on 5 February 2016. The grade descriptions were amplified to constitute the career development and progression of each grade and the requirement that eligible candidates, for General Service posts, must be familiar with the provisions of the *PAA* and *PSMC*. The distinction drawn in the *Manual on Resourcing Policies and Procedures* regarding the probationary period (Scale 10 or higher 12 months; Scale 11 or lower 6 months) was also factored in. Despite these changes, it is quite clear that the nomenclature and structure of the grades are very traditional and have strong influences from the traditional British grading system. However, one must conduct a thorough review to assess the extent to which these grades and the grading structures are still relevant to the current workforce trends.

There has been an increased effort for the Maltese civil service to meet customer expectations and to enhance their levels of efficiency and effectiveness in the delivery of results. Consequently, the way the civil service organises, manages and rewards the workforce is a crucial aspect. As a result, a well-defined grading structure is crucial in ensuring that there is ease in distinguishing from one grade to the other and that job titles and their corresponding job descriptions are clearly defined. This measure would assist HR practitioners and the selection board in the recruitment and promotions exercises since this measure would assist them in ensuring that candidates with the most suitable skills are being selected to the fill in the advertised grades. Modernising job titles and descriptions would serve as a tool in making such jobs appear more attractive for potential candidates. It has been observed that the entities which are equivalent to the HR arm of the Public Service have been re-branded and reformulated as a revamped HR entity with a philosophy that focuses on the humanistic dimension where the employee is valued as an individual rather than a resource. Consequently, the natural progression would be to proceed in modernising the job titles. Nonetheless, as it has been mentioned in the list of measures document prepared by the Strategy & Implementation Unit, such an exercise would require extensive consultation with the civil service unions. Other elements that must be considered are the manner that job titles and descriptions are being evaluated and if there is an adequate, objective basis for categorising jobs within the grade structure.

4.3   Structural Changes in the Human Resources Domain

A strategic workforce planning needs to be strengthened by a solid human resources backbone that provides enough infrastructural abilities from a human resources perspective. This section outlines two major structural changes that were implemented as from 2013 onwards.

4.3.1   Major HR Structural Change: The Transformation of PAHRO into People and Standards Division

The transformation of PAHRO into People and Standards Division was intended to inject a cohesive approach to the human resources leadership in the Public Service. This entailed a shift in human resources management culture from a record keeping mentality to an approach that is interlinked with the Government's national policies. Policies are supported by the introduction of Key Performance Indicators (KPIs) across the Public Administration. The offices within People and Standards Division comprise the following: People Resourcing and Compliance Directorate; the People Support and Wellbeing Directorate; the Research and Personnel Systems Directorate; the Industrial Relations Unit; and the Quality and Standards Directorate. These offices manage the tactical and operational aspects of recruitment, HR business planning and strategic management, research, conditions of service and well-being within Public Administration. Through delegation of authority, the People and Standards Division strive for the fulfilment of holistic HR policies and management systems, their implementation, monitoring and constant re-evaluation. The continuous improvement of public officers' performance and wellbeing, and sustaining quality service are its two major priorities.

   In practice this human resource structural move meant that, on one hand, public servants are valued and motivated through various human resources management programmes and, on the other hand, standards of quality and accountability are set in order to achieve the Public Service objectives. The underlying concept is that the transformed governing structures such as People and Standards are complemented with other significant managerial changes that include recruitment, promotions and industrial relations.

4.3.2   Transformation of the Centre for Development, Research and Training into an Institute for the Public Services

In October 2016, another major structural change was implemented regarding the research and training arm of the Public Service – the Centre for the Development of Research and Training (CDRT). CDRT was transformed into an Institute for the

Public Services (IPS). As part of the restructuring process, a tripartite agreement was signed between the Public Service, the University of Malta (UM) and MCAST in the form of a public-public partnership for the setting up of an Institute for Public Services. The objective of this structural move was to strengthen the collaboration with Higher Education Institutions (HEIs). An IPS Board was established including representatives from both the UM and MCAST. This enforces one of the governing principles, that of stakeholder engagement. The IPS was established to identify and develop the full potential of public officers through research, training and development. It is the focal point on all matters related to the personal and professional development of public officers, and research initiatives for the Public Service in Malta. The training programmes offered are designed according to career streams, covering ICT, Finance, Procurement, People Management and Well-being, and Customer Care. To ensure career progression, IPS also offers courses that are tailored to particular life events, such as returning to work after long absence. A graduation ceremony is held annually for public officers who successfully complete accredited course.

The aim of the restructuring was twofold: first, to offer high-level training to Public Service employees in order to augment their skills and capabilities and to develop several study-units in public administration within UM's and MCAST's courses. In connection with the first aim, the IPS continued to administer psychometric testing to candidates for headship positions at a Director and Director General level. The results of the test are used by the Senior Appointments Advisory Committee (SAAC) for headship positions. In practice, this structural transformation entailed closer links between training and career development in different career streams and in incorporating academic training in the courses offered by IPS. As a result, professionals from the Health, Education and Business Sectors have a basic understanding of the Public Service.

Of particular interest is the development of training courses for lower grades (industrial and manual workers) that are intended to broaden the skills and validating their experience. In terms of numbers, between 500 and 600 courses are organised each year by the Institute for the Public Services. The ultimate objective is that this initiative leads to an improvement in services provided by the civil servants to the public. Table 4.1 provides an analysis of the increase in the number of participants in a period of almost 10 years, from 2008 until 2017. The number of repeat participants increased by more than three times; from 4171 to 13,511. Such a significant increase has been fuelled by EU funding, specifically ESF funding.

Table 4.1 Number of repeat participants registered for courses delivered by IPS for period 2008–2017

Year	2008	2009	2010	2011	2012	2013	2014	2015	2016	2017
No. of courses	4171	5136	5370	5578	7296	9024	9033	9563	8875	13,511

Source: Data provided by the Institute for Public Services (IPS)

4.4 Attracting and Retaining the Brightest and Ablest

The aim of attracting and retaining the brightest and ablest recruits dates back to the Public Service reform of 1988. At that time, both structural reforms as well as initiatives that bring the best talent to Malta's Public Service were given significant importance.

4.4.1 Attracting the Best Talent

Fast forward to the pre-COVID scenario, Malta's employment situation has been presenting a very challenging period for employers given that the unemployment figures are at all-time low levels. The unemployment levels are amongst the lowest in the European Union. In fact, Malta's unemployment level is 3.9% and is the fifth lowest unemployment figure recorded in May 2018 (Eurostat, 2018). Such an external environment dictates that the Public Service is to be creative in creating new and practical ways on how to attract new employees.

A new mobile application entitled 'Join the Public Service' was launched in April 2018. Through this innovative Mobile App, a prospective Public Service applicant could be connected to the online recruitment site of the Public Service. The app enables the user to choose his/her preferred type of employment from 12 different categories. The system built within the app then alerts the prospective applicant that a particular call for applications has been published. This innovative reaching-out mobile app was launched after a newly designed online recruitment website that enables a person to register and apply online for Public Service job-posts. The plan was to automate the entire selection process for increased efficiency. In addition to IT online applications, as from the year 2015, the Public Service careers were being made visible amongst University of Malta students during the Freshers week.

4.4.2 Retaining Valuable Public Service Employees

Recruitment was only one facet of the human resources domain to attract employees. Specific HR tools are intended to motivate and retain public servants. The online performance appraisal system that was introduced in August 2016 did not only provide a user-friendly and efficient platform to public servants but served the entire Public Service to have a holistic assessment feedback. Such a comprehensive fully integrated HR systems enhances job satisfaction, accountability and provides valuable feedback for training and development. The integrated HR Management System consists of an online skills and qualifications module that provides a holistic and detailed overview of the knowledge capacity of the Public Service. These initiatives that were steered by the Research and Personnel Systems Directorate combined well with the initiatives of another governing structure: the newly formed Institute for Public Services (IPS) that is responsible for research and training across the Public Service.

Human resources governance has also been strengthened from an adaptability perspective to the external environmental that also helps to attract and retain the existing Public Service staff. The measures include: first, facilitating the mobility between the Public Service and the public sector; second, the recognition of unpaid leave when calculating the years of service for progression and promotion purposes; and third, the updating of the policy regarding re-employment, re-instatement and re-integration of ex-public officers. Several other measures were introduced that deal specifically with the welfare of the Public Service employees. The possibility to take 50% of the year's entitlement leave as hours and the special paid leave to assist a relative receiving medical treatment are practical examples of welfare-based human resources initiatives that give a human face to the Public Service and serve as an incentive to retain existing staff. Efforts related to staff welfare were structured through the Employee Support Programme that was awarded the 2014 Good Practice award by the Occupational Health and Safety Authority. Initiatives that were undertaken within the umbrella of this programme included the organisation of bereavement support groups for public employees, the training organised to health and safety representatives focusing on managing stress and mental health at the place of work and the dissemination of information documents to employees regarding several welfare issues.

4.5   The Evolution of Performance Management

Public Service Motivation (PSM) and keeping high morale is an essential factor in reforming the Public Service. Perry, Hondeghem & Wise (2010) highlighted the notion that a motivated staff is key towards achieving a performing Public Service while Van der Wal (2015) argues that highly motivated employees can increase the effectiveness of Public Service delivery.

The Performance Management Programme was introduced in the Public Service way back in 1994. This programme aimed to improve working relationships between managers and their employees and to improve performance. In line with the Government's commitment towards the renewal and strengthening of the operational capability of the Public Service, a new Performance Appraisal System within the Public Service was launched in 2016. The main objective of this new Performance Appraisal System is the holistic assessment of the individual as part of the overall Public Service Performance Management Programme. It is also a tool that is aimed at enhancing accountability, job satisfaction whilst giving visibility on training and development needs. The aim was to create an environment of motivation with an eagerness for higher achievement but also help to identify and develop future leaders. (OPM Circular No 20/2016). This system is web based and fully automated, where all employees can log in with their username and password. The employee is evaluated by his or her Next Level Supervisor and Supervisor. The main goal is to create a holistic approach in assessing individuals and encouraging sense of shared ownership. Such a measure will motivate employees to achieve higher, and it will also identify and develop future leaders.

This model is similar to the 360-degree feedback. However, this feedback system allows for a more comprehensive performance review system since feedback is provided from the immediate manager, peers and subordinates. The goal of such as system is for the employee to have a balanced view on how others view his or her contribution and performance in several areas such as leadership, teamwork, communication, interpersonal skills and work habits. The 360 review tends to focus more on how the employee affected the work of other employees than on whether the work was accomplished. The new online appraisal system was based on the SMART ways and process that is Specific, Measurable, Achievable, Realistic, Time Bound which will go beyond, towards a SMARTER way for Evaluation and Relevance to reach the Organisation's objectives and Budget measures on the basis of accountability and governance. Quality of output was to be taken into consideration rather just the Quantity.

Using the competency framework in performance appraisals involves collecting information and performance against competencies and thus one can identify immediately what are the missing objectives or the needs for the necessary training of the same appraisee. Also, the fact that the system is online and to input all relevant data, a team of supervisors was created where they could monitor the individual's performance and finally the next level supervisor finalises the grading, would strengthen the three-way relationship from bottom to top and vice versa between all ranks of the Public Service. The format was changed according to the needs and exigencies of the holistic approach to appraisals. In fact it does not deal with the duties of the employee only but its component is divided into four main parts: first, personal attributes – the inter-personal, organisational, social skills and work ethics and values; second, the work-plan – duties; third, the motivation and initiatives: going the extra mile; and fourth, career development.

The Performance Appraisal system, which is fully automated and web-based, will allow users to log into the system through their active Directory account, that is through their login and password, and consequently fill in the job-plan related to their appraisal directly into the system. Supervisors will then be required to check all and go through all criteria and award accordingly both the mid-year and final reviews. At the end of the reviewing period, and upon agreement between parties on the ratings and feedback, given the process for that particular period will be concluded. The automated process will include a system of alerts to remind supervisors when mid-year and final review periods are due. A helpline and a generic email had been set up by the People and Standards Division to assist all ranks of users for all queries they might have. This shows accountability and commitment to implement successfully the system and that it will be reachable to all. The new elements that can be clearly seen in the new appraisal system are the use of the numeric rating system instead of the alpha-numeric ratings. The introduction of a bi-annual

Table 4.2 PMP quantity audit in all ministries

Year/ indicators	Total PMPs planned in all ministries	Total PMPs completed	Compliance percentage rate (%)
2014	3987	3677	92
2015	4038	3750	93

Source: People & Standards Division, OPM, Head Count Data & percentage figures

Table 4.3 Performance appraisals (PA) statistics in all ministries

Year/ indicators	Total PMPs planned in all ministries	Total PMPs completed	Compliance percentage rate (%)
2016	3521	3314	94
2017	3848	3574	93
2018	3779	3110	82

Source: People & Standards Division, OPM, Head Count Data & percentage figures

assessment was perceived better than quarterly, as it does not make sense re-assessing on the same duties and projects after 3 months.

The Performance Management Programme (PMP) was suspended, as from 1st January 2016, in preparation for the introduction of the new online system which was in line with Government's commitment towards the renewal and strengthening of the operational capability of the Public Service, as well as with the continuous development of its HR skills and competences. During this period of suspension, the Interim Performance Management Programme Form was used as a substitute for PMPs. This document served the same purpose as any PMP document required for the period 1 January to 30 June 2016 (OPM Circular No 23/2015). As from 1st August 2016, the new online Dakar Performance Appraisal System was launched within the Public Service.

Data in Tables 4.2 and 4.3 portray that the amount of performance management and performance appraisals conducted as well as the compliance ratio within all Ministries, as from the year 2014 until 2018. The natural compliance rate, comparing the planned and completed, varied from 92% to 94% in all years except in 2018, which was 82%.

4.6   The Efforts Undertaken by the Public Service to Promote Family-Friendly Measures and Inclusiveness

To motivate and to retain a high morale of the Public Service employees, it is fundamental that the Public Service, through its work structures and management strategies, provide employment conditions and opportunities that best ensure employee retention, motivation and loyalty.

4.6.1   Gender Mainstreaming: A Policy Perspective

From a purely policy perspective, in 2017, the Ministry for European Affairs and Equality (MEAE) set up the Consultative Council for Women's Rights (CCWR) consisting of representatives of women's rights civil society organisations in order to serve as a platform for the development of policy and legislative proposals. Subsequently, in 2019, the Minister for European Affairs and Equality (MEAE) established the Gender Mainstreaming Unit (GMU) within the Human Rights and Integration Directorate (HRID) with the aim of developing and implementing the first national strategy and action plan in relation to gender equality mainstreaming, and the introduction of corresponding legislation.

The Gender Equality Mainstreaming Strategy and Action Plan as well as the Gender Equality Mainstreaming Bill focus on eight pillars: (1) Right to equal treatment; (2) Equal access and opportunity to the workplace and the combating of the gender pay gap; (3) Financial independence; (4) Equal access and opportunity to knowledge and education; (5) Co-responsibility and balance of work, private and family life; (6) Equal access and opportunity to positions of authority for women and men; (7) Equal access and opportunity to health and general wellbeing; and (8) Intersectionality.

4.6.2   Employee Support Programme

This initiative had been introduced by PAHRO back in 2011 and has been taken over and safeguarded by the People and Standards Division. The Employee Support Programme (ESP) provides a wide range of free and confidential support services to public officers designed to assist them in managing their work and life difficulties, which, if left unattended, could adversely affect their work performance and quality of life. Among the services offered to public officers are, training and awareness initiatives; counselling and psychological support; return to work support; and support in critical situations.

4.6.3   Sustaining Work-Life Balance

Inclusivity has become a key term within today's society. Consequently, it is no surprise that work-life balance measures are inclusive and not only targeted for those mothers who have children but also for fathers and for those who have health issues or elderly dependents. Measures such as teleworking, reduced hours, job sharing, compressed working week and flexible work schedules have been introduced and have become increasingly popular with employees.

The Collective Agreement 2017 covered a set of family-friendly measures, including marriage leave for spouses and partners in a civil union, maternity leave, paternity leave, unpaid parental leave, career breaks to take care of a child, leave for family reasons, urgent family leave, unpaid responsibility leave, bereavement leave, reduced working hours, teleworking, flexible working hours and pre-retirement leave. To complement the national education strategy, each public officer enjoys the best opportunities for learning and academic advancement, while being supported by flexibility in employment. These include unpaid leave to accompany a spouse or partner abroad on government sponsored assignments or courses, paid leave to participate in international sports events, unpaid leave to take up temporary employment with EU institutions, unpaid leave to take up a post with an international organisation, unpaid leave to try alternative employment in the private sector, unpaid leave to settle in a new country, paid cultural leave, unpaid special leave and donation of vacation leave. In 2017 alone, 6889 public officers have benefitted from the measures.

Therefore, the Public Service has undertaken a concerted effort to encourage female employees to return to the workforce with the introduction of free childcare and by encouraging organisations to adopt family-friendly measures. Consequently, it is no surprise that the Public Service strives to create a balance between the needs of the workplace and the individual and provides a leading example to other organisations. These measures encourage mothers to resume duties at an earlier stage after having a child and facilitate the process to return to the workforce. A fundamental and basic indicator to determine the level of gender equality is by counting the number of males and females working at the Public Service. Table 4.4 shows that the number of males and females in the Maltese Public Service is quite balanced. Both the head count and the percentage number of females have been on the increase as from the year 2014. It has increased from 49% to 52%, three percentage points in the span of 5 years.

The main conclusion is that the participation of women in the labour market has gradually increased. Nonetheless, this remains below EU average and Malta still has the highest gender employment gap in the EU. However, significant progress is being made. Currently, 46% of top public service posts are occupied by Women, from 21% in 2013. Consequently, one of the primary commitments of the Ministry for the Family and Social Solidarity was to continue increasing the rate of employment amongst women, especially in the public sector by focusing on more

Table 4.4 Number of male and female public service employees

Year	Male	Female
2014	15,908 (51%)	15,101 (49%)
2015	15,882 (50.6%)	15,516 (49.4%)
2016	15,561 (49.6%)	15,794 (50.4%)
2017	15,560 (48.6%)	16,440 (51.4%)
2018	15,569 (48%)	16,896 (52%)

Source: People & Standards Division, OPM, Head Count Data, Percentage figures adjusted to one decimal place

Table 4.5 Number of public service employees on reduced hours, maternity and parental leave, and teleworking

Year	Reduced hours	Maternity leave	Parental leave	Teleworking
2014	1316 (4.2%)	1031 (3.3%)	486 (1.6%)	872 (2.8%)
2015	1403 (4.5%)	1143 (3.6%)	476 (1.5%)	1035 (3.3%)
2016	1298 (4.1%)	1291 (4.1%)	498 (1.6%)	1158 (3.7%)
2017	1273 (4%)	1158 (3.6%)	480 (1.5%)	1234 (3.9%)
2018	1086 (3.3%)	986 (3%)	465 (1.4%)	1321 (4.1%)

Source: People & Standards Division, OPM, Head Count Data, Percentage figures adjusted to one decimal place

family-friendly measures and work-life balance initiatives. It is critical that a more equal representation of women in decision-making processes, including in government appointed Boards and Committees, is present and that women are provided with more opportunities to participate in political decisions. Malta still holds one of the lowest representations in female representation in comparison with EU nations.

Table 4.5 reveals that the percentage number of employees who are on reduced hours, maternity leave and parental leave has been quite stable with average percentages of 4%, 3.5% and 1.5% respectively. On the other hand, the percentage of Public Service employees who are making use of teleworking has increased from 2.8% in 2014 to 4.1% in 2018. These percentages show that a very little percentage has benefited from family-friendly measures. While it is important to consider the work exigencies of the Public Service, family-friendly measures are crucial means to attract and retain Public Service employees and the percentages recorded are still on the low side.

There are other work-life balance measures that assist the Public Service employees on occasions that require specific help for family or other personal reasons. The list is indeed quite comprehensive and include marriage or civil union leave, release to attend ante-natal examinations, maternity leave, paternity leave, leave for medically-assisted procreation (I.V.F. leave), adoption leave, bereavement leave, urgent family leave, leave to accompany spouse or partner in a civil union on government sponsored courses or assignments, parental leave (applicable to parents, legal guardians and foster carers), career break, responsibility leave and leave for a special reason. Another significant measure was the introduction of the free childcare scheme in 2014, which subsidised childcare in the case that parents were employed on a full-time basis and on a part-time basis. Entitlement to this scheme is calculated on the number of hours worked by the parent. This scheme was also extended to parents who are pursuing education leading to a recognisable qualification and thus boosting their employment prospects. Parents on parental leave are not considered eligible. This measure also increased the disposable income of women with children, facilitated a speedier return to the labour market after giving birth and increased the likelihood of mothers getting into sustainable employment. Currently there are around 95 childcare centres registered with the Ministry for Education and Employment. This measure proved to be successful since an increase in the mothers returning to employment within the same year of giving birth was observed in 2015 after this measure was introduced.

As from April 2014 until the end of December 2018, a total of 16,000 children have been enjoying free childcare. A total of 21,000 parents have benefited as a result of this measure. The number of childcare centres increased from 69 to 129 and the total government investment was 63 million. Furthermore, other services were introduced such as the *Klabb 3-16*, which is an after-school hour service and the Breakfast Club; two services geared towards bridging the gap between school and the parents' working hours and providing supervision to children before and after traditional school hours. Another measure was the tax exemption for females joining the labour market, which are provided with income tax deductions and extending the parental income tax computation for parents with children under the age of 23 who are still in tertiary education. The duration of maternity leave was also increased to 18 weeks. Mothers are provided with 14 weeks, which are compulsory and an additional 4 weeks that are optional.

Despite of all these positive measures, the scale seems to be tilted towards the mother of the child. In Malta, by law, the father is provided with one day of paternity leave, whereas the Public Service provides 5 days. Paternal leave refers to the leave entitlement reserved for fathers. Throughout Europe, the current uptake of paternity and parental leave by fathers is low and most of the leave is still taken up by mothers.

Several EU countries provide more gender-neutral options and have paternity leave that spans over an average of 2 weeks rather than days. The average length is 12.5 days. In comparison, new fathers in countries such as Spain and Austria receive 1 month of leave and 64 working days in Slovenia. Compensation varies when paternity is longer than 7 days. In the new EU work-life proposal currently being discussed, the EU aims to have a compulsory 10 days paid paternity leave for each member state. Fathers taking leave is of key importance for female labour force participation. It is critical to increase the leave uptake by fathers since studies display that this would encourage gender equality and would help enable dual-earner families to reconcile work and family responsibilities in a sustainable manner. Prolonged leave by mothers weakens their link with the labour market, with the repercussions on career progression and earnings. Nonetheless there are few policies in Malta that encourage the sharing of parental responsibilities.

This is becoming more important since the dual-family model has become the most common family structure in Malta, due to increased labour participation of women and the increased living costs. Consequently, in such a model, the overarching aim is for these families to support a sustainable working pattern for both parents and be able to develop themselves professionally throughout their working lives. This would lead to the retention of trained and experienced employees and the enhanced wellbeing of the employees. There are several discrepancies between what is provided by the Public Service and public entities. For instance, the Public Service provides three working days of marriage leave and 5 days of paternity leave, however the University of Malta provides seven working days of marriage and paternity leave. Nonetheless, the Manual on Work-Life Balance Measures is more detailed and several entities in the public sector make use of the measures outlined in this manual when these measures are not included in their Collective Agreement.

In Malta, parental leave is granted to parents on an unpaid basis. Once again when compared to other EU nations there is a clear discrepancy and there are no policies to encourage fathers to undertake parental leave. Several EU nations divide the parental leave up into a shared part and a non-shared part. Studies have shown that the following policies encouraged fathers to take up leave: any type of leave should be on an individual basis, targeted specifically for fathers on a use-it-or-lose-it basis, timed leave around the birth of child or return of mother to employment and high-income replacement. The average amount of parental leave is 87 weeks. Malta is one of the six EU nations that do not offer any form of compensation. The average compensation rate is 50 percent of earnings or by offering a flat rate. Portugal, Denmark, Italy, Poland, France, Germany and Romania offer paid leave. Other countries such as Belgium, Luxembourg and United Kingdom offer a fixed amount.

4.6.4   One-Stop-Shop for Public Officers: Giving a Human Face to the Public Service

Two essential measures were introduced that promote inclusiveness in the Public Service. The first measure involves the One-Stop-Shop for public officers that were set up in 2017 in order to provide quality guidance and assistance to Public Service employees for a wide range of services. It aims to ensure that public officers are given timely information, support with work and work-life balance related issues and guidance on entitlements or services accessible to them. Furthermore, the One-Stop-Shop provides support through the Grievance Help Desk to public officers who believe to be victims of some injustice. This sub-unit within the People & Standards Division provides guidance and assistance for public officers so that they would be able to provide informed and correct service to the general public. This is crucial since knowledgeable public officers would help in reducing bureaucracy and in providing a satisfactory service. Otherwise, the set-up of new structures would just result in the duplication of effort and in frustrating further citizens who do not feel that they are being provided with a high-quality service. Another function of this One-Stop-Shop is the Grievances Unit which investigates cases of alleged injustice or discrimination *vis-à-vis* a public officer. As it is the case with the One-Stop-Shop for the general public, this unit also serves as a quick channel for public officers' grievances as an alternative to the Ombudsman and the Law Courts.

4.6.5   The IDEA Initiative

IDEA is an initiative that was launched in 2014, whereby public officers of any grade can make suggestions directly to the Office of the Prime Minister, was another means of promoting inclusiveness in the Public Service. Ideas can be submitted any time through a website which is exclusively accessible to public officers. The ideas that were eventually implemented were recognised during the award-giving events held during the annual 'Public Service Weeks' in 2015, 2016 and 2018.

4.7 Delegation of Authority: Managing Human Resources Better

The delegation of authority lies at the core of the Public Service reform. Delegation is essentially the transfer of decision-making powers within an agreed framework of lines of authority. The New Public Management (NPM) discourse created great expectations of delegation (Hood, 1991; Osborne and Gaebler, 1992; Pollitt, 1993). The challenge is how human resources management can be used as a tool to delegate authority. Two tools were introduced to delegate authority.

4.7.1 A Shift Towards Delegation of Authority

In 2014, through Directive 7, delegation of authority was introduced to governmental departments to provide them with the ability to recruit new employees and to conduct promotion exercises in the Public Service entities. This resulted in a significant improvement in the efficiency and effectiveness to issue a call for applications and to promote public sector staff. The interesting notion is that a balance was achieved between adhering to the bureaucratic framework of the Public Sector and introducing effective mechanisms so that the Public Sector could attract the necessary employees in a rapidly changing labour market without any further delays. This measure has the objective of transferring resources and competencies nearer to the points of service delivery, and consequently HR decentralisation, which is viewed as a major trend in Public Administration modernisation.

Public Sector entities require prior approvals from central entities such as the Industrial Relations Unit (IRU), People and Standards Division and the Ministry responsible for Finance prior to when the human resources exercise takes place. This change was only applicable to already existing positions within the department concerned. The notion of the delegation of authority was spread to other human resources functions such as the empowerment of permanent secretaries to extend or terminate the probationary period and the submission as well as the approval of 3-year business and HR plans.

4.7.2   *Industrial Relations: Further Delegation of Authority and Strengthening of the Regulatory Process*

Industrial relations are another human resource dimension that experienced further delegation of authority as well as the strengthening of the consultation process and of the regulatory process. These characteristics are fundamental variables for better governance. Directive 9.1 entitled *Delegation of Authority to Conduct Industrial Relations and to Conduct the Selection and Appointment Process under Delegated Authority* provided the possibility to permanent secretaries to conduct industrial relations. This delegation of authority, from the centre to the ministry level, came in force over and above the selection process that was also decentralised.

The Industrial Relations Unit within the newly formed People and Standards Division organised a series of consultative meetings with unions and was involved in the discussions held regarding the Public Service collective agreement. The regulatory process was given an impetus through several verification processes that were carried out by the Department of Industrial Relations and Employment relations (DIER) in Public Service and public sector entities: 19 and 25 respectively. As it was the case with other functions, a coordinate and collaborative aspect could be noticed between several Public Service units in order to improve the industrial relations situation.

4.8   Conclusion: Way Forward to Consolidate HRM Developments

The Civil Service Systems and HRM Public Service Reforms have surely strengthened the drive towards increased professionalism in HRM practices although much more is needed to be done to strike a balance between the exigencies of the Public Service and the improvement of the wellbeing and performance of public officers through telework, work-life balance, family-friendly measures and training. As the largest employer in Malta, this balance is not easy to achieve especially when considering the reliance that a small island state has on the Public Service. This challenge is further accentuated with unforeseen circumstances, prominently the crisis of COVID-19 that has highlighted the need to invest more in human resources management.

Programmes intended to induce motivation in Public Service employees are to be more accentuated. Motivational techniques vary from the performance management programmes specifically performance appraisal to a robust flexible work-life balance arrangement. The former has seen a radical improvement in the last 6 years, but the latter needs a more solid framework in an era where teleworking and flexibility is dominating the labour market. The reform in the IPS is to be continued and consolidated especially regarding the aspect of instilling the Public Service values and excellence in all training provided by the Institute. The long-term vision of the Institute is to transform itself into an Academy that marks the professional status of a rapidly evolving Public Service.

References

De Freitas Bradley, C. (2017). Human resource reforms in public administration: The importance of the reward system. *HOLISTICA – Journal of Business and Public Administration, [online]*, 8(2), 49–58. Available at: https://content.sciendo.com/view/journals/hjbpa/8/2/article-p49. xml. Accessed 21 Apr 2020.

Eurostat (2018). *Employment rates and Europe 2020 national targets.* Available at: https:// ec.europa.eu/eurostat/statistics-explained/index.php/Employment_rates_and_Europe_2020_ national_targets. Accessed 27 Apr 2020.

Heichlinger, A., Thijs, N., Hammerschmid, N., & Attström, K. (2018). *Public Administration Reform in Europe: Conclusions, lessons learned and recommendations for future EU policy. [online]*. European Commission. Available at: https://ec.europa.eu/social/main.jsp?catId=738 &langId=en&pubId=8140&furtherPubs=yes. Accessed 1 Apr 2020.

Hood, C. (1991). A public management for all seasons? *Public Administration, 69*(1), 3–19.

Osborne, D., & Gaebler, T. (1992). *Reinventing government: How the entrepreneurial spirit is transforming the public sector*. New American Library.

Perry, J. L., Hondeghem, A., & Wise, L. R. (2010). Revisiting the motivational bases of public service: Twenty years of research and an agenda for the future. *Public Administration Review, 70*(5), 681–690.

Pollitt, C. (1993). *Managerialism and the public services: Cuts or cultural change in the 1990s?* (2nd ed.). John Wiley and Sons Ltd..

Van der Wal, Z. (2015). "All quiet on the non-western front?" A systematic review of public service motivation scholarship in non-western contexts. *Asia Pacific Journal of Public Administration, 37*(2), 69–86.

Chapter 5
Service Delivery and Digitalisation Reforms

"The sustainable success of digital transformation comes from a carefully planned organisational change management process that meets two key objectives, one being the organisational culture, and the other one is empowering its employees."

Enamul Haque
Author, Researcher and Managing Consultant

Information Communications Technology (ICT) has provided the means for the Public Service to provide service of excellence. Over the years, the Government has invested a significant amount in ICT to enable the Public Service to deliver its services on a 24/7 basis from anywhere. Thus, the Public Service in Malta has seen an enormous increase in the quality of services provided through the traceability of service requests; convenience; timely delivery; fewer errors using ICT systems; better communication; and continuous improvement through an analytics-based performance management system. The eGovernment Benchmark 2019 Report issued by the European Commission shows that Malta is a European front-runner in eGovernment. However, even though Malta is outperforming on digitalisation, it is still underperforming in how much the online services are being used by the public. Hence, the Public Service needs to implement a strategy for increasing the eGovernment systems penetration rate amongst the public. The spread and usability of online services rests on two main fronts, namely, more citizens need to be digitally literate and become aware and acquainted with the government online services; and the government is to continue its robust campaign to educate more the general public with regard to the advantages that emanate when using the vast array of online services.

F. Bezzina et al., *Public Service Reforms in a Small Island State*,
Public Administration, Governance and Globalization 22,
https://doi.org/10.1007/978-3-030-74357-4_5

5.1   Introduction: Parallel Reforms in Service Delivery and Digitalisation

New developments in Information and Communications Technology (ICT) are fundamentally changing the way we live, work and interact with each other. Shifts to digital technology such as the rapid rise in the use of mobile devices and other technological devices as well as the widespread information mean that citizens' expectations for technology enabled government services to have risen significantly in recent years. This shift in expectations coupled with the financial pressure on Government to transform and 'do more and better with less', presents new opportunities to deliver better outcomes for citizens, businesses and public servants (Fishenden & Thompson, 2013). The aim of this chapter is to analyse the improvements achieved in public service delivery and, in parallel, the digital revolution that has influenced the operations of the Public Service. Over the past two decades, service delivery and digitalisation have been a centre piece in improving Public Service performance (Roy, 2017). Investment in technology has been the backbone of reforms but it must be analysed in parallel with the way technology was a means towards improving service delivery. The citizen, as the ultimate beneficiary, has also played an important role in designing Government service delivery. Public Service providers have reviewed their mode of operations with the aim of providing a more efficient and effective service delivery resulting in the provision of cost-effective services through improved quality.

5.2   Initiatives Created to Enhancing Quality and Improving the Service Delivery

One silent reform that could bring a real change in the day-to-day lives of EU citizens is the way Public Services are offered and managed. Public services are expected to meet the aspirations and the needs of the various spectra of groups within a society in a timely manner. Red tape and bureaucracy have become commonly used 'buzz words' and such a perception are weakening the good work done by the respective public administrations of the EU member states. A holistic performance management approach incorporating Key Performance Indicators (KPIs) could be the answer to streamline and improve the quality of public services while strengthening the efficiency and effectiveness in the way the services are offered to the citizens (Bezzina et al., 2017: 5).

5.2.1   *Key Performance Indicators for the Public Service*

The use of KPIs in public administration was high on the agenda of the Maltese Presidency of the European Union between January and June 2017 and a specific EUPAN report was commissioned to study this subject. KPIs were a tool to instil a sense of a performing organisation in the Public Service. Between the years 2017 and 2018, a total of 30 Key Performance Indicators (KPIs) were launched for the Public Service as part of a new concept that provides clear targets to be reached within a specific timeframe. They are aimed at delivering a high-quality service and at bringing services nearer to citizens. The KPIs cover a wide span of sectors that affect citizens directly. In the energy sector, the KPIs were introduced to ensure that when a new application for electricity is submitted, the service is given by not later than 23 days from submission. Another KPI sets a specific timeframe for water service to be resumed in case of maintenance or damage. In the education sector, a KPI is tackling absenteeism in state schools while another one provides for personalised help to be given to 700 students with difficulties. In 2017, 12 KPIs were launched and subsequently introduced the concept of providing clear and specific measurable targets at a departmental, ministerial and national level. The pilot KPIs project included the following (Public Service, 2020c):

- Time to set up a new business in Malta was reduced drastically, cover a wide span of sectors affecting citizens directly;
- When a new application for electricity is submitted, the service is given by not later than 23 days from submission – meaning the waiting time is reduced by more than half;
- Timeframe for water service to be resumed in case of maintenance or damage;
- In the education sector, a KPI is tackling absenteeism in state schools while another one provides for personalised help to be given to 700 students with difficulties;
- Specific timeframe to be adhered to once a consumer lodges an official complaint;
- Setting up of a One-Stop-Shop where business owners find all the services, they need under one roof;
- In cases of long-term illness, patients who are assessed by a medical board will no longer have to present a certificate every week, meaning that certificates will be reduced by half. Also, the Pink Card will be renewed automatically for non-contributory benefits – a measure affecting some 4700 families;
- In the justice sector, two KPIs were launched: the setting up of a Commercial Court and a new system whereby law amendments are accessible online;
- Number of parks having a free wi-fi service will increase to seven. A free wi-fi service is also being introduced on some bus routes, in a KPI reaching some 200,000 commuters; and
- Technical help and advice for farmers in order to become more competitive.

A further 18 KPIs that were aimed particularly at the strengthening of operations in government departments were launched in May 2018. KPIs are not a magic wand to bring about the desired public service results. The use of KPIs is to be conducted with caution. The EUPAN report authored by Bezzina, Borg & Cassar (2017) highlighted the limitations in using KPIs which essentially involve counting the uncountable, the limitations in central-local relations, technical deficiencies in having too much data and the contextual limitations of a small island state to use at the maximum the designed KPIs.

5.2.2   Enhancement of Quality Service Charters for All Public Services

Public Services are enhanced not just by the setting of specific indicators that are measurable and achievable. The commitment towards a service of excellence required the drawing up of Quality Service Charters for all Public Services in 2016. The concept of quality service charters was not new to Malta. They have been around since the turn of the new millennium when various government entities drew up their own quality service charters. The main aim of Quality Service Charters is to act as a vehicle to improve consumer trust in government activities. Charters act as an interface between government services and end users, that is, consumers.

The 2016 reform consisted of an internal business process re-engineering exercise to improve quality, design and delivery. The Public Service Management Code (PSMC) was simplified, shortened by 25% by eliminating outdated elements, certain technicalities and the ambiguity of contradicting chapters. The renewed Public Service has even received a new definition of quality, which is based on four pillars – 'Voice, Design, Delivery and Accountability'. A 5-year strategic plan is currently being formulated that focuses on providing the highest quality service possible, referred to as a "Service of Excellence." A visible and significant change in the service being delivered by the Public Service was the set-up of new structures pertaining to One-Stop-Shops. One-Stop-Shops were created in order to cater for three different circumstances: the general public, businesses and the public servants themselves.

5.2.3   One-Stop-Shop Through servizz.gov

Through the implementation of the above-mentioned KPIs, several new One-Stop-Shops were set up where the client can find all the services required under one umbrella or public infrastructure. The first kind of One-Stop-Shop was the *servizz. gov* in local communities. The Maltese Government has made significant investments in ICT to improve service delivery. The 'joined-up' customer-facing services project commenced in 2016. All Government services were brought together on *servizz.gov* and categorised by sector to facilitate access. servizz.gov acts as a bridge between the Public Service and the citizen, makes life easier and saves time since its available online 24 × 7. servizz.gov and 153 has become the standard bearer for providing service of excellence, thus raising the notion of public service quality to a significantly higher level. An important aspect of servizz.gov is the establishment of a Public Service innovation hub that tests all the processes before being implemented. To ensure that these services are equally accessible to offline citizens, a freephone service and five servizz.gov regional hubs have been set up in Qormi, Birgu, Qawra, Paola and Birkirkara. These regional hubs have now increased to 23. In 2017, servizz.gov was awarded the international Service Design Award and was acknowledged by the European Union for best practices regarding public procurement. This was a fundamental step towards the reduction of bureaucracy and in providing a better service to the citizens. Thousand five hundred government services and their respective administrative processes were gathered into a single user-friendly online One-Stop-Shop website. It is interesting to note that a 153-help line was established that started with about 2000 phone calls and in 2020 is estimated to reached one million calls. From a logistical perspective, five community hubs were set-up that transformed the service not only to an online portal but also a Public Service with a human face in case the query presented by the citizens require a detailed explanation and further support than what is possible from an online service. Nevertheless, the major advantage for citizens is that in most instances they do not require to be physically present in case they need to just apply for a service. The Public Service has also launched a mystery shopper system to ensure that the level of service provided is of a high standard and is being delivered efficiently.

The main services provided by *servizz.gov* involve request of information on government services, request an online service, schedule appointments with government entities, report administrative problems or lodge a complaint and provide feedback or suggestions on how the Public Service could be improved. The ability to lodge a complaint through *servizz.gov* has turned a new page for citizens since they are now able to have their voice heard without going through a more rigorous process of the Ombudsman. This means that, in this instance, citizens can have a quicker administrative redress. This is a typical example of how red tape has been curtailed for better governance of public administration. Further to the 5 community hubs, 3 specialised technical hubs were set-up in education, finance and social services. This move will continue to consolidate the *servizz.gov* initiative and strengthen the citizen's trust in the government services. The *servizz.gov* was nominated as the Best National Digital Solution for Malta for the international World Summit Awards. The World Summit Awards are a global initiative selecting digital innovation making positive impact on society.

5.2.4   One-Stop Shop Through Business 1st

The second type of One-Stop-Shop was formed for businesses in the shape of *Business 1st*. *Business 1st* was introduced in 2016 as a pilot project and became fully operational by 2018. *Business 1st* is the single point of contact for businesses and offers services, information and assistance to potential entrepreneurs and SMEs interested in setting-up their own business. The time required to set up a new business has been reduced from 2 months to an average period of 3 days. The forms required to set-up a business have been reduced from 22 to just one. Several steps have also been taken to reduce bureaucracy within the Public Service. Several trading licences were abolished while inspections for small businesses were reduced drastically to save time and money. In terms of qualitative data, in the first year of the *Business 1st* operation, more than 32,000 clients made use of the services, mostly through the freephone 144 and more than 4000 entrepreneurs were trained.

5.2.5   The Development and Launch of Mobile Apps: mGovernment Facilities

mGovernment is part of the 'joined-up' customer-facing services project. The scope of mobile services is to cut down on extra bureaucracy, speed up procedures and bring governmental services closer to the community by improving the quality of services being offered. Technological advances can be used to deliver a better service to the public in a personalised and user-friendly manner. In March 2017, 21 new mobile apps were launched by the Principal Permanent Secretary (Public Service, 2020b). The apps were intended to enable the public access to government services 24 hours a day. Apps covered a continuum of important services to the general public that include: rating the level of government service provided, customs information, Malta travel point, myGozo, Valletta 2018, clean and upkeep, Malta industrial parks, the national patent register, EU funding, grants, organ donation, students' maintenance grants, free childcare, student support services and eCourts. These day-to-day services have an influence on the citizens' lifestyle. Just 1 year after the first launch, in April 2018, 13 other mobile apps were introduced that were specifically focused on information related to the Public Service recruitment, services offered by Business 1st, information regarding health and safety at the workplace, the police conduct certificate, Esplora and information on agriculture and fisheries. Mobile apps are also used as an effort to maintain and improve the quality of service delivery. Citizens are invited to rate the Public Service through a mobile app (Public Service, 2020a). Any feedback allows for the constant monitoring of the satisfaction level for each governmental department and any necessary action is taken to improve the service.

5.2.6   Injection of Quality & Standards in the Services Provided to Public: Mystery Shopper

The Mystery Shopper initiative, also launched in 2017, has been introduced in order to identify shortcomings in service delivery and remedy the situation accordingly. It is a classic example of checking how well the managerial engine room is working. The Mystery Shopper involves constant monitoring and assessment of the *servizz.*

gov agent responses, to make sure that correct information is being given in the shortest time possible through knowledgeable replies. To complement this initiative, the Government has also invested in its people. The Public Service has created the Institute for Public Services to provide Public Officers with the training required to deliver good quality services. Details concerning this initiative are indicated in another chapter.

The mystery shopper project is a clear illustration of a check and balance in terms of quality and in improving the service provided to the citizen. The essence of governance is after all this particular notion: to offer a good quality service to customers. Public servants are assessed in terms of accessibility, responsiveness, courtesy, reliability, credibility, communication, security, competence and understanding. A report is generated by the mystery shopper and the department concerned is then expected to take the necessary actions within a specific timeframe in order to improve their respective service. The mystery shopper exercise was conducted not only vis-à-vis *servizz.gov* but throughout the public administration. The mystery shopper exercise was performed in 42 service sites in 6 ministries. A total of 131 recommendations were put forward and resolved. The recommendations were categorised into the following main themes: physical accessibility, improving service delivery, ownership of service delivery, customer privacy and confidentiality, health and safety, tangibles and training.

The Mystery Shopper is complimented by the Departmental Quality Service Assessments in customer service which were conducted across the public administration by using 10 determinants based on the SERVQUAL model. Both the Mystery Shopper and the Quality Service Assessments are conducted by surprise without any prior notice. The Quality Service Assessments are based on an advanced notice and involve the following criteria: access, communication, empathy, competence, courtesy, credibility, reliability, responsiveness, security, health and safety environment, and tangibles. Successful departments were awarded a Quality Label. As from July 2017, 63 departments in 10 different ministries were assessed. A total of 160 recommendations emanated from these assessments and the nature of the recommendations were generally divided into 12 different categories: updating of departmental websites, façade signing with business hours, the setting-up of a complaints system, physical accessibility, customer usage survey, improving service delivery, customer privacy and confidentiality, dress code, staff communication, health and safety, tangibles especially with regards to the physical appearance of the department and staff training. Furthermore, a cycle of 17 HR compliance inspection assessments were completed by the People Resourcing and Compliance Directorate within the People and Standards Division (P&SD) in 17 Ministries, in the year 2018, based on ratings of five (5) criteria on the following determinants:

- **Responsiveness:** adherence to timeframes established in directives and regulations that may emerge from time to time;
- **Competence:** people Management competence and adherence to the respective policies and procedures;

- **Courtesy:** respect and attitude of People Management staff towards P&SD officers, before and during the visit;
- **Reliability**: up-to-date pertinent records and files; and
- **Communication:** intra-Ministry, with other departments, with P&SD officers.

5.3   Improving Public Services Through Information Technology

The discussion of the use of information technology in the Public Service is to be analysed from two main perspectives: first, its influence on the service delivery and secondly, the broader impact on a national scale and from a policy stance. OECD (2017:3) report on government strategies emphasised this stance in that: 'Digital technologies are one of the most transformational factors of our time, including their impact on effective public governance and potentially economic competitiveness.'

A practical case-study of the effect of digitalisation on a macro scale is the introduction of electronic counting instead of the traditional manual counting, in 2018. Electronic counting for the first time in Malta paved the way forward in terms of digitalisation for all sectors, including electoral procedures. The new electronic method provides faster electoral results and minimises the chance of human error although a lot of trials had to be conducted to assure the necessary trust in the two main political parties. A compromise had to be reached to provide a semi-automated process rather than fully automated, therefore more improvement is to be reached in the coming years from an IT perspective in the counting process. This example reveals the interplay of several stakeholders when launching delicate improvements in the public service delivery.

5.3.1   A Policy Perspective of ICT: Digital Malta Strategy 2014–2020

From a strategic national perspective, Digital Malta (2020) is the national ICT strategic plan for the years 2014–2020. The aim is to transform Malta into a digitally enabled nation in all sectors of society. The strategy identifies any gaps towards becoming a digitised society and proposes measures to address them. From a citizen's perspective, the strategy will enhance their digital capability to better and more efficiently access healthcare and social services, connect the elderly and socially excluded, improve education for all, and create higher-quality jobs. From an economic perspective, digital competence and specialist ICT skills need to be widened, and national policy and strategies adjusted, to strengthen Malta's workforce and make its businesses more innovative and competitive. To name a few, some initiatives under the Digital Malta Strategy included:

- The provision of tablets to school children, so that every child is given an opportunity at being computer literate to mitigate the future concern regarding the digital divide;
- Launching device and user mobility in Government through cloud computing;
- Enhancing the eGovernment programme;
- Addressing national security concerns;
- Creating a common business database to make information easily accessible within the restrictions of the data protection legislation; and
- Expanding free internet hotspots throughout Malta for general public use.

5.3.2   The Digitisation of the Public Service: Mapping Tomorrow (2019–2021)

The focus of the digitisation, specifically in the Public Service, has been on improving the public services delivery, building trust, looking at the needs, expectations and pain points of citizens and businesses, improving and simplifying the administrative processes and easing access to services through the setting up of One-Stop-Shops and multi-channel service delivery. Data sharing across government is an ongoing challenge and at the heart of this digitalisation plan is the 'Once-Only Principle'. This principle tries to eliminate the frustration of having to give the same personal information repeatedly. Once data has been given to a Ministry or a Government Officially Appointed Body, it will be shared as permitted by law or through consent, a digital transformation that is truly connecting government. Mapping Tomorrow is a Strategic Plan for the Digital Transformation of the Public Administration for the years 2019–2021 (OPM & MITA, 2019). The Government's vision aspires to take Public Services to the next level of improvement through the adoption of digital technologies. This plan builds on previous achievements such as the drive to provide services which are available 24 × 7. Based on past achievements, this Strategic Plan sets three goals which build upon each other and form a continued improvement in service delivery. The three goals are: (1) *Take-Up*: which links to previous strategies and aims to bring simplified services which are digital end-to-end to increase take-up; (2) *Once-Only*: the core goal, aiming at internal sharing and re-use of data and information that has been previously provided by a citizen or organisation. The aim is to stop asking for information which already exists within Government; and (3) *Service of Excellence*: which brings Public Services in line with social trends and demands, and to the quality levels expected by citizens and businesses. It looks at the adoption of emerging technologies such as AI to bring Public Services that are personalised, user-friendly and timely. The goal is to exceed client expectations.

5.3.3   The eGovernment Context

Malta's Public Service rank high in EU eGovernment Benchmarking and is now providing online services 24 hours a day. The digital user experience has been improved further through the implementation of the Mobile Government Strategy 2017–2018, making various new and enhanced Public Services available anytime and anywhere via mobile devices. In the Digital Economy and Society Index 2017 (DESI), which was published by the European Commission, Malta has been reconfirmed as the European leader in the provision of digital Public Services. Malta was also confirmed as the best-performing country when it comes to broadband connectivity. This index is a tool that measures the progress made by individual EU member states in achieving a digital economy and society. It measures the progress in five key indicators, which are namely connectivity; human capital; the use of internet by EU citizens; the integration of digital technology by businesses and the provision of Digital Public Services. The usage of eGovernment services remains a challenge, both for Malta and for the EU member states. In this context, Malta has increased its impetus to make online services accessible also through mobile devices.

In this way, Government can keep its commitment to reach out to a wider spectrum of audiences, by using different channels. Regarding the provision of these services, Malta's performance was rated higher than the EU average. The challenge is to increase their take-up by citizens. In fact, 57% of the Maltese public use eGovernment services, compared to the 67% EU average. According to Eurostat, in 2019, 50% of individuals in Malta have used the internet to interact with public authorities (European Commission, 2019). Furthermore, 58% of eGovernment users submitted filled in forms through the internet in 2019. This is lower than the EU average which marks 64%, although Malta has registered the biggest improvement from among all EU countries with a significant increase of seven percentage points (European Commission, 2020). Malta also registered positive results in broadband connectivity; citizens' use of the internet and use of digital technologies by businesses. Our country was in fact the only Member State to have full coverage of very fast broadband and having subscriptions growing each year. This infrastructure also enabled a significant increase in the number of internet users which is only 3 percentage points less than the EU average. Although the number of users on the internet was slightly less than the EU average, those who were online had a larger presence that their EU counterparts. In fact, 82% of the internet users were highly active on social media and were also keen users of video call facilities. This was also the case for business engagement online. In fact, 20% of the Maltese Small and Medium Enterprises (SMEs) were selling online, compared to the EU average of 17%.

5.3.4   An Information System Strategic Plan (ISSP)

An Information System Strategic Plan (ISSP) was formulated in 2016 with the objective of enhancing performance, greater accountability and promoting decentralised services. The ICT strategy adopted is based upon five key centric pillars, namely the Citizen, Business, Civil Society, Government, Administration and Technology. The Citizen Centric pillar focuses on ICT accessibility to every citizen; enhancing student's ICT capabilities; advancing female participation at the workplace; harnessing the potential of senior citizens; developing the individual; and protecting the individual. The Business Centric pillar focuses on the creation of job opportunities; leveraging intellectual capital; fostering eWork in the business community; implementing R&D initiatives; and advocating new ways of conducting business. The Civil Society Centric pillar focuses on health eServices; exploring eVoting trends; promoting Green ICT initiatives; and providing 'Digital' outreach campaigns. The Government Administration Centric pillar focuses on enhancing governmental decision-making by leveraging the use of information being generated by the various systems; sustaining national ICT assets; consolidating public information by integrating Government systems; enhancing the accessibility to public information by the general public; and providing better eGovernment, eGovernance and eDemocracy facilities.

5.3.5   Strengthening the IT Aspect Through the Better Use of Websites

In addition to the launch of new mobile apps, the Public Service developed more than 20 Public Service responsive websites. This meant that citizens could now access public websites through their tablets and mobiles in a user-friendly manner. This is also an important technological feature since a lot of information that is accessible on a normal website would not be available on a mobile or tablet device without such a development. Citizens could now access and apply online at any time of the day within the comfort of their home. In parallel with these initiatives, the Mobile Government Strategy was launched for the period 2017 and 2018. This technological oriented strategy is part of the renewal process of the Public Service, with the aims of reducing bureaucracy, facilitating processes and increasing the quality of the services rendered.

5.3.6   CONvErGE Project

The CONvErGE Project was launched in 2017 to further strengthen Public Services through the development of its ICT systems. The aim was to create several new services that provided more benefits to citizens and businesses. Through this project, the Malta Information Technology Agency (MITA) supported ministries in their implementation of new eService applications that included: a new accounting system for Government; a new electronic system for customs; a national health infrastructure known as eHealth; a digital platform for the tourism sector; a new system for the management of activity related to national disasters; new systems for Maltese laws, the legal profession and notarial archives; an electronic system for social services; and a project analysing the need for and development of a portal for businesses. Some other initiatives were implemented by several ministries in a continuum of policy areas to improve their operations and eventually their services using IT. The Electronic Exchange of Social Security Information (EESSI) is a case in point. It is an IT system that helps social security institutions across the EU exchange information more rapidly and securely, as required by the EU Regulations on social security coordination. The paper-based exchanges were replaced by electronic exchanges as from June 2019, as Member States including Malta progress with connecting to EESSI. The benefits arising from such a system are significant. It allows a faster and more efficient message exchange between social security institutions. Furthermore, EESSI will speed up exchanges between national authorities. It also allows member states to handle individual cases more quickly and facilitate a faster calculation and payment of claims.

More accurate data exchange between national authorities was also be possible since social security institutions across the EU started to use standardised electronic documents translated into their own language, improving multilingual communication. EESSI will introduce safeguards to ensure that the data exchanged is correct and complete, helping institutions to combat fraud and error. EESSI will optimise case handling, introducing standard electronic procedures to be followed by institutions; this will further enhance the correct application of social security coordination rules. There will be more secure handling of personal data given that EESSI will introduce the use of a common secure infrastructure for cross-border data exchange between social security institutions. It will enable message exchange between national institutions, but the system will not create a database to store such messages and personal data centrally. The content of the messages will only be available to the relevant institutions, and Member States will remain responsible to ensure a high standard of data protection, in line with EU rules. EESSI will follow the latest standards in IT security. From a citizen interface perspective, Malta through Connecting Europe Facility (CEF) funding for EESSI will be implementing citizen interfaces within its National Application which includes mobile apps, interactive website and check entitlement database. These applications will ensure that citizens' rights are respected through availability of information. Other IT oriented projects include the Cross-Border e-Health Services, a national electronic health record system (NEHR), an electronic patient record primary health care (EPRPHC), a patient consent management system (PCMS) and a health data exchange system (HDE).

The Ministry responsible for Agriculture is another case study of a major technological improvement. The Ministry identified smart farming and data analysis amongst the main technological implementations that can contribute to enhance the profitability and sustainability of farming in Malta. With the right technological infrastructure and the introduction of new digital solutions the Ministry will be introducing tools to assist farmers in their day-to-day business. Farmers can already view information related to their fields through augmented reality and on-site information can be seen superimposed on the actual image of the field. Such systems will be enhanced, and new projects will introduce automated tools that will generate alerts related to the crops by using satellite imagery, temperature, humidity data and other information about the field. The Ministry aims to improve the quality of Public Services to stakeholders including farmers, through the implementation of new online systems and mobile apps and provide up-to-date information about status of applications, payments and other obligations in areas such as waste management and applications for EU funding. Systems will be integrated so that data is shared, and users will be required to submit data only once. The Ministry is also adopting geo-database solutions consisting of data related to valleys and water catchment areas in Malta and Gozo. This information will be used in the decision-making process related to the management and planning of interventions in valleys and areas of water catchment.

5.3.7 myHealth Portal

myHealth is another ICT related project that has reengineered the way information is transmitted and available to the health care professionals and the patients. The objective behind the myHealth portal, which was created in 2017, is for patients and doctors to access healthcare efficiently. The benefits include the sharing of medical records and information on admissions and appointments. Emerging technologies such as robotics and artificial intelligence are being integrated into healthcare service provision. The Ministry will implement further technological changes to replace paper documents and minimise bureaucracy. It will strengthen the efficiency and effectiveness of resources and processes through timely and accurate data. Future projects will help patients gain more access to health records and provide the capability of managing consent. The myHealth portal provides citizens with secure online access to selected medical records, such as laboratory test results, reports on X-rays and other medical images, summaries of admissions to Government hospitals, appointments at Government hospitals and health centres, entitlement to Pharmacy of your Choice (POYC) medicines, POYC prescriptions and POYC dispensing records, and details of vaccinations. Patients can link with their family doctor through myHealth and give their doctor access to their data. Doctors can order blood tests and X-rays for their patients online and send forms to the public health authorities about notifiable infectious diseases and vaccinations. Both patient and doctors can be notified by email and SMS when new data becomes available in myHealth. Figure 5.1 reveals the total number of users who have directly accessed the myHealth portal since 2012, an increase from 2018 to 28,485 in 7 years.

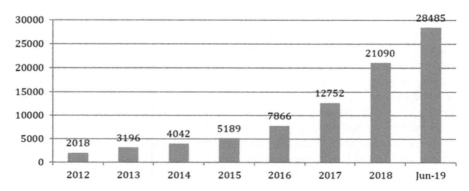

Fig. 5.1 Number of myHealth Users for Period 2012–2019

The main benefits of myHealth are improved continuity of care for patients between hospital (secondary care) and the community (primary care); empowerment of patients by giving them direct access to their own personal health data; and the digitisation of processes that were previously slower and paper-based. The uptake of myHealth has been monitored continuously since the launch of the myHealth service.

5.4 Conclusion

The Public Service in Malta has seen a huge leap in quality through the traceability of service requests, convenience, timely delivery, fewer errors using ICT systems, better communication and continuous improvement through an analytics-based performance management system. The *eGovernment Benchmark 2019 Report* released by the European Commission revealed that Malta is a European front-runner in eGovernment. However, although Malta is outperforming on digitalisation, it is still underperforming in how much the online service are used by the public. The usability of online service rests on two main fronts: first, more citizens need to be digitally literate and become acquainted to the government online services and, second, the government is to continue its robust campaign to educate more the general public with regard to the advantages that emanate when using the vast array of online services.

References

Bezzina, F., Borg, C., & Cassar, V. (2017). *The public service as a performing organisation.* International Report prepared for the Maltese Presidency of the Council of the European Union, published by the European Public Administration Network.

Digital Malta. (2020). *National strategy* 2014-2020. Available at: https://digitalmalta.org.mt/en/Pages/Home.aspx

European Commission. (2020). *Digital economy and society index (DESI) 2020 – Digital public aservices.* Available at: https://ec.europa.eu/digital-single-market/en/digital-public-services-scoreboard

European Commission. (2019). *Digital government factsheet 2019 – Malta.* Available at: https://joinup.ec.europa.eu/sites/default/files/inline-files/Digital_Government_Factsheets_Malta_2019.pdf

Fishenden, J., & Thompson, M. (2013). Digital government, open architecture, and innovation: why public sector IT will never be the same again. *Journal of Public Administration Research and Theory, 23*(4), 977–1004.

OECD. (2017). *OECD digital government studies: Benchmark digital government strategies in MENA countries.* OECD Publishing. Available at: https://doi.org/10.1787/9789264268012-en

Office of the Principal Permanent Secretary, Office of the Prime Minister (OPM) & MITA. (2019). *Mapping tomorrow – A strategic plan for the digital transformation of the public administration 2019-2021.* https://publicservice.gov.mt/en/Documents/MappingTomorrow_StrategicPlan2019.pdf

Public Service. (2020a). *Rate the public service.* Available at: https://publicservice.gov.mt/en/Pages/Initiatives/RateApp.aspx

Public Service. (2020b). *Public Service Renewal.*, Available at: https://publicservice.gov.mt/en/Pages/Initiatives/PublicServiceRenewal.aspx

Public Service. (2020c). *12 new KPIs for the public service.* Available at: https://publicservice.gov.mt/en/Pages/News/2017/20170515_KPISigning.aspx

Roy, J. (2017). Digital government and service delivery: An examination of performance and prospects. *60*(4), 538–561, the Institute of Public Administration of Canada.

Chapter 6
Organisation and Management Government Reforms

"Fit no stereotypes. Don't chase the latest management fads. The situation dictates which approach best accomplishes the team's mission."

Colin Luther Powell
American politician, diplomat and retired four-star general

This Chapter is about the various Organisation and Management government reforms that have been implemented in the Public Service. It reviews and considers these government reforms from a broad organisational and management perspective by focusing on three main reform features, namely, the structural reforms that have directly and indirectly impacted the Public Service; the national government policy reforms that required the complimentary coordination of Malta's public administration; and the specific organisational and management reforms within the Public Service. The research reveals that the Public Service by implementing these various organisation and management government reforms have optimistically responded to the emerging challenges by proposing and initiating both policy-oriented and legislative solutions. The ultimate objective of the Government was to mitigate the bureaucratic administrative process and, in parallel, evolve a dynamic vertical and horizontal service-based approach. Thus, satisfying the citizens and businesses needs at a highly advanced level to support the government's strategy to deliver a service of excellence. These organisational and management reforms are not a one-time occurrence but rather are part of a coherent, consistent and continuous change process. However, much more is required to be accomplished, if the Public Service is to keep up with the rapidly changing environment.

© The Author(s), under exclusive license to Springer Nature Switzerland AG 2021   141
F. Bezzina et al., *Public Service Reforms in a Small Island State*,
Public Administration, Governance and Globalization 22,
https://doi.org/10.1007/978-3-030-74357-4_6

6.1 Introduction: Organising and Managing Better the Government

The purpose of this chapter is two-fold: first, to outline the rationale for a strategic approach to the organisation and management of government and, second, to describe the approach adopted in Malta in terms of legislation, policies and structures. The introductory part of this chapter explains the rationale for a strategic approach to government which is a complex business to manage and that requires high quality, sophisticated decision-making. A critical determinant of successful government is the ability to make good decisions and to ensure an effective implementation through a well-functioning public administration. This is not an easy task since the national government's tasks are extremely complex especially in an era of multi-level governance. Modern governments are required to take thousands of decisions in a rapidly changing environment and scenarios. (Matheson et al., 1996). The ripple effect of these decisions is enormous, due to the size and pervasiveness of government, especially in small island states such as Malta.

The complexity of reforming government was also echoed by OECD member countries. Reforming the public sector is a complex matter and this was highlighted by OECD member and non-member countries which are facing increasing challenges to make change happen in an unpredictable environment. Adopting innovative reforms in order to respond adequately to social demands and the way that society is developing is no longer enough; governments need to accompany their reforms with a holistic strategy to organise and manage better. This is an essential pillar to achieve the desired success in a reform process (Huerta Melchor, 2008).

It is crucial to highlight a point for consideration. The point concerns the role of public servants in the reform process. Practice has shown that public servants are not neutral actors but have vested interests in the system. Malta's Public Service in today's realities is the sector that trade unions remain strongest. Therefore, when proposing reforms and reorganisations, trade unions play an important role at the formulation or pre-implementation stages. At times, finding a balance between the interests of political executives, public servants, public opinion and interest groups such as trade unions is the biggest headache experienced by national governments and international institutions.

6.2 The Creation and Enhancement of Structure: Managing Better for a Flourishing National Economy

When analysing reforms in the government and Public Service structures, a broader perspective is to be considered especially with regards to the influence of public administrative structures on the national economy. In the case of Malta, more structures were created to respond to the fast and robust development of Malta's economy, which in the period 2014–2017 grew at an average rate of 7% of the Gross

Domestic Product (GDP) (NSO, 2020). This chapter builds on the other chapters in describing how the government, through the decisions taken by the executive, has restructured the apparatus of the state, the public sector and specifically the Public Service. The first two reforms concerning the merging of the main revenue-generating departments and the establishment of the Institute for Public Services were mentioned in the previous chapters, but it is worth analysing the main facets of reform in these two crucial entities given that this chapter focuses on the better organisation and management of the government services:

6.2.1   Merging of the Main Revenue-Generating Departments

The Inland Revenue Department, the VAT Department and the Customs Department in 2018 have been merged into one entity. Several benefits were identified by this merger. An analysis conducted by the National Audit Office (2017), before the merger was accomplished, highlighted the consolidation of Malta's fiscal structure. The key specific benefits of this reform included the following: first, more efficient application of resources by eliminating duplication of functions and additional specialisation; second, better information sharing leading to more effective risk analysis by reducing data fragmentation; third, the fight to reduce tax evasion; fourth, more focus on a taxpayer-centred approach, resulting in the improvement of quality standards to provide equal treatment of taxpayers, concentrating further on service principles; fifth, better functionality for administration of all taxes; sixth, improved cash control management; seventh, centralisation of routine processes, which can be more easily automated; eight, improving compliance activities; ninth, increase in co-operation of staff and better career opportunities for employees; tenth, uniformity of forms and correspondence across taxes, new statements of accounts and direct electronic refunds; and eleventh, making maximum use of electronic transactions.

6.2.2   Institute for the Public Services

Another important reform is the establishment of the Institute for Public Services (IPS) in 2016, the central training organisation of the Public Service. Nevertheless, IPS acts as the research arm of the public service, as well as guides and direct research on Public Administration issues, with reference to those areas that are relevant to training and development needs, strategic human resources, leadership and good governance. IPS also contributes towards good governance by fostering beneficial relationships between academia and Government, for the benefit of maintaining standards within the Public Administration.

6.2.3   Office of the Arbiter for Financial Services

The Office of the Arbiter for Financial Services was established in 2016 by virtue of Chap. 555 of the Laws of Malta. It is an autonomous and independent body with the power to mediate, investigate and adjudicate complaints filed by customers against all financial services providers. Sound administrative and governance practices were established and continued evolving and improving in pursuit of high standards of governance. In the first year of its operation, more than 500 complaints were considered (Times of Malta, 2017). The main advantage of the new Office of the Arbiter over the law courts is that the procedures are not too legalistic and are not bound by the Code of Organisation and Civil Procedure. The procedures are only bound to provide equal fair hearing to both sides.

6.2.4   College of Regulators

The set-up of the Office of the Arbiter was complemented by the College of Regulators, which is a consultative body composed of 15 regulators from entities or departments related to business and enterprise, introduced in 2017. The main aim of the College is for all stakeholders to have full visibility of the enterprise sector, thus ensuring more efficiency. The functions of the College are, among many others: to ensure better use of regulation to promote efficiency, economy and competition within the enterprise sector; to make recommendations to Government in respect of reviews of policies; to develop measures for the promotion of efficiency, better economy and competition within the enterprise sector; and to publish an annual report of matters discussed during meetings.

6.2.5   National Skills Council

Another crucial body that seeks to improve the governance of skills anticipation and coordinate work that was previously fragmented across several Public Service departments is the National Skills Council which was set-up in December 2016 to review past and present available skills within the labour work force (CEDEFOP, 2020). Therefore, in practice, the National Skills Council, which works closely with the Ministry responsible for Education and Employment (MEDE), evaluates the changes required to meet current and future needs.

The three-year strategic plan of the Council has identified three priority areas:

- Bringing together the worlds of education and industry through work-based learning;
- Digital skills; and

- Research and development with the goal to create better conditions and incentives for lifelong learners.

This is another real-life example of how the organisation of the government can help a growing economy, which consequently has resulted in labour market shortages. It intends to minimise the skill gaps that exist in some of the demanding and rewarding sectors such as the digital, technical and financial sectors. To fulfil its role, the Council is to liaise not only with the Public Service and the wider Public Sector but all the stakeholders that are involved in education and employment to improve the skills governance. In fact, the National Skills Council brought together the University of Malta, MCAST, ITS, Jobsplus, Malta Chamber of Commerce and Malta Enterprise, as well as representatives from the Civil Society and lifelong learning specialists (MEDE, 2020).

6.2.6 Interactive Science Centre

Other means of government organisation in collaboration with EU funding can be observed in the dynamic set-up of the interactive Science Centre (Esplora) which was part of a programme created in 2016 entitled '*Investing in Competitiveness for a Better Quality of Life*'. The programme aimed to sustain a growing, knowledge-based and competitive economy and to improve Malta's attractiveness and the quality of life. The programme was funded by the European Regional Development Fund (ERDF). Worth noting is that although *prima facie* this project can be seen as a temporary investment, it has a permanent legacy in the contribution towards the future economy. The core concept of Esplora is Science, an academic discipline that is fundamental for tomorrow's economic advancement (Esplora, 2020).

6.2.7 Appointment of a Commissioner for Simplification

The economy and the improvement in the business environment have been a priority for the current Government, in most of the initiatives mentioned in this section. The appointment of a Commissioner for Simplification in 2014 to minimise bureaucracy was another step towards this direction. Several business reengineering exercises have taken place, including the implementation of numerous simplification measures, some of which are presented in the next section. The Commissioner for Simplification was initially considered as a catalyst for change in Public Administration to efficiently serve the citizen and the business community by eliminating any unnecessary bureaucracy (Commissioner for Simplification, 2020). However, in a practical sense the Commissioner for Simplification was not considered effective and has not been reappointed. The Public Service has currently established an innovation hub that has the responsibility for streamlining and testing all processes resulting from Business Process Reengineering exercises before their implementation.

6.3   Reforming Processes in the Creation of a Better Working and Business Environment

A variety of Public Service reforms were implemented that focused upon the Creation of a Better Working and Business Environment. These are described in the following sections.

6.3.1   Public Administrative Reforms to Help the Economy

The structural reforms, that provide the backbone of the public realm in its execution of the government priorities, were complemented by reforms in the managerial processes that were also intended to create the necessary business climate for enterprises to develop their respective business. Therefore, the interesting notion is that the public administrative machinery is used to improve the economic and social fabric of a state (Matei & Matei, 2010), as has been the case in Malta.

The following mosaic of Public Service reforms in the administrative processes can be significantly interlinked to developing a better business environment that in turn results in a better economic growth. The first three reforms were directly linked to businesses in three main realms: first, aiding businesses; second, simplifying the processes; and third, improving business inspections to ascertain that the necessary quality and standards are maintained.

6.3.1.1   MicroInvest

MicroInvest, as part of Malta Enterprise business infrastructure, was set-up in 2016 with the aim of encouraging undertakings to invest in their business, innovate, expand, and implement compliance directives, or to develop their operations (Malta Enterprise, 2020). Eligible undertakings, including self-employed persons, are supported through a tax credit representing a percentage of the eligible expenditure and wages of newly recruited employees. This scheme is intended to help many small and business enterprises flourish in their business endeavours, especially when considering that 80% of Malta's businesses fall in this category.

6.3.1.2 Simplification of Processes: Reducing the Time for Setting-up a New Business

The procedure to set-up a business in Malta was reviewed and facilitated in 2016. Bureaucratic burdens were significantly eased for business owners, in a manner that registrations could now be done through a single unified form. Malta Enterprise and MITA coordinated the task, as most processes have been automated. Business process reviews were carried out at the Inland Revenue Department and the VAT Department, allowing for the registration procedures (as a taxpayer and as an employer) to be automated, and for the VAT, Income Tax and Employer (PE) numbers to be issued online. Other business-related activities can also be done online, such as changing the address and expanding the business. The Inland Revenue Department and the VAT Department have also consolidated their call centres with those of *Servizz.gov* so that the customer care perspective is also strengthened in parallel.

6.3.1.3 Improving Business Inspections

Businesses in Malta are subjected to inspections to protect the interests of society and safeguard its future sustainability (OPM, 2015). In 2018, sector-specific inspections have been amalgamated into a single robust inspection, therefore mitigating the disruption to the business owner and staff, saving both time and money in the process. The number of inspectors required to carry out the on-site inspection has also been reduced. The Common Policy Framework focuses on four key outcomes *vis-à-vis* compliance: first, relevant inspections are to be conducted in terms of the legal framework; second, businesses are to be empowered to ensure that they have the necessary tools and information in attaining compliance; third, fewer and more robust inspections are conducted to not lose focus and overlaps are minimised; and fourth, improved transparency to ascertain transparency in inspections through the provision of standardised information and reporting mechanisms.

6.3.1.4 Simplification of Dispositions in the VAT and Income Tax Legislation

The intention behind this reform that was introduced in 2014 was to simplify operations and conformity with national fiscal laws. The essential aim of the Government was to assist businesses to pay their fair share without adding new excessive administrative burdens. When VAT returns are submitted in time, together with the payment, the amount paid is not deemed to set off old balances due. This encourages conformity and helps taxpayers who could not conform due to liquidity problems. Under the Value Added Tax Act and the Income Tax Act, the prescribed rate of interest on tax payable or refundable has been reduced and rendered more flexible.

6.3.2   Public Administrative Reforms from a General
           Policy Perspective

In addition to the strengthening of processes that were particularly directed to the economy, a number of other public administrative reforms were introduced in a continuum of general policy realms ranging from disabled persons to pension reforms, sustainability, the environment, the energy sector and transport. The cross-cutting argument that can be elicited in these policy reforms initiated by Malta's national government is that any policy decision requires the public administrative machinery to be effectively implemented and monitored.

As Raipa (2002) argues, public policy incorporates a process about selecting strategies and making choices. In order to achieve the intended results, governments embark on a series of public programmes and projects. Svara's (2002) complimentary model shows the close interconnection between the political executives and public administration in the examination of the strategies, the formulation and particularly the implementation of public policy. In practice, there is no clear separation between administration and politics in the development of government policy and public administration. The policies that Malta's government embarked on, show this close interlink between policymaking and the necessary administration framework stemming from the Public Service. Any legislative and policy decision requires a public administrative engine that is functioning effectively. This section outlines the main policy decisions that the government initiated as from 2013 onwards.

6.3.2.1   Enforcing the 2% Law to Employ Disabled Persons

In 2015, the Persons with Disability (Employment) Act was enforced to balance out the drawbacks and barriers which persons with disability face when seeking employment. The 1969 Act which required organisations employing more than twenty employees should employ at least a 2% quota of disabled persons was enforced by introducing an amount of €10,000 per employer for every person that should have been employed. Furthermore, organisations employing persons with disability are exempted from paying social security contributions related to these employees. They are also entitled to an income tax credit capped at a maximum of €4500 for each person with disability employed. These measures helped the government to achieve the intended results since the number of persons with a disability who were registering for work decreased by 71 when compared to the previous year, reaching 215 (NSO, 2019).

6.3.2.2   Pension Reforms (2015–2017)

The Government ventured to diversify retirement income and reduce dependency on state pensions. State dependency on pensions is unsustainable when considering that the demographic old-age dependency ratio is projected to increase from 29.1%

to 55.8% over the projection period, with the peak year being 2066 (European Commission, 2017). The third pillar personal private pension schemes were launched in 2015 and tax benefits for such products were introduced. Savers undertaking these plans can receive tax rebates on their savings for retirement. In 2016, the Government adopted two measures to strengthen the long-term sustainability of public finances. The first measure encourages later retirement and the second measure links the contributory period to the period spent in retirement. In 2017, the Government also implemented a measure intended to incentivise the take-up of voluntary occupational pensions. Such schemes provide tax credits to both employees and employers (including self-occupied persons). Furthermore, the Government launched the Home Equity Release, which allows home-owners pensioners to raise their annual financial income and improve their standard of living. Such income serves as a financial supplement to the pension, by allowing pensioners to convert part of their residential value into a stream of income.

6.3.2.3   Sustainable Development Framework

Malta is one of the few countries having a specific Sustainable Development Framework model in place which is underpinned by the Sustainable Development Act of 2011 (Legislation Malta, 2020). This legislative framework mandates Government to 'mainstream sustainable development across the workings of Government, to raise awareness of sustainable development issues and practices across society and to promote the adoption of sustainable development practices, as well as to set up a Guardian of Future Generations'. The Act requires the Ministry for the Environment, Sustainable Development and Climate Change (MESDC) to ensure the development and implementation of Malta's Sustainable Development Strategy and to revise the said Strategy in line with national, EU and international developments (MEAE, 2020).

The Permanent Secretary within each Ministry is the Sustainable Development Coordinator. Every Government Department, Agency or Entity has a Sustainable Development Focal Point to assist the Sustainable Development Coordinator in developing the Ministry's position in respect of any request by the Competent Authority. The Guardian of Future Generations has the role of safeguarding intergenerational and intra-generational sustainable development in Malta. The Guardian has the mandate to promote sustainable development advocacy across national policymaking, legislation and practices. Furthermore, the Guardian is empowered to request any Government entity in order to provide data or information or to collect data or information about any topic that could have a bearing on sustainable development. The Guardian can also propose goals and actions to Government entities for them to take up in order to contribute towards the goal of sustainable development. The Act also provides for the Sustainable Development Network aimed at promoting sustainable development in Malta. The Network brings together representatives from NGOs, Government and the private sector to work together toward more sustainable economic, environmental and social solutions. Whilst there has been no budget allocation for Sustainable Development in previous years, the Budget for 2014 has dedicated a budget for the Revision of the National Sustainable Development Strategy.

6.3.2.4   Schemes for Greener Vehicles

As from 2014 onwards, Transport Malta (2020), in conjunction with the Ministry for Transport and Infrastructure, has launched various schemes to incentivise the purchase of new environment-friendly vehicles. The Scheme for the scrapping of old and polluting vehicles is aimed at reducing the number of old motor vehicles from the road and thus reducing pollution. The Scheme for electric vehicles favours the purchase of new electric and hybrid vehicles as well as electric bikes, motor-bikes, mopeds and quads. A grant is also offered to new car importers who would like to upgrade their garage to service electric vehicles and train their staff on this new technology. The Scheme to convert vehicles to Autogas incentivises the conversion of vehicles to Autogas/LPG, which is a cleaner fuel when compared to petrol. As from 2018, the Government has removed the registration tax for all new and used electric vehicles including motorcycles, battery-driven electric mopeds, hydrogen fuel cell electric vehicles, plug-in hybrid electric vehicles and range extender electric vehicles used by individuals, private and commercial companies, NGOs and Local Councils as well as Government Departments. The annual circulation licence fee is also free for the first five years.

6.3.2.5   New Public Transport System

The year 2015 was an eventful year for the Maltese Public Transport. The route network saw the introduction of 24 new routes, modifications on 43 existing routes, 80 new bus stops, 14 new bus bays at the Valletta Bus Terminus and an increase of an average 400 daily trips. 3000 seats were added into the network, creating a 20% increase in capacity. New ticketing systems were installed, and new drivers were recruited locally. 2015 also saw the introduction of a new fare structure and the *tallinja* card, which brought about several benefits to commuters such as faster boarding times leading to reduced journey times, as well as reduced fares for Concessionary Card holders. The new buses are all low floor, have two doors thus making alighting and boarding of passengers quicker, and are better suited to Maltese roads since they are narrower than the remainder of the fleet. By 2019, over 320,000 individuals had a personalised *tallinja* card. Bus use increased by around 20% following the introduction of the card (Times of Malta, 2017).

6.3.2.6   Reform in the Energy Power Generation Sector

Following a major reform of the energy system brought up by a Government policy, Malta implemented a number of measures in the power generation sector, namely: the sourcing of electricity through a sub-marine cable interconnector; the closure of the Marsa Power Station in March 2015; the decommissioning of the old generating units at the Delimara Power Station; the added plant in the Delimara Power Station was converted to run on natural gas instead of heavy fuel oil; and in 2017, Malta shifted to natural gas to generate electricity nationwide. This change has led to improved air quality and reduction in power generation costs nationwide. A further reform has been mentioned several times by the Government in the manner that bills are computed by ARMS Limited given that constant complaints have been lodged by customers when receiving their bills.

6.3.2.7   The SUNFISH Project

Being open to innovation, Malta joined the SUNFISH project in 2015. The project is financed by the European Union and aims to find new solutions for the Public Sector through the integration of cloud systems. The project also seeks to overcome legislative barriers that make the use of available commercial technology solutions difficult. Thanks to SUNFISH, the Taxation Department has merged the different public clouds, which collect data from taxpayers, employers, banks and SMEs, and performs the required calculations and validations while ensuring compliance with the secrecy, privacy and data protection legislations and regulations. SUNFISH reduced the cost for Tax Authorities to operate the systems that collect information from taxpayers and employers, and processes data in a more efficient and effective manner. It has also cut down compliance costs for all businesses.

6.3.3   Public Administrative Reforms to Improve the Internal Processes

The first two sub-sections were focused on national polices and the eventual processes that were introduced post-2013 era. What is crucial to consider is the notion that the competitiveness of a country depends on how effectively its public administration functions. In this respect, a series of reforms were introduced in both the human resources domain, total quality management and the financial aspect. Some of the reforms were mentioned in other chapters but this sub-section is dedicated to crucial Public Service administrative reforms that helped the Public Service to operate better in a manner that helped the Government to implement a series of public policies.

6.3.3.1   Simplification and Standardisation of HRM Policies

The objective of this reform was to reduce the administrative burden through the simplification and standardisation of HRM policies that was launched in 2014. The reviewed HRM policies were intended to enable a more flexible and responsive public administration. The change focused on: first, simplifying and streamlining existing HR procedures through the creation or improvement of SOPs and forms; second, identifying HR processes that can be grouped under one integrated system with a view to reduce duplication of effort; third, strengthening the IT infrastructure to align HR processes for the effective attainment of targets; and fourth, simplifying, through effective delegation, HR processes while ensuring compliance with directives and guidelines.

6.3.3.2   Simplification and Enhancement of eForms

In 2015, a string of eForms from various Government entities have been collected into a common eGovernment platform. The idea was to embark on a direction in which citizens have a single reference to access government services online. Information is collected once at source and is subsequently electronically distributed to the respective Government entity. To complement eForms, other services started to be delivered electronically using the common eGovernment Shared Services. These include application progress tracking; notification services via web, email or SMS; authentication of the citizen's identity through eID; and electronic payments through the Government payment gateway. This reform was a big step towards bringing the Public Service closer to citizens and reducing administrative burdens.

6.3.3.3   TQM to Enhance the Service Quality of Public Services: The Common Assessment Framework

The Common Assessment Framework (CAF) is a total quality management tool inspired by the Excellence Model of the EFQM and the model of the German University of Administrative Sciences in Speyer. The main purpose of the CAF is to support the European Public Sector Administrations in improving their performance through quality management techniques. It is an easy to use tool and is free of charge; available in the public domain and it has been intended to be used across all sections of the public sector applicable to local, regional, national/federal, European public organisations. According to the European Institute of Public Administration (EIPA), the CAF intends to be a facilitator for a full advancement process within the organisations and comprises of five principles: first, to introduce public administrations to the principles of Total Quality Management and thus instigate a culture of excellence; second, to continuously guide them to completely develop a Plan-Do-Check-Act (PDCA) cycle; third, to simplify the self-assessment of a public administration with the intention of identifying issues and proceed on improvement actions; fourth, to act as a bridge across the different quality management models both in private and public sectors; and fifth, to enable bench learning between organisations in the public-sector.

The strategic policy framework designed to develop quality management systems between 2014 and 2020 is based on a vision of a professional, expedient Public Service which is close to its service users. This falls part of Malta's *ex-ante* conditionality (no. 11) under 'Thematic Objective 11 – Enhancing institutional capacity of public authorities and stakeholders and efficient public administration'. Consequently, the promotion and implementation of the Common Assessment Framework (CAF) was identified as one of the four key strategic objectives that are the pillars of this strategic policy framework. The CAF is a crucial tool in order to encourage sustainability and high-quality performance. The underlying principle of this tool is based on leadership as being the driving factor in directing policy and strategy to deliver excellent results in performance, customers, people and society. The model is practiced in at least 3750 public organisations in 53 countries. Three types of training had been delivered:

- Specialised Training Programme in CAF, delivered by CAF experts, to MEU staff (14 in total);
- CAF Model Training Programme, delivered by CAF experts, to six groups of public officials;
- Procedure on External Feedback training and the CAF Label Training Programmes delivered to MEU staff and public officials.

The Management Efficiency Unit (MEU) oversees overseeing the implementation of this strategy. MEU (2020) have conducted a feasibility study to identify the most suitable management tool for the context of the Maltese Public Service. CAF was identified as a potential effective management tool since it is specifically targeted for public administrations, cost-effective, flexible and adaptable. MEU's goal is to become the Maltese CAF Centre of expertise by strengthening its in-house capacity. Furthermore, Public Service officials were provided with training. As can be observed in Table 6.1, a total of 365 officials have been trained, both locally and overseas. The number of participants gaining a qualification was extremely high: 98%. In all indicators, the actual results achieved exceeded the indicators set (Table 6.1).

Table 6.1 CAF Indicators

Indicators	Type	Target	Actual
Number of persons participating in training	Output	200	365
% of participants gaining a qualification/certificate	Result	74.6%	98%
Increase in the number of adult participation in lifelong learning	Impact	0.058%	0.095%

Source: Data extracted from the Project Closure Report of ESF4.159 – Developing Quality Management in the Public Administration through CAF

There are now 16 sites officially registered on the European Institute of Public Administration (EIPA): the Gozo Public Library, the Food Safety Unit, the Gozo Sports Complex, the Foundation for Social Welfare Services (FSWS), Sedqa, Sapport and Appoġġ Agencies, the European Union Programmes Agency (EUPA), the MEU, the Ministry for the Economy, Investment and Small Business (MEIB), the Department of Contracts, the Health Standards Directorate, Automated Revenue Management Services (ARMS) Ltd., the Medical Imaging Department, Programme Implementation Directorate within the Education Department and the Ministry for Finance. The Health Promotion and Disease Unit and the Water Services Corporation had finalised the self-assessment meetings. Considering all actions undertaken as well as the indicators achieved, the Common Assessment Framework (CAF) Certification has been completed. 10 CAF users and 2 Effective CAF Label have been targeted as per project ESF 4.159. MEU has introduced the CAF tool through additional training sessions to 15 entities. Four of the CAF User Organisations were awarded the 'Effective CAF User' Label.

6.3.3.4   The Financial Management Reform of the Public Service

There is an increasing focus on improving the quality of public financial management around the globe, with many countries making important achievements in strengthening public financial management and governance. Nonetheless, much remains to be done. The Public Service landscape is rapidly changing with an increasing emphasis on fiscal management and discipline, prioritisation of expenditure and value for money. As a result, it is even more important that governments, national and local institutions, including regulators and professional accountancy bodies, work together in partnership to achieve long-lasting improvements, transparency and accountability in public financial management. The introduction of the Fiscal Responsibility Act that was approved by the Maltese Parliament in 2014 was a milestone in terms of introducing controls on public expenditure. The aims of the law were to increase efficiency in expenditure, set ceilings and introduce more controls on public expenditure. Although the government had obligations with the EU, there had been no legal provisions on transparency locally before this law was enacted.

The Fiscal Responsibility Act is a guideline for those who work in the civil service, so that responsible decisions are taken with a sense of accountability and more awareness of the obligation to conduct financial affairs with transparency, stability and effectiveness. It is a bill to establish greater responsibility in government expenditure. The Bill imposes a statutory duty on the Treasury to meet specific targets for the reduction of government borrowing and debt. The Act communicates the government's commitment to ensuring the sustainability of the public finances.

In line with the new law, the government started to publish a three-year rolling plan listing its fiscal policy and priorities. A Fiscal Council was set-up which, as a main function, had the task to oversee the financial plan and prepare an annual report on its implementation. The council's chairman is appointed following consultation with the Opposition and could only be removed by a Parliamentary resolution. The main purpose of the Fiscal Council is to review and assess the extent to which the fiscal and economic policy objectives proposed by the Maltese Government are being achieved and thus contribute to more transparency and clarity about the aims and effectiveness of economic policy in Malta. Whereas in the budget the government look back at the preceding year, a detailed report in March or April is prepared, enabling the collection of data to cover a whole year. The law also stipulates the drawing up of a half-yearly report on that year's plan with details on any variances. This would be followed by the draft budget and then the budget. Although the law also stipulated contingency reserves to cover slip-ups or over-expenditure, these would have to be justified with the Fiscal Council. The Fiscal Council is subsequently answerable to the Public Accounts Committee.

Salient points of the Act include the 'Budget Rule' and the 'Debt Rule' – this will require that the budget, baring 'exceptional circumstances' should be in balance or in surplus, or the structural budget is converging towards medium term budget objectives in line with a set time frame. The 'Debt Rule' will require that when the debt-to-GDP ratio exceeds 60% of the gross domestic product, this would be reduced. Another major transformation of the Public Service from a financial management perspective is the implementation of accrual accounting, which the Government of Malta switched to in the year 2017. As a start, 10 pilot sites were considered and eventually integrated system testing phase. Three pillars were of fundamental importance for the transition to an accrual accounting system. The first pillar pertains to the transformation of the present cash-based Departmental Accounting System (DAS) which will be replaced by a full-accrual accounting package, the Corporate Financial Management Solution (CFMS). The second pillar rests on the assurance that a proper Finance Function exists within each ministry and department. The third pillar is essentially based on the introduction of Accrual Accounting standards. In 2011, the Malta Government Accounting Standards Committee agreed that the International Public Sector Accounting Standards (IPSAS) as a way forward for Malta.

The major challenges for the introduction of accrual accounting are various. From a system perspective, it is crucial that ministries are not allowed to keep on using their existing accounting practices since it would serve as a barrier to implement the accrual accounting system across the entire Public Service. From a process point of view, all financial transactions will need to be reviewed in order to transform the entire system to accrual accounting based on international standards. This would be an opportunity to address control mechanisms. From a people staffing perspective, relatively few staff within Government have the necessary accountancy qualifications. The finance function in some ministries is already stretched and, from a governing financial standpoint, this would lead to a weak financial control system. Therefore, the availability of qualified and experienced accounting personnel at all levels is of fundamental importance for the implementation of the accrual accounting system. The training of staff is to be coordinated in order to ensure effectiveness of the entire system. From a programme management outlook, a central leading driver is to lead the full transition to accrual accounting and a communications strategy is vital to the success of the system.

6.3.3.5   eProcurement

Reference to the eProcurement system has already been made in the context of enhanced structures. But since better financial management goes together with ICT improvements, it should be addressed in this regard too. The new eProcurement system ensures that the capital expenditure of Government is employed in an economical, transparent and accountable manner. In fact, it even records post-award transactions such as modifications and payments, eAuctions, framework agreements, dynamic purchasing systems and the publication of contract and award notices to the *Official Journal of the EU*

The Electronic Public Procurement System (ePPS) is the national platform for eProcurement (Public Service, 2020), designed and developed specifically for the Public Service Administration to procure supplies, services and works. It covers the entire procurement cycle, from notification of a call for tenders to the fulfilment of the contract. eProcurement has provided the opportunity to decentralise the function and responsibility for major procurement tenders to the individual Ministries and the Department of Contracts to act as the regulator to ensure the adherence of the procurement regulations. The main benefit of eProcurement is reduction of costs and bureaucracy.

6.4   Conclusion: Three Main Lessons Elicited from the Organisational and Management Reforms

This chapter revisited the government reforms from a broad organisational and management perspective by eliciting three main facets of reforms: first, structural reforms that have directly and indirectly influenced the Public Service; second, national government policy reforms that required the complimentary coordination of Malta's public administration and third, the specific organisational and management reforms within the Public Service. The conclusive argument is that the organisation and management of government reforms have responded to emerging challenges that required both policy-oriented and legislative solutions. The aim of the Government was to reduce the bureaucratic administrative procedures and, in parallel, evolve a dynamic vertical and horizontal service-based approach to fulfil the citizens and businesses requirements at a high sophisticated level in line with the government's strategy to deliver a service of excellence. The organisational and management reform is not a one-time occasion but rather a constant change. Much more is required to be done if the Public Service is to keep up with the rapidly changing environment. The reforms outlined in this chapter are largely supported by the policy making coordination and implementation reforms, which are elaborated further in the next chapter.

References

CEDEFOP. (2020). *Malta: The National Skills Council – Improving Skills Governance*. Available at: https://www.cedefop.europa.eu/en/news-and-press/news/malta-national-skills-council-improving-skills-governance.

Commissioner for Simplification. (2020). Available at: https://simplificationcms.gov.mt/en/Pages/home.aspx.

Esplora. (2020). *Esplora: Malta Interactive Centre – European Regional Development Fund 2007–2013*. Available at: https://esplora.org.mt/about/.

European Commission. (2017). *Malta: Country Fiche on Pension Projections (2016–2070)*. Available at: https://ec.europa.eu/info/sites/info/files/economy-finance/final_country_fiche_mt.pdf.

Huerta Melchor, O. (2008). *Managing Change in OECD Governments: An Introductory Framework*, OECD working papers on public governance, no. 12, OECD publishing, © OECD. https://doi.org/10.1787/227141782188

Legislation Malta. (2020). *Sustainable development act 2011*. Available at: http://justiceservices.gov.mt/DownloadDocument.aspx?app=lp&itemid=22669&l=1.

Malta Enterprise. (2020). *MicroInvest*. Available at: http://www.maltaenterprise.com/support/micro-invest.

Management Efficiency Unit (MEU). (2020). *CAF Malta: For a quality public administration*. Available at: https://meu.gov.mt/en/Pages/Projects-CAF.aspx.

Matei, L. & Matei, A. (2010). *The Economic and Social Impact of Public Administration Europeanization*, published in: 32nd EGPA conference "temporalities, public administration and public policies" proceedings, 7-10 sept.2010, Toulouse, France (10 September 2010).

Matheson, A., Scanlan, G. & Tanner, R. (1996). *Strategic Management in Government: Extending the Reform Model in New Zealand*, Paper presented to the OECD's Public Management Service. Available at: http://www.oecd.org/dataoecd/12/10/1902913.pdf.

Ministry for Education and Employment (MEDE). (2020). *National skills council*. Available at: https://education.gov.mt/en/Pages/National-Skills-Council.aspx.

Ministry for the Environment, Sustainable Development and Climate Change (MEAE). (2020). *Malta's sustainable development vision for 2050*. Available at: https://meae.gov.mt/en/Public_Consultations/MSDEC/Documents/Malta%27s%20Sustainable%20Development%20Vision%20for%202050.pdf.

National Audit Office (NAO). (2017). *Press release: An analysis on revenue collection*. Available at: https://nao.gov.mt/en/press-releases/4/183/an-analysis-of-revenue-collection.

National Statistics Office (NSO). (2019). *News release: Registered unemployed - February 2019*. Available at: https://nso.gov.mt/en/News_Releases/View_by_Unit/Unit_C2/Labour_Market_Statistics/Documents/2019/News2019_050.pdf.

National Statistics Office (NSO). (2020). *Gross domestic product*. Available at: https://nso.gov.mt/en/News_Releases/View_by_Unit/Unit_A1/National_Accounts/Pages/Gross-Domestic-Product.aspx.

Office of the Prime Minister (OPM), Office of the Principal Permanent Secretary. (2015). *Government response to public feedback on improving business inspections*. Available at: https://meae.gov.mt/en/public_consultations/opm/documents/1-17-2015%20improving%20business%20inspection/consultation%20outcome%20report%20-%20improving%20business%20inspections.pdf.

Public Service. (2020). *A National Platform for eProcurement*. Available at: https://publicservice.gov.mt/en/Pages/News/2020/20200219_EPPS.aspx.

Raipa, A. (2002). Public policy and public administration: Development, structure and reciprocity, public policy and administration, Mykolas Romeris University.

Svara, J. H. (2002). The myth of the dichotomy: Complementarity of politics and Administration in the Past and Future of public administration. *Public Administration Review, 61*(2), 176–183.

Times of Malta. (2017). *Over 500 complaints to the arbiter in one year*. Available at: https://timesofmalta.com/articles/view/over-500-complaints-to-financial-arbiter-in-one-year.645280.

Transport Malta. (2020). Schemes for Greener Vehicles. Available at: https://news.transport.gov.mt/schemes-for-greener-vehicles/.

Chapter 7
Policy Making, Coordination and Implementation Government Reforms

"Above the policies, above the law, above the government, above the constitution, there is a higher principle, that is the principle of individual integrity, without which no matter how much policies and laws we create, we cannot ensure health, safety and sanity in the society."

Abhijit Naskar
Neuroscientist and Author

This chapter provides a detailed review and analysis of all the major reforms that were initiated and subsequently implemented by Malta's Government from the year 2013 onwards, regarding policy making, coordination and implementation. It expands on the theme of the previous chapter that focused on the interaction of public policy with the public administrative framework. The Government's progressive and contemporary policy design augmented the quality level through the application of standards; the reprioritisation of the political agenda; and the revamping of how key policy sectors are managed. These have changed significantly the country's political direction. Significant advancement has been made in implementing national policies so that Malta is more compliant with EU directives. The structural reforms have resulted in a substantial increase in all revenue streams reflecting the sustained and robust performance of the Maltese economy. Despite all the policy reforms, the only constant feature is change. It is contended that much more policy reforms are required, especially in the new COVID-19 era, to transform the citizen's lives drastically for the better.

7.1   Introduction: Crafting, Coordinating and Implementing a Diverse Array of Policies

Policy coordination is one of the oldest challenges for governments (Peters, 2018), and remains a headache for all national governments especially in an era of multi-level governance where governments have to deal with both internal and external stakeholders emanating from the needs and aspirations of so many diverse pressure groups, and the external pressures emanating from international institutions and the EU. To complicate matters, governments have to confront the rapidly changing environment which presents a situation where the executive arm have to take decisions in a relatively short period of time, while in parallel ensuring that the necessary consultative process is being held in all policy areas. This is a dilemma that every government must face in a highly vibrant, complex and unpredictable world of policymaking.

This chapter presents a comprehensive analysis of the vast portfolio of policy changes that were introduced and implemented by Malta's national government as from 2013 onwards. The policy changes must be analysed as part and parcel of the concurrent public administration renewal, which was a top priority for the newly elected Government. This was the argument postulated in the previous chapters, specifically in Chap. 6. Reforms go together with Government policies that are defined, coordinated and implemented either through legislative action or administrative endeavours. The policy reforms are classified under six categories: first, policies supported by EU funds; second, the robust fiscal and economic reforms initiated by the government; third, the widespread social reforms especially in the eradication of poverty, childcare and civil rights; fourth, the reforms in the education sector mainly by integrating more education with employment; fifth, the dilemma of balancing the environmental concerns with the economic exigencies; and sixth, multi-level governing reforms.

7.2   Crafting Policies Supported by European Union (EU) Funds

The Public Service is the means towards helping national governments to absorb EU funds. Malta has always had a success, as from EU accession in 2004, in absorbing funding that translates into investment in so many policy areas. The level of absorption has been high, achieving an impressive rate of almost 100% (Malta Independent, 2017). EU funding is a classical illustration of the interoperability of policymaking, coordination and monitoring and provides an avenue of extensive stakeholder involvement both from within and from outside the Public Service. Malta's Public Service has benefited from EU Cohesion Policy through 'Thematic Objective 11' by investing in institutional capacity to be able to reinvest itself and, at the same time manage EU funds appropriately (European Commission, 2020a, 2020b). This example shows the repeated intertwining of policymaking with the strengthening of the public administrative capacity that was demonstrated in Chapter 6. To portray in a clear manner the interaction between the Public Service and EU funding, three important structures are being delineated.

7.2.1   Policy Development and Programme Implementation Directorate

The Policy Development and Programme Implementation Directorate contributes towards enhancing policy development and formulation by keeping abreast of the policies being proposed and discussed by the EU, as well as through the dissemination of documentation and any other related information emanating from both the EU and other international institutions. Besides, the Directorate is responsible for ensuring that policies at both EU and international levels are coherent and consistent with Government-wide policies.

7.2.2   The Planning and Priorities Co-ordination Division

The Planning and Priorities Co-ordination Division (PPCD) was set-up as part of the administrative infrastructure required to manage the pre- and post-accession funds allocated to Malta by the European Union. PPCD aims to ensure the efficient absorption and management of European assistance, particularly in relation to Cohesion Policy, through effective co-ordination across Government Departments, Authorities, Agencies and other stakeholders. PPCD is the Managing Authority for the European Structural and Investment Funds (ESIF) 2014-2020. During the 2014-2020 programming period, PPCD has embarked on setting up a results-based monitoring and evaluation system as a tool to track progress and demonstrate the impact of this programme. Elements of the results-based monitoring and evaluation system include: baseline data to describe the problem or situation before the intervention; data collection on results and whether they contribute towards the achievement of the outcomes stated in the Grant Agreement; systemic reporting with more qualitative and quantitative information on the progress toward outcomes; and capture of information on success or failure of strategy/programmes in achieving desired outcomes.

7.2.3   Measures and Support Division

The Measures and Support Division aims to ensure the effective administration and implementation of EU-funded support measures to enterprises, through effective liaison with internal and external stakeholders. Set-up in 2015, the Division is mandated to ensure the strategic management, administration and implementation of

EU funded measures to support enterprises by taking up the function of an intermediary body for measures funded through the European Regional Development Fund 2014-2020, and acting as the national contact point for the implementation of aid measures funded through the European Structural and Investment Funds (ESIF) 2014-2020.

7.2.4 Minister for European Affairs and Implementation of the Electoral Manifesto

After the General Elections of March 2013, when the Labour Government came into power, a new portfolio was created in the form of a minister responsible for European Affairs and Implementation of the Electoral Manifesto. This new portfolio anticipated the need that EU funding is exploited to the maximum allowable level and that measures announced in the Labour Party manifesto, and specifically in the Budget, including the Public Administration reform measures, are coordinated and realistically implemented. This new ministerial portfolio reveals the creation of new governing structures both at political level and at a purely administrative level.

7.3 Robust Fiscal and Economic Reforms Initiated by Government

Chapter 6 has assessed several fiscal and economic reforms that were initiated by the Government as part of its robust approach to generate economic activity. This sub-section analyses further initiatives that were meant to inject greater economic prosperity.

7.3.1 Global Residence Programme

The Global Residence Programme was launched in June 2013 with the baim to boost various economic sectors in Malta while attracting investment and talent of persons outside the European Union and outside the European Economic Area. The main aim of this programme was to revitalise the property sector by increasing property purchase in Malta, while allowing the country to get more money in taxes, increasing work, even to professionals in this sector such as lawyers and tax consultants. The Global residence programme also aimed to help three major economic sectors namely: the financial services industry, the leisure industry and the hospitality industry (Malta Government, 2013).

7.3.2   Malta Individual Investor Programme

Malta has invested in this highly controversial programme in 2014, also known as Citizenship by Investment, to enrich its human capital and attract market leaders who can provide added value by sharing their business acumen, know-how, experiences, skills and funding that contribute towards society by stimulating business, increasing job creation, increasing revenue and augmenting human capital. As of January 2020, the Malta Individual Investor Programme (MIIP) has reached the expected threshold of 1,800 Malta passport applications on behalf of investors from more than 40 different countries. The revenues generated from the programme had contributed significantly to the National Development and Social Fund (NDSF), which money was subsequently invested in large social projects such as social housing. A total of 50 million Euros were invested for the 500 new social housing units to be built at 22 different sites, across 12 localities around the Maltese Islands (Malta Government, 2019a, 2019b).

7.3.3   MicroInvest, JEREMIE and JAIME Schemes

The Government has extended the MicroInvest and JEREMIE schemes for SMEs as a policy to boast economic activity. MicroInvest encourages undertakings to invest in their business, innovate, expand and implement compliance directives or to develop their operations. These business undertakings, including self-employed persons, are supported through a tax credit representing a percentage of the eligible expenditure and wages of newly recruited employees. JAIME is a financing package that builds on the success of the preceding JEREMIE financing package. Both schemes support the SME sector by addressing challenges such as financing, guarantees and undercapitalisation. They provide financing for capital investment and related working capital at advantageous interest rates and reduced collateral obligations. These SME initiatives are funded by the European Regional Development Fund allocated to the Government of Malta and Horizon 2020 and by the European Investment Bank.

7.3.4   Macroeconomic Forecasts for the Maltese Economy

The creation of new ministerial portfolios and governing structures were not only created in European Affairs. In 2015, the Malta Fiscal Advisory Council (MFAC) was set-up in terms of the Fiscal Responsibility Act, 2014 (Cap. 534 of the Laws of Malta). The MFAC monitors the Government's compliance with fiscal rules and assesses both the macroeconomic and the fiscal forecasts presented within the Draft Budgetary Plan, prepared by various entities within Government, primarily the

Economic Policy Department within the Ministry for Finance. This new set-up was crucial to start monitoring the performance of the Maltese economy.

7.3.5   Barts Medical University in Gozo

In 2019, the Government has invested €35 million to transform the Gozo General Hospital into a medical hub. The project was aimed to further attract foreign investment to Malta and paved the way to amalgamate the economic and health sectors to gain a competitive advantage for a small island state such as Malta and specifically for the community of the sister island, Gozo. The new Barts Medical University is intended to not only create new jobs and improve the local health services, but would also turn Malta into a niche for medical tourism, given its fluent use of the English language and a health service that already enjoys international appraisal (Malta Government, 2019a, 2019b).

7.4   Social Reforms: Widespread Reform in Childcare and Civil Rights

National economic progress is a means towards ensuring the citizens have a better standard of living. This is achievable if economic growth is redistributed fairly to ensure that everyone is not suffering from relative poverty and to ensure an effective social safety net. To achieve this aim, the Government embarked on several policy reforms targeting poverty reduction, social inclusion, active aging, education, employability, civil rights for minority groups specifically LGBT and responsible gaming. Therefore, economic reforms were mitigated by a series of social initiatives. In order to introduce a series of social reforms, the government has embarked on a direction to improve the relationship between civil society and Government while maintaining transparency. The Government launched an online platform in 2015 in order to encourage the general public, civil society organisations, trade unions, business organisations, political parties and governmental institutions to participate in the process of public consultation.

7.4.1   National Strategic Policy for Poverty Reduction and for Social Inclusion

The Government was committed to pursue political and economic policies which provide for the weak and vulnerable members of its society. A national strategic policy framework against poverty and social exclusion was implemented, aiming at enhancing social protection systems and promoting activation measures, to creating more employment opportunities and facilitating mobility and de-segmentation in the labour market, to addressing educational inequalities, ensuring equal access to quality healthcare, promoting an environmental health friendly approach, decentralising and integrating social services at community level, developing evidence-based policies and practices that address emerging needs and challenges, and enhancing the potential for equality and social inclusion through everyday culture. An inter-ministerial committee has been set-up to monitor the progress and consolidate Malta's commitment in this sphere (MFSS, 2014). Worth noting is the fact that AROPE (at risk of poverty or social exclusion) rate in Malta stood at 20.1%, which is below the euro area average of 23.1%. When compared with 2010, this indicates a drop of 1.1 percentage points, which compares rather favourably with other Member States, the majority of which experienced an increase in poverty rates during the same period (Central Bank, 2018).

7.4.2   Free Childcare Scheme

The Government has raised the standard of living of families by providing the opportunity for employment to many female employees through the provision of free childcare services. In 2014, the Government has kept its electoral promise of providing free childcare services to parents or guardians who are in employment or are pursuing their education, with the aim to help families achieve a work-life balance. It also incentivises women, who stopped working in order to raise their children, to return to the labour market. As from April 2014 until the end of December 2018, a total of 16,000 children have been enjoying free childcare. A total of 21,000 parents have benefited as a result of this measure. The number of childcare centres increased from 69 to 129 and the total government investment was 63 million. Furthermore, other services were introduced such as the Klabb 3-16, which is an after-school hour service and the Breakfast Club; two service geared towards bridging the gap between school and the parents' working hours and providing supervision to children before and after traditional school hours.

7.4.3   National Strategic Policy for Active Ageing

Other policies and strategies were introduced to deal with sectors that form the societal fabric of a state and that require special attention. In 2014, the National Strategic Policy for Active Ageing: Malta 2014-2020 constitutes a turning point for the local ageing policy. This is especially in view of the baby boom generation (people born between 1946 and 1964) currently accounts for 25.9 per cent of the total Maltese population. The share of the elderly population (aged 65 and more) in total population has grown substantially in the past decades in comparison to the other age groups. Persons aged 65 or older accounted for 3.0 per cent of total population in 1980; this ratio increased to 19.1 per cent by 2016; and in 2070 it is projected to reach 30.6 per cent of total population. Furthermore, the share of older workers (55-64) in employment (20-64) is projected to increase from 14.1 per cent in 2016 to 18.3 per cent in 2070. (MFIN, 2019: 11). As a result, the need for a comprehensive policy for active ageing was important. The three cornerstones of the National Strategic Policy are: active participation in the labour market; participation in society; and independent living. The National Strategic Policy embraces the concept of active ageing as an ideal development where older citizens have ample prospects to participate in the formal labour market, as well as engage in other unpaid productive activities ranging from leisurely pursuits, informal care and volunteering while leading a healthy, independent and secure lifestyle National Commission for Active Ageing XE "Active ageing" 2014).

7.4.4   Social Policies Related to LGBT Rights

The change in Government in 2013 brought with it several other crucial and revolutionary social policies that specifically targeted LGBT groups. The Civil Unions Act was enacted in 2014 including the right to joint adoption. The Cohabitation Act went into effect in 2017, which recognises cohabiting couples who have been living together for at least two years and gives cohabitants more rights pertaining to parental and medical decisions, among others. Same-sex marriage has been legalised in 2017. In line with the Gender Identity, Gender Expression and Sex Characteristics Act, citizens can change their gender on official documents and records. Besides, an X identifier has been introduced to denote undisclosed/undetermined gender. The age of consent (16 years of age) has been made equal for all. In 2018, the Embryo Protection Act 2012 has been amended to allow IVF access for single women and lesbians.

7.4.5   Responsible Gaming Foundation

The economic progress and the advent of robust gaming sector has brought with it several social problems. In 2014, an independent Foundation emerged following the debate in Parliament on the amendments of the Lotteries and Other Games Act (Cap. 438 of the Laws of Malta) to introduce regulations governing land-based gaming parlours. The Responsible Gaming Foundation was founded to create a wider awareness of the extent, possible causes and consequences of problem gaming in Malta with a view to preventing it and to provide the necessary support and advice to problem gamblers and their dependents in their recovery efforts.

7.5 Reforms in Education: Integrating Further Education with Employment

The reforms that in the previous chapters referred to the setup of the Institute for Public Services (IPS) were focused on a public administrative strategic alliance that amalgamates the function of training and development with the academic and vocational learning of those employed in Public Administration, thus supporting the coordination, development and capacity building of its employees, in line with the corporate strategy of the current Government Administration. The IPS does not work in isolation, it coordinates the bulk of its courses in conjunction with Higher Education Institutions (HEIs) and Jobsplus (Government's employment agency), thus enabling participants to learn the practical aspects of the skills and trades. This shows the hybrid of training, education and employment that was reflected in education policies, as exposed in the following sub-sections.

7.5.1 Higher Education Strategy for Malta

The Higher Education Strategy (MEDE, 2014) recommends four priority areas for action: (1) To increase participation and higher education attainment rather than leaving school early; (2) To reduce gender differences in different areas of studies; (3) To encourage innovative content and programme design; and (4) To increase employability and entrepreneurship. To ensure the quality and relevance of higher education, a single national Quality Assurance Agency for the accreditation and licensing of higher education providers has been established. The NCFHE performs the role of this agency, is government funded and appointed, but has enough legal and operational independence to carry out its role. The strategy highlights the importance to match higher education with employment although the two main public HEIs in Malta, that have 75% of the entire market share, have a wider role to sustain their responsibility for Malta's social exigencies. As from 2015, a new University of Malta Act has been in discussion but until the time of writing the Act has still not been published. It must be seen how such an institutional act will be working in tandem with the current Education Act of 1988.

7.5.2 Policy on Inclusive Education in Schools

The Policy on Inclusive Education in Schools views inclusive education as a continuous developmental process focused on understanding how children learn, identification and removal of barriers to learning, and participation in all schools by facilitating organisational renewal and strengthening internal capacities. It aims at supporting school leaders to monitor the quality and standards in inclusive practice, and to identify strengths, school development priorities, staff training, improvements in teaching/learning strategies for all identified themes, and ways to enhance the inclusion process in schools (MEDE, 2019). The ultimate aim of this policy was that in line with the Education Strategy of the Ministry of Education and Employment (MEDE), as stated in the *Framework for Education Strategy for Malta 2014-2024,* it promotes the setting of an inclusive educational setting that ensures that all learners have the opportunity to obtain the necessary knowledge, skills and attitudes to be active citizens and to succeed at work and in society.

The intertwining of education, the economy, the labour market and ultimately the societal needs can be also observed in two policy initiatives, one that encompasses all youths, so that they are active in either education and employment, and the other on a specific economic sector, the construction industry. The construction industry is a major economic driver in Malta with the core construction activities contributing €694.12 million in gross value added. When considering the direct and indirect impact, the Construction and Real Estate sectors contribute around 13.5% of Malta's GVA. Moreover, from 2016 to 2017, direct, indirect and induced output grew by 8.9% to €2.56 billion. Full-time employment in the sector also grew by 8.9% to 37,428 (MDA, 2017).

7.5.3 Construction Industry Skill Card

The Construction Industry Skill Card (CISC) was implemented in 2015. The policy goal is to help address the shortage of skills in the construction industry. It also aims to improve quality standards, health and safety practices, and employment conditions in this sector. The policy instrument creates an official method of recognition for people that have worked in the construction industry for years and never had their technical knowledge recognised. Apart from this, construction workers can benefit from training that will, in turn, lead to higher construction standards, including in health and safety as well as employment conditions (CEDEFOP, 2020).

7.5.4 Youth Guarantee Scheme

The Youth Guarantee scheme, which was introduced in Malta in 2014, is an EU-funded project developed for young citizens aged 15 to 25. It consists of education and employment-related initiatives. Based on preventive and assistive measures, each opportunity is designed to help young citizens continue their education or increase their chances of finding satisfaction and success in the world of work. The aim is to increase the global percentage of employment rate. Over the decade, through this initiative and other measures, Malta has had the largest employment rate increase (by 13.8 % to 73 %) in the EU, exceeding their 2020 target and the EU average (72.1 %). The activity rate (75.8 %) rose but remains below the EU average (78 %). The unemployment rate (4 %) is well below the EU average, including for young people (15-24, 10.6 %) and for long-term unemployment (1.6 %) European Commission, 2020a: 4, 2020b).

7.6   The Dilemma of Bablancing the Environmental Concerns with the Economic Exigencies

The main criticism levelled at the Labour Government, as from 2013, was that the robust and aggressive economic development was gradually harming the environment especially in a micro-state which is the most densely populated state in the European Union with 1,380 inhabitants per square kilometre. The counterargument has been that several environment reforms have improved substantially the air quality as well as the waste management.

7.6.1   Energy Policy on Using Gas as an Alternative to Heavy Fuel Oil

The energy reform was indeed a main platform of the Government's electoral pledge that sought to implement through the introduction of a new Energy Policy in 2013, the Government have shifted from using heavy fuel oil in its electricity generation mix to natural gas. This shift was primarily intended to improve the air quality and reduce energy generation costs. The project included the building of a new plant in Delimara and the decommissioning of the old energy generating units. By shifting to an energy mix based on natural gas later this year, the Government had the primary objective of saving almost one million tonnes of CO^2 emissions, whilst other pollutants, including particulate matter, will decrease by 90%. Getting rid of this air pollution and its effects on residents in Marsaxlokk and other areas in the southern part of the Island, is one of the best environmental projects ever undertaken to improve air quality in Malta and Gozo (Enemalta, 2016a). In parallel with this mega project, in 2015, the Prime Minister of Malta and the Prime Minister of Italy inaugurated the Malta-Italy interconnector, linking the Maltese electricity grid to the European energy network. Apart from continuing a project that was initiated by the previous Nationalist Government, the Labour Government sought safety and stability in the energy provision through the interconnector.

7.6.2   Dismantling the Marsa Electricity Power Station

In 2015, the Marsa Power Station was switched off and put on cold standby, pending final decommissioning. The actual dismantling process started in 2014, just a few months before March of the year 2015. As the new gas fired Delimara plants were undergoing final testing and started generating electricity, the Marsa Power Station was no longer required to remain on cold standby (Enemalta, 2016b). In 2017, it was completely disconnected from the national grid and started to be demolished. Apart from its outdated and highly pollutant use, the Marsa power station was considered as creating an eye-sore at the south of Malta.

7.6.3   Dismantling the Oil Storage Tanks at Birżebbuġa

Safety and stability of energy provision was also a priority when the Government decided to dismantle the oil storage tanks in Birżebbuġa in 2017, which were used to store petrol and diesel for the domestic market. Instead, existing underground storage tanks have been refurbished and upgraded with modern safety features to be used for the storage of domestic fuels. Since existing infrastructure was used for this project, no environmental issues were created.

7.6.4   Malta's National Air Pollution Control Programme

In addition to tangible projects, in 2019, the National Air Pollution Control Programme (NAPCP) was deemed as another step towards achieving air quality objectives and ensures coherence with other relevant plans and programmes including climate, energy, agriculture, industry and transport policy areas. The NAPCP is intended to guide Malta to further reduce air pollution and its associated risks to the environment and human health. Pursuant to Article 6 of the National Emission Ceilings Directive, Malta must reflect its emission reduction commitments by submitting an NAPCP every four years. The pollutants targeted by the programme in line with EU Directives Nitrogen Oxides, Sulphur Dioxide, Ammonia, Non-methane Volatile Organic Compounds and Fine Particular Matter (Environment and Resources Authority, 2019).

7.6.5   New State-of-the-Art Waste Management Facilities

The second major environment reform introduced by the current Government was concerning Waste Management. Waste is another perennial problem that has been accumulating for decades. Under the EU targets, at least 55% of municipal waste must be recycled by 2025, rising to 60% by 2030. State-of-the-art waste management facilities were announced in 2020 intended to drive the country towards a circular economy, with all waste streams being reutilised to their full potential. This largest ever investment in the waste management sector will take Malta to a new level, not only in waste management, but also in the country's overall environmental performance and recycling targets. The investment includes pillars in waste management such as the much-needed waste-to-energy plant which will in itself significantly limit our landfilling volumes, a new plant for the management of dry recyclables, a plant to treat organic waste to extract energy and produce compost for use in agriculture, as well as the replacement of the clinical and abattoir waste incinerator. The required land for the infrastructure of this project was drastically reduced, having taken into consideration the valid pleas from local farming communities. In fact, the project will now have a footprint of 82,000m² as opposed to the original proposal of 279,000m². The original plan to turn 150,000m² of land in an extended landfill has been shelved. Instead, Wasteserv is aiming to have the waste to energy plant in place ahead of what was originally planned and current landfill sites within the existing footprint will be used to their full potential. The facilities will be situated at Magħtab in a bid to centralise Wasteserv's operations, thereby increasing efficiency and minimising any adverse environmental impacts of said operations (Malta Government, 2020).

7.6.6 Placement of iBins at Various Locations

Other reforms targeted to facilitate the separation of waste from households and the better use of plastic which is harming Malta's environment especially its sea. In 2018, iBins were introduced. The iBins constitute a smart technological solution to the waste problem by making recycling simpler and more convenient to citizens, and to also make the overflowing of recycling bins and bring-in sites a thing of the past. The iBins have the capability to monitor waste levels and feed information back to a central system which enables GreenPak's recycling service to prioritise and customise collection routes across Malta and Gozo. The signal is also available to the general public through an App, wherein citizens can find the closest bin to their location. The iBin can also detect its temperature and, in the case of a fire, a special signal is sent to the emergency services.

7.6.7 Single-Use Plastic Products Strategy for Malta 2020-2030

In 2019, the Single-use Plastic Products Strategy for Malta to further help the transition for Malta to move towards a more circular economy and hence closing the loop of products' lifecycles was introduced. This strategy is intended to help protect our environment and human health from plastic pollution while reducing litter and consumption of single-use plastic products and increasing the quality and quantities of single-use plastic waste collected and recycled (MEAE, 2019).

7.7   Multi-Level Governing Reforms

The interplay of policy and public administrative reforms can be further observed in the multi-level governing reforms that were experienced as from 2013 onwards.

7.7.1   Governance at an International Level: Malta's Presidency and Rate of Absorption of EU Funds

One of the major barometers of a country's public administrative strength is the rate of absorption of EU funds. The successful absorption of EU funds, thanks to the efforts of the public administration leads to significant positive externalities. In the programming period 2007-2013, all the available EU structural and cohesion funds were utilised successfully to the benefit of the Maltese citizens. With an absorption rate of 100 per cent for the European Regional Development Fund (ERDF), the Cohesion Fund (CF) and the European Social Fund (ESF), Malta registered the highest level of success in the use of EU funds as it utilised fully the €987 million allocation for the 2007-2013 period. Specifically, €136 million were allocated to education, €74 million to healthcare, €71 million to the environment and €51 million were allocated to the private sector.

The Maltese presidency, which occurred between January and June of the year 2017, was another challenge for the Maltese public administration from an international perspective. During the Presidency, at least 24 main legislative dossiers with the European Parliament were concluded. Several dossiers were of significant benefit to the citizen, from high-speed internet to energy-efficiency labelling of consumer products. Negotiations on nearly all the deals had started under the Slovak or Dutch presidency and were sealed in the final, and most delicate, negotiations between presidency and Parliament. From a purely public administrative perspective, a budget of 40 million was allocated for the six-month presidency. Despite being a relatively small public administration, when compared to other public administration in larger countries, Malta's public service handled 20,000 delegates from all over the EU, 2,500 journalists, a total of 1,500 meetings that were held at different levels in Brussels and Luxembourg, another 200 meetings that were organised in Malta, 910 high-level conferences, and 15 European Council meetings that were also held in Malta. The government, over a year and half before the Presidency, provided intensive training for large sectors of its public service, both in Malta and Brussels, under the direction of ENA, the renowned French School of Public Administration in preparation for the Presidency.

7.7.2   *White Paper on the Local Government Reform*

The string of policy reforms reviewed in this Chapter also includes a reform from a multi-level governing perspective, which reform had the aim to render Local Councils integrated more into the policy-initiatives steered by the National Government in the social, economic and environment realms in order to ensure a better quality of life for residents. The year 2018, when the White Paper on the Local Government Reform was launched, was the 25th anniversary of local councils in Malta (MJCL, 2018). After 25 years in operation, this was an opportunity to see how Local Councils could operate better and be levelled to a local government platform, an objective that was mentioned for decades but never materialised.

The proposals in White Paper were focused on: recognition of voluntary work, social measures, information about new legislation, a better quality of life for senior citizens and persons with special needs, consultation and reactions to complaints and suggestions by citizens, integration and social inclusion, as well as more information relating to services rendered by Local Councils, Government Departments and Public Authorities. The aim was to allow citizens to be more actively involved in the drawing up of the Action and Business Plan of their respective locality. A mobile App was designed to be launched to enable citizens to send complaints and suggestions to Local Councils and the Local Government Division in real time. Therefore, through technological innovation, the Local Councils can become even closer to the citizens. The Local Government Division will also be strengthened in order to ensure better monitoring of Local Government operations, thereby increasing accountability further to securing better value for money. The reform is also expected to address the cooperation with the Office of the Auditor General to secure the necessary improvements in Local Council operations, thereby ensuring compliance with the recommendations made by this Office. Regional Councils will assist Local Councils with delivering better services to citizens. Regional Councils would therefore be allocated enough financial resources to enable them to fulfil their obligations and responsibilities. The reform also seeks to deliver staff related measures, so that staff members are aware of services offered and that synergies between Local Councils, Regional Councils, Government entities and departments as well as Central Government are improved.

When applying the principle of regionality, the aim of the reform is expected to result in increased operational efficiency, as well as more transparent processes, accountability and good governance with due regard to citizen expectations. For this reason, training programmes will be formulated for elected councillors and clerical staff at Local and Regional Councils with a view to further improving the knowledge and skills of the officials concerned. At a local level, the Department for Local Government (within the Ministry for Justice, Culture and Local Government) has a coordinative function, and provides monitoring and support from a devolution, strategy, policy and planning perspective to local councils in a multitude of tasks that include projects. The Department also provides an advisory role to the Ministry responsible for Local Councils. The Governance of the Local Government is multi-dimensioned within a number of other bodies that include the Local Councils Association (at a local level), the EU Committee of Regions, the Congress of the Local and Regional Authorities of the Council of Europe and the Commonwealth Local Government Forum (at the international level). Several initiatives were undertaken by the Local Government Division (LGD) vis-à-vis their commitment in the *ex-ante* conditionality to strengthen Local Government.

7.7.2.1 Professional Development Award in Public Management and Governance at Local Level ESF 4.181

The ESF project entitled *Professional Development Award in Public Management and Governance at Local Level ESF 4.181* was implemented in 2014 and 2015. This training programme, part-financed by the European Union, was also accredited by the National Commission for Further and Higher Education (NCFHE) and pegged at level 5 of the Malta Qualifications Framework (MQF), i.e. at a Diploma level. The course, entitled *Professional Development Award in Public Management and Governance at Local Level*, was an obligatory course for the 68 Executive Secretaries in Local Councils in Malta and Gozo, the 5 Executive Secretaries in the Regional Committees, 1 Executive Secretary in the Local Councils' Association and to 10 LGD members of staff. This was an intense course which was delivered at identified local council venues, and it included the following modules which were delivered by qualified and experienced trainers. The delivered training modules included: Public Management and Governance, Collaborative Strategy, Performance Management, Public Policy Research and Policy Making, Community Governance and Leadership, Local Council Regulation, Good Governance in Local Government and Public Management.

7.7.2.2 Norwegian Financial Mechanisms 2009-2014: A Partnership for Creative Governance

Another project funded by the Norwegian Financial Mechanisms 2009-2014 entitled *A Partnership for Creative Governance*. This project was a partnership between Malta and Norway in the area of local government which created a set of initiatives that researched, examined, focused and created a number of measures to strengthen institutional capacity, strengthen people development within the respective departments responsible for local government, the elected and the executive arms of local and regional government, improve the quality and accessibility of services provided and create a professional programme for exchange of personnel. Specific project targets included: (i) the delivery and publication of a National Training Strategy and a Training Needs Analysis, tailor-made for Local Government in Malta; (ii) the establishment of performance management systems; (iii) the development of a Leadership Academy Programme; and (iii) the awarding of the European Label for Governance Excellence (ELoGE) in collaboration with the Council of Europe.

7.7.2.3 Norwegian Financial Mechanisms 2009-2014: Other Miscellaneous Projects

Another project financed by the EEA-Norwegian Financial Mechanism was dedicated to the training of local staff in principles of good governance, transparency and accountability as well as a small Grant Scheme for Urban Local Councils. The project addressed the inequalities and socio-economic challenges encountered particularly by localities considered as urban areas. The Local Government Division (LGD) is proposing to elaborate on a sustainable development strategy for urban localities (as a result of a pre-defined project on good governance) by adopting a bottom-up approach and therefore thus involving all the different stakeholders. The objective of the project is also the continuing enhancement of urban areas to improve the quality of life and sustainable living standards of deprived communities.

7.8 Conclusion

This chapter brought under one umbrella all the major policy reforms that were initiated and subsequently implemented by Malta's Government as from the year 2013 onwards. It builds on the previous chapter which focused on the interplay of the public policy with the public administrative framework. The Government's progressive policy design, the increased quality level through application of standards, the reprioritisation of the political agenda and the revamp of how key policy sectors are managed, have changed significantly the country's political direction. Progress has been made in implementing national policies so that Malta is more compliant with EU directives. The structural reforms have led to an increase in all revenue streams reflecting the sustained and robust performance of the Maltese economy. Despite all the policy reforms, the only constant thing is change and much more policy reforms are required especially in the new COVID-19 era that is changing the citizen's lives drastically.

References

Central Bank. (2018). *Poverty, social exclusion and living conditions in Malta: An analysis using SILC*, Article published in the Quarterly Review, p. 61–70.
Enemalta. (2016a). *Enemalta to dismantle oldest Delimara power station plant*. Available at: https://www.enemalta.com.mt/news/enemalta-to-dismantle-oldest-delimara-power-station-plant-2/.
Enemalta. (2016b). *Demolition of marsa power station gathers pace*. Available at: https://www.enemalta.com.mt/news/demolition-of-marsa-power-station-gathers-pace/.
Environment and Resources Authority (ERA). (2019). *Malta's national air pollution control programme*. Available at: https://era.org.mt/wp-content/uploads/2020/06/NAPCP_ISBN_PDF_web.pdf.

European Centre for the Development of Vocational Training (CEDEFOP). (2020). *Construction industry skill card*. Available at: https://www.cedefop.europa.eu/en/tools/matching-skills/all-instruments/construction-industry-skill-card.

European Commission. (2020a). *Efficient public administration*. Available at: https://ec.europa.eu/regional_policy/en/policy/themes/better-public-administration/.

European Commission. (2020b). *The youth guarantee country by country – Malta*, Employment, Social Affairs and Inclusion, Brussels: Belgium.

Malta Developers Association (MDA). (2017). *Construction industry still backbone of the economy*. Available at: http://mda.com.mt/pr050419/.

Malta Government. (2013). *The global residence programme is launched*. Available at: https://economy.gov.mt/en/globalresidence/Pages/home.aspx.

Malta Government. (2019a). *NDSF & Housing Authority sign MoU to invest €50 million for New Social Housing Project*. Available at: https://iip.gov.mt/2019/02/08/ndsf-housing-authority-sign-mou-to-invest-e50-million-for-new-social-housing-project/.

Malta Government. (2019b). *The barts medical school and anatomy centre will be unique in the mediterranean region*, Statement by the Office of the Prime Minister. Available at: https://www.gov.mt/en/Government/DOI/Press%20Releases/Pages/2019/May/15/pr191057.aspx.

Malta Government. (2020). *Largest ever investment in waste management with state-of-the-art facilities announced*, Press Release by the Environment, Climate Change and Planning. Available at: https://www.gov.mt/en/Government/DOI/Press%20Releases/Pages/2020/April/15/pr200668en.aspx.

Malta Independent. (2017). *Government manages to absorb 100% of EU funds allocated to Malta*. Available at: https://www.independent.com.mt/articles/2017-03-03/local-news/Government-manages-to-absorb-100-of-EU-funds-allocated-to-Malta-6736171177.

Ministry for the Family and Social Solidarity (MFSS). (2014). *National strategic policy for poverty reduction & for social inclusion: Malta 2014-2024*. Available at: https://family.gov.mt/en/Documents/Poverty%20Strategy%2014%20English%20Version.pdf.

Ministry for Education and Employment (MEDE) (2019). *A policy on inclusive education in schools: Route to quality inclusion*, published by MEDE.

Ministry for Education & Employment (MEDE). (2014). *Higher education strategy for Malta*. Available at https://ncfhe.gov.mt/en/resources/Documents/Strategy%20Documents/Higher%20Education%20Strategy%20for%20Malta.pdf.

Ministry for the Environment, Sustainable Development and Climate Change (MEAE). (2019). *Single use plastic products strategy for Malta 2020-2030*. Available at: https://meae.gov.mt/en/Public_Consultations/MSDEC/Pages/Consultations/PublicConsultationSingleUsePlasticProductsStrategyforMalta20202030.aspx.

Ministry for Finance (MFIN) (2019). *Long-term pension projections for Malta: 2016-2070*, published by the Economic Policy Division.

Ministry for Justice, Culture and Local Government (MJCL). (2018). *White Paper on the Local Government Reform*, White Paper published by the Parliamentary Secretariat for Local Government and Communities within the Ministry for Justice, Culture & Local Government.

National Commission for Active Ageing. (2014). *National strategic policy for active ageing: Malta 2014-2020*. Available at: https://family.gov.mt/en/Documents/Active%20Ageing%20Policy%20-%20EN.pdf.

Peters, G. (2018). The challenge of policy coordination. *J Policy Design Pract, 1*(1), 1–11. https://doi.org/10.1080/25741292.2018.1437946

Part III
Public Service Reform: The Research

It must be emphasised that our research into Public Service Reform was extensive and covers:

(a) Public Service Reform in the *"Distant Past"* that dealt with the Knights (1530–1798), the French Occupation (1798–1800), and British Rule (1800–1964);

(b) Public Service Reform in the *"Recent Past"* that included the Post-Independence Era (1964–1971), 1970s Social Reform Era until 1979, Reforms in the turbulent 1980s, and the Road to EU Membership and its Immediate Aftermath (1990 – March 2013);

(c) Public Service Reform in the *"Present"* dealing with reforms of the past seven years (2013–2020), which is the focus of this book;

(d) Public Service Reform in the *"Immediate Present"* that deals with the organisational internal and external impact of Public Service Reforms that is also a focus of this book; and

(e) Public Service Reform: Global *Future Trends* perspective.

The Public Service reforms of the *"Distant Past"* and *"Recent Past"* were covered in Part I, whilst the previous chapters related to Part II examined the various reforms that were implemented since March 2013, under the heading of the *"Present."* The chapters in Part III will examine the internal and external impact of the Public Service reforms, thus evaluating the Public Service reforms in the *"Immediate Present."* Finally, Part IV will examine the global future trends related to Public Service reforms. The research methodology varied depending on the period being examined. For example, Public Service reforms of the *"Distant Past"* was based upon secondary data from the available historical literature, whilst those reforms regarding the *"Recent Past"* were also based upon secondary using the Government Financial Estimates from 1964 to 1990. The Government Financial Estimates of that era contained invaluable information, since they also had a detailed description of the various government programmes being undertaken by the various Ministries and their respective Departments during that period. The research methodology for the Public Service reforms related to the *"Present"* (i.e. 2013–2020) was based upon secondary data, namely numerous Governmental reports and strategies that were considered relevant for this period.

However, it must be emphasised that the research methodology for Part III (*"Immediate Present"*) was based upon primary data through a survey approach. This provided a snapshot of the Public Service today in terms of various variables. The survey related to the internal impact of the Public Service reforms was carried out amongst Government employees with a sample of 500 being collected and analysed. The survey related to the external impact was conducted amongst the Maltese population with a sample of 600 being collected amongst this population. Both surveys were conducted during August 2020, with the results having a margin of error ±4%. The research into the internal impact of Public Service reforms had the objective of assessing work-related perceptions of employees in the public service and to determine whether these vary by demographic variables; assessing patterns between work-related perceptions; and to provide the implications for Public Service management. On the other hand, the research into the external impact of the Public Service reforms examined customer satisfaction; the level of Public Service trust; and assessed service quality by analysing numerous letters sent to the Editors of Newspapers regarding the Public Service (as distinct from government) and using the SERVQUAL methodology.

The research suggests that it is proper to describe the Maltese Public Service as being in state of continuous transition. Generally, the research findings show that the Maltese Public Service has always, throughout various eras, faced up to the countless challenges and succeeded in making Malta a better place for its citizens. As explained at the beginning of this book, transformational reforms do not just happen. They are highly dependent on the leadership attitude of those leading the Public Service at any specific point in time, especially those leading the government and predominantly, the vision and driving force of the Head of the Public Service. Without an innovative and dynamic vision, the Public Service reforms are likely to be merely incremental in nature and will not have a transformational impact on the Public Service organisations.

Public Service reform in a transformational environment supports the concept of reinventing government that is based upon the reorientation of the focus of government operations from an inward-looking approach to an outward-looking one by emphasising the concerns and needs of the diverse internal and external customer base. Hence, Public Service reform in the Malta Government is based on three fundamental principles: (a) citizens are regarded as clients who become the central focus in designing government service delivery; (b) the move towards embracing the values of catalytic government and community ownership; and (c) public officials are challenged to think about how to empower citizens to take ownership of community problems by urging them to partner with citizen groups and non-profit organisations to identify solutions and deliver public services effectively.

Chapter 8
Organisational Impact of Public Service Reforms: Assessing the Internal Impact

> *"My creed is that public service must be more than doing a job efficiently and honestly. It must be a complete dedication to the people and to the nation with full recognition that every human being is entitled to courtesy and consideration, that constructive criticism is not only to be expected but sought, that smears are not only to be expected but fought, that honour is to be earned, not bought."*
>
> Margaret Chase Smith
> American politician

Public administrations lay the foundation of how the country is run (Holmberg & Rothstein, 2012). As a result, public sector reform is an integral part of the governments' efforts and initiatives to modernise the Public Service by rendering it more citizen-centric and responsive to the rising aspirations of society. Any Public Service reform cannot be analysed in a vacuum, it must be reviewed in parallel with a contextual analysis of the external environment (Kaufmann & Zoido-Lobatón, 2010). The aim of this chapter is to expose the institutional reforms through the neo-institutional theory that provides a theoretical perspective of organisational behaviour that is influenced by other organisations, the key stakeholders, and the wider economic and social force (Greenwood et al., 2012). The societal and external impact of Public Service reforms are discussed in the coming chapter.

© The Author(s), under exclusive license to Springer Nature Switzerland AG 2021
F. Bezzina et al., *Public Service Reforms in a Small Island State*,
Public Administration, Governance and Globalization 22,
https://doi.org/10.1007/978-3-030-74357-4_8

8.1   Introduction: A Comprehensive Approach of the Key Principles of Public Sector Reform

Several internal organisational facets are analysed, stemming from Public Service reforms that were meant to reduce red tape and to make the service more efficient and to render it more customer-oriented, the significant investment to train staff at all levels, the introduction of the business planning process, the design of performance management programmes and the use of information technology to reengineer the administrative services available to the public. These internal Public Service organisational dynamics emphasised significantly the aspect of service delivery, which is considered to influence the external dimension of Public Service reform. The manner in which the general public started to access public services has changed significantly: most services have been transformed online and a number of Public Service departments or units made commitments with the general public on the level of service that they are expected to deliver through the quality service charters. Service delivery was specifically addressed through the setting up of One-Stop-Shops that focus on providing a specialised and customer-oriented service to the citizens.

Public Service reform and the arising organisational impact is a broad subject. The challenge for this chapter was to encompass all issues within a holistic strategic approach. The approach adopted was to build on the nine key guiding organisational principles that were designed by the Commonwealth Secretariat (2016: 8): first, a pragmatic and results-oriented framework; second, administrative structures; third, intelligent political strategies and engagement; fourth, goal-oriented competencies and skills development; fifth; experimentation and innovation; sixth, professionalization and improved morale; seventh, a code of conduct for public sector ethics; eighth, effective and pragmatic anti-corruption strategies and ninth, effective public financial management. For the purpose of this chapter, the Commonwealth Secretariat principles are compressed within seven actions of reform. The experience of member States who joined the EU after 2004 was that they were motivated to carry out significant administrative reforms which were partly dictated by their preparation for EU membership. However, several years after accession, many countries have lost the momentum and, consequently, many aspects of administrative change remained static, weak or fragmented (Meyer-Sahling, 2009). The sustainability of the public administrations was most often compromised by a lack of political consensus, a theme that leads us to the first consideration in Public Service reform, the contextual factors (European Commission, 2017).

8.2   Intelligent Political Strategies and Engagement: Consider the Context

This chapter is focused on the internal impact of organisational reforms but the very first consideration of the key officials driving the reform is to have a comprehensive and thorough knowledge on the context, trends, challenges and opportunities that exist in the state and even from a multi-governing perspective. Public Service reforms that did not consider the local context have a greater risk of ending in failure (Repucci, 2014). The OECD Development Assistance Committee conducted a review on public sector governance reform (PSGR) in 2011 and found that most often the political dynamics is not given the necessary importance when Public Service reforms are designed (Scott, 2011).

Setting the context extend from the political culture as well as the institutional cultures that exist in the country, the informalities and personal interactions that surround small states, the conditions in the labour market and the degree or tolerance of political patronage (World Bank, 2008). The conditions that are specifically attributed to small states, as it is the case of Malta, result in having a limited skills base to rely on, the difficulty to achieve the desired economies of scale, the financial limitation to provide extensive public services and the overreliance on central government to sustain a Public Service reform (Zenobia, 2019). These small states limitations have a direct correlation to implement human resources reforms such as performance management and ICT reforms that embrace eGovernment.

An extensive Public Service reform requires the involvement of all the stakeholders especially of the political executives running the country. Political leadership is necessary because it provides the necessary safeguards, motivational drive and can exert the necessary pressure when reform comes to a halt. Therefore, the proactive involvement of politicians is necessary to ensure accountability and to safeguard the smooth progress of the reform initiatives. Active and proactive political involvement is at times lacking given the considerable financial and political costs involved and provided that the benefits are reaped on a long-term basis. Other external stakeholders and governing instruments are crucial for the Public Service reform. In order to function properly, the Public Service requires ecology of governing instruments that extend from the Law Courts and the Legislature to the Ombudsman, from the National Audit Office to the Public Service Commission. Without the necessary reforms in the state's institutional apparatus, the state's instruments lack independence and resultantly the state's institutional framework will not be able to provide adequate oversight. If the state institutions do not have the necessary tools and independence, they risk being subject to political influence (Glassie, 2018). The risk would be that the Public Service becomes an instrument of politics and patronage and the prospects for good governance are significantly undermined (Hassall, 2018).

The Sustainable Governance Indicators (SGI) combines an analysis of Policy Performance, Democracy and Governance for 41 EU and OECD countries (Bertelsmann Stiftung, 2017). The index analyses the governments' capacity in order to deliver sound policies as well as the participatory capabilities of social actors. The results have highlighted large differences within the EU in terms of executive capacity and accountability. In terms of strategic planning and coordination, the weakest countries are Greece, Cyprus and Hungary. The best integrated policy process was found in Denmark, Finland and the United Kingdom. As a general conclusion, a significant number of countries are limited in the use of evidence in policy development and the quality of regularity impact assessment (RIA) is to be improved. Countries such as Greece, Hungary and Romania need to invest more in the active involvement of civil society, the external stakeholders and academia in order to boost policy development and evaluation.

Throughout the 14 EU Member States a downward trend in the overall governance index was observed, specifically in countries such as Estonia, Croatia, Latvia, Lithuania, Luxemburg, Hungary, Netherlands, Poland, Portugal, Slovenia, Slovakia, Finland, and Sweden. Only three countries, which are Italy, Cyprus and Malta, have showed a more substantial improvement in their executive capacity since the launch of the indicators. The executive capacity is of essential importance for Public Service reform (European Commission, 2017).

8.3   A Pragmatic and Results-Oriented Framework

The second consideration in a Public Service reform is the design of a results-oriented framework: the raison d'être of any organisational dynamics. Today's rising aspirations and the subsequent complexity of modern society have pushed towards the delivery of results (Morieux & Tollman, 2014). The delivery of results presents a multi-governing approach since performance indicators are nowadays set at an international, national and local level. The indicators set at a national and international political level must be managed by the civil servants through the Public Service results-oriented framework. The results framework is to be designed in a pragmatic manner to respond to the societal needs and expectations that evolve continuously.

Bezzina et al. (2017) conducted a European wide survey amongst 27 EUPAN public administration networks to investigate the introduction and the implementation of comprehensive (Key Performance Indicators). Their analysis highlighted the five most critical constraining factors in the various spheres of the public administration that inhibit the enactment and implementation of KPIs, as detailed as follows:

(a) Insufficient data, technological and managerial tools

- Lack of quality data
- Data not always readily available
- Lack of enough technological and managerial tools
- Ineffective human resources
- Lack of human resources with the necessary skills, knowledge and competences

(b) Unmotivated workforce, lack of commitment and low level of engagement

- Lack of leadership and management
- More focus on successful groups of employees rather than a collective effort throughout the organisation
- Lack of responsibility and accountability
- Unclear roles

- Lack of team effort
- Lack of training
- Lack of managerial freedom because of budget constraints
- Resistance to change keep status quo instead of injecting quality culture in public administration
- Lack of trust and co-ordination
- Focus is on the punitive rather the corrective or the incentives dimension of KPIs
- Administrative burden and weak administrative capacity
- Benefits are not clear to users

(c) Political, contextual and societal challenges

- Lack of public interest in performance measurement regimes
- Information overload and a complex process with a lot of financial detail that cannot be understood by the citizens
- Difficulty to use information in Parliament
- Difficult to measure the influence on central government policy or to link operational with national objectives
- Rigid Public Service legislation
- Lack of political interest and commitment
- Lack of political continuity
- A tendency to be too entrepreneurial rather than focusing on the society's welfare

(d) Strategic, structural and planning difficulties

- Lack of strategic planning, lack of central structure and different procedures within organisations
- Complex and large public administration, lack of co-ordination and the creation of silos
- KPIs not communicated effectively – not cascaded down the organisation
- No systematic use of evaluation and evidence-based policy-making culture
- Low quality and unclear goals or indicators

(e) Central-local relations

- Success depends entirely on departments with little control in the hands of the centre
- Lack of consensus from the central administration regarding the KPIs to be used

The first category embraces the lack of data available either because of timing or because there are not enough technological or managerial tools to capture the right data. If data or correct data is not available, the foundation and parameters of the KPIs exercise will be undermined.

The second category focuses on human resources who are the main players for a successful KPIs implementation. Countries mentioned several human resources inhibiting factors ranging from lack of training, team effort, accountability and lack of leadership. Lack of accountability and team effort could be perceived as contradictory or odd factors when considering that, to the contrary, KPIs are intended to induce these elements in the human resources function. These factors reveal that the intended outcomes of a successfully managed KPIs exercise could be the factors that are deemed as inhibiting HR to function appropriately, especially in cases of lack of co-ordination and unmotivated staff. The most crucial factor is to manage resistance to change, a change from a traditional oriented culture towards a results-oriented and evidence-based mechanisms. Injecting a quality culture could prove to be very challenging if it is not led by a competent leader.

A leader and a senior manager who is not capable to steer the KPIs at departmental level will inevitably lead to unmotivated workforce, lack of commitment and low level of engagement at all levels of the organisational hierarchy. Countries stressed the importance that departments are led by an effective leader who is surrounded by highly competent employees possessing the necessary knowledge and skills in order to understand the complexity and technical details of KPIs. Other major challenges highlighted are the management of the heavy administrative burden emanating from an overload of information and detailed KPIs processes. If this aspect is not given its due importance, Public Service employees will never perceive the KPIs process as beneficial. Overload of information is just one facet of the problem. The tendency to focus on successful employees could lead to the creation of factions within an organisation, distrust will become stronger and the sense of a collective effort is ultimately undermined.

The third category revolves around the political will to embrace KPIs and to have a societal engagement. The collaboration of political executives with the public administration could be a tricky exercise especially if there is a difficulty to see how KPIs at an operational level are translated into positive and tangible results at a political and national level. This is difficult to be achieved especially in policy areas that are complex and ambiguous. At times, lack of political continuity that may result from frequent ministerial changes inhibits the interest that is expected from the political class and instead creates an aura of instability *vis-à-vis* the KPIs framework. Disinterest from politicians most probably translates into lack of public interest from the citizens. Such a situation would render the KPIs exercise as a purely technical inward-looking mechanism rather than an exercise that is perceived as beneficial to the society.

A clear strategy and an effective structure are a must if the development of a KPIs framework is to be a successful exercise. This is core element of the fourth category. Lack of structural and central direction with clear guidelines creates weak coordination especially when considering the large and complex public administrations present in most countries. Countries underlined the importance to communicate effectively the details and benefits of KPIs within the department or agency and between the central and local agencies. The fifth category of KPIs inhibiting factors involves lack of communication, lack of effective co-ordination between the centre and the local and lack of consensus from the central point that could be the recipe for a KPIs implementation failure. The departmental initiative to steer the KPIs process is extremely important and the countries' public administrations are not to be tempted to centralise the process but a locus of control from the centre is essential for a well-functioning KPIs framework.

8.4 Governing Arrangements: A Closer Look at the Administrative Structures and Processes

The third consideration is centred on the shift towards a goal-oriented Public Service that requires a solid and a cohesive administrative structure. The state's institutional framework is composed of a plethora of different organisations in the form of ministries with several portfolios, agencies and other public authorities that act at a multi-governing level: national, regional or local level. The quality of interaction between these state's entities influences the effectiveness or inefficiency of the Public Service processes and performance (European Commission, 2017).

Structural arrangements aim to improving governance to address fragmentation and address the disconnected working units and sub-units; expanding the use of networks to bring together the key stakeholders of the Public Service; and increasing flexibility to allow managers to achieve outcomes rather than resources and for workers to help broaden their skills and competencies (OECD, 2008). To achieve these objectives, the strategic role of the centre and the subsequent relationship with the administrative structures of the Public Service within the periphery is of utmost importance. The scholarly literature concerning the transformation of public services is not limited to the structural perspective. Literature focuses also on enabling and developing the Public Service to modernise by embracing new management techniques, new structures and processes, new financial systems and new technologies (Institute of Public Administration, 2013). Public Service reform signifies the interplay of policy frameworks, governing structures and processes as well as managerial actions. Such interplay requires a complex web of networks, structures and several stakeholders that highlight the shift from a narrow idea of government to the concept of governance (Rhodes, 1996). Pollitt and Bouckaert (2011) describe Public Service reform as a deliberate change to the structures and processes of public sector organisations and/or services, with the objective of working better and to improve the results. The changes in the structures and the corresponding processes, in order to better adapt to the changing realities, are of intra and inter organisational nature: within and between the Public Service departments and ministries.

Public service reform has led to three main types of structural changes: a whole system change, an internal system change, and system change in the service delivery. A *whole system change* emphasises the perspective that reforms address specific parts of the governing and managerial engine of the Public Service. The parts are identified and explored in significant depth. However, reforming just some structural parts without enduring the challenge to join the engine pieces together to have a holistic perspective of the structural changes is a limited approach. The effective coordination of the different points of the dynamic Public Service systems is crucial for both the internal system change and the system change in the service delivery. An *internal redesign of the system* involves looking at how the bureaucratisation of the Public Service is working in terms of financial systems, the working arrangements of the public servants, the working environment and the use of information technology to improve the used processes and procedures. The aim of a reform of a systems approach is to improve the *service* in all aspects of public policy (Colgan et al., 2016).

The ultimate aim of structural reforms is to improve the quality of relationships and collaboration between the Public Service units, the strengthening of multi-level governance, the assigning of powers and responsibilities at every administrative level, the effective redistribution of resources amongst all networks and government levels, the streamlining and simplification of administrative process through the use of ICT and the strengthening of interoperability within and across administrations (European Commission, 2017).

8.5   Goal-Oriented Competencies and Skills Development

The development of a results-oriented framework and the reform in the institutional design need the input of Public Service employees, who are a crucial asset for the Public Service. This fourth theme rests on the premise that most organisations, both public and private, spend a significant amount of resources on hiring the ideal employees, in management and development staff (Hinkin & Tracey, 2000). Employees are the basic building block of organisations, the primary vehicle for organisational change (Ang, 2002) as well as in orienting the Public Service to become performance oriented.

The development of the employees' potential is significant in the EU, given that the public sector is EU's 'largest employer'. Data published by the European Commission shows that the EU's public sector is around 75 million people, or 25% of the total EU workforce. Public expenditure amounts to almost 50% of the Gross Domestic Product (GDP) (European Commission, 2017). The aging of civil servants is the biggest risk for public institutions across EU when it comes to talent management and skills development. Some countries such as Belgium, Spain and Italy will experience up to 45% of their civil servants retire in the next 15 years. This raises serious concerns about the institutional capacity, institutional stability and quality of services (Baltic Institute of Social Sciences, 2015). Skills development is of paramount importance from two perspectives: human resources are not only the most important resource of public organisations, but also the most sensitive Public Service dimension. High performance public organisations manifest their commitment to achieve KPIs by embracing a goal-directed vision and mission that has continuous performance measurement as a central value. To achieve this notion a Public Service is to invest in multi-skilled workers who have a broader perspective rather than narrow expertise. In times of complexity and unprecedented circumstances, Public Service jobs are to be enriched and Public Service employees are given the necessary space and latitude to develop their skills. In practice, this public administration vision entails job enrichment and dispersed decision-making as well as a policy promoting continuous learning at all organisational levels (Čiarnienė et al., 2006).

The question is how to match the organisational objectives with the skills of the Public Service employees. From a management perspective, skills profiling is a tool to identify adequately the skills gaps. Skills profiling is a technique that analyse the skills possessed by employees when compared to the skills needed by the organisation to carry out its mandate. It identifies measures to bridge identified gaps, especially through training, and redeployment, if necessary. From the employees' perspective, it is an opportunity for self-development as well as higher satisfaction and motivation at their place of work (Malta Public Service, 2020). Addressing talent management and building a cohort of qualified, skilled and competent public servants involves a comprehensive approach for training. The traditional-based learning approach was shifted towards a greater emphasis on the development of soft skills that are deemed necessary to have a problem-based learning mentality, a performance-oriented philosophy and situation-emergent challenges (Subban & Vyas-Doorgapersad, 2014). The discourse on skills development relates instinctively to the dimension of structural arrangements and on how the Public Service is to be organised to keep up with today's exigencies. From a specific specialised point-of-view, public administrations have developed training institutes to focus on the delivery of tailor-made training programmes for civil servants. From an umbrella general perspective, many public administrations have shifted towards more flexible structural dynamics that replace the tall and rigid organisational hierarchy. The debate ensuing from the decision to shift towards high-performance public organisation is concentrated on a managerial control that is characterised by less exercise of formal authority and more by leadership.

8.6   Improved Professionalization and Morale

The professionalization of the Public Service, the first consideration of Public Service reform, includes a continuum of facets: the ability of public officials to have discretion and autonomy in doing their work, being successfully evaluated, being intellectuals and having a capacity to control and regulate themselves. Professional public servants have expert and specialised knowledge in the field they work in and are excellent in relation to the profession they practice, they produce excellent work and have high standard of professional ethics (The Commonwealth, 2016). The question is how work morale and motivation can be improved in order to strengthen the professional attire of the Public Service.

Motivated employees are a key element to having a performing Public Service. The notion of Public Service motivation (PSM) research became very popular at the turn of the new millennium (Perry et al., 2010). Highly motivated employees, who are compelled by the idea that their service serves a societal purpose for the general public can increase the effectiveness of Public Service delivery, through a minimum use of government resources (Van der Wal, 2015). The issue that is of most interest to Public Service managers is how could the positive effects of Public Service motivation be optimised for a better performance? (Paarlberg & Perry, 2008). This section seeks to identify the major Public Service motivators, stemming from the sense of civic duty, performance management programmes to adequate compensation in the form of salaries and the adoption of family-friendly measures. The setting of clear goals, as discussed in the previous section, is the first condition that can provide a strong base for motivating Public Service employees. Careful consideration is to be given to the conditions in which public servants work and to the barriers that exist in the public domain to achieve the objectives, either because of diffused goals (Chun & Rainey, 2005) or goals that are difficult to achieve due to several constraints.

The second motivating factor revolves around the selection, recruiting and training those Public Service employees that promote the organisational values (Lewis & Frank, 2002; Mann, 2006). Apart from being highly competent, employees need to reflect the raison d'être and work towards the established esprit de corps of the organisation. The third motivator is about setting the right work environment. A centralised manner in which decisions are taken will impede employees to see how their efforts contribute to the mission of the organisation (Scott & Pandey, 2005). Research shows that direct and indirect staff participation is a key factor for driving public management reforms (Farnham et al., 2005). Increased participation in the workplace decision-making provides a feeling, that work in the public domain has an impact on the lives of the citizens (Dee et al., 2003). Participation is not to be limited in purely technical decisions but also in issues that relate to the core and strategic aspect of the job (Leisink, 2004).

The fourth motivator involves performance management programmes. A study conducted by Paarlberg and Perry (2007) revealed that performance appraisals include a broader consideration of the public work ethos, that include honesty, teamwork, commitment to the customer and being a good steward of the installation's resources. The fifth motivator is of an umbrella nature, it highlights the societal contribution of Public Service employee and their desire to serve the general public. Serving the citizens creates a sense of satisfaction amongst workers. The connection between serving the public and having a sense of satisfaction is dependent on the extent to which employees can connect to their contribution that they are having in serving the public (Grant, 2007). Several Public Service jobs provide this opportunity especially those who work at the front-end, such as those who work in vocationally oriented jobs. A more challenging connection is for those who work behind the scenes, at the back end of technical department such as ICT.

8.7 Code of Conduct and Anti-Corruption Strategies

Any activity emanating from the Government and implemented by the Public Service is expected to adhere to standards of integrity and ethical behaviour. The sixth aspect of the reform exposes the experience gathered in most countries, where citizens, the business community and the civil society expect high standards of ethical conduct, provided that the Public Service is administering public money. The rising expectations from the citizens is the result of better-focused media attention and public scrutiny, which expectation is not only limited to ethics but also to systems of corrupt practices. In many public administrations including in Europe, Australia, New Zealand and Canada, significant progress was achieved to develop effective Civil Service ethics, codes of conduct, transparency measures, integrity systems, and anti-corruption agencies (Whitton, 2001).

As a matter of principle, ethical conduct involves the following facets: first the anticipation of specific threats to ethical standards and integrity in the public sector, specifically those systemic threats that weaken the core of the public sector ethics values and the public servants commitment to good governance; second, the strengthening of the ethical competence of civil servants and strengthening mechanisms to support ethical behaviour. This principle is mainly focused on ethical decision-making and the promotion of ethical culture as well as competent decision-making; and third, the development of administrative practices and processes that promote ethical values and integrity as well as adherence to a system of checks and balances that promotes the rule of law (Whitton, 2001). Several practical reforms were implemented to ensure ethical behaviour and anti-corruption mechanisms. The introduction of the Freedom of Information Acts is an instrument that establishes a right to information held by public authorities in order to promote added transparency and accountability in Government (Ministry of Finance, 2020). This practice is in line with Article 15 of the treaty on the functioning of the European Union which provides citizens and residents of EU countries the right of access to the documents of the European Parliament, the Council and the European Commission. This means that citizens can obtain documents held by the Commission and other institutions Documents include legislative information, official documents, historical archives as well as minutes and agenda (European Commission, 2020).

The Whistle-blower protection law is an anti-corruption instrument that protects public employees who reveal information that leads to corruption investigations and prosecutions. Countries around the world, including European Union member states, have dealt with whistle-blower legislations in a different manner by articulating the law in accordance to their contextual realities. The success of public sector anti-corruption strategies and reforms depend on whistle-blower protection, especially in countries where public sector corruption is systemic and endemic (Popescu, 2015). The legal framework is embraced by the design of codes of conduct specifically for a Public Service that is moving towards a result-based management. With the advent of New Public Management (NPM), where the Public Service has experienced a decentralisation of authority that led to more autonomy and increasing discretionary powers at lower levels, the need for ethically correct behaviour became crucial. The essence of a code of conduct is to formulate ethical guidelines for all public officials in order to deal with corruption and unethical practice. The challenge is to achieve a balance between the requirements of results-based management and adhering to ethical standards of the highest level (Demmke & Moilanen, 2011).

Integrity in the behaviour of public officers has also its way in the financial audits conducted. OLAF (the EU Anti-Fraud Office) investigates fraud against the EU budget, corruption and serious misconduct within the European institutions, and develops anti-fraud policy for the European Commission (European Commission, 2020). At a national level, members states have their internal auditors, in the case of Malta IAID (the Internal Audit and Investigations Department) provides assistance to the Maltese Government to make the best use of public funds in order to achieve the results (IAID, 2020).

8.8 Public Financial Management

The financial crisis that emanated in 2008 has increased financial pressures on both the central governments and the public sector. This situation rendered financial management to the forefront of public sector reform, the seventh consideration that is outlined in this chapter. The responses to the crisis have been diverse and country-specific, depending on the exigencies of the contextual factors. The approach adopted by many member states was to cut their budget (European Commission, 2017). The effective functioning of the state and its Public Service machinery rests on sound and efficient public administration. This entails the ability to ensure high quality Public Services while strengthening competitiveness and progress, a public administration is based on the principles of reliability, accountability and transparency, knowledgeable Public Service workforce and financial sustainability (Benkovic, 2018).

Financial management does not happen in a policy vacuum. Public financial management (PFM) is about spending money in accordance to the government expressed policy. Therefore, public financial management (PFM) is central to Public Service reform and it cannot be analysed separately from the key arguments that are highlighted by scholars on the quality of Public Service delivery, extending from education, healthcare and infrastructure. The key concerns of PFM revolve around accounting and financial reporting, auditing, fiscal policymaking, cost analysis, cash management. PFM offers the ability to review in a much thorough detail the analytical tools, measurement strategies and practices, the conceptual frameworks, as well as other tools of substantial value to financial management (Kioko et al., 2011). The ethos of managerialism and professionalism in financial management has been evident in many European countries (Hyndman & Irvine, 2016; Pollitt, 2016). PFM enforces the neo-institutional theory which brings into light the institutional adaptation to the external environment. The introduction of accrual accounting can be viewed as a process of adaptation with the external environment and influential stakeholders (Hyndman & Connolly, 2011; Pina et al., 2009).

Within this perspective, accrual accounting has been implemented in order to achieve a much broader range of financial knowledge that is beyond cash flows (Christiaens et al., 2010; Hyndman et al., 2018; Ridder et al., 2006), the regimental method of accounting revenues when money is actually received and for expenses only when money is disbursed. The main advantage of accrual accounting is that it allocates revenues and expenditures to the period in which they are earned or used (Bushman et al., 2016).

8.9 Conclusion

The literature review conducted in this chapter revealed the common characteristics that are related to Public Service reform. The literature review was based on the experience gathered in European public administrations that share these common traits of Public Service reform. Despite the common characteristics, countries are to be cautious not to adopt a one-size fits all approach. The Public Service strategic and operational activities do not happen in a vacuum; their actions contribute towards the national policy priorities that emerge from the economic and social contextual realties. Therefore, the Public Service reform initiatives are rooted in the central political actions and the key for a working relationship between public servants and politicians is complimentary rather than dichotomy. The outlined key aspects of Public Service reform from an internal organisational impact are very much inter-related and cannot be considered in isolation. Public service strategies, structures and managerial actions are intimately related with each other to produce a broad and a complex picture of continuous Public Service reform process.

References

Ang, A. (2002). An eclectic review of the multidimensional perspectives of employee involvement. *The TQM magazine, 14*(3), 192–200. https://doi.org/10.1108/09544780210425856

Bezzina, F. Borg, C. & Cassar, V. (2017). *The Public Service as a Performing Organisation*, International Report prepared for the Maltese Presidency of the Council of the European Union, published by the European Public Administration Network.

Baltic Institute of Social Sciences, et al. (2015). *The study on the future role and development of the public administration*. Latvia.

Bertelsmann Stiftung. (2017). Sustainable Governance Indicators. Available at: https://www.sgi-network.org/2019/.

Bushman, R. M., Lerman, A., & Frank, Z. (2016). The changing landscape of accrual accounting. *Journal of Accounting Research, 54*(1), 41–78.

Chun, Y. H., & Rainey, H. G. (2005). Goal ambiguity and Organisational performance in U.S. Federal Agencies. *Journal of Public Administration Research and Theory, 15*(4), 529–557.

Christiaens, J., Reyniers, B., & R., & Rollé, C. (2010). Impact of IPSAS on reforming governmental financial information systems: A comparative study. *International Review of Administrative Sciences, 76*(3), 537–554.

Čiarnienė, R., Sakalas, A. & Vienažindienė, M. (2006) *Strategic Personnel Management in Public Sector: The Case Study of Kaunas Municipality*, ISSN 1392-2785 Engineering Economics, No 2 (47), Available at: https://inzeko.ktu.lt/index.php/EE/article/view/11342

Colgan, A., Rochford, S., & Burke, K. (2016). *Implementing public service reform – Messages from the literature*. Centre for Effective Services.

Dee, J. R., Henkin, A. B., & Duemer, L. (2003). Structural antecedents and psychological correlates of teacher empowerment. *Journal of Educational Administration., 41*(3), 257–277.

Demmke, C., & Moilanen, T. (2011). *Effectiveness of Good Governance and Ethics in Central Administration: Evaluating Reform Outcomes in the Context of the Financial Crisis*, study for the 57th meeting of the directors general responsible for public services in EU member states and European Commission, European Institute of Public Administration.

European Commission. (2020). *Freedom of Information*. Available at: https://ec.europa.eu/info/about-european-commission/service-standards-and-principles/transparency/freedom-information_en.

European Commission. (2017). European Semester Thematic Fact Sheet: Quality of Public Administration. Available at: https://ec.europa.eu/info/sites/info/files/file_import/european-semester_thematic-factsheet_quality-public-administration_en_0.pdf.

Farnham, D., Hondeghem, A., & Horton, S. (2005). *Staff participation and public management reform: Some international comparisons*. Palgrave.

Glassie, N. (2018). Public sector management and reform: Cook Islands experience. *Asia Pacific Journal of Public Administration, 40*(4). https://doi.org/10.1080/23276665.2018.1543083

Grant, A. M. (2007). Relational job design and the motivation to make a prosocial difference. *Academy of Management Review, 32*(2), 393–417.

Greenwood, R., Oliver, C., Sahlin, K., & Roy Suddaby, R. (Eds.). (2012). *Institutional theory in organization studies*. SAGE.

Hassall, G. (2018). Special issue on public sector lenhancement in pacific island states. *Asia Pacific Journal of Public Administration, 40*(4). https://doi.org/10.1080/23276665.2018.1553276

Hyndman, N., Liguori, M., Meyer, R., Polzer, T., Rota, S., Seiwald, J., & Ileana, S. (2018). Legitimating change in the public sector: The introduction of (rational?) accounting practices in the United Kingdom, Italy and Austria. *Public Management Review, 20*(9), 1374–1399.

Hyndman, N., & Connolly, C. (2011). Accruals accounting in the public sector: A road not always taken. *Management Accounting Research, 22*(1), 36–45.

Hyndman, N., & Irvine, L. (2016). New public management: The story continues. *Financial Accountability & Management, 32*(4), 385–408.

Hinkin, T. R., & Tracey, J. B. (2000). The cost of turnover: Putting a price on the learning curve. *Cornell Hotel and Restaurant Administration Quarterly, 41*(3), 14–21. Available at: http://scholarship.sha.cornell.edu/articles/445/

Holmberg, S., & Rothstein, B. (2012). *Good government: The relevance of political science*. Edward Elgar Publishing.

Institute of Public Administration. (2013). Fit for purpose? Progress report on public service reform. Institute of Public Administration, Dublin. Available at: http://www.ipa.ie/pdf/June2013Report9.pdf.

Internal Audit and Investigations Department (IAID). (2020). About the IAID. Available at: https://iaid.gov.mt/en/Pages/About-Us/About-the-IAID.aspx.

Leisink, P. (2004). *Do Public Personnel Policies Nourish Public Service Motivation?* Paper presented at the European Group of Public Administration Annual Meeting, Llubljana.

Lewis, G. B., & Frank, S. A. (2002). Who wants to work for government? *Public Administration Review, 62*(July/August), 395–404.

Kaufmann, D. K., & Zoido-Lobatón. (2010). *Governance Matters*. Policy research working paper no. 2196, Washington, DC: World Bank. Available at: http://documents.worldbank.org/curated/en/665731468739470954/Governance-matters.

Kioko, S., Marlowe, J., Matkin, D., Moody, M., Smith, D., & Zhao, Z. (2011). Why public financial management matters. *Journal of Public Administration Research and Theory, 21*, 113–124.

Malta Public Service. (2020). *Skills Profiling*. People and Standards Division. Available at: https://publicservice.gov.mt/en/people/Pages/ResearchandPersonnelSystems/SkillsProfiling.aspx.

Mann, G. A. (2006). A motive to service: Public service motivation in human resource management and the role of PSM in the nonprofit sector. *Public Personnel Management, 35*(1), 33–48.

Meyer-Sahling, J. (2009). *The sustainability of civil service reform in central and eastern europe five years after accession*, SIGMA paper, no. 44. OECD, Paris: France.

Ministry of Finance. (2020). *Freedom of Information.* Available at: https://mfin.gov.mt/en/Services/Pages/foi.aspx.

Morieux, Y., & Tollman, P. (2014). *Six simple rules: How to manage complexity without getting complicated.* Harvard Business Review Press.

OECD. (2008). *OECD public management reviews.* Towards an Integrated Public Service, OECD Publishing, Paris.

Paarlberg, L., & Perry, J. L. (2007). Values management, aligning individual values and organization goals. *American Review of Public Administration.*

Paarlberg, L. & Perry, J. L. (2008). *From Theories to Practice: Strategies for Applying Public Service Motivation*, Available at: https://www.academia.edu/17520441/From_theory_to_practice_Strategies_for_applying_public_service_motivation.

Perry, J. L., Hondeghem, A., & Wise, L. R. (2010). Revisiting the motivational bases of public service: Twenty years of research and an agenda for the future. *Public Administration Review, 68*, 445–458.

Pina, V., Torres, L., & Yetano, A. (2009). Accrual accounting in EU local governments: One method, several approaches. *European Accounting Review, 18*(4), 765–807.

Pollitt, C., & Bouckaert, G. (2011). *Public management reform a comparative analysis: Public management, governance, and the neo-Weberian state* (3rd ed.). Oxford University Press.

Pollitt, C. (2016). Managerialism redux? *Financial Accountability & Management, 32*(4), 429–447.

Popescu, A. (2015). A critical analysis of whistleblower protection in the European Union. *Journal of Public Administration, Finance and Law, 7*, 135–140.

Repucci, S. (2014). Designing effective civil service reform lessons from past experience. *Public Administration and Development, 34*(3), 207–218. published online in Wiley Online Library, Available at: wileyonlinelibrary.com

Rhodes, R. A. W. (1996). The new governance: Governing without government. *Political Studies, 44*, 652–667. Available at: https://journals.sagepub.com/doi/10.1111/j.1467-9248.1996.tb01747.x

Ridder, H., Bruns, H., & Spier, F. (2006). Managing implementation processes: The role of public managers in the implementation of accrual accounting–evidence from six case studies in Germany. *Public Management Review, 8*(1), 87–118.

Scott, Z. (2011) *Evaluation of public sector governance reforms 2001–2011: literature review.* Available at: http://www.psgr.org.

Scott, P. G., & Pandey, S. K. (2005). Red tape and public service motivation: Findings from a national survey of managers in state health and human service organizations. *Review of Public Personnel Administration., 25*(2), 155–180.

Subban, M., & Vyas-Doorgapersad, S. (2014). Public administration training and development in Africa: The case of the Republic of South Africa. *Journal of Public Affairs Education., 20*(4), 499–514.

The Commonwealth. (2016). Key principles of public sector reforms: Case studies and frameworks, Commonwealth Secretariat.

Van der Wal, Z. (2015). "All quiet on the non-Western front?" a systematic review of public service motivation scholarship in non-Western contexts. *Asia Pacific Journal of Public Administration, 37*(2), 69–86.

World Bank. (2008). *Public sector reform: What works and why?* World Bank.

Zenobia, I. (2019) *Public Sector Reform and Capacity Building in Small Island Developing States*, K4D (Knowledge, Evidence and Learning for Development) Report. Available at: https://gsdrc.org/wp-content/uploads/2019/08/583_Small_Island_Developing_States_Revised.pdf.

Chapter 9
Societal Impact of Public Service Reforms

> *"To give real service you must add something which cannot be bought or measured with money, and that is sincerity and integrity."*
>
> Douglas Adams
> Author, screenwriter and dramatist

This chapter critically reviews literature concerning several ideas, methodologies and instruments that have been used to understand the societal impact of public services and Public Service reform; or that can be associated with related potential. These are namely the Net Promoter Score (NPS), Service Quality (SERVQUAL), Customer Satisfaction (CSAT) and trust in Public Services. A plethora of studies document the relevance of these societal impact metrics to private enterprise; whilst there is evidence of a growing support for deployment in the public sector and in gauging users' experience of private and public e-services. A headline finding of the literature review is that conceptual complexities ought not to be ignored; for example, the many possible interpretations of 'satisfaction' and the empirically ambiguous association between trust in public services and trust in government. The use of the term 'customer' for users of public services emerged as debatable. Another main finding is that attention is due to methodological limitations of societal impact metrics. Thus, whilst CSAT measures customer satisfaction with a product or service at the moment of consumption, the more sophisticated NPS has the added value of capturing customer loyalty; whilst SERVQUAL illuminates different and versatile dimensions of the service-user experience. Whilst no metric alone is likely to be enough to gauge societal impact, hybrid tools should factor-in context. Ultimately, societal impact concepts and metrics should not be seen as an end, but only as an initial informant on Public Service reform.

F. Bezzina et al., *Public Service Reforms in a Small Island State*,
Public Administration, Governance and Globalization 22,
https://doi.org/10.1007/978-3-030-74357-4_9

9.1   Introduction

Besides having a constitutional role, the Public Service has a societal impact through its representativity, reputation and prestige (Gow, 2007). Societal impact involves the demonstrable intended contributions and collateral effects on society, as constituted by individuals, organisations or countries. When Public Service embarks on reform, levels of societal impact that can inform on reform outcomes include the instrumental level, conceptual level and capacity-building. The instrumental level constitutes influence on the development of a society's policy, practices or service provision, the shaping of legislation or the altering of instrumental social behaviour (Economic and Social Research Council (ESRC), 2020), such as an individual's engagement with tax payments (e.g. taking up online rather traditional payment methods). The conceptual level of societal impact comprises an enlarged, reframed or reviewed understanding of issues or debates, such as the distribution of responsibilities for occupational health and safety. Capacity-building is the level where impact would comprise the development of technical and personal skills, such as skills required to access Public Services online.

Effectiveness and efficiency of the public sector of a country are strongly associated with the success of the development activities undertaken by that country (The World Bank Independent Evaluation Group (IEG), 2008). Quantifying and qualifying societal impact contribute to validating efficiency and effectiveness. Moreover, the complexity of Public Service entailed in its rational-legal foundations and its relative autonomy, which is consequent to the degree of authoritative status it enjoys in a specific context, implies insularity limitations. Attention to the societal impact of Public Service reform mitigates insularity risks by paying due attention to the foundational rationale of Public Service reform, namely, the capacity to tackle social problems in modern societies (Kekez, 2018). This chapter critically reviews literature concerning several notions, methodologies and instruments that have been used to understand the societal impact of public services and Public Service reform; or can be associated with related potential. These are namely the Net Promoter Score (NPS), Service Quality (SERVQUAL), Customer Satisfaction (CSAT) and trust in Public Services. The examination of research approaches and designs, applications, limitations and implications of findings will be examined to identify empirically based takeaways from the reviewed body of literature.

9.2   Net Promoter Score (NPS)

The NPS measures the customer's willingness to recommend the product, service or enterprise as a whole (Laitinen, 2018). Introduced by Fred Reichheld in 2003 (Laitinen, 2018), the NPS is based on the relatively one simple question addressed by an enterprise to its customers, 'How likely is it that you would recommend us to a friend or colleague?' Responses are scored on a 0-to-10 scale with 10 representing 'extremely likely' and 0 representing 'not at all likely' (Reichheld, 2006a). The term Net Promoter Score (NPS) is trademarked by Satmetrix Systems Inc., and ownership of the trademark is shared by Satmetrix, Bain & Company, and Fred Reichheld (Reichheld, 2006a, 2006b.

Customer responses tend to group in three clusters and each cluster is associated with particular behaviours. The 'promoters', those giving a rating of 9 or 10 rating, behave almost as if they were adjuncts to the enterprise's sales team. They report the highest repurchase rates, account for more than 80% of referrals and source most of the enterprise's positive word-of-mouth (WOM) reviews. Those that rate with a 7 or an 8 are referred to as the 'passively satisfied' or 'passives.' Their repurchase and referral rates are considerably lower than those of promoters, often by 50% or more. Customers rating the enterprise from 0 to 6 are known as 'detractors'. These are the least likely to repurchase or refer. They account for more than 80% of negative WOM reviews (Reichheld, 2006a).

An organization's NPS is the percentage of 'promoters' minus the percentage of 'detractors'. The metric was found to correlate well with increases in an enterprise's growth rate (Reichheld, 2006a). The review of the literature illuminates that the success of NPS lies in the medium of referral namely, WOM. The value of WOM is 'undisputable' (Marsden et al., 2005, p. 2). Consumers systematically rate WOM advice above all other forms of communication when making purchasing decisions. 'The logic is simple; word of mouth reduces risk for the buyer – it is free borrowed experience perceived as trustworthy because, unlike advertising, it has nothing to sell but itself' (p. 2). Reichheld's salient accomplishment was the crystallization of WOM, which, at the time, took place primarily offline in traditional face-to-face situations, into a measurable phenomenon; thus, foregrounding the 'hard economics of buzz' (p. 2).

Rather than making NPS redundant, Internet penetration and social media added the quantity and diversity of communication channels and data sources; to the extent that academic and grey literature document the 'word-of-mouse' (Marsden et al., 2005) and 'word-of-finger' (Levy, 2012; Quinion, 2010) phenomena. Notwithstanding, the literature flags that compared to traditional WOM referrals, word-of-finger interactions lack certain visual cues associated with traditional WOM advocacy and typically take place with anonymous strangers (Levy, 2012). Consequently, these differences can alter the reach and impact of the referral, although not necessarily in a negative manner.

Various studies took interest in the correlation between NPS and company growth rate. A 12-point increase in NPS was found to correspond to a doubling of a company's growth rate, though the variation from one industry to another was found to be substantial (Reichheld, 2006a, 2006b). Another study scoped retail bank, car manufacturing, mobile phone networks and supermarket industries based in the United Kingdom (UK) and found that a 7-point increase in NPS correlated, on average, with a one percentage point increase in growth rate (Marsden et al., 2005). Additionally, findings of this study added value to the 'economics of buzz' by validating the principle 'more good buzz is good, less bad buzz is better' (p. 4) and thereby flagging that the potential of customers as voluntary salespersons can be enhanced by stimulating and incentivizing their advocacy, and their positive advocacy in particular.

The validity of NPS' analysis is dependent on the timing of data collection: if this takes place immediately after purchase the score would be tracking customers' initial excitement and the checkout experience; when the survey takes place a few weeks after the purchase, the score also informs on how satisfied customers are with products and services over time. Tracking the satisfaction of an enterprise's customers over time is also a possible useful yield of NPS methodology. Other main advantages of NPS include the relatively simple collection, interpretation and communication of the data (Customer.guru, 2020a). Grey literature underlines the relevance of following-up on the score provided by the customer to close the loop of NPS. This is often overlooked to the detriment of the exercise. Furthermore, it can cause frustration in customers because the structure of the question does not allow the personalization of the experience; and trademark issues limit adaptation (Customer Sure, 2019). Arguably harsher and certainly more empirically founded, were the critiques of Kai Kristensen and Jacob Eskildsen (2011). Further to setting up a real experiment in the Danish insurance industry, they found that the NPS 'is by far inferior' (Eskildsen & Kristensen, 2011, p. 253; Kristensen & Eskildsen, 2011, p. 257) to the American Customer Satisfaction Index (ACSI) and European Performance Satisfaction Index (EPSI). They found the NPS to be heavily influenced by gender differences. In their study, females rated higher than males within the promoter block, females tended to use the promoter categories more (Kristensen and Eskildsen, 2011). They concluded that the NPS is invalid, unreliable and non-robust. Thus, the NPS is not a new scientific number for business like the numbers we know from physics, e.g. Planck's constant, Avogadro's number, and Hubble's constant... The NPS has gained popularity because it is very pedagogical. This is an advantage, but it is not enough... it does not provide reliable information about customer satisfaction and customer loyalty. Hopefully companies will realize this before too much harm is done (Eskildsen & Kristensen, 2011, p. 253).

Literature documenting the use of the NPS in public sector organizations is not abundant (Laitinen, 2018; Hakola, 2016) and rather restricted to customer evaluation of services provided by public libraries. The first reported use of the NPS of public library services constitutes a test administered by the National Library of Estonia (Välbe, 2015, 2016). The concept of NPS will likely be adopted in the new International Standard ISO 21248 (Information and Documentation Quality assessment for national libraries) that is being developed by the International Organization for Standardization (ISO) (Múčka, 2014). Additionally, Laitinen (2018) tested the applicability of the NPS to data retrieved from 2014–2016 user surveys about the services of the National Library of Finland. However, Marek Arendarčík Múčka (2014) suggested that the concept of the NPS could also be applicable in the public administration and corroborated with a number of similarities such as objectives that include effectiveness, efficiency, managerial functions, as well as the relevance of quality, innovations, customer satisfaction, the inclusion of clients and the inclusion of employees. Notwithstanding Múčka also flagged arguable differences between private and public sectors such as limitations in measuring growth and loyalty, very limited competition and lack of process approach.

Juho Hakola's research (2016) zoomed in on adapting the NPS to public sector organizations. The study tested a Net Promoter Score customized for the public sector (PSNPS) Main results of this study included no significant difference in promoting between promoters and detractors; sharing of positive word-of-mouth (PWOM) in some form by detractors and of negative word-of-mouth (NWOM) in some form by promoters; most of the passives had shared either PWOM or NWOM. Additionally, most of the given feedback was communicated face-to-face at customers' working place or with respective families. Indeed, only few of the respondents had shared WOM publicly in social sites. Notably, respondents' age and gender did not correlate with the NPS. In conclusion, the study claimed that the NPS is a needed tool in the public sector.

Notably, there is little evidence of use of the NPS in Malta, except for the flag carrier airline Air Malta; which was one of the first organisations in the country to have introduced the NPS in 2015. Across the quarters of this same year, excellent scores included +44 and + 54. These scores were also shared with employees as part of the efforts to make customer focus an integral part of the company culture (Airmalta plc, 2019). Further research did not yield more recent data on the use of the NPS in this company (Airmalta plc, 2019; Customer.guru, 2020b) or other industries based in Malta.

9.3 Service Quality (SERVQUAL)

The SERVQUAL model, initially developed by Parasuraman et al. (1988), is one of the tools used to test customer satisfaction. The model assumes that the quality of the service is determined by the discrepancy between the perception of the consumer and his expectations of the service. This method was also created in response to the fifth gap of the Five Gaps Service Quality Model, created by the same team of researchers (Fig. 9.1 – Parasuraman et al., 1985). The fifth gap is the difference between the consumer's expectations and the perception of the product.

The original SERVQUAL scale had 10 dimensions, which were then revised to the following five quality dimensions: reliability, referring to the ability to perform the promised service reliably and accurately; assurance, referring to the knowledge and courtesy of employees and their ability to convey trust and confidence; tangibles, referring to the physical facilities, equipment and appearance of personnel; empathy, which covers the provision of caring and individualized attention to consumers; and responsiveness, referring to the willingness to help consumers and to provide prompt services (Parasuraman et al., 1988).

Various researchers further modified the original scale's dimensions and items during their empirical research, mainly because the number of SERVQUAL dimensions varies from one industry to another and from one country to another.

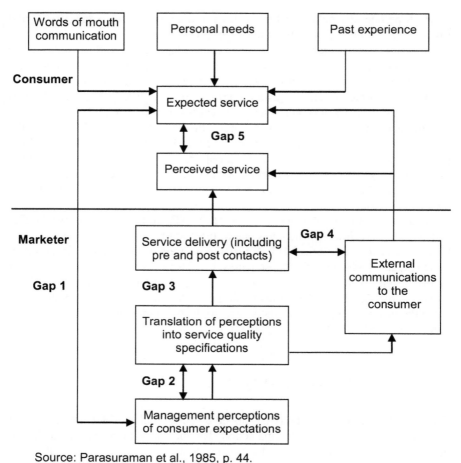

Source: Parasuraman et al., 1985, p. 44.

Fig. 9.1 Five gaps model of service quality

Customization of the tool's name features amongst adaptations, such as the DINESERV method used to measure quality performance of restaurants (Hansen, 2014). In Iran, to compensate for ambiguity and poor information about consumer opinions (referred to as the Grey system), SERVQUAL was adapted to include a 5-point Likert-type scale of dis/agreement to access expectations and perceptions of the consumers in using green products (Souri et al., 2018). Additionally, comparative research focused on examining the SERVQUAL scale and its dimensions from customers' perspectives by comparing two customers' samples (Ladhari et al., 2011; Arasli et al., 2005). However, comparative research studies that investigate the SERVQUAL dimensions and items from customers' and employees' perspectives alike are scant (Abu-El Samen et al., 2013).

SERVQUAL's relevance to e-service quality transpires from its numerous researched applications, such as the seven dimensions of online service quality (efficiency, reliability, fulfilment, privacy, responsiveness, compensation and contact) identified by means of e-SERVQUAL in the measurement of e-service quality (Zeithaml et al., 2000). The literature also documents an e-core service quality scale (E-S-QUAL) that examines website service quality using 22-item scales covering four dimensions (efficiency, fulfilment, system availability, and privacy) (Parasuraman et al., 2005); as well as the development of E-S-QUAL to gauge website service quality in the context of filing tax returns in Ireland using (Connolly & Bannister, 2008). In Malta, increased financial literacy and demands of financial services' clients rationalised a study on perceptions about retail finance that focused on service quality and internet banking. Its findings illuminated the emphasis of clients on reliability and access. The study also found that cost, security, convenience and having the service recommended by acquaintances significantly encouraged or inhibited the adoption of internet banking services (Camilleri et al., 2013).

Compared to the NPS, SERVQUAL has been associated with measurement of quality of different public services, such as education (Yousapronpaiboon, 2014) and healthcare (Al-Borie & Sheikh Damanhouri, 2013; Purcarea et al., 2013). In the late 1990s, public health care organizations, emergency services, local government and police were among public sector entities that manifested cognizance of customer service and quality as critical strategic issues. However, it is also widely recognized that such public sector organizations face difficulties in measuring service quality, primarily because of the multiplicity and characteristics of 'customers', to the extent that appropriateness of the term 'customers' has also been questioned. Notwithstanding, this corroborates the need for quality assurance that public services match customer expectations as accurately as possible (Wisniewski & Donnelly, 1996). Public sector services are also striving to identify customer needs and to monitor customer perceptions of services provided (Wisniewski & Donnelly, 1996), primarily because public services' customers are decreasingly perceived as passive users with limited voice and influence (Skelcher, 1992).

Studies that adopted and adapted the SERVQUAL model to public sector services, include research with users of public library services in the UK (Campbell et al., 1995; Dalrymple et al., 1995). More recently, Wan Zahari et al. (2008) developed the FM-SERVQUAL instrument using an empirical basis to evaluate the quality of services provided by local authorities in Johor Baharu City Council (Malaysia) to the public; whilst Kokku Randheer, Ahmed A. AL-Motawa and Prince Vijay. J (2011) administered a SERVQUAL scale to examine commuters' perception on service quality offered by the public transport services of the cities of Hyderabad and Secunderabad in India.

In Malta, as early as in the 1990s, SERVQUAL methodology was used to compare public and private hospital care service. This study identified sixteen service quality indicators and used these to develop two questionnaires. The first questionnaire measured patient pre-admission expectations for public and private hospital service quality (in respect of one another) and determined the weighted importance given to the different service quality indicators. The second questionnaire measured patient perceptions of provided service quality. Results showed that, at the time of the study, private hospitals were expected to offer a higher quality service, particularly in the hotel services, but it was the public sector that was exceeding its patients' expectations by the wider margin (Camilleri & O'Callaghan, 1998). Notably, use of SERVQUAL methodology also illuminated shortcomings in reliability and responsiveness of another Maltese private sector industry, namely motor insurance (Cassar, 2012).

SERVQUAL model criteria that included responsiveness, competence, courtesy, reliability and communication also featured in the cycle of seventeen human resources compliance inspection assessments carried out in 2018 by the People Resourcing and Compliance Directorate within the People and Standards Division. More recently, the Quality Award is a distinction awarded to departments and entities within the Public Administration that deliver services to customers at standards that address four pillars: voice and understanding the customer, design and implementation of policies and services that meet customer expectation, delivery of a quality service and accountability, where people become part of the excellence of the service provided. The award process is based on a SERVQUAL model of ten quality service determinants, namely: reliability, responsiveness, competence, access, courtesy, communication, credibility, security, understanding (i.e. knowing the customer and tangibles) (Government of Malta, 2020a, 2020b). At the time of writing the holders of the Quality Award included the Agriculture and Rural Payments Agency (ARPA), Business first, servizz.gov hubs, Aġenzija Żgħażagħ, the Malta-European Union Steering Action Committee (MEUSAC) and the National Blood Transfusion Service (NBTS) (peopleandstandards.gov.mt, n.d.)

Notably the Quality Award compliments a broader Mystery Shopper checks and balances exercise to assess quality and identify possibilities for improvement in the service provided to the citizen. As part of the Mystery Shopper exercise, the SERVQUAL methodology is adopted to assess public services (and servants) in terms of accessibility, responsiveness, courtesy, reliability, credibility, communication, security, competence and understanding. Limitations that are associated with using SERVQUAL in the public sector include that while overall service quality might indicate that the service matches customer expectations, there is no guarantee that service quality is high. This is particularly relevant to public sector organizations where customers may have developed low expectations for a variety of reasons. Notwithstanding, an adapted SERVQUAL instrument can highlight where expectations are low (Wisniewski & Donnelly, 1996).

9.4   Customer Satisfaction (CSAT)

CSAT involves asking customers what their experience or rating of the service or product in question is (Customer Sure, 2019, Infiniti, 2019). In other words, it's a measurement or a key performance indicator (KPI) that looks at how well a product or service experience meets a customer's expectation (Qualtrics, 2020). CSAT is measured by one or more variation of this 5-point Likert scale question that usually appears at the end of a customer feedback survey: 'How would you rate your overall satisfaction with the [goods/service] you received?' The results can be averaged out to give a composite customer satisfaction score, although CSAT scores are usually expressed as a percentage scale: 100% representing customer satisfaction, 0% total customer dissatisfaction. To do this, only responses of 4 'satisfied' and 5 'very satisfied' are included in the calculation because research shows that using the two highest values on feedback surveys is the most accurate predictor of customer retention (Qualtrics, 2020). Whilst literature on the deployment of CSAT in the private sector is very abundant, a closer look at published studies unravels how CSAT was often deployed as an entry point for researchers, who then combined use of NPS or SERVQUAL to gauge customer satisfaction. For example, in an empirical study of customer satisfaction with bank payment card services in Ho Chi Minh (China), CSAT informed the critical operationalisation of 'satisfaction' which was then gauged using a SERVQUAL-based model (Nguyen, Tran & Wang, 2014).

A similar combination of CSAT and SERVQUAL was used in Malta as a mediational model linking service quality to service loyalty via customer satisfaction in retail banking. The CSAT part of this study used a four-item scale that looked at post-purchase, global affective summary responses measured using a five-point Likert-type scale. The study concluded that customer satisfaction played a mediator role in the effect of service quality on service loyalty. More specifically, service quality affected service loyalty through customer satisfaction. Additionally, service quality was an important gateway to customer satisfaction and explained 53% of the variance (Caruana, 2002). Notably, evidence of the deployment of CSAT to examine customer satisfaction with public services is practically inexistent at a global level.

Compared to other tools surveying customer satisfaction or ratings, CSAT is considered to be relatively simple to understand by customers, those implementing it and those interpreting the results. CSAT question or questions may be articulated in various ways because CSAT is not owned by a particular entity and this is an advantage because it can be used in a more flexible manner (Customer Sure, 2019). CSAT can also use multiple questions to focus on specific parts of the customer experience, e.g. 'How would you rate your overall satisfaction with the telephone service you received /helpfulness of assistant/delivery?' (Qualtrics, 2020). The implied risk is that this makes it open to interpretation (Customer Sure, 2019), thus raising concerns of interpretation and comparability. The implications of CSAT's methodology include that as a KPI it gauges customers' reaction to the 'here and now' of a specific interaction, product or event (Qualtrics, 2020). 'Satisfaction is fragile and fickle, highly linked to the moment. It provides a general impression, but gives little understanding about the true experience' (Plaskoff, 2015, p. 20). This limits its potential of measuring a customer's ongoing relationship with a company (Qualtrics, 2020).

9.5   Trust in Public Service

This chapter's discussion has so far illuminated that surveying customer satisfaction with public services has been gaining ground (Van De Walle & Bouckaert, 2003). Literature makes an arguable association between scores attained by government entities in customer satisfaction surveys and the level of trust in Public Service, such as US government agencies' participation in American Customer Satisfaction Index (ACSI) surveys on a voluntary basis and Europe-based government agencies' participation in the Kundenmonitor (Bouckaert & Van De Walle, 2003). The association is arguable because in the relationship between the public sector and respective users other factors contribute to trust formation and maintenance; whilst performance of public administration and satisfaction of its users are not necessarily co-related (Van De Walle & Bouckaert, 2003).

Another association that requires further corroboration is the equivalence between trust in Public Service and trust in government that seems to be suggested by certain sources. Additionally, when trust in government can be measured, it is not at all clear whether changes in the level of trust are actually the outcome of government-related factors (Bouckaert & Van de Walle, 2003). This also implies that should the equivalence between trust in Public Service and trust in government be robustly corroborated, the linkages between trust in government and good governance would remain unclear. Furthermore, existing attempts to measure trust and satisfaction in government have been reviewed as misleading when claiming to be measuring good governance because satisfaction is difficult to measure, and it is also very service specific. Indeed, researchers have also shown interest in empirically substantiating the distinction between satisfaction with public service delivery and trust in government (e.g. Van De Walle & Bouckaert, 2003): the first might not necessarily lead to the trust in government; nor be a prerequisite to it. Related and relevant questions also include: (a) is government a simple summation of agencies and is it perceived as such by Public Service-users? (b) Do the users' perceptions of Public Service delivery influence trust levels and if so, to what extent? (c) Are they in a direct, inverse (Van De Walle & Bouckaert, 2003) or sporadic manner? Additionally, are users' perceptions concerning every single Public Service entity of comparable influence on trust levels, or is the perception of the service of some public entities more significant to perception formation than that of others? (Van De Walle & Bouckaert, 2003) There is also critique flagging that terms such as 'trust', 'confidence', 'perception' and 'image' of government are often used interchangeably as catchall terms and as buzzwords in political discourse (Van De Walle & Bouckaert, 2003, p. 893).

Apart from the above complexities, sampling bias, response bias, question design bias and lack of questions on people's actual experiences in dealing with different public institutions or their behaviours and attitudes towards government have been flagged as shortcomings of existing international perception survey measures (Lonti, 2014). In response, the five dimensions suggested as 'amenable to government actions' (p. 7) are reliability, responsiveness, openness and inclusiveness, integrity and fairness. Notwithstanding the above limitations, a number of research studies offer insights relevant to the rationale of this chapter. For instance, empirical research identified trust as a prerequisite to 'continuance use' of Public Service (Belanche et al., 2014). Another question that piqued interest to the point of empirical research asked whether it is low quality of Public Service that yields unfavourable evaluations of government in general, or whether it is the negative attitude towards government in general that leads people to evaluate the quality of its public services in a negative manner. In other words, can 'causality actually work in both directions, or does it then concern two entirely different causal relations?' (p. 893). The study found that modernisation of public services can only partially enhance government legitimacy. Actual performance is not equivalent to perceived performance; whilst there is no unanimity among citizens on the definition and requirement of public service performance. Consequently, focus on performance would not suffice. Ultimately, citizens' perceptions and definitions of government performance are not only created in government-citizen interactions, but also in everyday citizen-citizen relations. Restoring trust in government cannot just be based on a managerial action-plan but requires social engineering as well (p. 909).

The literature also documents interest in the development of a scale of trustworthiness, as was the case of Stephan Grimmelikhuijsen and Eva Knies (2017) who adapted and validated the Citizen Trust in Government Organizations scale in a public administration context using nine items measuring three dimensions: perceived competence, benevolence and integrity. Trust in e-Public Service has also attracted research interest, particularly further to the rise and sophistication of cybercrime, as well as recent leaks threatening trust in public entities' ability to securely provide electronic services (e-services). The UK's National Health Service (NHS) accidentally lost millions of digital medical records, while former Central Intelligence Agency (CIA) employee Edward Snowden leaked wilful exchanges of personally identifiable information between government entities based in the UK and in the United States' (US) (Belanche et al., 2014). In this context, Belanche et al. (2014) found that interpersonal and public administration recommendations and e-service quality enhanced user trust. They also found that trust in the Internet is a driver of trust in e-Public Services and related continuance intentions. As a result, public e-services should be well secured. Related good practices include easily recognizable government websites, also through use of government domain names (e.g. .gov), clear display of a privacy statement, procurement from respectable technology partners, testimonials of reliability, FAQ pages and contact pages (Wu & Chen, 2005).

Notably, at the time of writing the Maltese Public Service classified in first place in the European Commission's yearly e-government benchmarking for the online Public Services it provides from the participating thirty-six countries (European Union plus Iceland, Norway, Montenegro, Serbia, Switzerland, Turkey and the United Kingdom). The criteria included technical elements, quality and design of the online service, transparency adopted in the services provided, as well as the accessibility of online services – even when citizens are far away from their country and accessibility for businesses beyond Malta's shores (Government of Malta, 2020b).

9.6 Conclusions

This chapter reviewed literature documenting the development, application and limitations of NPS, SERVQUAL, CSAT, as well the understanding and measurement of trust in public services. A plethora of studies substantiates the influence of these societal impact metrics on the success of private enterprises; whilst there is evidence of a growing support for deployment in the public sector. The review illuminated that uptake of NPS and CSAT in the public sector in Malta is negligible. Conversely, there is abundant evidence of increasing systemic deployment of the SERVQUAL methodology across the public sector; which also brought to the fore the public sector's outstanding performance, particularly in the ratings of its e-government services. In this regard, the chapter also reviewed various studies that engaged with societal impact metrics to gauge the experience of users of e-services. More generally, conceptual complexities emerged as relevant, such as the many possible interpretations of 'satisfaction' and the empirically ambiguous association between trust in public services and trust in government. The use of the term 'customer' for users of public services has also been contested.

A second headline finding of this chapter is that attention is due to methodological limitations of societal impact metrics. For instance, CSAT measures customer satisfaction with a product or service at the moment of consumption, a limitation that is countered by the more sophisticated NPS, which has the added value of capturing customer loyalty; and SERVQUAL, which illuminates different dimensions of the service-user experience, which have also been adapted to specific contexts. This suggests that no metric alone is likely to be enough, whilst hybrid tools should factor-in context. Ultimately the buck cannot stop at measuring experience. It is what an entity does with the findings to drive reform that fulfils the rationale of societal impact concepts and metrics.

References

Abu-El Samen, A. A., Akroush, M. N., & Abu-Lail, B. (2013). Mobile SERVQUAL. *The International Journal of Quality & Reliability Management, 30*(4), 403–425. http://dx.doi.org. ejournals.um.edu.mt/10.1108/02656711311308394

Airmaltaplc.(2019).AirMaltaSurveysover10,000CustomersInNewCustomerSatisfactionSurvey. Accessed 21 October 2020, at https://www.airmalta.com/information/about/news-overview/ news-detail/air-malta-surveys-over-10-000-customers-in-new-customer-satisfaction-survey

Al-Borie, H. M., & Sheikh Damanhouri, A. M. (2013). Patients' satisfaction of service quality in Saudi hospitals: A SERVQUAL analysis. *International Journal of Health Care Quality Assurance, 26*(1), 20–30.

Arasli, H., Katircioglu, S. T., & Mehtap-Smadi, S. (2005). A comparison of service quality in the banking industry: Some evidence from Turkish- and Greek-speaking areas in Cyprus. *International Journal of Bank Marketing, 23*(7), 506–526.

Belanche, D., Casaló, L. V., Flavián, C., & Schepers, J. (2014). Trust transfer in the continued usage of public E-services. *Information & Management, 51*(6), 627–640.

Bouckaert, G., & Van de Walle, S. (2003). Comparing measures of citizen trust and user satisfaction as indicators of 'good governance': Difficulties in linking trust and satisfaction indicators. *International Review of Administrative Sciences, 69*(3), 329–343.

Camilleri, D., & O'Callaghan, M. (1998). Comparing public and private hospital care service quality. *International Journal of Health Care Quality Assurance, 11*(4), 127–133.

Camilleri, S. J., Cortis, J., & Fenech, M. D. (2013). Service quality and internet banking: Perceptions of Maltese retail Bank customers. *Bank of Valletta Review, 48*(Autumn), 1–17.

Campbell, S. J., Donnelly, M., & Wisniewski, M. (1995). A measurement of service. *Journal of the Scottish Libraries Association, 50*, 10–11.

Caruana, A. (2002). Service loyalty: The effects of service quality and the mediating role of customer satisfaction. *European Journal of Marketing, 36*, 811–828. https://doi.org/10.1108/03090560210430818

Cassar, B. (2012). *Service quality in the Maltese motor insurance industry* (unpublished b.com (hons.) marketing dissertation). Malta: University of Malta.

Connolly, R., Bannister, F. (2008). eTax Filing & Service Quality: The case of the revenue online service. *Proceedings of World Academy of Science, Engineering and Technology 28* (April), issn 1307-6884.

Customer Sure. (2019). Customer Experience Metrics: NPS, CSAT or Customer Effort: Explained! Accessed 15 April 2020, from https://www.youtube.com/watch?v=feqVpMtRyMU

Customer.guru. (2020a). *Public service enterprise group net promoter score 2020 benchmarks*. Accessed 2 April 2020, at https://customer.guru/net-promoter-score/public-service-enterprise-group

Customer.guru. (2020b). Air Malta net promoter score 2020 benchmarks. Accessed 1 October 2020, at https://customer.guru/net-promoter-score/air-malta

Dalrymple, J. F., Donnelly, M., Wisniewski, M., & Curry, A. C. (1995). Measuring service quality in local government. In G. P. Kani (Ed.), *Total quality management: Proceedings of the first world congress* (pp. 263–266). Chapman and Hall.

Economic and Social Research Council (ESRC). (2020). What is impact? Accessed 2 April 2020, at https://esrc.ukri.org/research/impact-toolkit/what-is-impact/

Eskildsen, J. K., & Kristensen, K. (2011). The gender Bias of the net promoter score. In *2011 IEEE international conference on quality and reliability (conference proceedings)* (pp. 254–258).

Government of Malta. (2020a). The Quality Award. Accessed1 1 October 2020, at https://deputyprimeminister.gov.mt/en/nbts/Pages/About-Us/Quality-Award.aspx.

Government of Malta. (2020b, September 29). Press Release by the Office of the Principal Permanent Secretary the Maltese Public Service ranks first yet again for E-government in Europe (PR201810en). Accessed 1 October 2020, at https://www.gov.mt/en/Government/DOI/Press%20Releases/Pages/2020/September/24/pr201810en.aspx

Gow, I. (2007). Whose model is realistic, whose [sic] unrealistic? *Optimum Online, 37*(4), 4.

Grimmelikhuijsen, S., & Knies, E. (2017). Validating a scale for citizen Trust in Government Organizations. *International Review of Administrative Sciences, 83*(3), 583–601.

Hansen, K. V. (2014). Development of Servqual and Dineserv for measuring meal experiences in eating establishments. *Scandinavian Journal of Hospitality and Tourism, 14*(2), 116–134.

Hakola, J. (2016). *Adapting Net Promoter thinking in public sector organizations*. Master's thesis, Organizational Communication and PR, Department of Communication, University of Jyväskylä.

Infiniti research posts article focused on measuring customer satisfaction. (2019, Feb 07). *Professional Services Close – Up*. Accessed 2 May 2020, at https://search-proquest-com.ejournals.um.edu.mt/docview/2176641175?accountid=27934

Kekez, A. (2018). Public service reforms and clientelism: Explaining variation of service delivery modes in Croatian social policy. *Policy and Society, 37*(3), 386–404. https://doi.org/10.1080/14494035.2018.1436505

Kristensen, K., and Eskildsen, J. (2011). *Is the Net Promoter Score a reliable performance measure?* IEEE International Conference on Quality and Reliability, 2011, pp. 249–253, https://doi.org/10.1109/ICQR.2011.6031719

Ladhari, R., Ladhari, R., & Morales, M. (2011). Bank service quality: Comparing Canadian and Tunisian customer perceptions. *International Journal of Bank Marketing, 29*(3), 224–246.

Laitinen, M. A. (2018). Net promoter score as Indicator of library customers' perception. *Journal of Library Administration, 58*(4), 394–406. https://doi.org/10.1080/01930826.2018.1448655

Levy, K. (2012). *Consumer Decision Making and Word of Mouth Communication.* Unpublished master of arts in recreation and leisure studies dissertation. Ontario: University of Waterloo. Accessed 4 October 2020: https://uwspace.uwaterloo.ca/bitstream/handle/10012/7026/Levy_Kristen.pdf?sequence=1&isAllowed=y

Lonti, Z. (2014). *The OECD work program on trust: Understanding the key drivers for better policy making.* OECD. Accessed 2 May 2020, at http://www.cdeunodc.inegi.org.mx/unodc/articulos/doc_conf2/p_ZsuzsannaLonti.pdf

Marsden, P., Samson, A. & Upton, N. (2005). Advocacy drives growth. Journal of Brand Strategy.

Múčka, M. A. (2014). Process mapping and feasibility of its practical implementation within the public administration in Slovak republic. *Ad Alta: Journal of Interdisciplinary Research, 4*(2), 26–29. Accessed 10 April 2020, at http://www.magnanimitas.cz/ADALTA/0402/papers/A_mucka.pdf

Parasuraman, A., Berry, L. L., & Zeithaml, V. A. (1985). A conceptual model of service quality and its implications for future research. *The Journal of Marketing, 49*(4), 41–50.

Parasuraman, A., Berry, L. L., & Zeithaml, V. A. (1988). Servqual: A multiple-item scale for measuring customer perceptions of service quality. *Journal of Retailing, 64*(1), 12–40.

Parasuraman, A., Zeithaml, V. A., & Malhotra, A. (2005). E-S-QUAL: A multiple-item scale for assessing electronic service quality. *Journal of Service Research, 7*(3), 213–233.

Peopleandstandards.gov.mt. (n.d.). The Quality Award. Accessed 1 October 2020, at https://public-service.gov.mt/en/people/Pages/TheQUALITYAWARD.aspx

Plaskoff, J. (2015). *eleVate The Citizen ExperienceTM – Transforming Government Customer Service.* HighPoint global government solutions. Accessed 2 May 2020, at https://www.high-pointglobal.com/wp-content/uploads/2016/10/HighPoint-Global-White-Paper-10-03-16.pdf

Purcarea, V. L., Gheorghe, I. R., & Petrescu, C. M. (2013). The assessment of perceived service quality of public health care services in Romania using the Servqual scale. *Procedia Economics and Finance, 6*, 573–585.

Qualtrics. (2020). What is a Customer Satisfaction Score (CSAT)? Accessed 2 May 2020, at https://www.qualtrics.com/uk/experience-management/customer/customer-satisfaction/?rid=ip&prevsite=en&newsite=uk&geo=MT&geomatch=uk

Quinion, M. (2010). World wide words: Word of finger. Accessed 10 April 2020, at http://www.worldwidewords.org/turnsofphrase/tp-wor1.htm

Randheer, K., AL-Motawa, A. A., & Prince, V. J. (2011). Measuring commuters' perception on service quality using SERVQUAL in public transportation. *International Journal of Marketing Strategies, 3*(1), 21–34.

Reichheld, F. (2006a). The microeconomics of customer relationships. *MIT Sloan Management Review, 47*(2), 73–78.

Reichheld, F. (2006b). *The ultimate question: Driving good profits and true growth.* Harvard School Publishing.

Skelcher, C. (1992). *Improving the Quality of Local Public Services. The Service Industries Journal*, 12:4, 463–477, https://doi.org/10.1080/02642069200000059

Souri, M. E., Sajjadian, F., Sheikh, R., & Sana, S. S. (2018). Grey SERVQUAL method to measure Consumers' attitudes towards green products – A case study of Iranian consumers of LED bulbs. *Journal of Cleaner Production, 177*, 187–196.

The World Bank Independent Evaluation Group. (2008). *Public sector reform: What works and why? An IEG evaluation of World Bank support.* The International Bank for Reconstruction and Development / The World Bank. Accessed 3 April 2020, at https://www.cmi.no/publications/file/3042-public-sector-reform-what-works-and-why.pdf

Välbe, K. (2015). *What is the probability of recommending library service to a friend or colleague? Possibilities of using promoter index as a library performance indicator.* Conference paper given in 7th qualitative and quantitative methods in libraries international conference (QQML2015) 26–29 may 2015, Paris, France.

Välbe, K. (2016). Net promoter score — *The best way to compare yourself to... yourself. Using NPS for identifying potential impact of a library*. Conference paper given in 8th qualitative and quantitative methods in libraries international conference (QQML2016) 24-27 May 2016, London UK.

Van De Walle, S., & Bouckaert, G. (2003). Public service performance and Trust in Government: The problem of causality. *International Journal of Public Administration, 26*(8–9), 891–913.

Wang, C.N., Nguyen, N.T. & Tran, T.T. (2014). An empirical study of customer satisfaction towards bank payment card service quality in Ho chi minh banking branches. *International Journal of Economics and Finance, 6*(5), 170. https://doi.org/10.5539/ijef.v6n5p170

Wisniewski, M., & Donnelly, M. (1996). Measuring service quality in the public sector: The potential for SERVQUAL. *Total Quality Management, 7*(4), 357–366.

Wu, I. L., & Chen, J. N. (2005). An extension of Trust and TAM model with TPB in the initial adoption of on-line tax: An empirical study. *International Journal of Human-Computer Studies, 62*(6), 784–808.

Yousapronpaiboon, K. (2014). Servqual: Measuring higher education service quality in Thailand. *Procedia-Social and Behavioral Sciences, 116*, 1088–1095.

Zahari, W., Yusoff, W., Maziah, I., & Graeme, N. (2008). FM-SERVQUAL: A new approach of service quality measurement framework in local authorities. *Journal of Corporate Real Estate, 10*(2), 130–144.

Zeithaml, V. A., Parasuraman, A., & Malhotra, A. (2000). *A conceptual framework for understanding eService quality: Implications for future research and managerial practice: Working paper (report number 00–115)*. Marketing Science Institute. Accessed April 30 2020, at https://www.msi.org/reports/a-conceptual-framework-for-understanding-e-service-quality-implications-for/

Chapter 10
Fair Deals in the Maltese Public Service: Linking Psychological Contract Breach to Attitudinal Outcomes

> *"Public service must be more than doing a job efficiently and honestly. It must be a complete dedication to the people and to the nation."*
>
> Margaret Chase Smith
> American politician

The Maltese Public Service is in a constant state of evolution and change. This continuous state of transformation brings with it not only risks and challenges but also opportunities. Normally change is associated with resistance and potential negative outcomes. Our research study, which was conducted in a double wave of change related to the internal and external environment, did not demonstrate the expected negative reactions and pessimistic ratings by employees. To be more precise, our research results suggest that the Maltese Public Service is coping and managing well the various changes being implemented as it becomes more people-oriented and embraces a new corporate identity. Furthermore, our study demonstrates how specific factors are associated to others and hence require leadership skills and abilities to steer people management in ways that ensure the maintenance of effective working relationships and therefore positive attitudes at work.

10.1 Introduction

The modern Public Service has become a complex organisation that has increasingly moved from paper pushing and a highly bureaucratic institution to a more performance-driven and customer-centric organisation. These changes have demanded shifts in operational modes leading to structural dynamics and culminating in new work structures and relationships of how to do work. Therefore, modern

F. Bezzina et al., *Public Service Reforms in a Small Island State*,
Public Administration, Governance and Globalization 22,
https://doi.org/10.1007/978-3-030-74357-4_10

public services have moved towards working models that allowed them to be more visible, subject to public scrutiny and checks-and-balances; at the same time transforming themselves into more efficient and effective systems of public administration. Public officers have also become more versatile with modern ways of organisation and, while adhering to strict legislative frameworks and policy guidelines in their call of duty, have become obliged to achieve higher standards of performance. Hence, we can construe the Public Service and its employees as being a good example of a transforming organisational system.

The Public Service is the context of our investigation and we examine the quality of the employment relationship by evaluating the degree of psychological contract breach on salient attitudinal outcomes. Therefore, our central concept is the psychological contract. The psychological contract represents an important index to evaluate the quality of the perceived employment relationship (Coyle-Shapiro et al., 2019). It becomes critical when evaluating an organisation's performance and employee reactions especially in times of transformation and change (Murray et al., 2002).

We organize this chapter as follows. First, we provide an appreciation of the context under investigation namely the Maltese Public Service. We then present the various pathways linking the various factors leading to several hypotheses. This will be followed by a description of the method and presentation of results. Finally, we provide an integrated discussion that includes insights from our findings and several recommendations.

10.2   The Maltese Public Service: A Journey of Transitions

Johns (2018), like others (e.g. Kozlowski & Klein, 2000), makes a solid emphasis on the appreciation of context in order to understand the way a phenomenon unfolds and shapes itself over time. As Rousseau and Fried (2001) correctly point out, 'contextualizing entails linking observations to a set of relevant facts, events, or points of view that make possible research and theory that form part of a larger whole' (p. 1). Of course, one should be careful not to go overboard and risk partitioning phenomena as overly context sensitive as this may risk theoretical parsimony and our ability to generalise from our findings. Rather, in line with Johns (2018), we argue that being sensitive to context can demarcate theoretical boundaries and therefore provide a more precise view of what may be happening that is salient to one's specific research location.

The context for our study is the Maltese Public Service. Most of the Maltese Public Service tradition is a result of British rule that lasted from 1800 to 1964. Malta became an independent state in 1964 and a Republic in 1974. Like most public services in democratic and free societies, the Maltese Public Service went through a host of changes and reforms with a major one being in 1989. These reforms have not only been strategic but also structural and operational. These reforms have not always been plain sailing and, given the size of Malta, they have often conflicted with the motives and agenda of the higher political class giving rise to certain dysfunctionalities (Pirotta, 1997). Indeed, Polidano (1996) argues that Malta's administrative reforms have produced mixed results. While they have achieved more than any previous initiatives, vital elements of the reform program were not carried out and results fell short of initial expectations. Partly, this is due to the need for sustained political backing and partly because of competing structures that struggle for their *raison d'etre*, a position also supported by other scholars (e.g. Warrington, 2002). Cassar and Bezzina (2005) argue that the Maltese Public Service is typically characterised by a high sense of legitimate authority with Warrington (2002) describing it as 'largely staffed by career officials appointed, disciplined and removable by the Prime Minister acting on the recommendation of a constitutionally recognised Public Service Commission' (p. 7).

Over the years, the Maltese Public Service has had to constantly transform itself to meet the needs of Malta's economic growth and changing social fabric while at the same time aligning itself to required obligations of the European Union following Malta's full membership in 2004. According to Cassar and Azzopardi (2019), the Public Service sought to shift from an administrative-centric institution to one that is more people-centric. In their words, 'the view that would lead to a new strategy was based on the belief that people are central and unique, different than all other resources' (p. 371). This strategy sought to achieve more through the people. Indeed, one important development in this episode was the creation of a new corporate brand captured in a four-pillar model namely 'voice' (i.e. a system open to new ideas and concepts), 'design' (i.e. setting structures that maximise one's ability to gather listening from stakeholders and customers), 'delivery' (i.e. ensuring getting results within set time frames and reaching standards) and 'accountability' (i.e. the ability of the Public Service to expose a degree of credibility in the eyes of those it serves).

Based on a host of other literature that calls for the transformation of the Public Service (e.g. Boyle, 2006; Martin & Smith, 2005; Osborne & Gaebler, 1992), Bezzina et al. (2017) evaluated the extent the European-based public service institutions were likely to implement performance indicators to ensure that they are objective-driven through their people. As expected, emphasis was given to financial thresholds where tight budgets may preclude public institutions achieving their objectives (Martin & Smith, 2005) and also the possible conflict between purely driven organisational objectives and broader national objectives of a political nature (Pirotta, 1997). In addition, complex policy procedures could impact the degree that public officers could achieve specific targets. This scenario presents a dual tension instance in typical public service organisations. On the one hand, public officers are expected to abide to specific and strict codes of practice; on the other hand, they are required to become agile in their operations to ensure they can achieve high level organisational goals that reflect efficiency and effectiveness. These may look incompatible to each other and sometimes contradictory. Research shows that high-performance work systems require very fluid work structures (Peiró et al., 2020). Even though the work environment structures may determine how people achieve their goals in a public service organisation (Camilleri, 2007), intentionally designed high-performance work systems can have negative effects on employees (Han et al., 2020).

Thus, given these scenarios, we may argue that the Maltese Public Service is in a state of flux oscillating between a purely administrative machine but, at the same, time pushing ahead to re-engineer a more performance-driven climate. As Cassar and Azzopardi (2019) rightly claim, 'The overall goal continues to be the continuous modernisation of the public administration…this is an ongoing and comprehensive project. It calls for measures for timely decision-making, simplified and more user-friendly processes, and strategically planned recruitment considering operational requirements' (p. 387). In doing so, employees must constantly adapt while redefining their deal with their employer. This model of adaptation and reconfiguration is our building block for this study, and it is to this that we now turn.

10.3   Research Model and Theoretical Justification: A Brief Overview of the Nature of the Psychological Contract

A psychological contract is defined as the perceived exchange relationship between employer and employee (Rousseau, 2011). It provides us with a strong index of the quality and state of the employment relationship. People in an employment relationship construe an exchange process whereby they expect specific returns for service provisions. Indeed, the basis of the employment relationship is often captured in a social exchange relationship (Blau, 1964) and the employment relationship is best seen through the lens of social exchange theory. The set of terms in the exchange relationship may often be written or contractually agreed but the different parties provide their own interpretation of how and when these are fairly provided or otherwise. Such terms constitute the obligations (e.g. training, salary, etc.) and inducements (e.g. day's work, loyalty, etc.) that are perceivably agreed in the contractual exchange relationship. Psychological contracts provide a strong sense of anticipation and clarity of future transactions between the parties (Rousseau, 1995). It is known that a healthy and stable employment relationship is important for organisational effectiveness (Coyle-Shapiro & Conway, 2004) and, given it is a perceived exchange (beyond the parameters of a mere collective agreement), wrong interpretations can give rise to unwanted reactions.

We base our conceptual pathways from a number of theoretical underpinnings but largely inspired by a number of propositions defined by Tomprou et al., (2015) who demonstrate, once again, the important and impactful influences of having one's exchange deal (the psychological contract) breached. The model highlights the distress caused by breach and the possible disengagement and demotivation that people are likely to experience because of that distress. The model also amplifies on several negative consequences that may result due to an employer failing to fulfil one's exchange relationship and the processes people go through in redefining their relationship with their employer. These dynamics are pertinent to contexts that are undergoing fundamental changes just like the Public Service (Cassar & Azzopardi, 2019). Therefore, we deem it warranted that the point of departure is the degree of

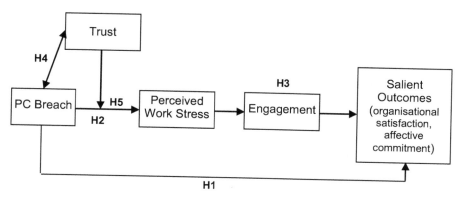

Fig. 10.1 Hypothesised research model

breach an employee is likely to perceive in a changing context. Our research model takes the shape of a hypothesised moderated mediation model (Preacher et al., 2007) and is presented in Fig. 10.1.

In essence, in line with the psychological contract literature in general (e.g. Rousseau, 2011) and the model shaping our thinking in this study (Tomprou et al., 2015), we argue that the quality of the employment relationship, as envisaged by the state of the fulfilment of the psychological contract, is associated to the level of perceived stress that employees manifest due to potential breach. This association is exacerbated by the level of trust employees have in their institution. While it is expected that breach impacts negatively salient organisational attitudinal outcomes, we suggest that breach may potentially impact negatively a host of other important variables before having negative consequences on outcomes through two mediators: perceived stress and engagement. We also postulate that this mediating pathway leading to outcomes is moderated by the level of trust employees have in their organisation. We now dissect the model into its various parts for the ease of explanation and provide separate hypotheses.

10.4   Breaches on Outcomes: Direct Effect

Psychological contract breach happens when employees feel that what was promised or is obliged by their employers, is actually not delivered (Morrison & Robinson, 1997; Robinson & Wolfe Morrison, 2000). Some studies also demonstrate that, often, employees are likely to report breach irrespective of promises made indicating how sensitive employment relations can be (Montes & Zweig, 2009). For example, Cassar (2001) found that employees in the Public Service were more likely to report job security as being breached given that it was implicated from other non-institutional sources rather than being explicitly told that their job could be on the line.

Psychological contract breach is very much likely to alter one's attitudinal reactions towards their organisation. Because breach is fundamentally a shift from the implicitly agreed exchange relationship, people who perceive breach are likely to reduce their investment in important outcomes that will benefit the organisation. In a meta-analysis, Zhao et al., (2007) found a strong correlation between breach and most salient organisational outcomes. Hence, we propose that:

Hypothesis 1 There is a negative association between psychological contract breach and salient organisational attitudinal outcomes; i.e. affective commitment (H1a) and organisational satisfaction (H1b).

10.5   Breaches on Outcomes Via Stress and Engagement: Indirect Effects

Drawing further from Tomprou et al.'s (2015) conceptual model thinking, we argue that perceptions and experiences of psychological contract breach is generally manifested by a series of negative emotions of anger, betrayal and disbelief (Morrison & Robinson, 1997). This is often coined as psychological contract violation and this emotional upheaval is likely to generate negative reactions on salient outcomes. This is well documented in the literature that events that are emotionally evoking can alter the state of one's evaluation of the work environment. For example, the influence of breach on outcomes is generally mediated by the intensity of the emotional turmoil (Suazo et al., 2005). This perceptual alteration seems to be higher for negative events than positive ones (Taylor, 1991). Such instances are likely to deplete internal resources (that is conditions that are valued by the person such as salient work conditions that get breached) and increase one's perception of stress (Hobfoll, 1989). This is also much in line with Tomprou et al. (2015) who argue that following violation experiences (hence experiences that are salient to the person; see e.g. Rousseau, 2011), people are likely to report higher levels of stress. Hence, we hypothesise that:

Hypothesis 2 There is a positive relationship between psychological contract breach and perceptions of work-related stress.

In addition to this, stress levels are likely to cut down short on people's willingness to look for intrinsic resources to function properly. In other words, people become disengaged. Work engagement is a multitude of positive dimensions that describe an employee's association to one's work. First mentioned by Kahn (1990), engagement is characterized by energy, involvement and efficacy. These dimensions were re-evaluated and typically include vigour, dedication and absorption (Schaufeli & Bakker, 2003; Schaufeli & Bakker, 2010). Work engagement is distinct from a myriad of other related concepts like commitment and flow (Schaufeli & Bakker, 2010). Systematic reviews and meta analyses have found its overall effect to be significant although rather small (Knight et al., 2017). Despite this, work engagement is still considered as a relevant feature that defines the quality of an employee's relationship to one's work. It can be construed as a form of intrinsic motivation. For example, low work engagement may contribute towards decreased well-being and work performance (Harter et al., 2002).

It has also been strongly associated to aspects like positive emotions and mental health (Cassar et al., 2018). It is deemed to be an element that mobilises workers to utilize actively and effectively their internal and external resources as captured in the Job Demands-Resources model (Bakker & Demerouti, 2008). Given its intrinsic qualities of 'mobilising' workers to energise themselves on their job, we view engagement as a potential mediator that is influenced by degrees of perceived work stress (therefore increased demands) and, in turn, impacts negatively salient outcomes. Multitudes of research have already established a strong association between perceived stress at work and salient organisational outcomes (Hart & Cooper, 2012) and we thus postulate that:

Hypothesis 3 *Psychological contract breach leads to heightened levels of work stress which, in turn, is likely to reduce levels of work engagement and, in turn, decreases organisational attitudinal outcomes i.e. affective commitment (H3a) and organisational satisfaction (H3b).*

10.6 Trust as a Moderator

One fundamental precursor of whether employees are likely to report breach, is the level of trust employees have in their employer. We take some time to clarify who best represents the 'employer' in this research domain. There is no firm evidence that indicates that top management are the sole representatives of the 'organisation' in other people's minds (except for the study by Guest et al., 2000). For example, Shore and Tetrick (1994) state that 'the employee is likely to view the [immediate] supervisor as the chief agent for establishing and maintaining the psychological contract' (p. 101). In addition, although agency theory is concerned with a general theory of the relationship based on a strict bilateral contract between principal and agent, and hence can be applied to all sorts of relationships (e.g. lawyer-client; buyer-supplier) (Eisenhardt, 1989), it becomes reductionist when it is applied to the employer-employee relationship. Research reveals that employees vary about whether they believe their psychological contract is with their immediate supervisor, top management or someone else (Rousseau, 1998). In order to reduce ambiguities with the referent representative of the 'organisation', we postulate that the immediate superior represents the employer. Moreover, this referent representation is more factual as employees tend to build and establish trust with other people they frequently encounter, and with specific referent and legitimate power in the organisation rather than with an anthropomorphic institution.

Trust has several direct effects on a number of aspects of work (Dirks & Ferrin, 2001). Because psychological contracts are firmly based in the norm of reciprocity

(Gouldner, 1960), this reciprocal process generates trust. We thus present trust as a reciprocal dynamic process whereby people can anticipate the credibility of future transactions based on previous ones (Lewicki & Brinsfield, 2017). Given that trust is a reciprocal process between parties in an exchange relationship, trust has strong relationships with the state of perceived breach with people lower in trust reporting more psychological contract breach. Hence we argue that the current state of trust amongst public officers is likely to determine the degree of perceived psychological contract breach has on people's level of stress (Tomprou et al., 2015). This is because lower trust is likely to render people more vigilant and possibly more suspicious on whether the exchange relationship is being honoured or otherwise (Carol, 2007; Robinson, 1996). Hence, we hypothesise that:

Hypothesis 4 *There is a negative relationship between trust and psychological contract breach*

In addition, and following from hypothesis 4, we argue that the level of trust will specifically impact the association between breach and stress in the 'breach → stress → engagement → outcomes' pathway. Earlier, studies have indicated that initial trust moderates the impact of breach on later trust, thus suggesting that the exchange relationship implicit in the employment relationship is paramount to enhancing the level of subsequent trust (Robinson, 1996). Trust may be considered as a form of support resource that employees have in view of potential transgressions and may enable to cushion the influence of distress due to perceiving the employer to have failed to fulfil its part of the bargain. We therefore hypothesise that:

Hypothesis 5 *Levels of trust will moderate the mediating pathway specifically in the relationship between psychological contract breach and perceived work stress.*

10.7   Justification for the Choice of Attitudinal Outcomes and 'Adaptability to Change' as Control for this Study

Before presenting the details of the study, a word is warranted for the choice of outcome variables and the reasons why we opted to keep 'adaptability to change' as a control. Our two outcomes include satisfaction with the organisation and affective commitment.

Employee (or job) satisfaction is defined as the way people feel about their jobs and different aspects of their jobs (Spector, 1997). Locke's (1976) value theory of job satisfaction suggests that such salient discrepancies, which take the form of contract breach, are more likely to generate dissatisfaction (Bunderson, 2001) than less salient ones. The hypothesis that a negative correlation exists between employee satisfaction and contract breach has been consistently upheld both in cross-sectional (e.g. Cassar, 2001; Turnley & Feldman, 2000) and longitudinal studies (e.g. Bunderson, 2001; Robinson & Rousseau, 1994). One must highlight that a measure of 'organisational' satisfaction may be more relevant for inclusion in this research than 'job' satisfaction. For example, Robinson and Rousseau (1994) used two items; one of which was directed at the job (presumably the task) and the other was directed at the organisation. However, the choice of wording in the measure may direct the respondent's attention to different aspects; in this case one focuses on the task and the other on the organisation. But the psychological contract resides in the perceived relationship between the employee and the representatives of the organisation (Rousseau, 1989) and not the task (or job) one actually does. Assessments of organisational satisfaction may be more suitable in psychological contract research than simply 'job satisfaction', which can be taken to mean one's satisfaction with the immediate task at hand.

With regards to commitment, this may be defined as an 'individual's psychological attachment to an organisation - the psychological bond linking the individual and the organisation' (O'Reilly III & Chatman, 1986, p. 492). Several models of commitment exist. Mowday et al. (1982) suggest that commitment is composed of one's acceptance to an organisation's goals, a willingness to exert considerable effort on behalf of the organisation and a strong desire to maintain membership. Meyer and Allen's (1991) three-component model of organisational commitment is currently the one mostly cited (Meyer, 1997). This model constitutes: (a) affective commitment (linked to a person's emotional attachment to an organisation); (b) continuance commitment (linked to a person's perception of the costs and risks associated with leaving an organisation); and (c) normative commitment (linked with a person's felt obligation and responsibility towards one's organisation). Studies suggest that these three dimensions are relatively independent of each other but can also co-exist (Meyer et al., 1993). In this investigation, we specifically assess affective commitment given that it is the construct most popularly associated to the phenomenon of commitment. Why should contract breach be associated with commitment? Psychological contracts serve to channel employees' behaviours in a certain manner that would require less monitoring and links organisational goals with personal goals (Shore & Tetrick, 1994). In doing so, they facilitate the exchange process ensuring that obligatory expectations are met and enhance a person's fitness in the organisation (Meyer, 1997). Breach is likely to create a rift in this employment balance creating perceptions of disassociation with the organisation. It is important to note that this does not occur in all circumstances except in those that are perceived as critical to the employee (Schalk & Freese, 1997). Studies reveal a relationship between assessments of commitment and assessments of psychological contract fulfilment. For example, Coyle-Shapiro and Kessler (2000) showed that employees who reported the fulfilment of employer obligations were also likely to score high on commitment. Similar results have been obtained by other studies (e.g. Cassar, 2001; Guzzo et al., 1994).

Finally, we opted to control for adaptability to change. At the time of the study, the Maltese Public Service was undergoing major operational changes (Cassar & Azzopardi, 2019) such as telework, digitalization, One-Stop-Shop commitments, and the elimination of excessive bureaucratic procedures and research shows that change has very significant impact on people's attitudes at work (Shin et al., 2012). Given that this investigation was not strictly interested to investigate change but the state of employees' exchange relationship with their employer and how this impacts attitudes at work, we did not want to have unwanted fluctuations in attitudes due to extraneous factors related to change. To this end, we decided to control for people's perception of adaptability to change in the Maltese Public Service and thus reduced the possibility of nuisance variance.

10.8   Research Method

The research method is based on a quantitative methodology that is described in the following sections.

10.8.1   Population and Sample Characteristics

This study targeted Maltese Public Service employees, aged 18 to 65, occupying the following grades: senior management (scales 2 to 5), management (scale 6 to 11) and administrative/clerical (scales 12 to 16). With a population of 28,002 employees, a confidence level of 95.0% and a confidence interval of 5.0%, the minimum sample size required for this study was 379. Although 1812 employees participated in the study, some provided incomplete responses, resulting in a net sample of 1314 employees. With this sample size, the margin of error reduces to 2.6%. Table 10.1 provides a breakdown of population (where available) and sample sizes by demographic characteristics.

The largest demographic categories were (i) female; (ii) ages ranging from 36 to 45 years; (iii) tenure of 12–15 years of experience in the Public Service; and (iv) occupying a managerial position. To assess the representativeness of the sample, the Chi-square Test of Independence was used. This revealed that the population and sample distributions did not differ significantly from each other with respect to the available demographic characteristics: namely, by gender ($\chi^2 = 3.01$, $df = 1$, $p = 0.08$), age-group ($\chi^2 = 5.24$, $df = 2$, $p = 0.07$), job tenure ($\chi^2 = 4.54$, $df = 2$, $p = 0.10$) and job grade ($\chi^2 = 5.57$, $df = 2$, $p = 0.06$).

10.9   The Instrument

A self-administered questionnaire was purposely designed for the present study. An email containing a cover letter highlighting the purpose of the study, the time window, instructions for filling the questionnaire and a web-link to an online questionnaire was sent by the People and Standards Division within the Office of the Prime Minister. Confidentiality and anonymity were guaranteed. This instrument contained two sections. In Section A, the respondents were provided with 28

Table 10.1 Population and sample distributions

	Population	Sample
Job Grade	*N (%)*	*n (%)*
Senior Management (scale 2–5)	1996 (7.1%)	112 (8.5%)
Management (scale 6–11)	16,105 (57.5%)	765 (58.2%)
Administrative/clerical (scale 12–16)	9901 (35.4%)	437 (33.3%)
Gender	*N (%)*	*n (%)*
Female	15,030 (53.7%)	737 (56.1%)
Male	12,972 (46.3%)	484 (43.9%)
Age Group	*N (%)*	*n (%)*
18–30	6020 (21.5%)	300 (22.8%)
31–50	13, 675 (48.9%)	604 (46.0%)
51–65	8, 287 (29.6%)	410 (31.2%)
Job Tenure	*N (%)*	*n (%)*
0–5 years	7397 (26.4%)	256 (23.0%)
6–15 years	7636 (26.8%)	205 (15.6%)
16–30 years	9352 (33.4%)	284 (21.6%)
31+ years	3617 (13.4%)	569 (43.3%)
Total	*28,002 (100.0%)*	*1314 (100.0%)*

NA not available

randomised Likert-type items covering 7 established constructs that were adapted from various sources (see Table 10.2). The original items were slightly modified to ensure that the referent point was the Public Service. For example, 'I am satisfied with my job' was adjusted to 'I am satisfied working in the Public Service'. The Cronbach alpha coefficient for each construct exceeded the 0.70 threshold for good internal consistency reliability (Hair et al., 2010). In Section B, the respondents were requested to specify their age, gender, job tenure, and job grade.

10.10 Data Analysis Procedure

After composite variables were extracted, the data was subjected to statistical analysis. In preliminary analysis, we generated descriptive statistics and zero-order correlations between the study variables. To test for direct and indirect effects, we used Andrew F. Hayes' PROCESS macro for SPSS, Version 3.5 (Hayes, 2018). This path analysis modelling tool can be used to assess simple, parallel and sequential mediation. To investigate direct effects, the regression coefficient and the corresponding *p*-value for a predictor are interpreted; a significant predictor is indicative of a significant direct effect. To investigate indirect effects, the 95% bootstrapped confidence interval for the unstandardized indirect effect was interpreted; mediation was present when '0' does not fall within this confidence interval. Finally, to test for moderation, we looked for a significant interaction between the moderator and the

Table 10.2 Questionnaire constructs, sources and number of items

Construct (Code)	Source	Number of Items	Cronbach alpha
Psychological Contract Breach (PCB)	Takleab & Taylor (2003)	3[b]	0.78
Trust[a] (T)	Yamagishi & Yamagishi (1994)	6[b]	0.92
Perceived Work Stress	Marcatto et al. (2015)	4[c]	0.81
Employee Engagement (EE)	Schaufeli et al. (2019)	3[b]	0.71
Affective Commitment (AC)	Meyer et al. (1993)	6[c]	0.77
Organisational Satisfaction (OS)	Robinson and Rousseau (1994)	3[b]	0.87
Adaptability to change (A)	Griffin et al. (2007)	3[b]	0.83

[a]Items were slightly modified to ensure that the referent point was the direct superior
[b]scale ranges from 1 = strongly disagree to 5 = strongly agree
[c]scale ranges from 1 = never to 5 = always
[d]original scale referred to as Individual Task Adaptivity

independent variable on the dependent variable, after mean centring both the moderator and the independent variable to reduce multi-collinearity issues and facilitate interpretation.

10.11   Results

A detailed description of the results from the study is found in following sections.

10.11.1   Preliminary Analysis

Table 10.3 provides descriptive statistics for the study variables while the various distributions are exhibited by the boxplots in Fig. 10.2.

The descriptive statistics revealed that on average, employees:

(a) Disagreed (to some extent) that the Public Service has failed to fulfil obligations associated with perceived mutual promises;
(b) Neither agreed nor disagreed that they experience work stress; and
(c) Agreed that they are trustful of their direct superiors, are emotionally attached and committed to an extent to their organisation, are satisfied working in the Public Service, and have been able to adapt during operational changes and the COVID-19 pandemic.

Additionally, the boxplots revealed that the respondents provided a wide range of scores for each scale which ranged from 1 = strongly disagree to 5 = strongly agree.

Table 10.3 Descriptive statistics for study variables

Construct (Code)	Median (Min – Max)	Mean (SD)
Psychological Contract Breach (PCB)	2.67 (1.00–5.00)	2.58 (.91)
Trust in superior[a] (TS)	4.17 (1.00–5.00)	3.97 (.86)
Perceived Work Stress	3.00 (1.00–5.00)	2.94 (.77)
Employee Engagement (EE)	4.00 (1.00–5.00)	3.83 (.74)
Affective Commitment (AC)	3.50 (1.00–5.00)	3.47 (.78)
Organisational Satisfaction (OS)	4.00 (1.00–5.00)	3.92 (.88)
Adaptability to change (A)	4.33 (1.00–5.00)	4.29 (.71)

It is worth noting that outliers were retained since they do not represent procedural errors but valid observations in the population (Hair et al., 2010). Table 10.4 provides zero-order correlations between the study variables. It shows that all correlation coefficients are statistically significant ($p < 0.01$) and in expected theoretical direction.

10.11.2 Path Analysis of Direct and Indirect Effects

We started by generating a moderated mediation model using Hayes' PROCESS macro (Model 83). The regression of perceived work stress on psychological contract breach, trust and their interaction, (after controlling for adaptability) revealed that the interaction term was not statistically significant ($b = .0097$, $s.e. = 0221$, $t = .4388$, $p = .6609$). This suggests that trust in superiors does not moderate the effect of psychological contract breach on perceived work stress. In the presence of a non-significant interaction effect, the moderated mediation model was reduced to a sequential mediation model. Tables 10.5 and 10.6 provide path analysis output for direct and indirect effects respectively using Model 6 (the PROCESS macro for sequential mediation). Table 10.5 shows that there were significant direct effects of:

(i) Psychological contract breach on perceived work stress (positive), employee engagement (negative), organisational satisfaction (negative) and affective commitment (negative);

(ii) Perceived work stress on organisational satisfaction (negative) and affective commitment (negative);

(iii) Employee engagement on organisational satisfaction (positive) and affective commitment (negative).

However, the direct effect for the path from perceived work stress to employee engagement was not statistically significant. An analysis of indirect effects (see Table 10.6) revealed that:

(i) The effect of psychological contract breach on organisational satisfaction was moderated by perceived work stress and employee engagement;

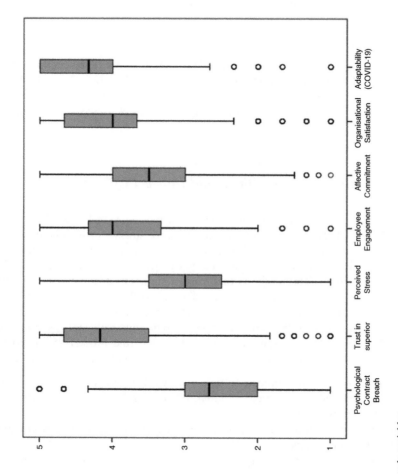

Fig. 10.2 Boxplots of study variables

Table 10.4 Correlations between construct measures

Factors	Factors						
	PCB	TS	PS	EE	AC	OS	A
Psychological Contract Breach (PCB)	1.00						
Trust in Superior (TS)	−0.48	1.00					
Perceived Work Stress (PS)	0.35	−0.31	1.00				
Employee Engagement (EE)	−0.46	0.44	−0.16	1.00			
Affective Commitment (AC)	−0.60	0.43	−0.25	0.63	1.00		
Organisational Satisfaction (OS)	−0.67	0.50	−0.34	0.67	0.74	1.00	
Adaptability to change (A)	−0.23	0.27	−0.08	0.30	0.25	0.25	1.00

Note: all correlation coefficients are significant at the 0.01 level (2-tailed)

Table 10.5 Parameter estimates for direct effects

Paths	Unstandardised Estimate	t-statistic S.E.		p-value
PCB→PS	0.2974	0.0225	13.2303	<0.001
PCB→EE	−0.3312	0.0214	−15.4899	<0.0001
PS→EE	−0.0052	0.0257	−0.2124	0.8318
PCB→OS	−0.3984	0.0195	−20.3944	<0.0001
PS→OS	−0.1360	0.0207	−6.5614	<0.0001
EE→OS	0.5460	0.0232	23.5241	<0.0001
PCB→AC	−0.3289	0.0195	−16.8560	<0.0001
PS→AC	−0.0414	0.0207	−1.9992	<0.0001
EE→AC	0.4617	0.0232	19.9169	<0.0001

(ii) The effect of psychological contract breach on affective commitment was mediated by employee engagement but not by perceived work stress;

(iii) The effect of psychological contract breach on outcomes did not flow through perceived work stress and employee engagement, implying that there was no evidence of sequential mediation.

Based on these findings, we can now determine whether the proposed hypotheses have been supported or rejected:

(a) Hypothesis 1 was supported since a negative and significant association was found between psychological contract breach and both organisational attitudinal outcomes – affective commitment (H1a) and organisational satisfaction (H1b).

(b) Hypothesis 2 was supported since a positive and significant association was found between psychological contract breach and perceived work stress.

(c) Hypothesis 3 was not supported since the sequential mediation chain was broken due to the insignificant pathway between perceived work stress and employee engagement was insignificant.

(d) Hypothesis 4 was supported since a negative relationship was found between psychological contract breach and trust.

Table 10.6 Indirect effects (sequential mediation)

Hypothesis	Effect[a] (s.e.)	Bootstrap 95% CI		Significant
		Lower	Upper	
PCB→PS→OS	−0.0404 (0.0075)	0.0561	0.0265	Yes
PCB→EE→OS	−0.1808 (0.0174)	−0.2154	−0.1479	Yes
PCB→PS→EE→OS	−0.0009 (0.0048)	−0.0107	0.0086	No
PCB→PS→AC	−0.0123 (0.0066)	−0.0255	0.0010	No
PCB→EE→AC	−0.1529 (0.0136)	−0.2154	−0.1479	Yes
CB→PS→EE→AC	−0.0007 (0.0041)	−0.0085	0.0074	No

[a]unstandardised regression weight indirect effect

(e) Hypothesis 5 was not supported since trust did not moderate the mediating pathway in the relationship between psychological contract breach and perceived work-related stress.

Finally, given that the results did not support sequential mediation suggests parallel mediation (Model 4). In other words, although psychological contract breach had a direct effect on perceived work-related stress and employee engagement, there was no direct effect from perceived work stress to employee engagement while both stress and engagement were related to organisational attitudinal outcomes. Thus, one can logically deduce the possibility of parallel mediation, wherein perceived work-related stress and engagement compete in the relationship between psychological contract breach and outcomes. The direct and indirect effect estimates, however, remain the same as those presented in Tables 10.5 and 10.6 but the path from perceived stress to employee engagement becomes redundant. The resulting path diagrams (with unstandardized regression weights) representing parallel mediation with affective commitment and organisational satisfaction as outcomes, are illustrated in Figs. 10.3 and 10.4 respectively.

10.12   Discussion

This study explored the relationship between various important factors in line with important theoretical underpinnings. It examined the level of agreement of these factors and the extent to which their associations are upheld in a large sample of Maltese Public Service employees. In interpreting our results, it is right to point out three important caveats. First, unlike other typical organisations, public organisations have a higher degree of formality and protocol and less flexibility for manoeuvre; however, in more recent years such form of organisation has been questioned in the light of new realities both in terms of what they stand for and what they intend to achieve in terms of performance (Cassar & Azzopardi, 2019; Cassar & Bezzina, 2005; Pirotta, 1997). This means that public organisations have become closer to operate like business organisations (Osborne & Gaebler, 1992) although their distinct role and deeper motivation should be kept in mind. Second, the study was

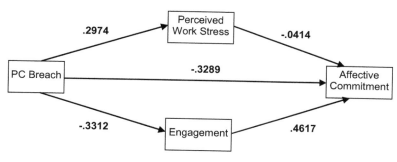

Fig. 10.3 Parallel mediation models with affective commitment as outcome variable

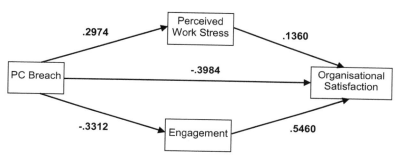

Fig. 10.4 Parallel mediation models with organisational satisfaction as outcome variable

conducted under instances of major upheaval and unprecedented scenarios given the global COVID-19 pandemic. We controlled for any unexpected fluctuations by keeping constant adaptability to change.

Hence, one is warned that the results could have come different under other more normal conditions and this is especially true given our analysis was based on cross-sectional data. Having said this, descriptive data indicated that the great majority of employees surveyed are positive about the Public Service. For example, average scores were on the agreement side with regards to trust in their superiors, their state of engagement, commitment and satisfaction. It is relevant to state that during the pandemic, the Public Service was very well organized in terms of resources and protocols for working from home and this was also reflected in the very high score on adaptability to change. In addition, psychological contract breach was also rated very low which implies that employees do not perceive major breaches in their employment relationship by their organisation. It is worthwhile to note though that the spread of scores here was higher than in all the other factors implying that while breach is low, the degree of heterogeneity in terms of agreeability was high and thus a larger percentage of respondents would have scored higher on breach compared to the other factors. By and large, the situation at the Public Service can be described as adequate to very acceptable and, despite the changes happening (Cassar & Azzopardi, 2019), employees are generally coping effectively well. Third, our study departed from the notion that the centrality of an effective work organisation resides in the quality of the exchange relationship between employer and employee. We may be biased in this notion but our argument is firmly grounded in the literature and the research (Coyle-Shapiro & Kessler, 2000).

The findings pertaining to the associations were in line with theoretical expectations. For example, our study found a negative association between breach and attitudinal outcomes (Zhao et al., 2007), an association between the propensity of breach on stress (Tomprou et al., 2015), and an association between breach and trust (Robinson, 1996). These findings indicate that maintaining a healthy open channel of communication between employees and their superiors will lead to increased favourable perceptions about the quality of their employment relationship and subsequently could improve favourable outcomes and reduce unwanted factors like work-related stress.

On the other hand, we failed to find that improvement in the state of the psychological contract has any impact on the state of engagement by following a reduction in stress. It seems that engagement is not necessarily dependent on people's evaluation of work demands but rather dependent on the available resources and the meaning an employee gives to one's task at hand. In some ways, this is not surprising; when we assessed the direct impact of breach on engagement, we did find that breach may impact engagement which then impacts outcomes. A breach can be considered as a motive towards depleting people's will to search for adequate resources to accomplish their tasks and given that engagement is an interplay of resources over demands (Schaufeli & Bakker, 2010) then it is no surprise that breach impacts negatively engagement. In fact, this pattern was found in our additional analyses except that engagement had an impact on commitment but not on satisfaction. As already hinted, the value given to engagement per se in the workplace has already been highly questioned by other researchers, implying that organisations need to ensure well-motivated and diligent employees by enhancing other factors besides engagement (Knight et al., 2017).

In fact, perceived work stress was also a mediator, *besides* engagement. This implies that focusing on mere engagement *and* reducing stress at work has a bigger impact on outcomes than handling either one or the other separately. In terms of practical management, this turns out that managers should ensure that employees are empowered by quality resources that intrinsically drive them to engage them better with their tasks while providing support to help reduce the heightened demands of tasks. This is very much in line with Schaufeli and Bakker's (2010) propositions. Put differently, in instances where an organisation may fail for any reason to maintain its promises (typically during change), the impact on outcomes is less likely to be felt should the organisation ensure that (1) employees are able to deal with exceeding or unexpected stressors at work and (2) resources are made available to ensure employees can handle effectively their tasks. Of course, we do not exclude that over time, stress may impede people's sense of engagement but that would require more longitudinal data to establish and therefore any suggestions in this direction would be purely speculative.

Similarly, our findings did not uphold the hypothesis that trust moderates the association between breach and trust. Given its central role in organisational life (Lewicki & Brinsfield, 2017), and its powerful determining effect on how people assess and evaluate breach and their corresponding reactions (Robinson, 1996; Tomprou et al., 2015), this finding was a slight surprise. There could be two explanations for our finding. The first is that most studies have explored initial and subsequent trust (e.g. Robinson, 1996) and hence emphasis is on the *change* in trust levels rather than the current state of trust. The second explanation is that trust is a redundant factor in this case because breach per se is based on the notion of reciprocal exchange which is fundamentally grounded in trust (Carol, 2007; Gouldner, 1960) and hence covered implicitly by a measure of breach. Indeed, breach and trust were highly correlated in this study suggesting a significant overlap between the two constructs.

10.13   Implications and Recommendations from the Findings

The current investigation's implications should be considered in the light of its limitations which are mainly two: The first is that the study is a cross-sectional study and hence it is difficult to provide firm conclusions on causality. Our model took a theoretical perspective that positions variables in a causal mode, but causality can only be ascertained with a more longitudinal design. The second is that, while our sample was representative of the clerical/managerial grades within the Public Service, we did not survey employees below a specific grade. Hence, we can only draw conclusions and implications drawing from data based on surveying a specific, albeit large and significant, chunk of the Public Service.

We draw four specific implications from our investigation and that are pertinent especially to the specific context of the study (Johns, 2018), namely the Maltese Public Service (Cassar & Azzopardi, 2019). First, in spite of the fact that the current state of the Public Service is in a mode of change (coupled with unexpected changes due to COVID-19), respondents were exceptionally very positive in their responses and perceive the Public Service as a fair and reliable workplace providing a degree of certainty about the future especially in uncertain times. Second, it is clear from the pattern of the results that the Public Service is handling change effectively and this may be attributable to the degree of improved and enhanced communication channels that exists across the various hierarchies. The notion of becoming more people-centric and adopting an enhanced corporate framework model (voice, design, delivery and accountability) may be responsible for this rather positive state in times of major change. Third, although trust did not moderate the association between breach and stress and for possible reasons stated above, trust was still rated highly.

Trust is a determining factor for many subsequent behaviours and outcomes, and our study indicates that respondents scored very high on trust in their superiors. This is a positive stance and all measures should be taken to maintain this. Transparency and a sense of fair play while enforcing procedures to facilitate a perception of trust, is essential to make this possible. Fourth, stress and engagement seem to coexist in our sample and it would be best for management to ensure practices that both keep levels of stress low (e.g. by promoting further services like the Employee Support Programme) and also ensure high levels of engagement by providing all the necessary resources be them extrinsic (e.g. work environment) and intrinsic (e.g. personal development).

10.14 Conclusion

The Maltese Public Service is in a constant flux of change. Change presents several challenges and opportunities and generally change is perceived as an instance of resistance and possible negative reactions. Our study, conducted in a double wave of change (internal and external), did not show typically negative reactions and ratings by employees. Rather our results indicated that the Maltese Public Service is coping and managing well its changes as it becomes more people-oriented and embraces a new corporate identity. Moreover, our study illustrates how specific factors are associated to others and hence require leadership skills and abilities to steer people management in ways that ensure the maintenance of effective working relationships and therefore positive attitudes at work.

References

Bakker, A. B., & Demerouti, E. (2008). Towards a model of work engagement. *Career Development International, 13*(3), 209–223. https://doi.org/10.1108/13620430810870476

Blau, P. M. (1964). *Exchange and power in social life*. John Wiley.

Boyle, R. (2006). *Measuring public sector productivity: Lessons from international experience* (Vol. 35). Institute of Public Administration.

Bunderson, J. S. (2001). How work ideologies shape the psychological contracts of professional employees: Doctors' responses to perceived breach. *Journal of Organisational Behavior: The International Journal of Industrial, Occupational and Organisational Psychology and Behavior, 22*(7), 717–741.

Camilleri, E. (2007). Antecedents affecting public service motivation. *Personnel Review, 36*(3), 356–377. https://doi.org/10.1108/00483480710731329

Carol, A. (2007). Trust and the psychological contract. *Employee Relations, 29*(3), 227–246. https://doi.org/10.1108/01425450710741720

Cassar, J., & Azzopardi, M. (2019). Public service and the public sector (Part 1). In G. Baldacchino, V. Cassar, & J. G. Azzopardi (Eds.), *Malta and its human resources: Management and development perspectives*. Malta University Press.

Cassar, V. (2001). Violating psychological contract terms amongst Maltese public service employees: Occurrence and relationships. *Journal of Managerial Psychology, 16*(3), 194–208. https://doi.org/10.1108/02683940110385749

Cassar, V., & Bezzina, C. (2005). People must change before institutions can: A model addressing the challenge from administering to managing the maltese public service. *Public Administration and Development, 25*(3), 205–215. https://doi.org/10.1002/pad.358

Cassar, V., Bezzina, F., & Buttigieg, S. (2018). Investigating the psychometric properties and assessment capabilities of the short version of the Health and Safety Executive's Management Standards Indicator Tool. *The International Journal of Human Resource Management*, 1–26. https://doi.org/10.1080/09585192.2018.1431955.

Coyle-Shapiro, J. A. M., & Conway, N. (2004). *The employment relationship through the lens of social exchange.*

Coyle-Shapiro, J., & Kessler, I. (2000). Consequences of the psychological contract for the employment relationship: A large scale survey. *Journal of Management Studies, 37*(7), 903–930.

Coyle-Shapiro, J. A. M., Pereira Costa, S., Doden, W., & Chang, C. (2019). Psychological contracts: Past, present, and future. *The Annual Review of Organizational Psychology and Organizational Behavior, 6*(1), 145–169. https://doi.org/10.1146/annurev-orgpsych-012218-015212

Dirks, K. T., & Ferrin, D. L. (2001). The role of trust in organisational settings. *Organisation Science, 12*(4), 450–467. https://doi.org/10.1287/orsc.12.4.450.10640

Eisenhardt, K. M. (1989). Agency theory: An assessment and review. *Academy of Management Review, 14*(1), 57–74.

Gouldner, A. W. (1960). The norm of reciprocity: A preliminary statement. *American Sociological Review, 25*(2), 161–178. https://doi.org/10.2307/2092623

Griffin, M. A., Neal, A., & Parker, S. K. (2007). A new model of work role performance: Positive behavior in uncertain and interdependent contexts. *Academy of Management Journal, 50*(2), 327–347.

Guest, D. E., Conway, N., Guest, D., & Conway, N. (2000). *Can an organisation have a psychological contract? A conceptual and empirical analysis.* Annual Meeting of the Academy of Management.

Guzzo, R. A., Noonan, K. A., & Elron, E. (1994). Expatriate managers and the psychological contract. *Journal of Applied Psychology, 79*(4), 617.

Hair, J. F., Black, W. C., Babin, B. J., & Anderson, R. E. (2010), *"Multivariate data analysis: A global perspective"* Pearson Prentice Hall.

Han, J., Sun, J.-M., & Wang, H.-L. (2020). Do high performance work systems generate negative effects? How and when? *Human Resource Management Review, 30*(2), 100699. https://doi.org/10.1016/j.hrmr.2019.100699

Hart, P. M., & Cooper, C. L. (2012). Occupational stress: Toward a more integrated framework. In *Handbook of industrial, work & organisational psychology – Volume 2: organisational psychology* (Vol. 2, pp. 93–114). https://doi.org/10.4135/9781848608368.n6

Harter, J. K., Schmidt, F. L., & Hayes, T. L. (2002). Business-unit-level relationship between employee satisfaction, employee engagement, and business outcomes: A meta-analysis. *Journal of Applied Psychology, 87*(2), 268–279. https://doi.org/10.1037/0021-9010.87.2.268

Hayes, A. F. (2018). *Introduction to mediation, moderation, and conditional process analysis.* (2nd ed.). The Guilford Press.

Hobfoll, S. E. (1989). Conservation of resources: A new attempt at conceptualizing stress. *American Psychologist, 44*(3), 513.

Johns, G. (2018). Advances in the treatment of context in organisational research. *The Annual Review of Organizational Psychology and Organizational Behavior, 5*(1), 21–46. https://doi.org/10.1146/annurev-orgpsych-032117-104406

Kahn, W. A. (1990). Psychological conditions of personal engagement and disengagement at work. *Academy of Management Journal, 33*(4), 692–724. https://doi.org/10.5465/256287

Knight, C., Patterson, M., & Dawson, J. (2017). Building work engagement: A systematic review and meta-analysis investigating the effectiveness of work engagement interventions. *Journal of Organisational Behavior, 38*(6), 792–812. https://doi.org/10.1002/job.2167

Kozlowski, S. W. J., & Klein, K. J. (2000). A multilevel approach to theory and research in organisations: Contextual, temporal, and emergent processes. In *Multilevel theory, research, and methods in organisations: Foundations, extensions, and new directions.* (pp. 3–90). Jossey-Bass.

Lewicki, R. J., & Brinsfield, C. (2017). Trust repair. *The Annual Review of Organizational Psychology and Organizational Behavior, 4*(1), 287–313. https://doi.org/10.1146/annurev-orgpsych-032516-113147

Locke, E. A. (1976). *The Nature and Causes of Job Satisfaction*. In Handbook of Industrial and Organizational Psychology. Vol. 1. ed. by Dunnette, M. D., and Hough, L. M. Chicago: Rand McNally.

Marcatto, F.; Di Blas, L.; Luis, O.; and Ferrante, D. (2015). *The perceived stress-at-work scale*. Conference paper: Trieste Symposium on Perception and Cognition, November 2015.

Martin, S., & Smith, P. C. (2005). Multiple public service performance indicators: Toward an integrated statistical approach. *Journal of Public Administration Research and Theory, 15*(4), 599–613.

Meyer, J. P. (1997). Organisational commitment. *International Review of Industrial and Organisational Psychology, 12*, 175–228.

Meyer, J. P., & Allen, N. J. (1991). A three-component conceptualization of organisational commitment. *Human Resource Management Review, 1*(1), 61–89.

Meyer, J., Allen, N., & Smith, C. (1993). Commitment to organisations and occupations: Extension and test of a three-component conceptualization. *Journal of Applied Psychology, 78*, 538–551.

Montes, S. D., & Zweig, D. (2009). Do promises matter? An exploration of the role of promises in psychological contract breach. *Journal of Applied Psychology, 94*(5), 1243–1260. https://doi.org/10.1037/a0015725

Morrison, E. W., & Robinson, S. L. (1997). When employees feel betrayed: A model of how psychological contract violation develops. *Academy of Management Review, 22*(1), 226–256. https://doi.org/10.5465/amr.1997.9707180265

Mowday, R., Porter, L., & Steers, R. (1982). Organisational linkages: The psychology of commitment. *Journal of Vocational Behavior, 14*(4), 224–247.

Murray, G., Belanger, J., Giles, A., & Lapointe. P. A. (2002). *Work and employment relations in the high performance workplace*. Continuum.

O'Reilly, C., III, & Chatman, J. (1986). Organisational commitment and psychological attachment: The effects of compliance, identification, and internalization on prosocial behavior. *Journal of Applied Psychology, 71*(3), 495–499. https://doi.org/10.1037/0021-9010.71.3.492

Osborne, D., & Gaebler, T. (1992). *Reinventing government: How the entrepreneurial spirit is transforming the public sector from schoolhouse to statehouse. City Hall to Pentagon*, Addison-Wesley.

Peiró, J. M., Bayona, J. A., Caballer, A., & Di Fabio, A. (2020). Importance of work characteristics affects job performance: The mediating role of individual dispositions on the work design-performance relationships. *Personality and Individual Differences, 157*, 109808. https://doi.org/10.1016/j.paid.2019.109808

Pirotta, G. A. (1997). Politics and public service reform in small states: Malta. *Public Administration and Development, 17*(1), 197–207. 10.1002/(SICI)1099-162X(199702)17:1<197::AID-PAD921>3.0.CO;2-U.

Polidano, C. (1996). Public service reform in Malta, 1988-95: Lessons to be learned. *Governance, 9*(4), 459–480. https://doi.org/10.1111/j.1468-0491.1996.tb00252.x

Preacher, K. J., Rucker, D. D., & Hayes, A. F. (2007). Addressing moderated mediation hypotheses : Theory. *Methods and Prescriptions, 42*(1), 185–227.

Robinson, S. L. (1996). Trust and breach of the psychological contract. *Administrative Science Quarterly, 41*(4), 574–599. https://doi.org/10.2307/2393868

Robinson, S. L., & Rousseau, D. M. (1994). Violating the psychological contract: Not the exception but the norm. *Journal of Organisational Behavior, 15*(3), 245–259.

Robinson, S. L., & Wolfe Morrison, E. (2000). The development of psychological contract breach and violation: A longitudinal study. *Journal of Organisational Behavior, 21*(5), 525–546. 10.1002/1099-1379(200008)21:5<525::AID-JOB40>3.0.CO;2-T.

Rousseau, D. (1995). *Psychological contracts in organisations: Understanding written and unwritten agreements*. Sage Publications.

Rousseau, D. M. (1989). Psychological and implied contracts in organisations. *Employee Responsibilities and Rights Journal, 2*(2), 121–139. https://doi.org/10.1007/BF01384942

Rousseau, D. M. (1998). The'problem'of the psychological contract considered. *Journal of Organisational Behavior*, 665–671.

Rousseau, D. M. (2011). The individual–organisation relationship: The psychological contract. In *APA handbook of industrial and organisational psychology, Vol 3: Maintaining, expanding, and contracting the organisation.* (pp. 191–220). American Psychological Association. https://doi.org/10.1037/12171-005.

Rousseau, D. M., & Fried, Y. (2001). Editorial: Location, location, location: Contextualizing organisational research. *Journal of Organisational Behavior, 22*(1), 1–13. http://www.jstor.org/stable/3649603

Schalk, R., & Freese, C. (1997). New facets of commitment in response to organisational change: Research trends and the Dutch experience. *Journal of Organisational Behavior (1986–1998)* (p. 107).

Schaufeli, W. B, & Bakker, A. B. (2003). *UWES–Utrecht work engagement scale: test manual.* Unpublished Manuscript: Department of Psychology, Utrecht University (p. 8).

Schaufeli, W. B., & Bakker, A. B. (2010). Defining and measuring work engagement: Bringing clarity to the concept. *Work Engagement: A Handbook of Essential Theory and Research, 12*, 10–24.

Schaufeli, W. B., Shimazu, A., Hakanen, J., Salanova, M., & De Witte, H. (2019). An ultra-short measure for work engagement the UWES-3 validation across five countries. *European Journal of Psychological Assessment, 35*(4), 577–591.

Shin, J., Taylor, M. S., & Seo, M.-G. (2012). Resources for change: The relationships of organisational inducements and psychological resilience to employees' attitudes and behaviors toward organisational change. *Academy of Management Journal, 55*(3), 727–748.

Shore, L. M., & Tetrick, L. E. (1994). The psychological contract as an explanatory framework. *Trends in Organisational Behavior, 1*, 91–109.

Spector, P. E. (1997). *Job satisfaction: Application, assessment, causes, and consequences* (Vol. 3). Sage Publications.

Suazo, M. M., Turnley, W. H., & Mai, R. R. (2005). The role of perceived violation in determining employees' reactions to psychological contract breach. *Journal of Leadership & Organisational Studies, 12*(1), 24–36. https://doi.org/10.1177/107179190501200104

Taylor, S. E. (1991). The assymetrical impact of positive and negative events: The mobilization-minimization hypothesis. *Psychological Bulletin, 110*(1), 67–85.

Tekleab, A. G., & Taylor, M. S. (2003). Aren't there two parties in an employment relationship? Antecedents and consequences of organization-employee agreement on contract obligations and violations. *Journal of Organizational Behavior, 24*(5, SpecIssue), 585–608. https://doi.org/10.1002/job.204

Tomprou, M., Rousseau, D. M., & Hansen, S. D. (2015). The psychological contracts of violation victims: A post-violation model. *Journal of Organisational Behavior, 36*(4), 561–581. https://doi.org/10.1002/job.1997

Turnley, W. H., & Feldman, D. C. (2000). Re-examining the effects of psychological contract violations: Unmet expectations and job dissatisfaction as mediators. *Journal of Organisational Behavior, 21*(1), 25–42.

Warrington, E. (2002). *A revolution in governance? A review and assessment of changes in Maltese Public Administration.* Unpublished document (p. 1–18).

Yamagishi, T., and Yamagishi, M. (1994). Trust and Commitment in the United States and Japan. *Motivation and Emotion 18*(2):129–166.

Zhao, H. A. O., Wayne, S. J., Glibkowski, B. C., & Bravo, J. (2007). The impact of psychological contract breach on work-related outcomes: A meta-analysis. *Personnel Psychology, 60*(3), 647–680.

Chapter 11
Societal Impact of Public Service Reforms: Cross-Sectional Surveys and the Media

"The best way to find yourself is to lose yourself in the service of others."

Mahatma Gandhi
Indian lawyer, anti-colonial nationalist, and political ethicist

This chapter provides a deeper understanding of the success and the degree of impact attained by the introduction and implementation of a variety of public services. It also contributed towards suggesting improvements that may be made to enhance the user-oriented relationship by focusing on the particular needs of each demographic sector. This Chapter is based upon original research and is organised into two major segments. The first segment evaluates the methodology and other demographic considerations; and the second segment analyses and discusses the research findings. The results suggest that generally the respondents' perception reflects a positive outlook on the provision and execution of government-provided services to the wider community over recent years. Respondents, specifically Government employed individuals, appeared to be highly conscious of major projects, measures and initiatives implemented by the state, particularly those that relate to digital and social measures. Moreover, the findings suggest that accessed services by income and status demographic were found to be in line with a priori expectations and reflected the various group-specific needs of each sub-category. Those who registered non-usage of services were more critical of provided services, most prevalently within the Maltese population sub-sample. However, there is general consensus across all sub-samples that government has exerted a high level of effort in introducing a vast mixed array of digital, social and forward-thinking measures. The findings suggest that there is a need for government to implement better good governance and bureaucratically transparent processes, particularly with stronger views among the lower-income and unoccupied status cohort. Overall, respondents confirm the government's success in introducing, facilitating and implementing various measures and initiatives. This had a positive resulting effect on community level service provision and, consequently, quality of life on all fronts.

11.1   Introduction

It is ostensible that, over recent years, current state administration has set forth several measures developed in various strategic reports that aim towards a more technology-driven and efficient country-level evolution. While this proves a direct way forward to modernisation, it does not necessarily reflect the extent to which such initiatives have been publicised and utilised to their full potential by the wider general population. As such, the purpose of this chapter is to evaluate and analyse Maltese citizens' awareness, uptake and perception on government-provided services during recent years. This includes evaluations on various facets and considerations of good governance, social, digital and other financial measures and incentives that have been introduced and implemented over the past seven years under the current administration, all within the wider national context.

In part, this will thus provide further insight into both the success and impact of the introduction and implementation of certain services, together with a user-oriented rapport of what can be improved and catered to each demographics's particular needs. This all to the end of creating a basis on which these services are analysed to better serve, guide and support the administering of current and proposed services and initiatives for the wider community. The remainder of the chapter will be segregated as follows: (a) Evaluation of the methodology and other demographic considerations; (b) Analysis and discussion of the findings; and (c) Discussion of different themes and conclusion.

11.1.1   List of Acronyms

The following list of acronyms will be used throughout this chapter:

(a) GPS Government-Provided Services
(b) GEI Government Employed Individuals
(c) MP Maltese Population
(d) NWI Nation Wide Individuals
(e) CDRT Centre for Development, Research and Training
(f) IPS Institute for Public Studies

11.2   Research Methodology

The study employs a mix of qualitative and quantitative methodological analysis. The qualitative element features in the two main surveys that were conducted, both for government-employed individuals (GEI) and the wider national Maltese population (MP). Both open-ended and closed-ended questions were posed with varying metrics being applied to each question. Particularly, questions 10–13 feature a three and five-point scale metric ranked lowest to highest, further detailed as notes to each respective table for each question, further quantitatively analysed and presented as main findings in this chapter. Undertaken during the month of August 2020, the study involves a total sample of 1100 participants, 500 of which refer to the GEI while the remaining 600 constitute the wider national Maltese Population.

Data filtering, cleaning and other statistical techniques were employed at initial stages to ensure that the integrity of the data is maintained. Given the nature of the responses by participants, particularly with reference to the more open-ended questions, major groupings were employed whereby only a condensed view of all categories were presented as findings. Supplementary explanations of each condensed constituent category are discussed in main general text albeit not formally presented in the results for comparability and ease of evaluation. Results were further analysed first at face value by its own metric, thereafter against distinct demographics for a more comprehensive and in-depth evaluation of findings, segregated as follows; GEI data was primarily investigated against government-scale level while MP data was further analysed by age, gender, income-bracket, education level and status attainment.

11.2.1   Questions Administered in the Surveys

The questions administered in the surveys are as follows:

1. Can you mention 3 projects related to the Public Service, on which the Government has worked for the past 7 years?
2. Have you ever used an online Government service? (Yes/No)
3. If 'Yes' (Q2), which online service do you use most?
4. If 'No' (Q2), what is the reason why you have never used online services?
5. Have you ever used a mobile Government service? (Yes/No)
6. If 'Yes' (Q5), which mobile service do you use most?
7. If 'No' (Q5), what is the reason you have never used mobile services?
8. Have you taken any training offered by the Government in the past 7 years? (Yes/No)
9. If 'Yes' (Q8), which training course was most beneficial to you?
10. Have you heard of any of the following Government Initiatives in the past 7 years? (Yes/No)

   (a) Whistleblower's Act
   (b) Financing of Political Parties Act
   (c) Appointment of a Commissioner for Standards
   (d) Public Sector Reform
   (e) Centre for Development, Research and Training (CDRT)/Institute for Public Services (IPS)
   (f) IDEA

(g) One-stop-shop for public officers
(h) My Personal Kiosk
(i) Quality Service Charters
(j) Servizz.gov
(k) myHealth Portal
(l) Mystery Shopper
(m) Mobile Government Services
(n) Business First
(o) Appointment of a Commissioner for Simplification
(p) Arbitration Office for Financial Services
(q) Individual Investor Programme
(r) Free Childcare

11. From 1 to 5 (1-No effort at all, 5-Great effort), how much effort do you think the Government has put into the following since 2013?

(a) Introduce Government services online?
(b) Introduce mechanisms to ensure transparency in Governmental operations?
(c) Enhance citizens' rights, including participation in Government's decisions?
(d) Introduce mechanisms so that public officers are accountable for the performance of their duties?
(e) Introduce mechanisms to reduce bureaucracy in Governmental operations?
(f) Introduce mechanisms so that citizens are served with improved/efficient Government services?
(g) Introduce systems/programmes to improve the performance of public officers?
(h) Introduce mobile apps to facilitate access to Government services to citizens?
(i) Introduce online health systems so that citizens are served better?
(j) Introduce systems for businesses to improve their operations in Malta?
(k) Introduce mechanisms to simplify Governmental operations?
(l) Introduce systems to simplify Government services offered to citizens?
(m) Introduce systems/programmes to improve Malta's economy?
(n) Introduce systems to increase working opportunities to citizens?

12. Since 2013, do you think that the following has improved, remained the same or deteriorated?

(a) Type of Government services in the Public Sector
(b) The way the Government operates in providing services to the citizens
(c) Decisions taken by Government on the services offered
(d) The way public officers are kept accountable for the performance of their duties

(e) The way public officers are professional in the performance of their duties
(f) Government's efficiency in the Public Service
(g) Services offered by Government for business operations in Malta
(h) The country's regulatory system
(i) Government online services
(j) Bureaucracy within the Public Service

13. How satisfied are you with the following (1-Extremely unsatisfied, 5-Very satisfied):

(a) Bit Type of Government services in the Public Sector
(b) The way the Government operates in providing services to the citizens
(c) Decisions taken by Government on the services offered
(d) The way public officers are kept accountable for the performance of their duties
(e) The way public officers are professional in the performance of their duties
(f) Government's efficiency in the Public Service
(g) Services offered by Government for business operations in Malta
(h) The country's regulatory system
(i) Government online services
(j) Bureaucracy within the Public Service

14. Are you aware that in the past 4 years the Government has introduced some 600 measures related to the simplification of processes? (Yes/No)
15. Can you name any measures related to the simplification of processes introduced by the Government?
16. Since 2013, has the level and quality of your life improved, deteriorated or remained the same?
17. Age
18. What is your highest level of education?
19. Gender

11.2.2 Demographic Context

As depicted in Figs. 11.1, 11.2, and 11.3, the data shows a representative and unbiased sample population with a parallel distribution across all demographics. For a more detailed demographic analysis refer to Sect. 11.5. Given the political nature of the study being undertaken, additional checks were employed to assert an equal share of political views within both samples, preserving both the integrity and reliability of data being gathered and analysed.

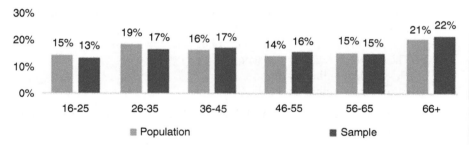

Fig. 11.1   Age distribution

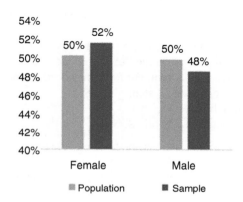

Fig. 11.2   Gender distribution

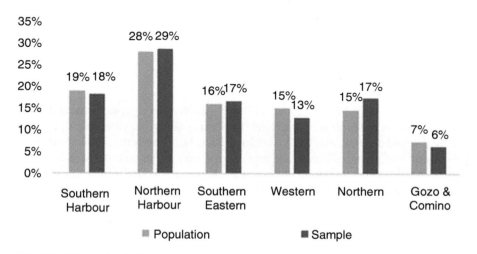

Fig. 11.3   District distribution

11.3 Results

The following section will present, evaluate and discuss the results found through this study, initially at face value, thereafter by identified key demographics pertinent to each sample group that provide further sub-sectoral insights reflective of a full analysis. As such, findings from this study will be segregated into five distinct themes that emerge from the qualitative survey review, namely; knowledge and exposure, uptake, initiative, progress and outcomes that are created, maintained and/or result from government-provided services (GPS).

11.3.1 Knowledge of and Exposure to Government-Provided Services, Initiatives and Measures

The first theme explores the general level of knowledge and awareness that citizens have of government-provided services deduced from survey questions 1, 10, 14 and 15 (listed in Sect. 11.2). Comparison is drawn from respondent answers between government-employed individuals GEI and the wider population MP to deduce whether directly being within government employment increases the likelihood or level of awareness of government-provided services.

On a general level, respondents from both surveys were found to have enough knowledge on various major projects undertaken by the Government in the past 7 years, as shown in Table 11.1 and Fig. 11.4. Most notably by GEI are the 'Marsa Flyover Project' and the digital introduction of online 'servizz.gov' services. In fact, these form part of a wider category of projects under 'Infrastructure' and 'Digital Measures' sub-categories, constituting 13% and 49% of all mentioned project groups respectively. Similarly, infrastructural projects constituted the major part of Maltese population sample responses at 30%, closely followed by other social measures such as 'Free Childcare'. It can also be noted that a relatively large group of the MP sample cohort only listed an average of 1 project with the remainder being classified under 'N/A' reflective of answers that show no knowledge of the topic. This in comparison to a relatively low percentage of 'N/A' by GEI that are then accounted for in other various project groupings such as 'business-related projects' indicative of higher levels of knowledge and awareness of state provided projects.

More specifically, when queried on knowledge of individual initiatives set up by local government over the past 7 years, some discrepancy can be seen between GEI and the general Maltese population, with the former having more knowledge of such initiatives on almost all fronts. Furthermore, it can be noted that initiatives which had a high awareness rating i.e. a high-count level of 'Yes' Responses tallied between GEI and the general Maltese population with the more social and digital measures such as 'Free Childcare' and Online Government Services proving

Table 11.1 Can you mention 3 projects related to the Public Service, on which the Government has worked for the past 7 years?

	Government employees	Maltese population
Digital related project	48.6%	4.4%
Infrastructural Projects	13.3%	30.1%
Social Measures/Projects	8.3%	29.1%
Others	8.2%	4.6%
Family measures	7.1%	6.0%
Academic sponsorships	6.2%	3.9%
Healthcare related projects	4.2%	5.4%
Business Related	3.1%	1.2%
Don't know	1.0%	13.5%
New Policies/Projects	0.0%	1.8%

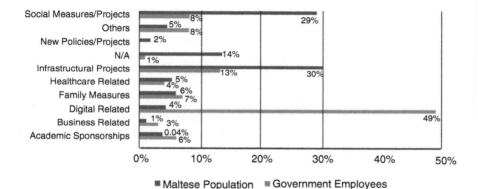

Fig. 11.4 Question 1 general analysis

prominent amongst the sample population as depicted in Table 11.2 and Fig. 11.5. Further data tables by Demographics are included in Sect. 11.5.

From further demographic analysis refer to Sect. 11.7.1. Respondents within the Maltese sample population that fell within a higher income tax bracket seemed to be more knowledgeable on government initiatives particularly those that involve any financial or online services alongside a general trend that awareness tends to increase as income increases. This analysis is also present when evaluated by level of education, whereby generally, as attained education levels increases, so does awareness of government initiatives with the exception of individuals having an 'A Level/ Diploma' level of education that did not register to be as familiar with such initiatives. This could in part also correlate to statistics obtained when analysed against

Table 11.2 Have you heard of any of the following Government initiatives in the past 7 years?

	Government employees	Maltese population
Whistleblower's Act	92.3%	78.1%
Financing of Political Parties Act	73.2%	71.5%
Appointment of a Commissioner for Standards	77.4%	52.0%
Public Sector Reform	87.3%	63.7%
Centre for Development, Research and Training (CDRT)/Institute for the Public Services (IPS)	74.9%	N/A
IDEA	48.5%	N/A
One-stop-shop for public officers	81.1%	N/A
My Personal Kiosk	83.7%	N/A
Quality Service Charters	49.9%	24.5%
Servizz.gov	97.8%	76.9%
myHealth Portal	89.1%	57.1%
Mystery Shopper	55.0%	14.9%
Mobile Government Services	61.9%	35.6%
Business First	45.2%	47.1%
Appointment of a Commissioner for Simplification	39.6%	38.0%
Arbitration Office for Financial Services	37.9%	42.1%
Individual Investor Programme	45.7%	30.7%
Free Childcare	97.2%	96.0%

Notes: Values reflect the percentage of which respondents listed 'Yes' in response to Q10

status levels of individuals, whereby students registered the lowest (little to no) levels of initiative awareness whilst those who registered being unemployed listing near to full awareness of all queried initiatives. Out of those employed with government institutions, those at lower-scale levels recorded having more awareness on such initiatives than those within higher ranks.

In line with a priori expectations, individuals within lower and middle-aged group brackets recorded being more aware of the more digital-oriented initiatives such as 'Servizz.gov' whilst the older population recorded having more knowledge on initiatives set out within social measures such as 'Free Childcare'. No significant difference in proportions can be recorded between responses as categorised by gender, with a more equal registered distribution.

Contrary to this, the general level of awareness was specifically low for measures relating to the simplification of process implemented by Government. In fact, only 35% of GEI and 27% of the general Maltese Population listed having knowledge of such measures, the majority of which related to 'Digital Measures' such as online applications and online form/certification downloads and payments, as depicted in

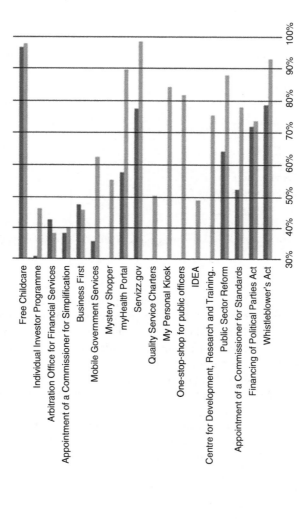

Fig. 11.5 Question 10 general analysis

Table 11.3 Are you aware that in the past 4 years the Government has introduced some 600 measures related to the simplification of processes?

	Government employees	Maltese population
Yes	34.5%	27.1%
No	65.5%	72.9%

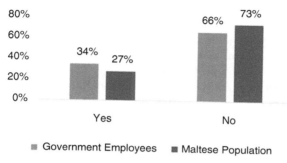

Fig. 11.6 Question 14 general analysis

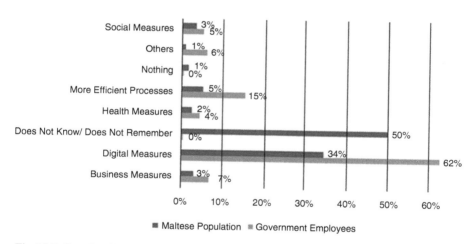

Fig. 11.7 Question 15 general analysis

Table 11.3 and Figs. 11.6 and 11.7. A huge proportion of respondents (at 50%) declared that they were not aware of or could not remember any specific measures relating to simplification of processes that are implemented by Government, tallying to the low 'Yes' count levels of general awareness of simplification of processes. Noteworthy of mention is the general significantly higher level of awareness of such measures by GEI rather than the general-wide population albeit in parallel trend.

11.3.2   Uptake of Government-Provided Services

Thus far, it has been deduced that GEI record significantly higher levels of awareness of government-provided services, initiatives and measures than the general Maltese sample population, specifically with regards to recently provided digital and online services. This subsequent theme therefore delves deeper into whether this level of knowledge is translated into higher levels of uptake of such services by similar demographic analysis, deduced from analysis of survey questions 2–9.

Initially, results seem to indicate that GEI have generally made more use of both online and mobile services, albeit utilising the latter to a lesser extent, outlined in Tables 11.4 and 11.5, and Figs. 11.8 and 11.9 respectively. This could be partially due to the fact that they registered being more aware of government incentives, measures and other services as discussed in the previous section. From the previous section, it was recorded that respondents from the Maltese population sample were more knowledgeable on online services rather than application-specific measures, this further confirmed through higher levels of usage of online rather than mobile-based government services by the same population demographic, suggestive of correlation between knowledge and uptake of such services.

From those respondents that listed having used government's online services, different service usage can be seen between each population group, further depicted in Figs. 11.10 and 11.11. While the general usage was spread over various service

Table 11.4 Have you ever used an online Government service?

	Government employees	Maltese population
Yes	84.6%	45.6%
No	15.4%	54.4%

Table 11.5 Have you ever used a mobile Government service?

	Government employees	Maltese population
Yes	42.8%	25.9%
No	57.2%	74.1%

Fig. 11.8 Question 2 general analysis

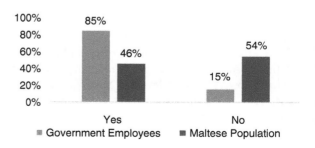

Fig. 11.9 Question 5
general analysis

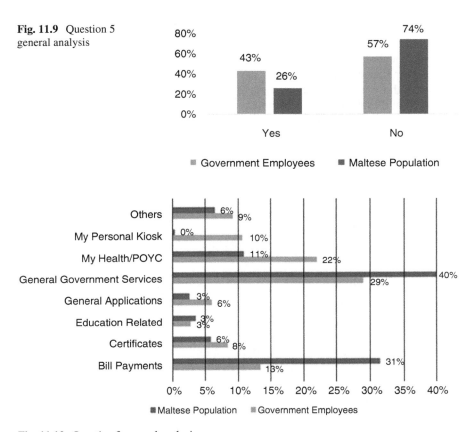

Fig. 11.10 Question 3 general analysis

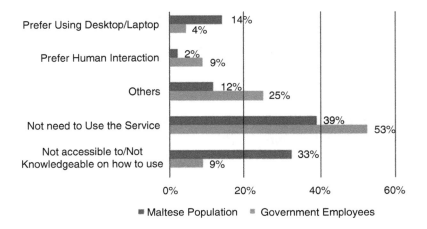

Fig. 11.11 Question 4 general analysis

provisions, both groups listed health and financial related services as being mostly utilised. Particularly prevalent within the Maltese population being the general use of government services that on the larger part all mentioned the service 'servizz. gov'. Other services such as online payment facilities were also highly utilised, mostly by those in higher income brackets and those registered as being currently employed and male. Other health-related services were mostly accessed by those registered as being unemployed and by those in higher age groupings. It is also evident that with better knowledge of government services, GEI were less critical of why online services were not utilised, with most responses as blank or referring to the 'others' sub-category which includes listings such as those who seek the involvement of third parties to sort out all related affairs on their behalf. Maltese population sub-groups listed not having access to and/or the lack of need of usage of such services as a main reason for non-usage. It should be noted that the evaluations for Q3, 4, 6, and 7 needs to be assessed with caution, with low levels of responses, constituting inflation of average percentages. Further analysis by demographic can be found in Sect. 11.7.2.

In contrast to online services, most respondents made use of a mix of services available via mobile applications as depicted in Figs. 11.12 and 11.13. Most of them related to the recent COVID-19 pandemic for the general population sub-sample accessed mostly by those in older age groups, followed by sporadic listings condensed into the 'others' sub-category. GEI, showed a more dispersed uptake of mobile services including a mix of education and health-related services together with the highest-ranking service being 'General Government Applications' involving the aforementioned service 'servizz.gov', mostly used by respondents within lower age brackets.

Distinctively, with reference to education-related services, GEI recorded having a sample majority confirmation of circa 58% of individuals who confirmed having taken up some form of government-provided training in the past 7 years, depicted in Table 11.6, and Figs. 11.12 and 11.13. Out of which, 37% related to business, financial and other administrative sectors followed by IPS and Digital-related measures, equally at 17%. Note that the relatively significant 'Others' category includes a vast array of responses including First Aid and other career-specific courses (Figs. 11.14 and 11.15).

11.3.3   Initiative by Maltese Government on the Provision of GPS

Evident from responses thus far, awareness seems to be in correlation to levels of uptake albeit the low levels of usage of online and app-based government services by the general sample groups, reasons in favour and against of which have varied significantly. This next section further determines whether, despite such low levels of uptake, it is the case that the general perception includes government having put

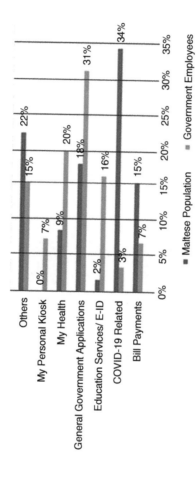

Fig. 11.12 Question 6 general analysis

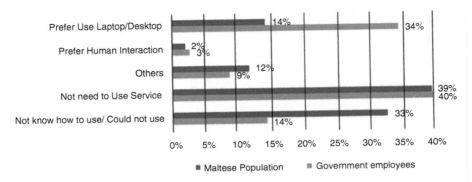

Fig. 11.13   Question 7 general analysis

Table 11.6 Have you taken any training offered by the Government in the past 7 years?		Government employees
	Yes	57.5%
	No	42.5%

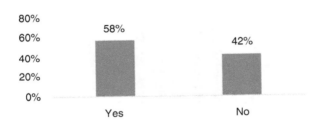

Fig. 11.14   Question 8 general analysis

in significant effort in the efficiency of process and digital transformation. In other words, whether the level of uptake of listed services affects and/or is influenced by a perception of lack of initiative and user-friendly processes or rather by simply lack of awareness.

From Table 11.7 there is tallying evidence of consensus on all fronts by both sub-samples, that government has inserted a high level of effort, in introducing and implementing the various listed digital services and simplification of processes over recent years, with GEI reflecting a higher distribution of agreement than the wider Maltese population. Further analysis by demographic can be found in Sect. 11.7.3. Highest percentage ranking themes where high effort was allocated, mostly involve the transformation of online and digital services, while greater effort is reflected to be needed in more social-oriented measures particularly those that refer to good governance. Nonetheless, the overall general level of confidence seems to be above average ratings of effort within GEI sub-group, and a neutral-high level of confidence for the Maltese population sub-sample.

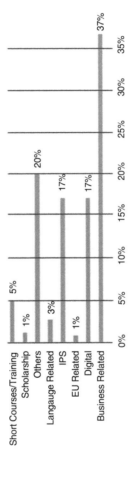

Fig. 11.15 Question 9 general analysis

Table 11.7 How much effort do you think the Government has put into the following since 2013? (1-Lowest effort, 5-Highest effort)

	GEI	MP	GEI	MP	GEI	MP	GEI	MP
	Low	Low	Neutral	Neutral	High	High	Ave.	Ave.
Introduce Government services online?	4.0%	13.2%	8.4%	30.3%	87.6%	56.5%	4.2	3.6
Introduce mechanisms to ensure transparency in Governmental operations?	16.8%	31.2%	27.8%	31.0%	55.4%	37.8%	3.5	3.1
Enhance citizens' rights, including participation in Government's decisions?	22.8%	35.4%	32.5%	32.9%	44.7%	31.7%	3.3	2.9
Introduce mechanisms so that public officers are accountable for the performance of their duties?	24.6%	36.3%	27.4%	26.3%	48.0%	37.5%	3.2	3.0
Introduce mechanisms to reduce bureaucracy in Governmental operations?	24.7%	34.5%	26.4%	26.1%	48.9%	39.4%	3.3	3.0
Introduce mechanisms so that citizens are served with improved and efficient Government services?	10.1%	21.7%	12.0%	25.6%	77.9%	52.7%	4.0	3.4
Introduce systems/programmes to improve the performance of public officers?	13.2%	23.4%	20.0%	29.9%	66.8%	46.8%	3.8	3.3
Introduce mobile apps to facilitate access of Government services to citizens?	7.1%	13.2%	21.0%	25.2%	71.9%	61.6%	3.9	3.7
Introduce online health systems so that citizens are served better?	6.6%	13.2%	18.3%	25.5%	75.1%	61.3%	4.0	3.7
Introduce systems for businesses to improve their operations in Malta?	7.6%	15.6%	34.6%	34.3%	57.8%	50.1%	3.7	3.5
Introduce mechanisms to simplify Governmental operations?	14.7%	20.0%	31.6%	32.4%	53.7%	47.7%	3.5	3.4
Introduce systems to simplify Government services offered to citizens?	11.6%	14.5%	20.9%	36.4%	67.5%	49.1%	3.8	3.5
Introduce systems/programmes to improve Malta's economy?	5.7%	18.2%	19.0%	24.5%	75.4%	57.3%	4.1	3.5
Introduce systems to increase working opportunities to citizens?	10.4%	17.6%	17.5%	17.0%	72.0%	65.4%	3.9	3.6
Introduce Government services online?	4.0%	13.2%	8.4%	30.3%	87.6%	56.5%	4.2	3.6

When evaluated against deterministic demographics, it is a general belief across the board that government has exerted a neutral-high level of effort in implementation of the above listed service, unchanged by gender filtering. Participants with higher levels of education that also fall within lower age brackets also seemed to lean towards awarding a higher level of effort category on average, most especially when it comes to measures directly impacting Malta's economic make-up. This to the exception of individuals registered as unemployed who attest a relatively negative scoring rate of 2 (little effort) for the implementation of good governance measures such as transparency and accountability of processes. From GEI sub-sample, high effort ranking is placed for government efforts in introducing several measures, most prominently online services listings, closely followed by similarly high effort rankings for all other services. This possibly comes as a result of increased awareness and usage of services that merit such scoring, in contrast to other participants who may have not yet reaped the fruits of such advancements and consequently submitted neutral-average scoring.

11.3.4   Subsequent Progress on the Sufficiency of GPS

While results thus far indicate a good level of confidence in government's ability and effort to introduce and implement new, efficient and effective measures and services, this does not necessarily reflect recent state of play and progress within already existing GPS. As such, this theme evaluates the progress levels as perceived by the wider general population specifically with respect to various social facets that directly and/or indirectly affect the participants' standard daily living environment.

It is the general perception on almost all listings by both sub-groups that various GPS have in fact improved over recent years, with GEI submitting more optimistic views than those within MP data, depicted in Table 11.8. Further analysis by demographic can be found in Sect. 11.7.4. Categories that received significantly lower percentage levels, despite still constituting almost half of total rankings alone, related to accountability and bureaucracy within public office, elements of good governance, also put to question in previous themes.

There is no record of any service to be awarded a deteriorating rating across any demographic, with improvements on all fronts mostly noted by participants within higher income brackets and higher levels of education. Little to no change was detected by participants within older-age groups, reflective also of neutral ratings when data is analysed by status. Noteworthy of mention is the fact that across all GEI, at all scale levels, there is a general agreement that almost all services, social or otherwise, have generally improved, possibly due to the nature of information that such participants are privy to as directly being involved within a government environment. This to the exception of previous sections highlighted as having remained neutral by almost all demographics, namely; accountability and bureaucracy within public office.

Table 11.8 Since 2013, do you think that the following has improved, remained the same or deteriorated? (1-Improved a lot, 5-Deteriorated a lot)

	GEI	MP	GEI	MP	GEI	MP	GEI	MP
	Imp	Imp	Same	Same	Det	Det	Average	Average
Type of Government services in the Public Sector	77.7%	61.4%	16.8%	33.3%	5.6%	5.4%	1.3	1.4
The way the Government operates in providing services to the citizens	72.4%	61.7%	21.8%	32.3%	5.9%	6.0%	1.3	1.4
Decisions taken by Government on the services offered	62.8%	53.5%	32.4%	34.7%	4.9%	11.7%	1.4	1.6
The way public officers are kept accountable for the performance of their duties	47.3%	41.7%	43.9%	43.6%	8.8%	14.7%	1.6	1.7
The way public officers are professionals in the performance of their duties	59.9%	44.9%	33.8%	43.9%	6.3%	11.3%	1.5	1.7
Government's efficiency in the Public Service	64.2%	57.5%	29.4%	35.8%	6.4%	6.7%	1.4	1.5
Services offered by Government for business operations in Malta	63.7%	63.6%	31.8%	31.6%	4.5%	4.8%	1.4	1.4
The country's regulatory system	45.1%	48.0%	42.1%	39.7%	12.9%	12.3%	1.7	1.6
Government online services	86.2%	74.2%	9.7%	22.9%	4.1%	2.8%	1.2	1.3
Bureaucracy within the Public Service	39.6%	42.0%	48.4%	42.0%	12.0%	16.0%	1.7	1.7

11.3.5   Outcome Completion of GPS

In order to fully evaluate the full-encompassing impact of all GPS being introduced and implemented over recent years, respondents further gave insight into the extent to which such services have provided low, neutral or high levels of personal satisfaction. In line with a priori expectations, overall neutral-high rankings of improvements within all GPS across the board, parallel to similar scoring patterns in previous progress questions, depicted in Table 11.9. Further analysis by demographic can be found in Sect. 11.7.5 of Government-Provided Services (GPS). Conclusively, this suggests that noted improvements within the provision of GPS have led to higher levels of user satisfaction most predominantly among GEI sample population, with MP respondents remaining relatively neutral on the topic within a general sense.

All scoring patterns were almost identical for evaluations between gender and income bracket groupings. Conversely, respondents with higher recorded levels of education and the younger-aged cohort tend to assert a higher level of satisfaction

Table 11.9 How satisfied are you with the following? (1-Lowest, 5-Highest)

	GEI	MP	GEI	MP	GEI	MP	GEI	MP
	Low	Low	Neutral	Neutral	High	High	Average	Average
Type of Government services in the Public Sector	8.6%	20.7%	17.7%	29.2%	73.8%	50.1%	3.8	3.4
The way the Government operates in providing services to the citizens	9.9%	22.3%	19.3%	26.7%	70.8%	50.9%	3.8	3.3
Decisions taken by Government on the services offered	10.0%	22.8%	27.1%	34.1%	62.9%	43.1%	3.7	3.3
The way public officers are kept accountable for the performance of their duties	19.3%	25.3%	31.6%	35.7%	49.1%	39.0%	3.4	3.2
The way public officers are professionals in the performance of their duties	12.8%	23.0%	27.2%	33.0%	60.1%	44.0%	3.6	3.2
Government's efficiency in the Public Service	10.9%	21.3%	27.1%	31.8%	62.0%	46.9%	3.6	3.3
Services offered by Government for business operations in Malta	7.4%	16.6%	36.4%	32.3%	56.2%	51.1%	3.6	3.4
The country's regulatory system	17.8%	21.1%	39.8%	38.7%	42.4%	40.2%	3.3	3.2
Government online services	5.5%	14.4%	12.2%	24.5%	82.3%	61.0%	4.1	3.6
Bureaucracy within the Public Service	6.8%	15.7%	24.7%	29.1%	68.5%	55.1%	3.9	3.5

with the manner in which government services are provided possibly in correlation to higher levels of uptake of those same services coupled with their above average knowledge of availability of GPS in comparison to the wider population sample. There is further evidence of correlation between knowledge of GPS that translates into uptake and thereafter satisfaction ratings by respondents who recorded being unemployed – listing above average rankings on all three segments. Noticeably, higher levels of satisfaction were associated with the state's transition and provision of digital services almost within all sub-categories. Noteworthy of mention is that, contrary to other respondent's concerns, higher rates of satisfaction were given to the government's level of good governance, accountability and bureaucracy despite their averagely neutral ratings in previous progress and imitative questions. Higher levels of satisfaction were also recorded for GEI, as is the trend on nearly all themes, almost identical across all scale levels.

It is of populist opinion by both sub-samples that since 2013, respondents' quality of life has in fact increased, at average responses in agreement surpassing the

Table 11.10 Since 2013, has the level and quality of your life improved?

	Government employees	Maltese population
Improved	64.5%	55.1%
Deteriorated	6.0%	11.4%
Stayed the same	29.5%	33.5%

Fig. 11.16 Question 16 general analysis

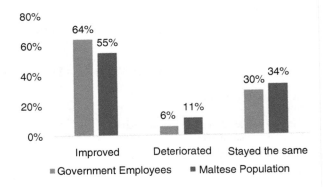

mid-point mark (refer to Table 11.10 and Fig. 11.16). This seems to be paralleled across all groupings with near-equal proportions identified between each sub-sample.

11.4   Newspapers Analysis

This part of the research is about examining newspapers letters to the editor within the period from year 2008 to year 2019. The analysis focuses on whether the letters were positive, negative or of neutral opinions, in relation with the services being offered by the public service.

11.4.1   The Methodology

The research methodology involved scrutinizing about 22,000 newspapers over the spam of 12 years. Hence, this analysis included articles that were written during 2 different administrations; the Nationalist administration (2008–2013) and the Labour administration (2013–2019). The data collection included four daily newspapers, one weekly and seven that are published every Sunday. The four daily newspapers included; two that are written in the English language: The Times and The Independent and the other two are written in the Maltese language: *Orizzont* and *Nazzjon*. The weekly newspaper is in English: The *Malta Today* midweek which is published every Wednesday. On Sundays, there are three English newspapers: *The*

Sunday Times, The Independent on Sunday and the *Malta Today,* and four Maltese newspapers: *It-Torċa, KullĦadd, Mument* and *Illum.* There are another two newspapers which are published weekly on a Thursday: *Business Weekly* and *Business Today.* However, these newspapers never boosted any letters within their issues.

The work involved consisted of searching letters within hard copies of the newspapers. All letters were categorised and classified by positive, negative and neutral theme. Following this, a random sample of 40 letters per month were selected from different newspapers and their topic/theme was noted to be included as part of the analysis. Such letters over the years started to lose its popularity as citizens started opting to other means of communication, such as the social media to reach their objective and to raise their opinions. An example is that, since the year 2017, the *KullĦadd* and *Illum* newspapers are not including any letters to the editor and, since 2018, *Torċa* has also ceased to feature such letters. This trend is visible in the number of letters that were being published over the years. For example, in 2008, there were 12,407 letters published while in 2019, there were only 2990 letters to the editor published.

Regarding the 'positive', 'negative' and 'neutral' factor, people tend to complain more rather than praising about several government services. In fact, this is evident in the number of negative letters (related to government services) over these 12 years: 5834 from a total of 87,809 (this is the total letters to the editor, including all types of letters). On the other hand, there were only 1400 positive letters, mostly were personal experiences related to good service from the government departments. The majority were related to hospitals and other health services. In general, the newspapers are dying out slowly, mostly due to the spread of digital and social news portals. Most of the newspapers that publish a hard copy also manage a news portal with live news on 24/7 basis. This is far cheaper to the consumers and more reachable than the hard-copy newspapers.

11.4.2   Time Series Analysis

The number of articles for different categories decreased since 2008. In fact, the number of articles related to Government service from 1200 in 2008, to 494 in 2019. As mentioned above, this decrease is mainly due to shift from the traditional printed newspaper to the online portals. The decline is reflected for the different categories (Fig. 11.17). For example, the number of neutral articles decreased from 541 (in 2008) to 136 (in 2019). The number of negative articles decreased from 553 (in 2008) to 309 (in 2019) and the number of positive articles decreased from 106 (in 2008) to 49 (in 2019).

The distribution between positive, negative and neutral articles changed over the years (Fig. 11.18). Mainly there was a shift of an increase in percentage points for the negative articles and a decrease in the neutral articles. There was always a slight increase percentage wise with regards to the positive articles. The percentage distribution increases regarding the negative articles; one factor can be attributed due to

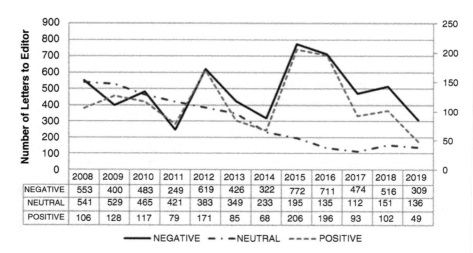

	2008	2009	2010	2011	2012	2013	2014	2015	2016	2017	2018	2019
NEGATIVE	553	400	483	249	619	426	322	772	711	474	516	309
NEUTRAL	541	529	465	421	383	349	233	195	135	112	151	136
POSITIVE	106	128	117	79	171	85	68	206	196	93	102	49

——— NEGATIVE   — · —NEUTRAL   — — — POSITIVE

Fig. 11.17 Number of letters to the editor by category

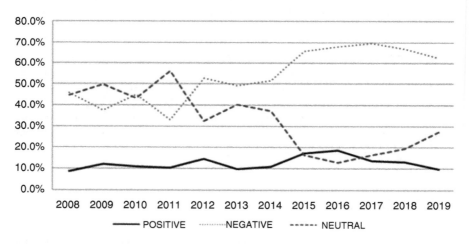

——— POSITIVE   ·········NEGATIVE   — — — — NEUTRAL

Fig. 11.18 Percentage of the letters to the editor by category

the fact that three major weekly newspapers KullĦadd, Torċa and Illum stopped the letter to the editor. The last three (latter) newspapers are more pro-government leaning. Furthermore, almost half of the letters to the editor are coming from the newspaper Times of Malta, which is more critical to the current government.

11.4.3   Thematic Analysis

As part of the analysis, we analysed the themes of the respective letters to the editor. A sample of 480 articles was selected for every single year including in this analysis. From Table 11.11, one can see that the main concerns amongst those who wrote the letters to the editor between 2008 and 2013 were issues related to:

* Malta Environment and Planning Authority (MEPA)
* General Public Hospital (Mater Dei)
* National Airline (Air Malta)
* Automated Revenue Management Services Ltd (ARMS – Utilities Bill Entity)
* Transport Malta

However, the main prominent issues were related to MEPA.

Between 2014 and 2019 we saw a change in the main prominent issues mentioned in the letters to the editor (Table 11.12). In fact, the negative letters related to 'Transport Malta' ranked on top in four from the six years. During these six years, we saw a change in some of the above themes. For example, 'ARMS' and 'Air Malta' became less of an issue. On the other hand, we saw the theme of 'Police' being mentioned more prominently. During the last three years the topic of 'Mater Dei' did not feature as one of the main three issues in the 'letters to the editor'. However, issues related to MEPA and the Planning Authority was prominent during the last six years.

Table 11.11   Negative themes between 2008 and 2013

Main themes in 2008	Main themes in 2009	Main themes in 2010	Main themes in 2011	Main themes in 2012	Main themes in 2013
MEPA	MEPA	ARMS	MEPA	Transport Malta	MEPA
Mater Dei	Transport Malta	MEPA	Transport Malta	MEPA	Public Broadcasting
Air Malta	Air Malta	Air Malta	Air Malta	ARMS	Mater Dei
Transport Malta	Water Services	Mater Dei	ARMS	Housing Authority	Transport Malta
Water Services	Gozo Channel	Police	Mater Dei	Mater Dei	Air Malta
Police	Police	Public Broadcasting	Gozo Channel	Police	ARMS
Public Broadcasting	Mater Dei	Transport Malta	PBS	Air Malta	Parking
Shipyards	MTA	WSC	Waste Services	Public Broadcasting	Law Courts
Road Works	Gozo Law Courts	Animal Welfare	Road Safety	Road works	Police
Malta Tourism Authority	Animal Welfare	Road Safety	Housing Authority	Animal Welfare	Enemalta

Table 11.12 Negative themes between 2014 and 2019

Main themes in 2014	Main themes in 2015	Main themes in 2016	Main themes in 2017	Main themes in 2018	Main themes in 2019
Police	Transport Malta	Transport Malta	Transport Malta	Transport Malta	Planning Authority
Mater Dei	MEPA	MEPA/PA/ERA	MEPA/PA/ERA	Planning Authority	Transport Malta
Transport Malta	Health	Mater Dei	Police	Public Cleansing	Road Works
MEPA	Gozo Affairs	Police	Traffic	Pavements	Air Malta
ARMS	Police	Road works	Roads	Wasteserv	Housing Authority
Gozo Channel	Road works	ARMS	Mater Dei	Police	Pensions
Pharmacy of your choice	Traffic management	Pavements	Air Malta	Roads	ARMS
Public Broadcasting	Public Cleansing	Traffic	Public cleansing	Health	Wasteserv
Traffic	ARMS	Air Malta	Road maintenance	ARMS	Gozo Malta Tunnel
Parking	Justice	Pensions	Pavements	Education	Traffic

On the other hand, most of the praise during the years 2008 and 2013 in the letters to the editor was related to the topics of 'Mater Dei', 'Air Malta' and 'Police' (Table 11.13). The first two topics were also the most that were criticized for the same period.

Similarly, as above, the main positive articles during 2014–2019 were related to the topics of 'Mater Dei', 'Air Malta' and 'Police' (Table 11.14). To a lesser extent, the topics related to 'Transport Malta', 'Education' and 'Road works' were also ranked on top of the lists.

11.5   Supplementary Demographic Tables

The supplementary demographic tables consist of demographic by Age, Gender and District. These Tables support Sect. 11.2.2 (Tables 11.15, 11.16, and 11.17).

11.6   Conclusive Remarks

Conclusively, it is without question that the overarching perception reflects a positive outlook on both the provision and execution of government-provided services to the wider community over recent years. Respondents, specifically GEI, seemed to be very aware of major projects, measures and initiatives implemented by the state, particularly those that relate to digital and social measures. This cemented

Table 11.13 Positive themes between 2008 and 2013

Main themes in 2008	Main themes in 2009	Main themes in 2010	Main themes in 2011	Main themes in 2012	Main themes in 2013
Mater Dei	Mater Dei	Mater Dei	Mater Dei	Mater Dei	Mater Dei
Air Malta	Air Malta	Air Malta	MEPA	Police	St Vincent de Paule
AFM	Police	Police	Air Malta	MEPA	Air Malta
Police	Mosta Health Centre	Animal Welfare	Police	Gozo Hospital	Health
ITS	Zammit Clapp Hospital	AFM	Karen Grech Hospital	Mater Dei	MCAST
Education	Animal Welfare	ARMS	AFM	Transport Malta	Animal Welfare
St Vincent de Paule	Transport Malta	Gozo Hospital	ARMS	Air Malta	Police
Gozo Channel	Gozo Channel	St Vincent de Paule	Animal Welfare	Health	Hamrun Day Care Centre
Pharmacy of your choice	AFM	MEPA	Gozo Hospital	Education Department	Heritage Malta
National Orchestra	WSC	Siġġiewi Primary School	Pharmacy of your choice	Enemalta	Gozo Hospital

Table 11.14 Positive themes between 2014 and 2019

Main themes 2014	Main themes 2015	Main themes 2016	Main themes 2017	Main themes 2018	Main themes 2019
Mater Dei	Health	Mater Dei	Mater Dei	Mater Dei	Health
Police	Animal Welfare	Transport Malta	Education	Police	Road Works
Air Malta	Transport Malta	Air Malta	Police	ARMS	Public cleansing
Transport Malta	Police	MEPA/PA/ERA	Public cleansing	Valletta 18	Cremation
AFM	Education	Police	Gozo Hospital	Road Works	Transport Malta
National Book Council	Air Malta	Restoration	Health	Transport Malta	Mater Dei
Gozo Hospital	Gozo Affairs	Education	Gozo Affairs	Air Malta	Restoration
Road works	Road Infrastructure	Animal Welfare	Tourism	Gozo Affairs	Planning Authority
Mosta Health Centre	Tourism	Gozo General Hospital	Prisons	Planning Authority	WSC
Prisons	Prisons	Wasteserv	Valletta 18	Health	Beaches

Table 11.15 Demographic by age

Age	Population	Sample	Difference
16–25	15%	13%	−1%
26–35	19%	17%	−2%
36–45	16%	17%	1%
46–55	14%	16%	−2%
56–65	15%	15%	–
66+	21%	22%	1%

Table 11.16 Demographic by gender

Gender	Population	Sample	Difference
Female	50%	52%	1%
Male	50%	48%	−1%

Table 11.17 Demographic by district

Districts	Population	Sample	Difference
Southern Harbour	19%	18%	−1%
Northern Harbour	28%	29%	1%
Southern Eastern	16%	17%	1%
Western	15%	13%	−2%
Northern	15%	17%	3%
Gozo & Comino	7%	6%	−1%

with evidence of correlation between cohorts that documented an above average level of awareness to uptake of those same services, mostly serviced through an online rather than an app-based platform. Little to no knowledge was documented of measures that relate towards the state's simplification of processes from either sub-sample, with digital measures repeatedly being highlighted as a main service of interest.

Accessed services by income and status demographic were found to be in line with a priori expectations, and reflected the various group-specific needs of each sub-category, while those who registered a non-usage of services were more critical of provided services, most prevalently within the Maltese population sub-sample. Despite this, there is general agreement across all sub-samples that government has exerted a high level of effort in introducing a vast mixed array of digital, social and forward-thinking measures. Flagged across all demographics was the need for government to implement better good governance and bureaucratically transparent processes, particularly with stronger views among the lower-income and unoccupied status cohort.

Similarly, current provision and availability of state-provided services have on the larger part been perceived to have improved under the current administration over recent years, except for good governance and other state bureaucratic measures across all sub-group demographics. This is further reflected in the high-ranking levels of satisfaction that respondents documented with GPS overall, particularly among participants with higher levels of education as well as those in younger cohorts who recorded having made increased use of GPS services overall. Tallying to this same belief is a general high perceived level of quality of life that has been attested to have improved in recent years by both sample populations.

All things considered, respondents overall attested towards the government's success in introducing, facilitating and implementing various measures and initiatives. This had a positive resulting effect on community level service provision and, consequently, quality of life on all fronts.

11.7   Supplementary Statistical Analysis to Support Results and Conclusive Remarks

The following statistical analysis has the objective of providing supplementary information to support Sects. 11.3 and 11.6.

11.7.1   Knowledge and Exposure to Government-Provided Services (GPS)

This section provides further information regarding Government-Provided Services. Note that list of initiatives differs from the national to GEI sample population. Furthermore, for simplification and comparability purposes, only similar segments were analysed (Tables 11.18, 11.19, 11.20, 11.21, 11.22, 11.23, and 11.24). The first 5 tables are related to the 'Maltese population' and table 11.23 is related to the 'Government Employees'.

Table 11.18 Q10 by income tax bracket

	0%	15%	25%	35%
Whistleblower's Act	66.9%	71.1%	92.3%	91.4%
Financing of Political Parties Act	65.1%	49.3%	87.4%	96.6%
Appointment of Commissioner for Standards	45.1%	41.8%	60.0%	70.7%
Public Sector Reform	42.9%	57.7%	72.7%	81.0%
Quality Service Charters	14.9%	24.1%	37.2%	32.8%
Servizz.gov	65.1%	77.5%	90.7%	100.0%
myHealth Portal	40.6%	65.5%	74.7%	69.0%
Mystery Shopper	6.3%	17.6%	16.9%	31.0%
Mobile Government Services	25.7%	33.8%	42.9%	48.3%
Business First	34.9%	43.0%	56.3%	75.9%
Appointment of Simplification Commissioner	34.9%	22.5%	37.2%	62.1%
Arbitration Office for Financial Services	28.7%	34.5%	47.0%	50.0%
Individual Investor Programme	17.7%	27.5%	42.6%	51.7%
Free Childcare	97.7%	97.9%	100.0%	100.0%

Table 11.19 Q10 by gender

	Female	Male
Whistleblower's Act	78.3%	78.1%
Financing of Political Parties Act	70.3%	72.8%
Appointment of a Commissioner for Standards	50.8%	53.3%
Public Sector Reform	70.2%	56.9%
Quality Service Charters	22.6%	26.6%
Servizz.gov	80.9%	72.5%
myHealth Portal	60.2%	53.7%
Mystery Shopper	14.9%	15.0%
Mobile Government Services	34.9%	36.2%
Business First	48.2%	45.9%
Appointment of a Commissioner for Simplification	33.7%	42.3%
Arbitration Office for Financial Services	44.8%	39.4%
Individual Investor Programme	30.4%	31.2%
Free Childcare	97.3%	94.6%

Table 11.20 Q10 by level of education

	1st Degree	A-Levels/ Diploma	Masters/ PhD	Primary	Secondary
Whistleblower's Act	85.8%	74.3%	84.8%	67.3%	77.8%
Financing of Political Parties Act	77.6%	56.6%	91.3%	73.5%	71.9%
Appointment of a Commissioner for Standards	62.7%	43.0%	76.1%	40.8%	50.1%
Public Sector Reform	76.1%	59.6%	84.8%	52.9%	59.6%
Quality Service Charters	26.1%	16.3%	43.5%	13.3%	26.1%
Servizz.gov	87.3%	83.8%	97.8%	60.0%	70.2%
myHealth Portal	71.6%	64.7%	76.1%	26.5%	50.8%
Mystery Shopper	23.9%	6.6%	17.4%	4.2%	15.9%
Mobile Government Services	38.3%	27.2%	28.3%	25.0%	40.2%
Business First	65.7%	38.6%	60.9%	18.4%	45.6%
Appointment of a Commissioner for Simplification	50.7%	29.4%	52.2%	20.8%	36.7%
Arbitration Office for Financial Services	41.0%	32.4%	52.2%	40.8%	45.2%
Individual Investor Programme	52.2%	18.4%	47.8%	14.3%	27.5%
Free Childcare	97.8%	98.5%	100.0%	71.4%	97.2%

Table 11.21 Q10 by status

	Not Employed	Employee	Fulfilling domestic tasks	Pensioner	Student
Whistleblower's Act	100.0%	81.6%	79.4%	74.8%	28.0%
Financing of Political Parties Act	100.0%	72.4%	75.2%	70.9%	28.0%
Appointment of a Commissioner for Standards	80.0%	52.4%	47.7%	58.2%	16.0%
Public Sector Reform	90.0%	68.9%	71.9%	51.9%	12.0%
Quality Service Charters	20.0%	31.1%	18.3%	14.9%	12.0%
Servizz.gov	100.0%	87.6%	80.6%	49.1%	52.0%
myHealth Portal	70.0%	68.7%	48.8%	36.7%	36.0%
Mystery Shopper	20.0%	19.9%	7.0%	10.8%	0.0%
Mobile Government Services	20.0%	40.3%	38.8%	21.2%	36.0%
Business First	80.0%	55.1%	48.0%	29.1%	16.0%
Appointment of a Commissioner for Simplification	90.0%	39.6%	26.0%	42.0%	28.0%
Arbitration Office for Financial Services	90.0%	41.3%	46.5%	44.3%	0.0%
Individual Investor Programme	80.0%	37.0%	18.9%	24.1%	12.0%
Free Childcare	100.0%	99.3%	97.7%	87.3%	88.0%

Table 11.22 Q10 by age

	16–25	26–35	36–45	46–55	56–65	66+
Whistleblower's Act	60.0%	75.7%	83.1%	82.4%	90.3%	74.8%
Financing of Political Parties Act	30.0%	76.5%	82.3%	75.2%	85.1%	70.9%
Appointment of a Commissioner for Standards	36.7%	52.2%	52.0%	49.6%	59.0%	58.2%
Public Sector Reform	50.0%	59.1%	74.4%	62.8%	87.4%	51.9%
Quality Service Charters	26.7%	13.9%	27.2%	32.6%	35.4%	14.9%
Servizz.gov	83.3%	82.6%	96.0%	83.9%	75.2%	49.1%
myHealth Portal	66.7%	61.7%	64.0%	62.5%	59.6%	36.7%
Mystery Shopper	13.3%	17.4%	15.2%	15.3%	18.8%	10.8%
Mobile Government Services	36.7%	31.3%	44.8%	44.1%	38.6%	21.2%
Business First	43.3%	60.4%	53.6%	47.3%	55.4%	29.1%
Appointment of a Commissioner for Simplification	20.0%	48.7%	46.8%	27.7%	38.4%	42.0%
Arbitration Office for Financial Services	23.3%	20.9%	45.6%	54.0%	59.2%	44.3%
Individual Investor Programme	33.3%	20.9%	40.0%	35.0%	32.3%	24.1%
Free Childcare	96.7%	100.0%	100.0%	98.5%	96.0%	87.3%

Table 11.23 Q10 by Government Employed Individuals (GEI) Scale

	2–4	5–6	7–8	9–10	11–12	13–14	15+
Whistleblower's Act	100.0%	96.3%	97.5%	89.7%	88.1%	87.1%	100.0%
Financing of Political Parties Act	92.9%	85.2%	73.8%	70.7%	69.0%	71.0%	65.0%
Appointment of a Commissioner for Standards	96.4%	87.7%	81.3%	71.1%	65.9%	80.6%	70.0%
Public Sector Reform	92.9%	92.6%	83.8%	90.9%	80.5%	93.5%	90.5%
Quality Service Charters	21.4%	36.7%	48.1%	55.7%	55.0%	48.4%	78.9%
Servizz.gov	100.0%	96.3%	97.5%	98.7%	95.2%	100.0%	100.0%
myHealth Portal	82.1%	87.7%	91.4%	91.1%	80.5%	93.5%	90.0%
Mystery Shopper	89.3%	67.9%	60.3%	53.9%	26.8%	58.1%	47.4%
Mobile Government Services	85.7%	68.8%	63.3%	54.2%	43.9%	83.9%	60.0%
Business First	85.7%	58.2%	52.6%	37.0%	34.1%	45.2%	42.1%
Appointment of a Commissioner for Simplification	82.1%	55.7%	50.0%	29.2%	19.5%	41.9%	21.1%
Arbitration Office for Financial Services	67.9%	34.6%	38.5%	35.2%	39.0%	35.5%	31.6%
Individual Investor Programme	85.7%	56.4%	51.9%	32.4%	29.3%	41.9%	45.0%
Free Childcare	100.0%	97.5%	98.7%	96.2%	97.6%	100.0%	100.0%

Table 11.24 Can you name any measures related to the simplification of processes introduced by Government?

	Government employees	Maltese population
Business Measures	6.7%	2.9%
Digital Measures	62.4%	34.4%
Does Not Know/Does Not Remember	0.3%	49.8%
Health Measures	4.3%	2.4%
More Efficient Processes	15.2%	5.0%
Nothing	0.3%	1.4%
Others	5.9%	0.8%
Social Measures	5.1%	3.2%

11.7.2 Uptake of Government-Provided Services (GPS)

This section provides a detailed statistical analysis regarding the uptake of government provided services (Tables 11.25, 11.26, 11.27, 11.28, 11.29, 11.30, 11.31, 11.32, 11.33, 11.34, 11.35, 11.36, 11.37, 11.38, and 11.39). From tables 11.27 to 11.31 and 11.34 to 11.38 these are related to the 'Maltese population' and table 11.39 is related to the 'Government Employees'.

11.7.3 Initiative by Government on Provision of Government-Provided Services

This section provides a detailed statistical analysis regarding the initiatives taken by Government regarding the provision of Government-Provided Services (GPS) (Tables 11.40, 11.41, 11.42, 11.43, 11.44, and 11.45). The first 5 tables are related to the 'Maltese population' and the last table is related to the 'Government Employees'.

Table 11.25 If 'Yes' (Q2), which online service do you use most?

Usage	Government employees	Maltese population
Bill Payments	13.2%	31.2%
Certificates	8.3%	5.7%
Education Related	2.7%	3.5%
General Applications	5.9%	2.5%
General Government Services	28.8%	39.7%
My Health/POYC	21.7%	10.7%
My Personal Kiosk	10.5%	0.3%
Others	9.0%	6.35%

Table 11.26 If 'No' (Q2), what is the reason why you have never used online services?

	Government employees	Maltese population
Not accessible to/Not knowledgeable on how to use	0.6%	16.7%
Not need to Use the Service	1.2%	20.1%
Others	7.2%	6.0%
Prefer Human Interaction	1.2%	1.1%
Prefer Using Desktop/Laptop	3.4%	7.3%
Blank	86.5%	48.8%

Table 11.27   Q3 by income tax bracket

	0%	15%	25%	35%
Bill Payments	14.6%	20.0%	43.0%	53.8%
Certificates	0.0%	12.7%	7.9%	1.9%
Education Related	9.8%	10.9%	0.9%	0.0%
General Applications	9.8%	0.0%	0.0%	0.0%
General Government Services	46.3%	29.1%	43.9%	38.5%
My Health/POYC	17.1%	12.7%	3.5%	5.8%
My Personal Kiosk	0.0%	1.8%	0.0%	0.0%
Others	2.4%	12.7%	0.9%	0.0%

Table 11.28   Q3 by gender

	Female	Male
Bill Payments	20.7%	42.8%
Certificates	6.1%	5.3%
Education Related	3.0%	3.9%
General Applications	2.4%	2.6%
General Government Services	46.3%	32.2%
My Health/POYC	13.4%	7.9%
My Personal Kiosk	0.6%	0.0%
Others	7.3%	5.3%

Table 11.29   Q3 by level of education

	1st Degree	A-Levels/ Diploma	Masters/ PhD	Primary	Secondary
Bill Payments	33.3%	21.1%	39.0%	0.0%	33.9%
Certificates	4.4%	5.6%	14.6%	0.0%	3.6%
Education Related	1.1%	8.5%	0.0%	0.0%	3.6%
General Applications	3.3%	1.4%	9.8%	0.0%	0.0%
General Government Services	48.9%	38.0%	29.3%	66.7%	36.6%
My Health/POYC	8.9%	14.1%	7.3%	0.0%	11.6%
My Personal Kiosk	0.0%	1.4%	0.0%	0.0%	0.0%
Others	0.0%	9.9%	0.0%	33.3%	10.7%

Table 11.30 Q3 by status

	Not employed	Employee	Fulfilling domestic tasks	Pensioner	Student
Bill Payments	0.0%	35.6%	12.1%	42.9%	0.0%
Certificates	0.0%	6.8%	0.0%	7.1%	0.0%
Education Related	0.0%	2.8%	12.1%	0.0%	0.0%
General Applications	0.0%	1.6%	0.0%	0.0%	40.0%
General Government Services	0.0%	39.6%	48.5%	28.6%	60.0%
My Health/POYC	100.0%	6.0%	27.3%	7.1%	0.0%
My Personal Kiosk	0.0%	0.4%	0.0%	0.0%	0.0%
Others	0.0%	7.2%	0.0%	14.3%	0.0%

Table 11.31 Q3 by age

	16–25	26–35	36–45	46–55	56–65	66+
Bill Payments	5.6%	42.2%	25.6%	50.0%	19.2%	42.9%
Certificates	11.1%	0.0%	11.0%	1.7%	3.8%	7.1%
Education Related	0.0%	4.8%	7.3%	1.7%	0.0%	0.0%
General Applications	5.6%	4.8%	0.0%	1.7%	0.0%	0.0%
General Government Services	44.4%	43.4%	40.2%	37.9%	26.9%	28.6%
My Health/POYC	22.2%	0.0%	8.5%	3.4%	46.2%	7.1%
My Personal Kiosk	0.0%	0.0%	0.0%	1.7%	0.0%	0.0%
Others	11.1%	4.8%	7.3%	1.7%	3.8%	14.3%

Table 11.32 If 'Yes' (Q5), which mobile service do you use most?

Usage	Government employees	Maltese population
Bill Payments	6.9%	15.4%
COVID-19 Related	3.4%	34.2%
Education Services/E-ID	16.3%	1.7%
General Government Applications	31.0%	17.9%
My Health	19.7%	8.5%
My Personal Kiosk	7.4%	0.0%
Others	15.3%	22.2%
Bill Payments	6.9%	15.4%

Table 11.33 If 'No' (Q5), what is the reason why you have never used mobile services?

	Government employees	Maltese population
Not accessible to/Could not use	7.2%	16.7%
Not need to Use the Service	19.7%	20.1%
Others	4.4%	6.0%
Prefer Human Interaction	17.1%	1.1%
Prefer Using Desktop/Laptop	3.4%	7.3%
Blank	50.2%	48.8%

Table 11.34 Q6 by income tax bracket

	0%	15%	25%	35%
Bill Payments	20.0%	0.0%	13.3%	85.7%
COVID-19 Related	36.7%	50.0%	33.3%	0.0%
Education Services/E-ID	0.0%	0.0%	4.4%	0.0%
General Government Applications	16.7%	41.7%	20.0%	14.3%
My Health	6.7%	8.3%	0.0%	0.0%
Others	20.0%	0.0%	28.9%	0.0%

Table 11.35 Q6 by gender

	Female	Male
Bill Payments	17.1%	12.8%
COVID-19 Related	27.1%	44.7%
Education Services/E-ID	1.4%	2.1%
General Government Applications	17.1%	19.1%
My Health	12.9%	2.1%
Others	24.3%	19.1%

Table 11.36 Q6 by level of education

	1st Degree	A-Levels/ Diploma	Masters/ PhD	Primary	Secondary
Bill Payments	0.0%	0.0%	50.0%	0.0%	19.0%
COVID-19 Related	36.8%	27.8%	41.7%	75.0%	30.2%
Education Services/E-ID	0.0%	11.1%	0.0%	0.0%	0.0%
General Government Applications	63.2%	5.6%	8.3%	0.0%	11.1%
My Health	0.0%	16.7%	0.0%	25.0%	9.5%
Others	0.0%	38.9%	0.0%	0.0%	30.2%

Table 11.37 Q6 by status

	Not employed	Employee	Fulfilling domestic tasks	Pensioner	Student
Bill Payments	0.0%	10.0%	30.8%	0.0%	0.0%
COVID-19 Related	0.0%	28.3%	33.3%	60.0%	57.1%
Education Services/E-ID	0.0%	3.3%	0.0%	0.0%	0.0%
General Government Applications	0.0%	26.7%	2.6%	10.0%	42.9%
My Health	100.0%	3.3%	12.8%	20.0%	0.0%
Others	0.0%	28.3%	20.5%	10.0%	0.0%

Table 11.38 Q6 by age

	16–25	26–35	36–45	46–55	56–65	66+
Bill Payments	0.0%	0.0%	52.2%	21.4%	0.0%	0.0%
COVID-19 Related	0.0%	25.0%	0.0%	42.9%	58.1%	60.0%
Education Services/E-ID	0.0%	0.0%	4.3%	3.6%	0.0%	0.0%
General Government Applications	100.0%	25.0%	21.7%	7.1%	0.0%	10.0%
My Health	0.0%	0.0%	13.0%	0.0%	16.1%	20.0%
Others	0.0%	50.0%	8.7%	25.0%	25.8%	10.0%

Table 11.39 If 'Yes', which training course was most beneficial to you?

	Government employees
Business Related	36.6%
Digital	17.0%
EU Related	0.8%
IPS	17.0%
Language Related	2.6%
Others	20.0%
Scholarship	1.1%
Short Courses/Training	4.9%

Table 11.40 Q11 by income tax bracket

	0%	15%	25%	35%	Total Ave.
Introduce Government services online?	3.3	3.6	3.9	4.1	3.7
Introduce mechanisms to ensure transparency in Governmental operations?	3.1	3.3	3.1	3.1	3.2
Enhance citizens' rights, including participation in Government's decisions?	3.0	3.0	3.0	2.9	3.0
Introduce mechanisms so that public officers are accountable for the performance of their duties?	3.1	3.1	3.0	2.8	3.0
Introduce mechanisms to reduce bureaucracy in Governmental operations?	3.1	3.0	3.0	3.3	3.1
Introduce mechanisms so that citizens are served with improved and efficient Government services?	3.4	3.5	3.5	3.6	3.5
Introduce systems/programmes to improve the performance of public officers?	3.1	3.5	3.2	3.0	3.2
Introduce mobile apps to facilitate access to Government services to citizens?	3.3	3.9	3.7	4.2	3.7
Introduce online health systems so that citizens are served better?	3.3	3.7	3.8	3.8	3.7
Introduce systems for businesses to improve their operations in Malta?	3.3	3.8	3.5	3.4	3.5
Introduce mechanisms to simplify Gov. operations?	3.2	3.6	3.3	3.9	3.5
Introduce systems to simplify Government services offered to citizens?	3.3	3.8	3.3	3.6	3.5
Introduce systems/programmes to improve economy?	3.3	3.9	3.5	3.9	3.7
Introduce systems to increase citizen work opportunities?	3.3	3.9	3.7	3.6	3.6

Table 11.41 Q11 by gender

	Female	Male	Total Ave.
Introduce Government services online?	3.8	3.5	3.6
Introduce mechanisms to ensure transparency in Governmental operations?	3.2	3.0	3.1
Enhance citizens' rights, including participation in Government's decisions?	3.0	2.9	2.9
Introduce mechanisms so that public officers are accountable for the performance of their duties?	3.0	2.9	3.0
Introduce mechanisms to reduce bureaucracy in Governmental operations?	3.1	3.0	3.0
Introduce mechanisms so that citizens are served with improved and efficient Government services?	3.5	3.3	3.4
Introduce systems/programmes to improve the performance of public officers?	3.3	3.3	3.3
Introduce mobile apps to facilitate access to Government services to citizens?	3.8	3.5	3.7
Introduce online health systems so that citizens are served better?	3.9	3.5	3.7
Introduce systems for businesses to improve their operations?	3.5	3.4	3.5
Introduce mechanisms to simplify Governmental operations?	3.4	3.3	3.4
Introduce systems to simplify Government services offered to citizens?	3.5	3.4	3.4
Introduce systems/programmes to improve Malta's economy?	3.6	3.4	3.5
Introduce systems to increase working opportunities to citizens?	3.8	3.5	3.6

Table 11.42 Q11 by level of education

	1st degree	A-Level/ Diploma	Master/ PhD	Primary	Secondary	Total Ave.
Introduce Government services online?	3.9	3.8	4.2	3.2	3.5	3.7
Introduce mechanisms to ensure transparency in Governmental operations?	3.1	3.1	2.8	3.0	3.2	3.0
Enhance citizens' rights, including participation in Government's decisions?	2.9	2.9	3.0	3.0	3.0	2.9
Introduce mechanisms so that public officers are accountable for the performance of their duties?	3.1	2.9	2.8	3.1	3.0	3.0
Introduce mechanisms to reduce bureaucracy in Governmental operations?	3.1	2.8	3.2	3.1	3.0	3.0
Introduce mechanisms so that citizens are served with improved & efficient Government services?	3.7	3.3	3.9	3.1	3.3	3.5
Introduce systems/programmes to improve the performance of public officers?	3.3	3.4	3.1	2.9	3.3	3.2
Introduce mobile apps to facilitate access to Government services to citizens?	4.0	3.8	3.9	3.2	3.5	3.7
Introduce online health systems so that citizens are served better?	3.9	3.8	4.1	3.3	3.5	3.7
Introduce systems for businesses to improve their operations?	3.7	3.7	3.5	3.1	3.4	3.5
Introduce mechanisms to simplify Governmental operations?	3.4	3.4	3.6	3.1	3.3	3.4
Introduce systems to simplify Government services offered to citizens?	3.6	3.4	3.8	3.3	3.4	3.5
Introduce systems/programmes to improve Malta's economy?	3.7	3.7	3.9	3.1	3.4	3.6
Introduce systems to increase working opportunities to citizens?	3.5	3.9	4.0	3.4	3.6	3.7

Table 11.43 Q11 by status

	Not employed	Employee	Fulfilling domestic tasks	Pensioner	Student	Total average
Introduce Government services online?	4.1	3.9	3.4	3.2	3.7	3.6
Introduce mechanisms to ensure transparency in Governmental operations?	2.6	3.2	3.1	2.9	3.2	3.0
Enhance citizens' rights, including participation in Government's decisions?	2.4	3.1	2.6	2.8	3.4	2.9
Introduce mechanisms so that public officers are accountable for the performance of their duties?	2.4	3.0	2.8	2.9	3.6	3.0
Introduce mechanisms to reduce bureaucracy in Governmental operations?	3.7	3.1	2.7	2.9	3.6	3.2
Introduce mechanisms so that citizens are served with improved and efficient Government services?	4.2	3.6	3.0	3.0	4.0	3.6
Introduce systems/ programmes to improve the performance of public officers?	4.1	3.4	3.0	3.2	3.0	3.3
Introduce mobile apps to facilitate access to Government services to citizens?	3.4	3.9	3.5	3.3	3.7	3.6
Introduce online health systems so that citizens are served better?	4.9	3.8	3.5	3.3	3.9	3.9
Introduce systems for businesses to improve their operations in Malta?	3.7	3.7	3.1	3.3	3.4	3.4
Introduce mechanisms to simplify Governmental operations?	3.9	3.5	3.0	3.1	3.5	3.4
Introduce systems to simplify Government services offered to citizens?	4.0	3.6	3.1	3.2	3.4	3.5
Introduce systems/ programmes to improve Malta's economy?	3.2	3.8	3.1	3.1	3.5	3.3
Introduce systems to increase working opportunities to citizens?	3.8	3.9	3.3	3.3	3.5	3.6

Table 11.44   Q11 by age

	16–25	26–35	36–45	46–55	56–65	66+	Total average
Introduce Government services online?	3.6	4.1	3.8	3.6	3.7	3.2	3.7
Introduce mechanisms to ensure transparency in Governmental operations?	3.3	3.4	3.0	3.1	3.1	2.9	3.1
Enhance citizens' rights, including participation in Government's decisions?	3.0	3.4	2.8	2.9	2.7	2.8	2.9
Introduce mechanisms so that public officers are accountable for the performance of their duties?	3.3	3.3	2.8	2.8	3.0	2.9	3.0
Introduce mechanisms to reduce bureaucracy in Governmental operations?	3.1	3.3	3.0	3.0	2.9	2.9	3.0
Introduce mechanisms so that citizens are served with improved and efficient Government services?	3.9	3.8	3.3	3.4	3.2	3.0	3.4
Introduce systems/programmes to improve the performance of public officers?	3.6	3.4	3.1	3.1	3.2	3.2	3.3
Introduce mobile apps to facilitate access to Government services to citizens?	3.8	4.0	3.8	3.6	3.6	3.3	3.7
Introduce online health systems so that citizens are served better?	3.9	4.0	3.5	3.7	3.8	3.3	3.7
Introduce systems for businesses to improve their operations in Malta?	3.9	3.9	3.2	3.5	3.3	3.3	3.5
Introduce mechanisms to simplify Governmental operations?	3.5	3.8	3.4	3.3	3.1	3.1	3.4
Introduce systems to simplify Government services offered to citizens?	3.7	3.8	3.5	3.4	3.2	3.2	3.5
Introduce systems/programmes to improve Malta's economy?	4.1	4.0	3.5	3.5	3.1	3.1	3.6
Introduce systems to increase working opportunities to citizens?	4.0	4.0	3.7	3.6	3.4	3.3	3.7

Table 11.45 Q11 by Government Employed Individuals (GEI) Scale

	2–4	5–6	7–8	9–10	11–12	13–14	15+	Total average
Introduce Government services online?	4.3	4.5	4.3	4.3	4.1	4.2	4.7	4.3
Introduce mechanisms to ensure transparency in Governmental operations?	3.6	3.5	3.4	3.5	3.5	3.8	3.7	3.6
Enhance citizens' rights, including participation in Government's decisions?	3.4	3.4	3.1	3.2	3.1	3.7	3.7	3.4
Introduce mechanisms so that public officers are accountable for the performance of their duties?	3.5	3.3	3.2	3.2	3.4	3.7	3.5	3.4
Introduce mechanisms to reduce bureaucracy in Governmental operations?	3.9	3.5	3.3	3.2	3.4	3.5	3.6	3.5
Introduce mechanisms so that citizens are served with improved and efficient Government services?	4.4	4.2	4.0	3.9	3.9	4.1	4.3	4.1
Introduce systems/programmes to improve the performance of public officers?	3.9	3.9	3.7	3.7	3.8	3.9	3.8	3.8
Introduce mobile apps to facilitate access to Government services to citizens?	4.3	4.1	3.9	3.8	3.8	4.3	4.4	4.1
Introduce online health systems so that citizens are served better?	4.0	4.1	4.1	3.9	4.0	4.2	4.2	4.1
Introduce systems for businesses to improve their operations in Malta?	4.2	3.8	3.6	3.6	3.6	3.9	3.9	3.8
Introduce mechanisms to simplify Governmental operations?	4.0	3.6	3.4	3.5	3.5	3.6	3.6	3.6
Introduce systems to simplify Government services offered to citizens?	4.2	3.9	3.7	3.6	3.6	3.8	4.0	3.8
Introduce systems/programmes to improve Malta's economy?	4.3	4.2	4.0	4.0	4.0	4.1	4.4	4.1
Introduce systems to increase working opportunities to citizens?	4.1	3.9	3.8	3.9	3.6	4.0	4.2	4.0

11.7.4   Subsequent Progress on the Sufficiency of Government-Provided Services

This section provides a detailed statistical analysis regarding subsequent progress on the sufficiency of Government-Provided Services (GPS) (Tables 11.46, 11.47, 11.48, 11.49, 11.50, and 11.51). The first 5 tables are related to the 'Maltese population' and the last table is related to the 'Government Employees'.

Table 11.46   Q12 by income tax bracket

	0%	15%	25%	35%	Total Ave.
Type of Government services in Public Sector	1.5	1.4	1.4	1.2	1.3
The way the Government operates in providing services to the citizens	1.5	1.5	1.3	1.3	1.4
Decisions taken by Government on services offered	1.6	1.6	1.5	1.5	1.5
The way public officers are kept accountable for the performance of their duties	1.8	1.6	1.7	1.9	1.7
The way public officers are professional in the performance of their duties	1.7	1.5	1.7	1.6	1.6
Government's efficiency in the Public Service	1.5	1.3	1.5	1.4	1.4
Services offered by Government for business operations in Malta	1.5	1.3	1.4	1.3	1.4
The country's regulatory system	1.6	1.6	1.7	1.5	1.6
Government online services	1.4	1.3	1.2	1.1	1.3
Bureaucracy within the Public Service	1.6	1.7	1.8	1.7	1.7

Table 11.47   Q12 by gender

	Female	Male	Total average
Type of Government services in Public Sector	1.4	1.5	1.4
The way the Government operates in providing services to the citizens	1.4	1.5	1.4
Decisions taken by Gov. on services offered	1.5	1.6	1.6
The way public officers are kept accountable for the performance of their duties	1.7	1.8	1.7
The way public officers are professional in the performance of their duties	1.6	1.8	1.7
Government's efficiency in the Public Service	1.5	1.5	1.5
Services offered by Gov. for business operations	1.4	1.5	1.4
The country's regulatory system	1.6	1.7	1.6
Government online services	1.2	1.4	1.3
Bureaucracy within the Public Service	1.7	1.8	1.7

Table 11.48 Q12 by level of education

	1st degree	A-Level/ Diploma	Master/ PhD	Primary	Secondary	Total Ave.
Type of Government services in the Public Sector	1.2	1.2	1.3	1.7	1.6	1.5
Way the Government operates in providing services to the citizens	1.3	1.3	1.4	1.6	1.6	1.5
Decisions taken by Government on the services offered	1.5	1.4	1.5	1.9	1.6	1.6
The way public officers are kept accountable for the performance of their duties	1.7	1.7	1.6	1.7	1.8	1.7
The way public officers are professional in the performance of their duties	1.6	1.6	1.5	1.6	1.7	1.6
Government's efficiency in the Public Service	1.4	1.3	1.3	1.8	1.6	1.5
Services offered by Government for business operations in Malta	1.3	1.3	1.2	1.6	1.5	1.4
The country's regulatory system	1.6	1.7	1.5	2.0	1.6	1.7
Government online services	1.2	1.2	1.0	1.5	1.4	1.3
Bureaucracy within Public Service	1.7	1.7	1.8	1.8	1.8	1.8

Table 11.49 Q12 by status

	Not employed	Employee	Fulfilling domestic tasks	Pensioner	Student	Total Ave.
Type of Government services in Public Sector	1.0	1.3	1.7	1.6	1.3	1.5
The way Government operates in providing services to the citizens	1.0	1.4	1.7	1.6	1.1	1.4
Decisions taken by Government on the services offered	1.0	1.5	1.8	1.7	1.3	1.6
The way public officers are kept accountable for the performance of their duties	2.0	1.7	1.7	1.9	1.4	1.7
The way public officers are professional in the performance of their duties	1.8	1.6	1.7	1.8	1.4	1.6
Government's efficiency in the Public Service	1.2	1.4	1.6	1.7	1.2	1.5
Services offered by Government for business operations in Malta	1.0	1.3	1.5	1.6	1.2	1.4
The country's regulatory system	2.3	1.6	1.6	1.8	1.4	1.6
Government online services	1.0	1.2	1.4	1.4	1.1	1.3
Bureaucracy within the Public Service	1.0	1.7	1.9	1.8	1.4	1.7

Table 11.50   Q12 by age

	16–25	26–35	36–45	46–55	56–65	66+	Total Ave.
Type of Government services in Public Sector	1.2	1.4	1.5	1.4	1.6	1.6	1.5
The way the Government operates in providing services to the citizens	1.3	1.2	1.5	1.4	1.5	1.6	1.5
Decisions taken by Government on the services offered	1.4	1.4	1.5	1.6	1.8	1.7	1.7
The way public officers are kept accountable for the performance of their duties	1.6	1.6	1.6	1.9	1.8	1.9	1.8
Way public officers are professional in the performance of their duties	1.5	1.7	1.6	1.6	1.7	1.8	1.7
Government's efficiency in Public Service	1.3	1.4	1.4	1.5	1.6	1.7	1.5
Services offered by Government for business operations in Malta	1.2	1.2	1.4	1.5	1.5	1.6	1.5
The country's regulatory system	1.6	1.4	1.7	1.7	1.6	1.8	1.7
Government online services	1.2	1.2	1.2	1.3	1.3	1.4	1.3
Bureaucracy within the Public Service	1.6	1.6	1.8	1.8	1.9	1.8	1.8

Table 11.51   Q12 by Government Employed Individuals (GEI) Scale

	2–4	5–6	7–8	9–10	11–12	13–14	15+	Total Ave.
Type of Government services in Public Sector	1.3	1.2	1.2	1.3	1.4	1.4	1.3	1.3
Way the Government operates in providing services to the citizens	1.2	1.3	1.3	1.4	1.4	1.4	1.3	1.3
Decisions taken by Government on the services offered	1.3	1.3	1.5	1.5	1.5	1.3	1.2	1.4
The way public officers are kept accountable for the performance of their duties	1.8	1.5	1.7	1.7	1.5	1.5	1.5	1.6
The way public officers are professional in the performance of their duties	1.5	1.4	1.4	1.5	1.5	1.3	1.4	1.4
Government's efficiency in Public Service	1.4	1.3	1.4	1.5	1.5	1.4	1.3	1.4
Services offered by Government for business operations in Malta	1.3	1.3	1.4	1.5	1.5	1.4	1.2	1.4
The country's regulatory system	1.5	1.7	1.8	1.7	1.7	1.6	1.3	1.6
Government online services	1.1	1.2	1.2	1.2	1.3	1.2	1.1	1.2
Bureaucracy within Public Service	1.5	1.6	1.8	1.8	1.9	1.7	1.6	1.7

11.7.5   Outcome Completion of Government-Provided Services

This section provides a detailed statistical analysis regarding outcome completion of Government-Provided Services (GPS) (Tables 11.52, 11.53, 11.54, 11.55, 11.56, and 11.57). The first 5 tables are related to the 'Maltese population' and the last table is related to the 'Government Employees'.

Table 11.52   Q13 by income tax bracket

	0%	15%	25%	35%	Total Ave.
Type of Government services in Public Sector	3.2	3.4	3.5	3.5	3.4
Way the Government operates in providing services to the citizens	3.2	3.3	3.4	3.5	3.3
Decisions taken by Government on the services offered	3.1	3.4	3.4	3.1	3.2
The way public officers are kept accountable for the performance of their duties	3.1	3.2	3.2	3.1	3.2
The way public officers are professional in the performance of their duties	3.1	3.2	3.2	3.4	3.2
Government's efficiency in Public Service	3.1	3.4	3.4	3.4	3.3
Services offered by Government for business operations in Malta	3.3	3.5	3.5	3.7	3.5
The country's regulatory system	3.0	3.2	3.3	3.2	3.2
Government online services	3.3	3.8	3.8	4.2	3.8
Bureaucracy within Public Service	3.2	3.6	3.6	4.2	3.6

Table 11.53   Q13 by gender

	Female	Male	Total Ave.
Type of Government services in Public Sector	3.5	3.3	3.4
Way the Government operates in providing services to citizens	3.4	3.2	3.3
Decisions taken by Government on services offered	3.3	3.2	3.3
The way public officers are kept accountable for the performance of their duties	3.3	3.0	3.2
Way public officers are professional in performance of their duties	3.3	3.1	3.2
Government's efficiency in the Public Service	3.4	3.2	3.3
Services offered by Government for business operations	3.6	3.3	3.4
The country's regulatory system	3.4	3.0	3.2
Government online services	3.7	3.5	3.6
Bureaucracy within the Public Service	3.6	3.4	3.5

Table 11.54 Q13 by level of education

	1st degree	A-level/ Diploma	Master/ PhD	Primary	Secondary	Total Ave.
Type of Gov. services in Public Sector	3.6	3.5	3.6	3.0	3.2	3.4
Way the Government operates in providing services to the citizens	3.4	3.4	3.7	3.1	3.2	3.4
Decisions by Gov. on services offered	3.4	3.4	3.4	2.9	3.2	3.3
Way public officers are kept accountable for performance of duties	3.1	3.2	3.4	3.1	3.2	3.2
Way public officers are professional in the performance of their duties	3.2	3.2	3.6	3.3	3.2	3.3
Govt's efficiency in Public Service	3.4	3.4	3.4	3.0	3.2	3.3
Services offered by Government for business operations in Malta	3.6	3.5	3.6	3.3	3.3	3.5
The country's regulatory system	3.1	3.4	3.6	2.9	3.1	3.2
Government online services	4.1	3.7	4.4	3.3	3.4	3.8
Bureaucracy within Public Service	3.8	3.5	4.2	3.1	3.4	3.6

Table 11.55 Q13 by status

	Not employed	Employee	Fulfilling domestic tasks	Pensioner	Student	Total Ave.
Type of Government services in Public Sector	4.7	3.5	3.1	3.1	3.6	3.6
Way Government operates in providing services to citizens	4.7	3.4	3.0	3.1	3.6	3.6
Decisions taken by Government on the services offered	4.7	3.4	3.0	2.9	3.6	3.5
Way public officers are kept accountable for the performance of their duties	3.4	3.2	3.3	3.0	3.4	3.2
Way public officers are professional in the performance of their duties	3.4	3.3	3.1	3.0	3.6	3.3
Government's efficiency in the Public Service	4.1	3.4	3.1	3.0	3.5	3.4
Services offered by Government to business operations in Malta	3.6	3.6	3.3	3.2	3.5	3.4
The country's regulatory system	3.0	3.3	3.1	2.9	3.4	3.1
Government online services	4.7	3.9	3.4	3.1	3.9	3.8
Bureaucracy within Public Service	4.1	3.7	3.3	3.0	3.8	3.6

Table 11.56 Q13 by age

	16–25	26–35	36–45	46–55	56–65	66+	Total Ave.
Type of Government services in the Public Sector	3.8	3.8	3.3	3.2	3.2	3.1	3.4
The way the Government operates in providing services to the citizens	3.6	3.7	3.3	3.2	3.1	3.1	3.3
Decisions taken by Government on the services offered	3.6	3.6	3.3	3.1	3.1	2.9	3.3
The way public officers are kept accountable for the performance of their duties	3.3	3.3	3.2	3.1	3.3	3.0	3.2
Way public officers are professional in the performance of their duties	3.3	3.4	3.4	3.1	3.3	3.0	3.2
Government's efficiency in Public Service	3.6	3.5	3.3	3.3	3.1	3.0	3.3
Services offered by Government for business operations in Malta	3.6	3.7	3.5	3.4	3.3	3.2	3.4
The country's regulatory system	3.4	3.5	3.2	3.1	3.3	2.9	3.2
Government online services	4.1	4.0	3.6	3.6	3.6	3.1	3.7
Bureaucracy within the Public Service	3.8	3.9	3.5	3.5	3.4	3.0	3.5

Table 11.57 Q13 by Government Employed Individuals (GEI) scale

	2–4	5–6	7–8	9–10	11–12	13–14	15+	Total average
Type of Government services in the Public Sector	3.9	4.0	3.8	3.8	3.7	3.8	3.9	3.8
The way the Government operates in providing services to the citizens	4.0	3.8	3.8	3.7	3.7	3.7	3.8	3.8
Decisions taken by Government on the services offered	3.9	3.7	3.5	3.7	3.5	3.7	4.0	3.7
The way public officers are kept accountable for the performance of their duties	3.2	3.5	3.2	3.4	3.4	3.4	3.6	3.4
The way public officers are professional in the performance of their duties	3.6	3.7	3.6	3.5	3.5	3.6	3.8	3.6
Government's efficiency in the Public Service	3.8	3.7	3.6	3.6	3.6	3.6	3.8	3.7
Services offered by Government for business operations in Malta	4.0	3.7	3.6	3.5	3.3	3.5	4.0	3.7
The country's regulatory system	3.5	3.2	3.1	3.4	3.1	3.3	3.6	3.3
Government online services	4.4	4.2	4.1	4.1	3.8	4.1	4.1	4.1
Bureaucracy within Public Service	4.2	4.0	3.8	3.9	3.5	3.9	4.1	3.9

Part IV

Public Service Reform: The Future

The focus of this section is the Public Service reform trends that are likely to impact public service delivery worldwide in the future. Only ultra conservative governments remain inactive and unchanging. Hence, it is with certainty that governments will be on the move. The issue is the speed at which a particular government will be moving at. However, the response to this issue also depends on the leadership at a specific point in time. As Eleanor Roosevelt appropriately philosophised, the future belongs to those who believe in the beauty of their dreams. The future will bring innumerable and unavoidable changes as the opportunities that the current conditions and technology are presenting us are incredibly never-ending. No matter how good the past has been, we need to dynamically embrace the great potential of the new ways of thinking. This, sustained by technology, will help us confront the challenges presented by the future. Walt Disney suggested that times and conditions change so rapidly that we must keep our aim constantly focused on the future.

Entities are influenced by their internal and external environments. The internal environment is mostly under the control of the entity and is impacted by the ability of management to meet head-on the challenges presented to it. However, the external environment is a free spirit that is shaped by global, regional and local circumstances, and the accumulated and independent diverse actions and reactions of countless others. Hence, it is the external environment that has the greatest impact on the pace of change that governments are likely to adopt. That is, whether governments take a proactive stand to anticipate change or take a wait-and-see reactive attitude. Whatever approach is adopted, the external forces will compel governments to introduce change. The difference between the tactics is that a proactive stand enables a government to define and influence its future, with an ensuing high return in terms of the benefits it may gain on behalf of its citizens. Whereas, a reactive approach pre-conditions and restricts Government's manoeuvrability to mould its future and thus the return in terms of benefits are much lower. A case in point is the outbreak of the Corona virus. Governments that had a teleworking policy supported by the appropriate technology already in place had little difficulty in continuing their services under complete or partial lockdown. However, those governments that did not have a teleworking policy had to take a reactive approach with a resultant panicked atmosphere leading to a severe crisis management scenario. Additionally, the Corona virus outbreaks made many governments recognise that teleworking had the potential to contribute towards a significant increase in air quality, better family quality time, less pressure on public transport systems, less office space and a general decrease in operational costs. Hence, it is perceived that teleworking is likely to be here to stay and will probably be refined and applied to a wider section of government workers.

A detailed study of employee attitudes at Malta government's employment agency, Jobsplus, revealed that these employees perceived the following future trends: empowering customers and employees through the provision of simplified computing services at anytime from anywhere; implementing green technology, leading to a paperless environment; use of business intelligence tools to analyse information and making use of decision support systems (Big Data Analytics); partner with diverse categories of customers to offer innovative solutions that suit their particular needs; establish a performance-focused culture that encourages employees to suggest ways on how their Division's performance may be assessed and improved; and permit greater citizen participation in community work and public policy. Most of these trends were found to be congruent with the literature related to the international future trends in Public Service reforms. These trends and others will be explored further to reflect on the future of the Public Service and how to contemplate the challenges and harness the opportunities presented by the hands of time.

Chapter 12
Public Service Reform: The Future (A New Beginning)

> *"Change is the law of life. And those who look only to the past or present are certain to miss the future."*
>
> John F. Kennedy, 35th President of the United States

This Chapter is about the future and is based upon extensive literature research regarding the future developing trends related to Public Service reforms. UNDP (2015) argues that most reforms in government are only partially successful not because, once implemented, they yield unsatisfactory outcomes, but because they never get past the implementation stage at all. They contend that learning lessons from experience, and applying them, is particularly essential. In this regard, information technology is viewed as an essential change agent. It has continued and will continue to provide opportunities for governments to initiate Public Service reforms, with the intention of improving the living standards of its citizens, in a variety of sectors. Information technology has paved the way to making the world flat in terms of creating a friendly and effective environment, where all the diverse stakeholders conduct their personal and business affairs on a level playing field in terms of conducting business and serving customers, wherein all competitors have an equal opportunity through the application of information technology. In such a scenario, governments are under unrelenting pressure to provide a much better service to their customers. Public service reforms and the systems they generate as a platform for service delivery are full of challenges and require sustained commitment from all levels of the Public Service. Public Service employees need to look for new ways of implementing change by taking advantage of the opportunities that technology provides in the day-to-day operations of government and its decision-making process. However, the most important factor for change to occur is to have strong, capable and above all visionary leadership. Visionary leaders see things and make sense of them and are not afraid to take the plunge.

F. Bezzina et al., *Public Service Reforms in a Small Island State*,
Public Administration, Governance and Globalization 22,
https://doi.org/10.1007/978-3-030-74357-4_12

12.1   Introduction

According to Lynn (2003), citizens around the world are awakened as never before to their right to an effective government, to a government that can perform honestly and efficiently. He argues that this awakening is the greatest source of pressure for better public policies, administrative reform, and a 'New Public Management'. Furthermore, he views administrative reform as an unquestioned priority of the international community, of OECD, of the World Bank, of the European Union, and of many regional bodies. The above views were put forward nearly two decades ago and the objective of having an effective government that performs honestly and efficiently is and will remain on the agenda of Public Service reform for the years to come. The basic reason for this is that no matter what institutional changes and reforms take place over the years; the bottom line is the motivational basis of those that administer.

12.2   The Concept of Time and the Initiation of Public Service Reforms

To talk about the future of Public Service reform is an extremely difficult task. What do we really mean when we refer to the future? In other words, is the future related to a specific length of time into what we expect to happen? There does not seem to be a consensus of the meaning of the word 'future'. One definition describes the future as the time or a period of time following the moment of speaking or writing; time regarded as still to come. The online MS Word thesaurus defines future as the prospect, outlook, potential, expectations, imminent, forthcoming and so on. To avoid any confusion, the future for the purpose of this chapter shall be taken to mean the probable outlook for the next decade or so. This will place into prospective the expectations of the Public Service reform developments that are emerging or are to emerge. Apart from time, another important issue that needs to be addressed is how do Public Service reforms come about? According to Bouckaert and Jann (2017), a study of Public Service reforms suggests that several clusters or typologies emerge in recent decades in the OECD-world that are based upon several drivers. These researchers have identified three key Public Service reform drivers, namely ideology, imitation and evidence based.

They view the first driver (ideology) as 'value' driven reforms that are supported by essentially the particular circumstances, or approximately 'the' market, or essentially based on networks. Bouckaert and Jann (2017) argue that there is a norm that the status, markets or networks will result in 'good' governance of systems, which in turn implies that 'values' are identified, accepted and explained, that actions are aligned with these values, ensuing in a shared hope of realized values. For example, the Public Service reforms recommended by the Venice Commission to the Maltese government, which have been mostly accepted, have the objective of supporting fundamental democratic values related to transparency, governance and rule of law. These reforms aim to strengthen the framework of the separation of powers between the government, Parliament, and the Judiciary in Malta; to strengthen the independence and accountability of State institutions; and to implement change in various areas of public administration and the State, including prosecution and the forces of law and order.

Bouckaert and Jann (2017) contend that imitation as the second driver may become the standard practice in organisations for initiating reforms. This approach is based upon identifying good or better practices, but instead of using them as benchmarks, they would be adopted as the practices for the particular entity, thus adopting a copy-pasting solution. However, they argue that while this imitative conduct may be attractive, it does not always provide the proper solution and is often unsuccessful in achieving the established objectives. Bouckaert and Jann (2017) argue that the reason for this is that the imitation approach assumes that good or better practices are known and that they may be implemented in a different operating environment without modification and achieve the same or very similar outcomes as the imitated practice. For example, New Public Management is used in government and Public Service institutions and agencies as part of an effort to make the Public Service more 'business-like' and to improve its efficiency by using private sector management models. However, emulating private sector practices may not always be suitable in certain conditions because government entities, in particular those utilising public funds, require greater scrutiny and do not have a profit motive. Additionally, a procedural system or policy that may be suitable in one jurisdiction may not be suitable in another due to different national cultures and development status. For instance, systems that are implemented in a developed country may not fit or function in a developing nation. Hence, one needs to be cautions with respect to one-size-fits-all solutions (Lynn, 2003, p.49).

The third driver identified by Bouckaert and Jann (2017) is 'evidence-based' reform and evaluation. They ascertain that this approach is based upon undertaking a critical and comparative study, relating to a particular phenomenon that occurs or change over a period of time. This enables an assessment to be made with an adequate degree of certainty about the particular situation to determine what needs to be done in the form of a 'to do' list for reforms. They argue that this would also include the study and appraisal of different alternatives. Bouckaert and Jann (2017) contend that this approach is based upon the aspiration that an evidence-based agenda has the capability to accomplish improvement. For example, the Third Pillar Pension scheme launched by the Malta Government in November 2014, which was aimed at encouraging earners to start saving for their retirement and maintain their future quality of life, was launched after a comprehensive study was conducted and evaluated. This scheme encouraged Maltese residents to invest in additional pension contributions in private products offered by local banks, life insurance companies and other financial institutions. Thus, their normal government pension would be supplemented by income from a private pension scheme on retirement. Bouckaert and Jann (2017) cautioned against having excessive rationality that may propose simplified hypotheses when applying this approach. They maintain that Public

Service reforms are normally identified by a hybrid approach that takes into consideration the three identified drivers of ideology, imitation and evidence. This position is supported by OECD's observation that there is no single model of reform, and there are no off-the-shelf solutions to the problems of the bureaucratic state (OECD, 1995, p.19).

In the light of the Corona virus outbreak, it is suggested that there may be a fourth factor driving Public Service reform, namely circumstances or exigencies. For example, since the outbreak of the Corona virus, governments (and private organisations) have adopted a more vigorous policy towards allowing employees to work from home through teleworking. Whereas in the pre-Covid-19 period, teleworking was restricted to special and particular cases, the virus outbreak forced governments to embrace teleworking on a much larger and wider scale because of the exigency during this period. Furthermore, it is argued that the Covid-19 outbreak made many governments recognise that teleworking had the beneficial potential to contribute towards a significant increase in air quality, enhanced family quality time, mitigate pressure on public transport systems, lower office space needs and a general decrease in operational costs. Hence, the exigency of the period has forced the reform towards teleworking due to its necessity rather than as a typical incentive to retain employees. Additionally, it is likely that this particular Public Service reform will be refined and applied to a wider section of government workers. In determining the future of Public Service reform, it is appropriate to discuss beforehand four phases, namely the strategies for change in implementing Public Service reforms; reforms from the recent past; present-day reforms; and the future.

12.3 Strategies for Change in Implementing Public Service Reforms

Under pressure from their own people, governments everywhere are engaged in self-conscious projects of administrative and managerial improvement (Lynn, 2003, p.50). The age of consumerism, which has encouraged the acquisition of goods and services in ever-increasing amounts, has over the decades enhanced people's discernment and preferences. Baker McKenzie (2018) argue that advances in telecommunications technology have transformed the tools used for marketing and consumerism, and ultimately the way that businesses operate, resulting in the end of the industrial era of consumption and into a consumer power-shift. Product and service providers no longer view people as consumers but also see them in the role of co-producers, thus the consumer power-shift has most definitely begun (Baker McKenzie, 2018). This consumer power-shift has also had an impact on the ways governments view and serve their customers. Customers expect the same level of service (if not better) from government as they receive from the private sector. In a comparatively short time frame, governments globally have endured enormous demands to address a fundamental issue regarding how public administration is to organise and implement governance that will fulfil the ambitions and needs of its customers, be they the citizens, businesses or civil society. To address this issue, two aspects will be examined, namely, New Public Management and the effect of globalisation.

12.3.1   New Public Management

According to Lynn (2003, p.50), in hindsight the 1980s and 1990s indicated that various governments worldwide appear to have particular common political motivations in the approach taken to implement Public Service reforms. On close examination, they argue that these commonalities reflected the embodiment of a new paradigm of governance and public management that is referred to as New Public Management (NPM). Hence, NPM dominated the 1980s and 1990s and was adopted by many governments as the norm that influenced the future trends in the implementation of Public Service reform at that time. The fundamental principle of NPM was to substitute administrative, hierarchical and professional traditions by a commercial and free market philosophy. In other words, the aim was for government public service organisations to emulate private sector practices. According to Kettl (2000, p.3), the drivers for Public Service reform under NPM had several key characteristics, namely:

(a) Doing more for less to enhance productivity and simultaneously make better utilisation of public revenues;
(b) Marketability by initiating market leaning motivation for creating public goods and services;
(c) Service orientation thus being quicker to respond to citizens as service recipients;
(d) Decentralization through the delegation of authority and accountability to a lower stratum of government, and to the private sector through privatisation of government assets;
(e) Policy formulation and direction by enhancing government's capability to define, execute, and determine the value of public policies;
(f) Responsibility for outcomes by replacing top down rule-driven systems with bottom-up, results driven mechanisms.

The acceptance of NPM and the common political motivations in the approach taken to implement Public Service reforms during this period suggests that the NPM trend corresponded to the 'imitation' reform driver depicted by Bouckaert and Jann (2017). One must note that while European Union (EU) countries must comply with EU policy and regulations, the EU member states were at liberty to decide how these policies and regulations were to be implemented and managed. Therefore, the observed convergence with NPM principles and the key characteristics described above may be complete, partial or selective, thus influencing particular entities more than others. The evidence suggests that the NPM principles were to various degrees adopted by many countries, including EU member states. Pollitt (2000) contends that there were five key intended outcomes of NPM, namely: (i) savings through reduced budget appropriations; (ii) better processes through business process reengineering to attain seamless services and one-stop service provision; (iii) improved efficiency by doing more with less, for example having the same number of business permits being issued with significantly fewer staff; (iv) greater administrative effectiveness, such as mitigation of poverty and illiteracy, lower drug abuse, and the creation of additional new jobs; and (v) a robust public administration system by increasing general capacity and flexibility, such as having more competent and committed Public Service employees.

According to Pollitt (2000), the intended outcomes of NPM have often not materialised as planned. Many government entities claimed that the reforms led to savings, but these claims were difficult to identify and assess. Pollitt (2000) argues that the so-called savings in one area may have been offset by increased expenditure in other areas. Hence, expenditure may have merely been transferred to another sector rather than reduced. Similarly, improved processes had been attained in some areas but there were trade-offs in others. For instance, eGovernment may have streamlined and reduced processes but the manual systems in many cases were retained due to the digital divide, with many customers being non-computer literate. Admittedly, foresight indicates that Smart phones have helped to bridge the digital divide, since they provide internet access to populations previously at a digital disadvantage. However, this improvement has been attained at a cost, which may not be affordable to a wide sector of the community, resulting in unintentional discrimination.

The same may be said for efficiency. It all boils down to trade-offs. Outsourcing services may have reduced the cost of some services but there have been indications in many countries that the quality of the services and more importantly, who is served, may have deteriorated. Whether increased effectiveness has been achieved under NPM is also questionable. Lynn (2003) argues that endeavours to verify whether effectiveness under NPM actually improved is impeded due to several factors. It is posited that the difficulty arises owing to the intricacy of identifying, and assessing with accuracy the deliverables (outputs) and the resultant consequences of these outputs (outcomes) due to a host of other influencing variables that may be leading to better effectiveness rather than the management reforms themselves. Pollitt (2000, p.194) contends that cases, where there is unmistakable evidence of management reform producing more effective government action, are rare. It is also difficult to determine whether NPM has positively impacted the public administration system transformation by a general increase in capacity and flexibility. Pollitt (2000, p.195) maintained that this aspect was not wholly pessimistic. However, he predicts that it would take time to assess the success rate of this aspect. Unfortunately, the time element brings with it other influencing variables, such as economic conditions, political environment and technological advances, which means that it becomes very complex to differentiate whether NPM is really the cause of any improvement. Pollitt (2000) contends that there has been a mixture of results from NPM across various countries. For instance, he maintains that measured efficiency has generally increased; downsizing has been attained in some countries due to privatisation of some government entities; and various specific services became more user-friendly and flexible. However, he argues that the complete cost effects and trade-offs is still questionable. Lynn (2003) suggests that NPM was oversold as a single best solution to the administrative problems of the many different nations that were under pressure to improve their governments.

12.3.2   Effect of Globalisation

Globalisation has had a profound impact on public administration and management. According to Guttal (2010) globalisation is the process of interaction and integration among people, companies, and governments worldwide. This definition views globalisation as a complex and versatile phenomenon that implies a capitalist expansionist style, which brings about the integration of local and national economies into a global, unregulated market economy. Globalisation is not a new phenomenon, but in the modern era, it has expanded due to the extraordinary rapid progress of transport and information communications technology. This has resulted in bringing nations – wherever their location – much closer together, resulting in increased global interactions, growth of international trade, and the exchange of ideas and cultures. Such an environment has presented all governments with comparable concerns and similar general paradigm of change. Nevertheless, how governments respond to these concerns may differ, depending on the vision, leadership, structure and the competencies of their particular public administration. Garvey (1995, p.87) argues that administrative action must maintain a suitable balance between capacity and control since these two factors are the central dynamic forces of administrative transformation in democratic countries everywhere.

Kettl (2000) identified several issues that may influence various democratic countries when confronting the practicality of administrative change. One such issue is delivering non-traditional services, particularly when these services depend on non-governmental bodies that are still reliant on government funding. The concern with this activity is institutional integrity and operating effectiveness of the public and private partners, given that the partnership is supported by public funds. Another important issue is the trend towards the delegation of authority by the decentralisation of certain functions to lower hierarchical levels of government. The concern here is to determine the new roles in government operations and how to exercise adequate controls. A critical issue is to initiate systems that cross traditional ministerial and organisational boundaries for the provision of seamless governmental services. The challenge with this issue is how to manage the increased burdens related to service coordination, particularly with the provision of integrated services through a one-stop shopping concept or the application of the Once Only Principle (OOP). In a practical sense, OOP means that citizens and businesses provide varied data only once when in contact with public administrations, while public administration bodies take the necessary actions to internally share and reuse these data, even across borders, always in respect of data protection regulations and other legal and ethical constraints (CEF Digital, 2020). The final issue identified by Kettl (2000) concerns national government management capacity in terms of managing its basic functions; reallocation of income; and gathering data and fostering information sharing. This issue stresses the importance of governments to think strategically and to building bridges. The concept of building bridges is complex because it deals with the identification and promotion of best practice, and policy that will create strong and closely coordinated partnerships and collaborations between a wide range of stakeholders, including families, youth, advocates, community and residential service providers, and oversight agencies (Building Bridges Initiative, 2020).

It is argued that globalisation is a driver for change, but the change it is likely to encourage is mainly related to liberalisation of certain sectors, such as dismantling or substantial weakening of command and control bureaucracy; privatisation of state owned enterprises; removal of all types of distortions in prices; and mitigating government interventions related to capital and labour mobility. However, it is also argued that notwithstanding globalization, the national, social, cultural and political pressures in each individual country are likely to have a major impact in the approach and objective that Public Service administrative reform will take. On the other hand, one must keep in mind that each democratic country is fundamentally based on acceptable norms of rule of law, legitimate regulation of markets through a democratic process, such as parliaments, and proficient bureaucracies, such as the public services that are subject to control by legislative bodies and judicial authorities that have the ability and authority to implement national policies. Moreover, these various processes within democratic countries are subject to certain standards and parameters that are seen as acceptable international standards, such as money laundering and financing of terrorism regulations, human rights and many others. Therefore, globalisation does have a great impact in the operation of governments in all democratic countries. Moreover, the bureaucratic process through a nation's Public Service is essential for all types of laws and regulations to be administered and enforced. The guru of democracy, Friederich (1940) argued that democratic governments have no chance of survival without bureaucracy (implying the Public Service) since it would not be possible to conduct the promises contained in the political manifesto of its elected leaders.

Hence, it is argued that the notion of John Donne (1572–1631) that 'No Man Is an Island', is applicable to nations as well in the context of Globalisation. No nation lives or exists alone, and all nations are all part of something greater (Globalisation). Each individual nation is like a part of the mainland or a piece of a bigger continent, rather than an island nation that is self-sufficient and cut off from the rest. Nations and their respective Public Service administration do not work in isolation they are subject to international laws, treaties and principles and therefore are greatly influenced by Globalisation. Bureaucratic excesses and arbitrary exercise of power must be curbed, transparency of operations must be assured, and competence and accountability must be institutionalized and made permanent (Lynn, 2003, p.54).

12.4   Reforms from the Recent Past (1993–2017)

The United States provides some excellent examples of Public Service reforms at a federal level. A major reform initiative in the 1990s was the National Performance Review, which was the Clinton-Gore Administration's initiative to reform the way the federal government works (Gore, 1997). Its goal was to create a government that 'works better and costs less'. According to Gore (1997), the reform programme was launched in June 1993 at the Reinventing Government summit and included 384 recommendations and detailing 1250 specific actions intended to save $108 billion, reduce the number of 'overhead' positions, and improve government operations. By December 1993, the President had signed 16 directives implementing specific recommendations, including cutting the work force by 252,000 positions (later amended to 272,900), cutting internal regulations by half, and requiring agencies to set customer service standards. Gore (1997) contends that by September 1995, agencies had saved $58 billion of the originally recommended $108 billion in savings through these reforms and had identified $28 billion a year in reduced regulatory burdens and proposed eliminating 16,000 pages of regulations. Gore (1997) claims that the fiscal year 1997 budget included other major reform initiatives:

(a) Convert to Performance-Based Organizations. Agencies would have greater autonomy from government-wide rules to deliver measurable services in exchange for greater accountability for results. Hence, agencies would focus on deliverables not policy making by recruiting a chief executive on a performance contract for a fixed term. It was claimed that this approach was used successfully in the United Kingdom to improve services and reduce costs.

(b) Improve Customer Service Dramatically. All agencies were to establish service goals that were significantly better to ensure that government service was getting better. Heads of agencies with the greatest customer contact made public commitments to improve selected services during that particular year (1996).

(c) Increase the Use of Regulatory Partnerships. Regulatory agencies initiated non-coercive partnerships that focused on meeting goals rather than forcing compliance with regulatory processes.

(d) Create Performance-Based Partnership Grants. Grants were utilised to fund federal-state-local partnerships based on achieving results rather than focus on processes. Thus, states and localities would be given greater flexibility in using and accounting for federal grant funds.

(e) Establish Single Points of Contact for Communities. This concept was based upon seamless government, so that services are provided without the service recipient having to determine who is responsible for what. The aim was to create integrated accountability for government's actions in large communities.

(f) Transform the Federal Workforce. The aim was to ensure that the civil service system would respond quickly to change or the varying needs of different organisations in the federal government. However, this initiative did not receive congressional support. A diluted version of this reform was introduced where there was bipartisan support, such as expanding existing authorities for agencies to tailor the system to their individual needs.

Light (1997) argues that the above reforms had four key themes, namely: (i) reducing red tape by streamlining the budget process, decentralising of HR policy, reorienting the inspectors general operations, and empowering state and local governments; (ii) placing customers first by ensuring that service providers compete and use market mechanisms to solve problems; (iii) empowering employees to get results by the decentralisation of decision-making power, forming a labour-management partnership, and exerting leadership; and (iv) cutting back to basics by eliminating redundant programs, investing in greater productivity, and re-engineering programs to cut costs. Thompson (2000, p.509) contends that the National Performance Review included a wide range of measures that addressed various but distinct goals. His survey-based study suggests that measures relating to downsizing, reducing administrative costs, and reforming administrative systems had been significantly attained. On the other hand, his findings indicated only some degree of success for the measures regarding decentralising authority within agencies, empowering front-line workers, promoting cultural change in agencies, improving the quality of Public Services and improving the efficiency of agency work procedures. He concluded that there was no evidence of any significant, systemic improvement in quality of services or culture (Thompson, 2000, p.510).

A major reform initiative was launched by President George Bush to promote performance management in all national agencies through a report entitled 'The President's Management Agenda: Fiscal Year 2002'. The report focused on fourteen areas of improvement to address the most apparent deficiencies where the opportunity to improve performance was the greatest (Bush, 2002, p.1). Bush (2002) placed emphasis on performance and results with the aim of ensuring that the federal government is well run and results-oriented, and that the resources entrusted to the federal government were well managed and wisely used. This reform was based upon five government-wide initiatives and nine programme initiatives. The focus of this reform review is mainly on the government-wide initiatives that included: strategic management of human capital; competitive sourcing; improved financial performance; expanded electronic government; and budget and performance integration. The President's vision for government reform was guided by three key principles, namely that government should be: (i) citizen-centred, not bureaucracy-centred; (ii) results-oriented; and (iii) market-based, actively promoting rather than stifling innovation through competition (Bush, 2002, p.4).

A main feature of this reform initiative was the mechanism to grade and rank the major departments on their performance on the five government-wide management initiatives. The grading of the departments was based on three categories: green for good; yellow for needing improvement; and red for failed. The ranking was to be conducted by the Office of Management and Budget (OMB). Initial results suggested that no greens and only a few yellows were awarded, meaning that most of the departments were failing on all five initiatives. The ranking exercise was to be conducted bi-yearly with a mid-year report to be issued around mid-year. Another important reform feature of the Bush Administration was the reformatting of the Federal Budget. Since, the reforms were performance (results) based, the budget was organised by cost-centres, namely by agency, instead of function or policy area. Functional or policy areas tended to cut across agencies/departments that made it difficult to assign specific accountability for the results achieved. Hence, having accountability focused on agencies or departments facilitated performance measurement. Thus, this reform throws the spotlight on individual agencies, with the budget document having a chapter that specifically highlights the agency's main activities, including an assessment of the agency's performance in meeting the objectives of particular programs. What's more, this reform incentivised good performance because an agency's performance assessment was taken into consideration in the budget allocation that was provided to it. Lynn (2003) argues that, overall, experts on public management reform view these reform initiatives as part of a political strategy and not as a major attempt to transform the management of government or to improve the budget allocation mechanism or performance. Lynn (2003) claims that even though agencies appear to be trying to support the reform priorities, they expected little change in agency culture or quality.

The Bush initiative resembles the system of Public Service Agreements in the United Kingdom (Lynn, 2003). He argues that the agreements establish expenditure limits, performance measures, and performance targets for service providers, but they tend to be complex and be inclined to centralise power over resource allocation and management in the Treasury. However, he maintains that, if implemented properly, they provide strong strategic and rational direction. Lynn (2003) contends that the American experience has been the same as the British experience in that both have failed to make significant use of the wealth of performance information, target setting, delivery agreements and the spending review process tends to be seen as secretive. In another example, Jose (2016) argues that the Government of India had successfully applied outcome budget as a performance measurement tool because it has been shown to facilitate: better service delivery; effective decision-making; the evaluation of programme performance and results; communicating programme goals; improving programme effectiveness; making budgets more cost effective; fix accountability; and better scheme management. Jose (2016) contends that this reform was implemented from 2007–08 onwards, with the previous Performance Budget being merged with the Outcome Budget, with all Ministries having to prepare outcome budgets. However, no evidence has been shown as to whether this key reform has actually improved government performance.

In 2001, the Finance Committee of the Scottish Parliament commissioned a study on outcome budgeting to help guide it on the possible introduction of these concepts (Flynn, 2001). Flynn (2001, p.5) in a survey of experience in other countries found the following:

(a) *Australian States*: The budget linked overall aims and outcome aspirations to the outputs, but the link was not adequate to be able to directly connect the expenditure of money on outputs to the achievement of outcomes.

(b) *USA*: The US system was found to take a great deal of effort and time to develop outcome-based budgets, even where there was legislation in place to make it happen. It shows that the solution is not to generate huge amounts of data and targets because this makes the process unmanageable.

(c) *New Zealand*: While it has been possible for the New Zealand government to specify outcomes and its aspirations for the effects of Public Services, the planning process was still concerned with outputs and it has discovered that it is not possible to make a watertight connection between a stream of outputs and the flow of outcomes that result from them.

(d) **Singapore**: The system does not attempt to integrate its outcome definition, quality programmes and special initiatives into the budget process, leaving the budget purely for resource allocation.

(e) *Sweden*: The government view that the generation of information does not in itself constitute a capacity to use that information in resource allocation or scrutiny. Giving managerial freedom to agencies in exchange for a definition of outcomes may simply mean replacing one set of detailed bureaucratic controls for another, such as the bureaucracy of outcome measurement replacing the bureaucracy of input controls.

The most recent US reform proposals of any significance were those put forward by President Obama in 2015. Since, Obama's Administration did not have a controlling majority in the Congress these proposals were not given due attention by them. However, Katz (2016) argues that Obama's reforms include several significant proposals to overhaul agency structures and programs. He also contends that despite the lack of support from Congress, some of the proposed reforms were undertaken unilaterally by the Administration, while others were prioritised when dealing with Congress. The major objective of Obama's reform roadmap was his desire to continue to invest in ways to make government run more efficiently (Katz, 2016). According to Katz (2016) the key Public Service initiatives proposed by Obama include the following:

(a) *Evidence-based programs*: This emphasised the importance of agencies making decisions based on proven evidence and data.

(b) *Reorganisation authority*: Having fast-track authority to move around or consolidate the exact function of federal components and offices by streamlining operations to meet changing circumstances and customer demand.

(c) *Funding flexibility*: To institutionalise cross-cutting management initiatives rather than dealing with them on a case-by-case basis.

(d) *Crowd-sourcing science*: More interaction with the public to solve problems by asking for more input and relying on the participation of the public to collect data over large geographic areas.

(e) *Shared services*: Having a Unified Shared Services Management to improve delivery and increase adoption of shared services, such as financial management, human resources, acquisitions, grants and information technology.

(f) **Cyber reforms**: To increase in IT security spending and the creation of a new U.S. chief information security officer, including having cyber-security professionals across government.

Moreover, Cobert (2017) in the US Office of Personnel Management (OPM) Cabinet Exit Memo declared that the overarching focus of the Administration's two four year terms were based on new ways of using data for supporting decision-making, investing in new tools and technologies, and streamlining processes. Cobert (2017) argues that OPM had focused on: IT security and modernisation; enhanced customer service delivery with a consistently high level of responsiveness and quality; and using data analytics to improve performance. Cobert (2017) also outlines the future focus in the government's reform policies, namely: (i) to accelerate IT modernisation for cost cutting, improve critical programs, and mitigate security risks in a world of continually evolving threats; (ii) continued improvements in customer service by expanding the use of online portals, using modern quality improvement techniques to streamline processes, and embracing new metrics to identify ways to improve the processes; and (iii) investing in technology that supports human capital management by initiating IT systems that support agencies' talent management goals by driving a more effective, efficient, and data-driven hiring and talent management process that improves performance. The above clearly indicates that the various Public Service reforms initiatives were basically aimed at ensuring the governments work more efficiently at less cost, with technology and modernisation being the fundamental facilitators. However, there is a lack of consensus and evidence as to whether the various reform programmes over the years have produced the desired results to any significant level.

12.5 Present-Day Reforms (2017–2020)

In the last few years, Public Service reform programmes have had a mixed destiny, ranging from being regressive to progressive. Poland's Public Service reforms regarding governance and the rule of law have regressed with the termination of the appointments of all Supreme Court judges and the appointment of new judges at the discretion of the government. According to The Guardian (2017), what makes matters worse is that the Supreme Court rules on the validity of elections, approves the financial reports of political parties and adjudicates on disciplinary proceedings against judges. The Polish government had already passed laws giving it control of the constitutional court and additionally has approved laws that give parliament control over the previously autonomous body appointing judges, with ministers having the power to appoint the president of each court, who decides which judge will sit in each case (The Guardian, 2017). The European Union has threatened to sanction Poland unless it drops legal reforms that undermine the independence of its judiciary (Grzymala-Busse, 2017). However, no such action has been forthcoming. The Polish legislation mirrors earlier changes in Hungary, leading many analysts to draw parallels between the broader challenges to liberal democracy by the two regimes (Grzymala-Busse, 2017). According to Grzymala-Busse (2017), both Poland and Hungary appear to be following the same template: First, target the highest courts and the judiciary, then restrict the independence of the media and civil society, and finally transform the constitutional framework and electoral laws in ways that enshrine their hold on power. These examples are in direct contrast, to the progressive Public Service reforms regarding governance and the rule of law instituted by the Malta government on the recommendation of the Venice Commission.

According to The Independent (2020), the Malta Government will be making a number of legislative amendments to strengthen governance, namely: the President of the Republic and Chief Justice will be appointed by a two-third majority in Parliament; the judicial appointments system will be made stronger by having a committee consisting of seven members, four of which will be members of the judiciary appointed by their own peers, with Cabinet and Parliament not being involved in the appointment or removal of candidates; the Ombudsman, the Commissioner for Standards in Public Life and the Auditor General will be able to directly report on corruption cases to the Attorney General; and the Permanent Commission Against Corruption will be strengthened by removing the power of appointment of its members from the Prime Minister to Cabinet. Furthermore, legal amendments are also being proposed in order to ensure that the Public Service Commission, which is an independent constitutional body, will make recommendations to the President of the Republic directly for the appointment of Permanent Secretaries after giving due consideration to the recommendation made by the Principal Permanent Secretary. Moreover, the appointment of the Principal Permanent Secretary shall be made by the President. The above illustrates the divergence of measures between EU Member states related to the issue of governance and rule of law.

Public service reform in the United Kingdom and the United States of America has been seriously disrupted in recent years. The United Kingdom has endured a lengthy period of uncertainty and political instability due to Brexit. There has been a change of leadership in the Conservative government followed by an election, which has resulted in the Conservative party being returned to power, with its focus on Brexit as a priority. In the United States, President Trump has faced a long impeachment process and a certain amount of controversy on various issues, including 'Black Lives Matter', which is described as a Movement to fight for freedom, liberation and justice. According to Price (2017), the Public Service under Trump is a dying field occupied only by the barest ranks needed to keep it afloat. According to Yochelson (2017), the loss of faith in Washington that has carried Donald Trump to the White House dims the future of the Public Service. Since, John F. Kennedy's inaugural address of 1961, the trust level of government to do the right thing most of the time, has plummeted from 70% to a current 20%, with the morale of career public servants having dropped to rock bottom, according to data collected by the Office of Personnel Management (Yochelson, 2017).

On the other hand, Korte (2019) contends that President Trump wanted to 'hire the best and fire the worst' federal government employees under the most ambitious proposal to overhaul the civil service in 40 years. However, the Federal employee unions fear that the pay-per-performance plan resulting from this measure will be used to reward loyalists and discriminate against women and minorities (Korte, 2019). Ironically, Yochelson (2017) argues that one of President Trump's first official acts when coming to power was to order an across-the-board federal job freeze except for the military, public safety and public health. This implies that the current concern with the low morale of career public servants and the general situation in the American Public Service is self-inflicted. It is argued that unlike his predecessors, President Trump has not proposed any major plan for a Public Service reform programme. For example, Katz (2020) itemises the eleven most significant agency reforms in President Trump's 2021 budget. However, a close examination of these reforms indicates the there are no substantial plans for a Public Service reform programme that is comparable to those proposed by President George Bush in 2002 (The President's Management Agenda: Fiscal Year 2002) and by President Obama in 2015.

According to Colgan et al. (2016, p.58) the Australian government has taken a different approach in that it has focused on the concept of 'connected government' and an increased emphasis on 'public value' in leadership development, along with modifications of earlier initiatives. These reform initiatives are based upon on a public reform programme entitled 'Australian Government Administration Ahead of the Game: Blueprint for the Reform of Australian Government Administration' that was published by the Advisory Group on Reform of Australian Government Administration (2010). The major initiatives include: (i) meeting the needs of citizens through more integrated services linking levels of government; (ii) strong leadership and strategic direction by strengthening strategic policy advisory, strengthening the role of departmental secretaries, and giving a stronger role to the Australian Public Service Commission; (iii) having highly capable workforce through career development, more investment in human resource management and return to central remuneration systems; and (iv) greater efficiency by strengthening governance arrangements, reduced 'red tape', and having systematic agency reviews (Colgan et al., 2016, p.58). It is argued that these reform initiatives place a great deal of emphasis on technology and business process reengineering, supported by appropriate leadership and competent employees.

The Government of Ireland is viewed as a key leader in Public Service reform amongst the EU Member States and therefore may be considered as a best practice model. The current Public Service reform plan is built on previous plans, namely Public Service Reform Plan 2011–2014 and more recently Public Service Reform Plan 2014–2016 (Colgan et al., 2016, p.15). According to Colgan et al. (2016, p.16), a programme of political and legislative reform has been under way and, in many instances completed, with the aim of improving openness, transparency and accountability, as part of the Government's objective of rebuilding the relationship with the citizen and restoring public trust in the institutions of the State. According to Government of Ireland (2017, p.8), the objective of the latest Public Service reform plan is summarised by six high-level outcomes for the Public Service, namely: increased customer satisfaction; increased public trust; greater use of digital approaches to do business with the Public Service; better government effectiveness; quality of certain Public Services; and greater employee engagement. It is argued that these objectives in many cases are very similar to other countries, with some notable exceptions (such as Poland and Hungary). However, there is very little evidence to suggest that these reforms have had a dramatic effect on public service performance in Ireland or anywhere else. According to a survey of top civil servants in 20 European countries on public sector reforms, changes in various EU Member States have been patchy (European Commission, 2015). This survey, which was an EU funded project COCOPS, received about 10,000 responses, providing one of the largest data records on the subject. The COCOPS survey allowed researchers to compare the attitudes and behaviours of top public managers in Austria, Belgium, Croatia, Denmark, Estonia, Finland, France, Germany, Hungary, Iceland, Ireland, Italy, Lithuania, the Netherlands, Norway, Portugal, Serbia, Spain, Sweden and the UK. The researchers also asked consultants, trade unions and public management academics to contribute their thoughts on the main challenges facing the public sector.

The COCOPS' analysis suggests that all groups agreed that cost efficiency, transparency and service quality have improved over the past five years; however, the respondents strongly agreed that the reforms have reduced citizens' trust in government, the attractiveness of a career in the Public Service, and social cohesion (European Commission, 2015). According to European Commission (2015), a review of previous surveys of citizens' attitudes to liberalised Public Services confirmed that some categories of disadvantaged citizens, such as the elderly and the less educated, are less satisfied with some services than other groups. Furthermore, the survey concludes that the big wave of typical NPM-style reforms, such as outsourcing, privatisation and the establishment of autonomous agencies, appear to be over; however some trends are emerging internationally, and new modes of governance are likely to emerge, ranging from coordination, to demand-driven and responsive government, and the virtualisation of the public sector through the growth of eGovernment (European Commission, 2015). Colgan et al. (2016, p.65) argues that it is necessary for the following key critical success factors to be in place when implementing Public Service reform:

(a) Having a compelling and explicit vision and purpose to guide reform.
(b) Strengthening policy development skills and integrating expertise on implementation to increase the success of Public Service reforms.
(c) Having a citizen-centric approach as being one of the characteristics of a highly productive public sector, but it must be real.
(d) Recognising that Public Service reform increasingly involves whole system, whole of government change to deliver needs-led services to citizens.
(e) Acknowledging that changes in governance arrangements and structures alone will not deliver Public Service reform.

(f) Conceding that Public Service change requires leadership geared to managing complex change.

(g) Investing in people by building capacity for managing complexity and continuous professional development are essential enablers of change.

(h) Recognising that Public Service values are tangible assets that should be harnessed to support reform.

(i) Accepting that achieving systems change takes time and resources and requires political and administrative leaders to have long-term goals and perspectives.

It may be generally concluded that Public Service reforms is a continuous renewal process with technology playing a major role as an outreach tool in providing the various government driven services to a diverse range of customers. However, the digital gap is still with us and is likely to take a generation or two before the digital gap can be fully bridged.

12.6   The Future: A New Beginning

Determining the future of Public Service reforms is a complex and difficult matter because there are so many variables that may influence what is to happen. According to Abraham Lincoln, the most reliable way to predict the future is to create it. It is likely that the drivers for change as depicted by Bouckaert and Jann (2017) and strategies for change in implementing Public Service reforms related to NPM, globalisation and exigency will remain the same or will be very similar. The uncertainty in forecasting the future related to Public Service reform is likely to be due to the strength and impact of several facilitators and barriers at any point in time. Generally, the facilitators and barriers are somewhat like the success-failure factors described by Camilleri (2011) related to the project success model. Implementing Public Service reforms is comparable to implementing any other major project and therefore the success or failure of the project depends on several key factors. It is argued that the extent of future Public Service reforms will be highly dependent on the forthcoming technological developments; strong, committed and visionary leadership; the competencies and receptiveness to change of government employees; the willingness and level of sophistication of those that use Public Services; and the particular circumstances at one point in time. All these factors, particularly technology, play an important role in future Public Service reforms.

The Covid-19 outbreak has provided important lessons related to implementing Public Service reforms. For example, the Malta government took a more vigorous approach to teleworking. Many government employees were able to serve their customers from home. All types of government employees, including clerical workers, and teaching and lecturing staff (including those of private schools) were able to work from home and provide most of the services required by their customers unhindered. It was also recognised that an important barrier at this stage was the digital gap. However, because most customers had no choice but to use online services through tablets or mobile apps, the digital gap immediately began to reduce. The Malta government also recognised that the digital gap stems from two major causes, namely computer illiteracy or/and the lack of financial means to secure the technology necessary. The issue related to computer illiteracy could not be resolved overnight, even though the government had initiated a policy some years ago to educate the general public, including the elderly in the use of computer technology and related application systems. However, the government ensured that those families that had school-aged children attending government or private schools and could not afford a laptop or tablet, including the supporting internet services were provided with these amenities at no cost. This ensured that all children maintained their education programme without disruption. This further reduced the digital gap to the extent that the only segment that had a digital concern was limited to several elderly citizens. This concern was resolved by supporting these elderly citizens through voluntary workers, who provided individual attention.

12.6.1   Global Technological Developments

Technology, like the past and the present is the most influential individual factor that will determine the future direction of Public Service reform in relation to service delivery. Camilleri (2019, p.325) contends that five key aspects will have a great impact on the future change in Public Service reform related to service delivery: (i) ethical responsibilities related to technological change; (ii) analytics and artificial intelligence; (iii) evolution of communications technology; (iv) growth of block chain technology; and (v) the expansion of mobile Apps technology.

12.6.1.1   Ethical Responsibilities Related to Technological Change

The Facebook–Cambridge Analytica data scandal that surfaced around March 2018 has raised serious concerns that are likely to have ramifications in the future, in relation to ICT ethical responsibilities. This scandal entailed the gathering of personally identifiable information of almost 90 million Facebook users since 2014. The data was purportedly utilised in an endeavour to influence voter opinion in several countries. On CNN, Facebook director (Mark Zuckerberg) described the incident as a 'breach of trust'. Trust was, is and will always be a key issue and has surfaced once again as being in the forefront when discussing the future directions of public service delivery. The private and public sectors have a corporate social responsibility (CSR) to protect citizens and all types of entities from the misuse of collected information through any media, particularly the social media. While voluntary CSR compliance is important, it is the governments that must regulate the ethical behaviour of those that hold information. Irrespective of whether individuals or entities make use of the various application systems, information is still being collected about them from numerous sources. Therefore, new ethical and legal safeguards are required to ensure that the rights of all are protected. Hence, it is likely that governments will take a more radical approach to resolving this issue by taking proactive measures to implement ethical standards and legal safeguards that keep the pace with the technological developments taking place.

Information and the dissemination capability through a Wide Area Network (WAN) has become a potent source of power. Under the disguise of 'freedom of expression', a WAN operates independently of particular individuals or computing facilities. Hence, there is no or very little control of WANs and the information content they disseminate, thus creating a quasi-lawless environment. The view in the United Kingdom (UK) is that internet traffic should not just be monitored, but also censored (Evens, 2018). Currently, individuals with minimum computing knowledge and resources can convey messages of hate and bigotry to millions of other individuals around the globe with very little means of government control. WANs have also developed into social networks, where individuals share their thoughts, create relationships with others and, at times, generate heated arguments about a diverse set of issues. These social networks have also developed into tools for bullying and spreading malicious gossip about individuals that in some case have led to suicides or/and the destruction of families and careers. According to Lynch (2014) a lack of face-to-face contact fosters virtual anonymity that allows interaction without any sort of commitment, thus the sense of shared responsibility that people must have in a real community does not necessarily exist on the Internet. Current legal provisions in individual countries that are meant to protect people do not apply, particularly if the source comes from a geographical location outside the legal jurisdiction of those being targeted. It is becoming evident that countries must form some kind of legal alliance to control such abuses.

Prediction-01 *It is likely, that governments from various countries will cooperate closely and take more assertive action to control cyber space against the various abuses generated through the internet.*

Disruptive commercialisation is rapidly becoming a serious threat. Runciman (2018) argues that companies such as Uber and Deliveroo seem to be undoing years of hard-won employment rights in the name of disruption. Moreover, he argues that artificial intelligence and robotics are transforming workforce practices and are claimed to be bypassing employment laws, which are viewed as the social safety net for ensuring a respectable living standard. Additionally, Runciman (2018) contends that we lived on the web, where it was possible to login and logout; but currently we live in a digital world where we don't logout anymore because the mobile phones constantly keep us online. He argues that senior executives and managers in the public and private sectors are expected to respond to emails or/and SMSs immediately, irrespective of the time of day. He contends that it is not digital innovation that is of concern but its governance. Runciman (2018) maintains that the current policy of many governments related to 'do first, repair afterwards' is erroneous and that a proactive stand is required. He argues that it is imperative that some kind of regulation is implemented otherwise the effort, which has been conducted over the years to introduce family friendly measures, will just go down the drain.

Prediction-02 *It is likely, that governments from various countries with the partici-pation of trade and labour unions will regulate so called 'disruptive technology' to strengthen and sustain family friendly measures.*

12.6.1.2 Analytics and Artificial Intelligence (AI)

According to Miller (2017), analytics and AI leverage the speedy nature of comput-ing to find relationships that might otherwise be proverbial haystack needles. Martinho-Truswell (2018) contends that applications of AI in a public sector envi-ronment are broad and growing, with early experiments taking place around the world. She claims that public servants in the United States are using AI to help them make welfare payments and immigration decisions, detect fraud, plan new infra-structure projects, answer citizen queries, adjudicate bail hearings, triage health care cases, and establish drone paths. Martinho-Truswell (2018) argues that the issues public servants will be confronted with are related to which tasks will be handed over to machines. State and local governments in the United States have also been experimenting with Chatbots for some time with various levels of success. For example, Miller (2017) cites applications in Los Angeles, where a city built Chatbot answers business-related questions for citizens; and in Mississippi, people can use the Amazon Alexa artificial intelligence service to plug into government informa-tion about things like taxes and vehicle registration.

There are government security agencies that are experimenting with AI to anal-yse the tone of emails and to endeavour to keep up with cyber-security threats even as they morph (change their outward appearance completely and instantaneously) and evolve. Miller (2017) maintains that as AI becomes ever-present, people who work both inside and with government are finding numerous innovative ways of applying AI. Martinho-Truswell (2018) claims that the most promising applications of AI use machine learning, in which a computer program learns and improves its own answers to a question by creating and iterating algorithms from a collection of data. For example, IBM's Watson is an IA application, which is a treatment recommendation-bot. Sometimes it can find medical treatments that a human doctor might not have considered or known about. Martinho-Truswell (2018) argues that because government workers are often following a set of rules (i.e. a policy or set of procedures), this scenario presents many opportunities for the application of AI.

Prediction-03 *The application of Analytics and Artificial Intelligence (AI) will become the norm for governments from various countries in resolving an assort-ment of concerns. A key issue that public servants worldwide will be confronted with is related to which tasks will be entrusted to machines.*

12.6.1.3 Evolving Communications Technology

Communications technology is the most significant driving force in the globalisation process, since it is the key vehicle for the provision of many of the services that people, and industries receive and use every day. Being connected is synonymous with growth, driving the industry value chain to its utmost limits, whereby consumers, suppliers, financial institutions, governments and other categories of individuals and entities all share the cyberspace to conduct their business in a virtual environment. The communications industry is highly competitive, with industry players seeking more and more traffic on their digital highways at a lower cost. The future appears to indicate that connectivity will remain the major thrust in the provision of services at cheaper rates. This is supported by the fact that in 2019 SpaceX delivered 10 new Iridium satellites into orbit. Iridium now has 75 new satellites in orbit, including nine spares, resulting in an investment of $3 billion in the Iridium NEXT project, thus replacing the entire original fleet.

Prediction-04 *Communications technology will remain the most significant driving force in the globalisation process. Governments will likely further regulate this industry to ensure that connectivity will remain the major thrust in the provision of services at cheaper and affordable rates.*

A major future trend (which has already commenced) is likely to involve an upsurge of connected devices. The IoT (internet of things) is likely to add billions of connected data sources in the near future, with a rapid increasing rate, thereafter, generating an enormous growth in data volumes of immeasurable proportions. However, extraordinary speed of transmission is needed for this growth to occur. Communications carriers will need to speed up the transmission speed and break the current 5G limit.

Prediction-05 *The growth of IoT (internet of things) will likely exert pressure on the communications industry (probably through governments and consumer demand) to break the current 5G transmission speed limit.*

Currently, the growth in mobile phone usage has surpassed fixed line connectivity. Furthermore, there are already indications that the growth in sales of laptop computers and tablets are falling, but those of the smart mobile phones are increasing at much more rapid rate. Mobiles are getting smarter and cheaper, enabling users to access all types of internet and app services. This is having a great impact in developing countries, particularly among the poorer populations, where the mobile is the cheapest way of being connected and being able to access internet services provided by the public and private sectors. Digital illiteracy amongst senior citizens is currently a major obstacle for increasing the penetration rate in the use of eServices. However, this concern is likely to be overcome through the assistance received at retirement homes to enable senior citizens to make use of digital and mobile technology. Moreover, anyone born in the 1970s (and after) is likely to have been affected by the home or personal computer boom of the 1980s and beyond.

Prediction-06 *The demand for smart mobiles will likely continue to grow since it is and will probably remain the easiest and cheapest method of being connected to cyberspace. Hence, it is likely that digital illiteracy will be significantly reduced because of this phenomenon resulting in a growth in the penetration rate of eServices.*

12.6.1.4   Growth of Block Chain Technology

The state of Delaware in the USA initiated the blockchain initiative in 2016, with the objective of establishing a suitable legal framework and associated infrastructure for distributed ledger shares, to increase efficiency and speed of incorporation services. This development is significant for blockchain technology because half of all publicly traded companies in the USA and 65% of the Fortune 500 companies are incorporated in Delaware. Malta, which has a growing eGaming industry and is recognised as a major financial centre in the Mediterranean, was the first country in the European Union that has regulated blockchain technology through a comprehensive legislative parliamentary process. Blockchain technology is viewed as a major breakthrough for providing diverse services in a public sector environment due to its ease of use, immediate scalability and its resilience to being hacked. WU GTPC (2017) argues that by its very nature, blockchain is able to tackle three key business issues: (a) trust, since through the use of blockchain, all the parties involved in a transaction only have to trust the blockchain without a need for a central intermediary; (b) transparency, since the blockchain ledger is distributed, all peers involved in the transaction network can view it subject to security rights; and (c) accountability, since all parties in the transaction can view the distributed ledger, everyone can agree on how the transaction is progressing while it is ongoing, and how it went once it is complete.

Moreover, blockchain technologies have the potential to be used for providing a diverse range of government services that involve by and large the processing and management of public documents. Blockchains may be used to support the general provision of various Public Services to citizens and stakeholders, particularly for those services that demand personal interaction and require individual identification. Blockchain technology has the potential to be applied to a wide range of applications but blockchain deployments in developing countries face complex challenges. Blockchain technology is at its infancy and will require a great deal of investment and development before the technology is widely accepted. A number of potential and futuristic blockchain application areas have been identified, including: (i) digital property rights, leading to multi-territorial licensing policies and improved legal certainty for both creators and purchasers of content; (ii) supply chain management used by Customs and Excise authorities through the ability to rely on the origin of the goods transported and the ease of sharing the customs related documentation between the various departments involved; (iii) land registration by secure deed titles while ensuring they are not transferred without authorization, including the ability to record and determine who owns the rights, including dispatching the property tax assessment for the property rights to the rightful person; (iv) asset management, including estate management by recording, tracking and monitoring moveable and immovable assets; (v) governmental financial management systems for bookkeeping of the various financial budgetary accounts to quickly provide the financial accounting statements, rationalize payment processing and enable full transparency of governmental transactions; (vi) identity services to authenticate and protect personal identity for use in managing passports, birth and wedding certificates, and national and electoral personal identity; and (vii) tax administration to enhance tax compliance by guaranteeing real-time, automated tax payments from the tax payer at the time when a transaction in being executed, particularly by incorporating the concept of Smart Contracts.

Prediction-07 *As blockchain technology matures and governments realise its advantages, particularly in relation to security and transparency, its use will grow and expand to enable networked public services on a very large scale.*

12.6.1.5 Expansion of Mobile Apps Technology

Apps are computer programs that are designed specifically for mobile devices like smartphones, tablets and wearables. Mobile apps technology is particularly important because it enables the application of technology to be targeted to an individual person's or individual entity's specific needs. Mobile apps are viewed as a paradigm shift, where citizens, civil society and businesses are requesting government services on demand from public agencies at anytime from anywhere. The use of apps is mitigating the digital divide because owning and using a mobile covers a wide spectrum of society from children to senior citizens, and from the wealthy to the low-income earners. Ganapati (2015) classifies government apps into two fundamental categories, depending on their utilisation, namely enterprise-focused apps and citizen-oriented apps. He views enterprise-focused apps as being mainly for internal use. In other words, these apps are accessible only to the employees of the public organization they are employed at and thus operate within a secure firewall established by the particular organization. Ganapati (2015) contends that enterprise-focused apps could potentially become a powerful tool for transforming a government organization through business process reengineering of the organisation's field operations by taking advantage of the robustness and flexibility of the apps applications.

Prediction-08 *Government employees will be able to access their departmental systems and perform their daily work through their mobile in a secure environment.*

On the other hand, citizen-oriented apps are intended for external use and are accessible to anyone seeking the immediate use of Public Services. The main challenge confronting this category of apps is the need for having compatibility across different devices that citizens commonly use. These apps have the primary objective of providing public services through direct citizen engagement at any time and from anywhere. mGovernment is emerging as the primary method for engaging the citizen due to a number of reasons, such as the wider acceptance of these type technologies by the public sector; high level of penetration of mobile devices across a wide spectrum of the population; user friendly for citizens; facilitates integration and interoperability of devices; offers personalised services to bring the government closer to its citizens; and user affordability and cheaper than computer-based services.

The applications for mobile apps are unlimited and are only restricted by one's imagination. Government at any level (federal, state or local) has the capacity to reach a broad spectrum of its citizens through a mobile app, because most people (estimated to be around 90% and increasing) own a mobile phone and use it as the principal means of communication. Moreover, mobile apps can appear to be personalised and it permits governmental services to be delivered from anywhere and anytime. For example, the government health service of Malta (the smallest EU member state) sends a message via a mobile SMS to patients reminding them of their medical appointment a week ahead and sends a final reminder two days before the appointment. Furthermore, the government of Malta offers more than 1500 services online and through mobile apps. In Singapore, the Land Transport Authority provides basic taxi data to apps developers that can help people travel around the city, giving users a choice of services. In Boston Massachusetts, citizens automatically report potholes in the roads they are driving on, through a mobile app named Street Bump. Street Bump uses the accelerometer and GPS data from mobile phones to detect any bumps that take place during their car journey. Single bumps are ignored, however if the same bump is registered several times at the same location by different mobiles, then a road crew is sent to repair the pothole. However, the use of mobile apps for public service delivery is still at its very early stages.

Prediction-09 *Public service delivery to citizens, civil society and businesses is likely to be dominated by mobile apps that specifically cater for a diverse range of the individuals' personal needs.*

It should be noted that government organisations deal with highly sensitive information, therefore it is imperative that they address the concerns created by mobile technology, particularly those related to security. The mobile device itself has several security features to protect the device itself; the data that is stored within it; and the applicable logon and authentication method for the apps which reside on it. However, a government entity that allows its workforce to use their own personal mobile device for work must ensure that internal information on the device cannot be accessed by non-trusted mobile devices and can be audited, updated, remotely wiped and blocked from network access by the government entity.

12.6.2   Global Public Service Specific Reform Developments

There is no doubt that technology or digitisation will remain the central focus as a facilitator for future government Public Service reform around the world. However, there are also factors, apart from technology that push public sector reforms forward. For instance, Robertson Foundation for Government (2020) highlights how cross-sector collaboration can drive progress toward a future characterized by impacts across multiple domains, particularly, where citizens will drive government services and performance; government delivery will be carried out by multi-organizational networks; technology platforms will enable integration of new innovation; volunteers will support government activity; and data will drive progress. Some of these aspects, specifically related to technology platforms and data, have been discussed in the previous section. It is a well-known fact that the application and utilisation of data has rapidly escalated becoming greater with every passing time.

However, not all governments have embraced the power that data can provide. Public service management must confront the difficulties of transforming data into inferences that can be directly moulded into a response, thus providing the necessary impetus for employees to carry out the necessary activities to bring about change. However, harnessing the tremendous volume of data brings with it its own challenges. Data must be managed, accessible, and supported by experts to establish and maintain the necessary data warehouse so that this wealth of information may be shared across organisational boundaries that may even be external to governments. This will create the basis for information resource management and, together with the appropriate data mining and intelligence engine, permit the full exploitation of data by transforming it into information, knowledge and wisdom for complex decision making.

Prediction-10 *Public service entities will progressively embrace information resource management concepts, data warehousing and data mining techniques, by making use of an appropriate business intelligence engine for complex decision making.*

There is no doubt that the social media has dominated and has made a great impact in relation to internet usage amongst the digital population. As a result, governments at a federal, state and local level have been given an opportunity to have an open dialogue and engage directly with its citizens on a mixture of social media platforms regarding a host of topics. Governments have recognised that the social media is an effective multi-channel communication tool not only for engaging citizens but even government employees. Social media, if harnessed and managed well, is viewed as a valuable governance tool for participative government and may be used by government employees for initiating, defining and formulating government and management policies. However, current social media practices would need to be refined and to some extent regulated to mitigate the risk of allowing it to be used to instigate hate and bullying.

Prediction-11 *Social media is likely to be exploited for improving the citizen's experience and engagement for initiating, defining and formulating policies to encourage and improve participative government (for citizens) and management (for government employees) through collaborative governance.*

Although government entities have been implementing systems for many years, Helfrich (2019) contends that in 2019 and beyond, management at government entities will continue reimagining how work gets done, what skills are needed, and how people might spend more time on the value-added work. He refers to this trend as Future of Government Work, where employees spend more time on valuable and mission-critical work. He maintains that government roles will change in the future, giving its employees more time to focus on more complex tasks and advancing how, when and where work gets done.

Prediction-12 *The trend known as Future of Government Work is likely to increase the convergence of the government workforce and automation by changing government roles that give employees more time to focus on new complex tasks and advancing how, when, and where work gets done.*

Eggers and Turley (2019, p.4) identify nine significant trends that have three things in common, namely: (a) they all focus on government operations, not policy issues; (b) each trend has been tested and is now at a stage of penetration into many government administrations; and (c) all trends are global in scope, occurring in developing and developed nations. A discussion of each of these nine key trends in Public Service reform is provided below.

12.6.2.1 AI-Augmented Government

Eggers and Beyer (2019, p.9) argue that the way governments react to AI, both as a regulator and as a user, will affect societies and geopolitics for many years in the future. To some extent this development has been addressed at *Prediction-03* when discussing Global Technological Developments. Eggers and Beyer (2019) contend that since AI requires volumes of data, it is likely that it will work well for government, since governments tend to have volumes of data. They identified more than 25 countries that have already developed national AI strategies. For instance, they cite that the UK government initiated the AI Sector Deal in May 2018, which has the objective of leveraging government-industry partnerships for a wider adoption of AI. Other examples cited are related to Sweden's national approach for AI that focuses on developing standards and principles governing AI, whilst Estonia has developed an AI action plan that will include ethical implications, potential economic incentives, and priority areas for pilot programs (Eggers & Beyer, 2019, p.10). The Malta Government is in the final stages of releasing its National AI Strategy that has an ambitious objective of placing Malta amongst the top 10 nations for managing and regulating AI related matters. Eggers and Beyer (2019, p.12) maintain that the growth rate for AI spending in central governments globally up to

2022 is estimated to be approximately 44 percent, which is faster than spending in personal and consumer services. However, they argue that progress in AI-augmented government will depend on getting the government workforce ready for the AI era; controlling the growing complexity of AI technologies; providing adequate funding for AI technologies; and resolving the growing concerns over algorithmic risk, black box and bias.

Prediction-13 *The trend towards AI-augmented government in terms of spending is likely to be faster than spending in personal and consumer services (also see Prediction-03).*

12.6.2.2 Digital Citizen: Improving End-to-End Public Service Delivery via a Unique Digital Identity

Hutchinson et al. (2019, p.17) claim that for decades, governments have depended on a sizeable mix of systems that identify and manage people, using assorted methods, such as passwords, smart cards and biometrics; moreover, in developing countries over a billion persons worldwide have no formal way of substantiating their identity. Eggers and Turley (2019) maintain that unique digital identifiers may be a way for achieving integrated data and a seamless citizen experience, enabling a huge increase in service quality, immense efficiency gains, and a sustainable move to a digital delivery model. Hutchinson et al. (2019, p.17) argue that a unique digital identity for citizens may assist to drive financial and social inclusion by providing citizens access to health care, education, and other government benefit programs. They cite Estonia as having an advanced model, where Estonia's digital infrastructure enables every part of the government to easily identify citizens and offer services more efficiently. They maintain that the Once Only Principle is adhered to so that basic citizen information is entered just once and shared across agencies, with the result that an Estonian citizen preparing a tax return has a pre-populated tax form, rather than a blank slate. They argue that Estonia's model is so advanced that Estonians can vote online, access their e-health records, and conduct just about every government transaction online (barring marriage, divorce and real-estate transactions); they even allow citizens of other countries to become an 'e-resident' of the country, thus making it easier for them to do business in Estonia.

Hutchinson et al. (2019, p.20) maintain that 24 of 28 EU member countries have already begun implementing the Once-Only initiative, which is expected to save around 855,000 hours for citizens and 11 billion Euros for businesses annually, and that Estonia's use of digital signatures helped achieve 2 percent in annual GDP savings. However, they also identified two major risk factors, related to the growing risk of state surveillance, and cyber-security and privacy concerns.

Prediction-14 *The trend towards improving end-to-end public service delivery via a unique digital identity has commenced and will continue to disperse in the public sector due to the maturity of digital authentication technologies in the private sector.*

12.6.2.3 Nudging for Good – Using Behavioural Science to Improve Government Outcomes

Shah et al. (2019, p.25) contend that better decisions may be made in situations where individuals have unbounded cognitive abilities and no self-control problems, if the choice environments are design in ways that work in harmony with human psychology. They argue that as the field of behavioural economics advances, our understanding of how people make choices, 'nudging' is replacing incentives and punishments. For example, if we know our neighbours are recycling, then we are more likely to recycle. Shah et al. (2019, p.26) explain that in 2010, the United Kingdom's Behavioural Insights Team became the first governmental 'nudge unit' to study and harness behavioural patterns for more informed policymaking and improved government services. They argue that since then, there has been an abundance of both formal and informal nudge groups within government, as hundreds of countries, states, and cities have applied the concepts of nudge thinking to improve outcomes. They claim that recent years have seen nudges develop from something that is unique to being a commonly applied approach due to the creation of hundreds of government nudge units and their notable outcomes. They claim that nudges have increased tax compliance in the United Kingdom and the United States; reduced littering in Scotland; encouraged citizens to save more for their retirement in Oregon; and more businesses to comply with regulations in Ontario, Canada. Shah et al. (2019) maintain that nudge units have been established in 200 governments worldwide, but there are still a huge number of untapped opportunities.

Prediction-15 *Using behavioural science ('nudging') to improve government outcomes is likely to expand in intensity and spread within governments at every level (federal, state and local).*

12.6.2.4 The Rise of Data and AI Ethics: Managing the Ethical Complexities of the Age of Big Data

Information is power, and power can be used for good or ill (Eggers & Turley, 2019, p.4). Eggers and Turley (2019, p.4) declare that governments will need to address the data ethics issue from two perspectives, that as an 'owner' and custodian of considerable volume of data, and as a national regulator of corporate data use. It is argued that as technology gathers data with intelligence and therefore increases its knowledge about individuals and entities, it must be ensured that issues of privacy, equity, and transparency are addressed to protect individuals and entities in the process. To some extent this issue has been addressed at *Prediction-01 and Prediction-03* when discussing Ethical responsibilities related to technological change under the heading of Global Technological Developments. Dalmia and Schatsky (2019, p.33) argue that whole concept related to data and AI ethics has highlighted the escalating role and importance of this issue to the daily lives of individuals, businesses and governments.

A combination of technologies, such as IoT and associated sensors, mobile devices, image identification systems, analytics and AI have the ability and capacity to monitor, trace and keep track of people every minute of their daily lives. Dalmia and Schatsky (2019, p.33) contend that as AI systems develop and can decide on more situations, AI ethics becomes even more important and relevant to public policy. As an example, they cite a situation of a self-driving car when faced by a perilous circumstance: should the self-driving car choose a course of action that mitigates the risk to the passengers or to the pedestrian, even if the pedestrian is at fault? Hence, they argue that data ethics is a complex issue that is not well articulated by existing legislation. Dalmia and Schatsky (2019, p.34) have examined the status of various actions taken by some countries related to data and AI ethics:

(a) *European Union*: The General Data Protection Regulation (GDPR) makes it mandatory for private and public entities to provide 'data protection by design' and 'data protection by default'.
(b) *Japan*: The Ministry of Internal Affairs and Communications initiated guidelines for AI research and development with the focus on protecting the interests of citizens by mitigating risks of AI systems.
(c) *United Kingdom*: The Centre for Data Ethics and Innovation has been instituted as an advisor to government on the application of AI and other technologies to benefit society.
(d) *Canada*: Government has released a decree on automated decision-making to ensure that decisions made by automated systems are interpretable, transparent and mitigate risk to Canadian citizens.
(e) *Singapore*: An advisory council has been established to advice on the responsible development and deployment of AI, particularly related to ethical application of AI and data.

As one may observe, the actions taken by various countries all aim to protect the citizen but there is still little legislative control of AI and Data concepts and associated applications. The reasons for this appear to be a lack of understanding of how these technologies work and the means to control and regulate them without stifling innovation that may be of great benefit to many countries.

Prediction-16 *It is likely that governments worldwide, individually and in a collaborative manner, will be establishing task forces and specialized ethics units to scrutinise algorithms for biases, and to make legislative proposals to control and regulate AI and Data exploitation (see also Prediction-01 and Prediction-03).*

12.6.2.5 Anticipatory Government – Preventing Problems Through Predictive Analytics

Perricos and Kapur (2019) maintain that data analytics, sensitivity analysis through scenario modelling, and simulations provide a means of examining and keeping in check concerns before they break out and become a serious problem. They claim that these types of preventive tools may be applied to a whole range of conditions, from highlighting possible fraud to revealing extensive overuse of opioid medications, both from medical prescriptions and from illegal sources (known as the opioid epidemic). Perricos and Kapur (2019, p.41) argue that governments, by analysing their voluminous data warehouses of structured and unstructured data and using data mining techniques to identify patterns, can anticipate latent problems. They contend that this allows governments to take proactive preventative action by allocating resources to address problems before they occur. For example, they cite the case of how the US Air Force is exploiting this approach to determine the period that an aircraft is likely to break down so that they may conduct the appropriate preventive maintenance, thus avoiding a breakdown and mitigating aircraft downtime and preventing major repair costs. Perricos and Kapur (2019, p.42) have identified the following examples of how this anticipative government approach is helping governments in their decision-making process:

(a) *Canada*: Revenue agency is applying predictive analytics to highlight likely tax evaders and enhance compliance.
(b) *United Kingdom*: Revenue and Customs Office is using predictive models to improve the precision of tax audits and expose tax avoiders.
(c) *China*: Integrated Joint Operations Platform utilises predictive technologies to predict potential instances of crime before being committed.
(d) *Singapore*: Civil Authority in partnership with the IATA (International Air Transport Association) is initiating a Global Safety Predictive Analytics Research Centre for revealing possible aviation risks.
(e) *Australia, Queensland*: Public hospitals are using a Patient Admission Prediction Tool to examine patient admission data to optimise patient flow rates.
(f) *New Zealand*: Ministry of Social Development initiated a predictive model to identify children that are at risk of abuse and mistreatment.

Perricos and Kapur (2019, p.45) argue that there is still a long way to go due to a general shortage of competent employees in government; concerns related to data privacy; concerns related to the complexity and openness of data; and the possibility of partiality of the algorithm (computer model).

Prediction-17 *Anticipatory government is likely to grow as governments worldwide recognise and harness the power of information and find new innovative ways of applying it (see also Prediction-09 and Prediction-12).*

12.6.2.6 Cloud as an Innovation Driver – The Basis for Employing Emerging Technologies in Government

Cloud computing has been used in the private sector for some years but there is still a long way to go before it becomes a standard for governments. Mariani et al. (2019) view cloud computing as a window of huge opportunities for governments, particularly in developing countries. Mariani et al. (2019, p.49), claim that the cloud has become the focus of attention worldwide because it is viewed not only as a cost saver but of adding greater value. They argue that the cloud is adding greater value because governments are progressively applying a combination of technologies that make use of AI, robotic process automation, IoT, and big data analytics. The cloud is viewed as resolving one of the greatest concerns faced by governments regarding the structure and management of data, particularly the common practice of having data silos. Mariani et al. (2019, p.49) contend that the cloud is an enabler of future innovations because it can facilitate the breakdown of data silos and thus help in the implementation of AI by linking various stakeholders and giving them the potential to access unlimited data. They maintain that the US federal government has adopted a new 'Cloud Smart' policy and both Bahrain and the United Kingdom have implemented cloud-first policies to stimulate innovation, improve responsiveness, and enhance service delivery for citizens.

In their research, Mariani et al. (2019, p.50) have also identified that the governments of Australia, Canada, Norway, Switzerland, India, New Zealand and Singapore amongst others have adopted a cloud strategy, with a number of these countries having Cloud-First policies. The reason for implementing Cloud-First policy varies from government to government. The government of India views the cloud as a means of hastening eServices delivery, faster way of developing and utilising applications, and optimising infrastructure cost; the Australian government sees it as way of implementing new platforms, enhancing services quickly, and mitigating maintenance; whilst the New Zealand government anticipates faster deployment of services, enhanced security, and the optimisation of cost. Mariani et al. (2019, p.53) identify four inhibitors to implement Cloud computing, namely, securing the appropriate funding for cloud migration; resolving mounting cyber-security concerns; many governments lack a cloud strategy, governance structures, and standardised cloud acquisition procedures; and divergent governmental (federal, state and local) and international regulations regarding privacy, data use and security, amongst others.

Prediction-18 *Cloud computing will likely to expand in usage as governments worldwide recognise its full potential. Cloud computing has the potential to facilitate the Collaborative Governments concept.*

12.6.2.7 Innovation Accelerators – Creating Safe Spaces for Government Innovation

Eggers and Turley (2019, p.5) argue that iterative, reality-tested, and safe experimentation is critical to innovation, in every government sector, from health care to financial systems. They maintain that accelerators, incubators, and government 'labs' are all part of an emerging trend that require regulatory sandboxes as a way to permit private innovations much greater flexibility within a restricted space. Henry et al. (2019, p.57), argue that a secure, entrepreneurial environment that permits and encourages risk-taking together with the process of learning from failure is essential to innovation, particularly when the innovation efforts are revolutionary. However, they contend that the more the innovation is transformative, the greater the likelihood that it will be viewed as a threat and therefore be opposed.

They further argue that this is especially applicable to government, where public funds are under closer scrutiny and failures are unacceptable, leading to a situation where risk taking is discouraged and innovation stifled. To overcome this risk-averse environment, public sector entities are setting-up formal innovation units that cautiously consider how to align their objectives, activities and supporting capabilities (Henry et al., 2019, p.57). They maintain that an innovation unit needs to be designed based on whether it is focused on getting its ideas from the internal or external environment or whether it is focused on developing solutions or driving innovation amongst various stakeholder groups. Henry et al. (2019, p.58) identify various initiatives taking place in various countries:

(a) **Canada**: Instituted the Impact and Innovation Unit that operates across departments to create and utilize better financing approaches, innovative partnership models and innovative systems to assess impact.
(b) **United Kingdom**: Established the Open Innovation Team to improve links with academics and make the most of their expertise to encourage innovation.
(c) **Denmark**: Instituted the National Centre for Public Sector Innovation that acts as hub for sharing knowledge with other stakeholders thus increasing the rate of innovation across the government.
(d) **Taiwan**: Initiated the Public Digital Innovation Space to encourage an open innovation methodology to policymaking by accessing the shared intelligence of citizens, academics and civil servants.
(e) **Singapore**: Created the Transformation Office and Innovation Lab that aims to disseminate the ethos of innovation across all public entities.

Malta, the smallest EU member state, established the Malta Life Sciences Park to provide an international centre of excellence facility for life sciences and information technology innovation. This centre of excellence was co-financed through the European Regional Development Fund and supported by Malta Enterprise. Malta Life Sciences Park is designed to promote research and development and to spur the growth of the life sciences sector in Malta, building on the base that the country developed in the pharmaceutical industry during the last decade. The Life Sciences Park, which is comprised of the Malta Life Sciences Centre and the Malta Digital Hub provides access to experienced and professional business, and financial advice, as well as assistance for internationalization.

Prediction-19 *The trend towards having innovation accelerators to create safe spaces for government innovation is likely to escalate at a fast rate in the coming years.*

12.6.2.8   Smart Government – Smart City Solutions for the Public Services Landscape

Eggers and Turley (2019) contend that governments will intensify their efforts to implement technology for serving citizens in a collaborative and inclusive approach to enhance the way people live. They argue that while cities were initially targeted to become smart cities, this trend has now expanded to regions, universities, and rural communities, amongst others. Sen et al. (2019) argue that what started with the idea of 'smart cities' by having integrated, connected and sustainable neighbourhoods, has now grown to include a multiplicity of 'smart' sphere of influence that includes all types of communities, such as university campuses, states and counties. They contend that these locations exploit technology for serving their citizens in a very all-inclusive way to improve various facets of public life, including their mobility, quality of life, security, education, economy and environment.

Sen et al. (2019) claim that the smart government concept has many potential benefits, including improved quality of life for those living within the smart zone, including their visitors; provides better economic competitiveness to attract industry and talent; and ensures environmental sustainability. However, for the concept to flourish it requires measures to mitigate the potential of a substantial cyber risk; ensure robust smart city governance, particularly data governance; secure sufficient funding and financing to initiate and sustain the concept; and ensure strong and visionary leadership.

Prediction-20 *The trend towards Smart government and smart city solutions for the public services landscape is likely to attract interest in the coming years, but general progress is likely to be slow due to the technical complexities, governance, substantial funding and lack of strong and visionary leadership.*

12.6.2.9   Citizen Experience in Government Takes Centre Stage – Treating Citizens like Customers to Drive Triple Value Impact

Eggers and Turley (2019, p.5) argue that governments need to recognise that 'one size fits all' is not a solution. They contend that governments need to establish and understand the needs of the individual to ensure that large public systems deliver services that meet these needs. They maintain that Customer Experience tools are available and can be effectively exploited to serve not only government's customers but also government employees, regulated entities and businesses. Chew et al. (2019, p. 73) argue that successful companies provide an exceptional customer experience (Cx) because they place the customers at the centre of everything they do, which in turn leads to improving overall performance. They argue that governments around the world are beginning to recognise the significance of Cx and some are allocating resources to improve the current status.

Chew et al. (2019, p. 73) claim that whilst the public sector has been striving to improve customer satisfaction over the years, these endeavours have met with resistance. However, they argue that contemporary advances in digital technologies, together with modern developments related to behavioural science, have enabled various governments to experiment and engage in Cx with added effort. They maintain that government leaders are progressively focusing on Cx as a core function of government since they view it as a means of enhancing customer satisfaction, improving efficiency, and strengthening mission-effectiveness. Chew et al. (2019, p. 73) assert that government agencies worldwide are accepting the concept of Cx, but are utilising different but highly complementary approaches that reflect different starting points, missions and challenges. For instance, they cite the Design for Europe programme that is cosponsored by the European Commission, which has the objective of elevating Cx by promoting design awareness and knowledge exchange. Another example that is cited is that of the United States, the Office of Management and Budget, which directed all executive branch agencies to incorporate Cx into their strategic decisions, culture and design of services.

Chew et al. (2019, p. 76) reveal that substantial progress is being made, for instance 18 out of 28 EU countries have government-funded national design centres for policy and service design; the United Kingdom's cross-government design community that works on human-centred design and user experience has more than 800 employees; and the US Office of Personnel Management, has trained more than 2000 government employees in human-centred design. However, this is viewed as only the beginning. They claim that Cx has several potential benefits, namely, encourages greater citizen trust; enhanced customer satisfaction; increased employee engagement; reduced costs; better efficiency; and enhanced mission focus. However, there are several associated risks that include the failure to sustain rising expectations; lack of funding to upgrade the necessary technology; difficulty of harmonising across silos and agencies; and delays in implementation because of repeated testing.

Prediction-21 *The trend towards citizen experience in government is likely to grow and is likely to be narrowly deployed in government.*

12.6.3 Summary of Identified Predictions Related to Worldwide Public Service Delivery

Table 12.1 provides a summary of all the identified predictions related to the worldwide public service delivery. Moreover, the above trends in public service delivery will invariably depend on international circumstances and developments.

Additionally, these trends are profoundly associated with current technology and therefore they are doable, and the likelihood of further technological developments will make it even more probable that the identified trend in public service delivery will come about at a much more feasible effort. However, for these predictions to come about, each country must have strong, capable and visionary leaders that are able to push these Public Service reforms forward.

Table 12.1   Identified predictions related to worldwide public service delivery

01	Governments from various countries will cooperate closely and take more assertive action to control cyber space against the various abuses generated through the internet.
02	Governments from various countries with participation of trade and labour unions will regulate 'disruptive technology' to strengthen and sustain family friendly measures.
03	The application of Analytics and Artificial Intelligence (AI) will become the norm for governments from various countries in resolving an assortment of concerns. A key issue that will need to be confronted is which tasks will be entrusted to machines.
04	ICT will remain the most significant driving force in the globalisation process. Governments will further regulate this industry to ensure that connectivity will remain the major thrust in the provision of services at cheaper and affordable rates.
05	The growth of IoT (internet of things) will exert pressure on the communications industry to break the current 5G transmission speed limit.
06	The demand for smart mobiles will likely continue to grow since it is and will probably remain the easiest and cheapest method of being connected to cyberspace. Hence, digital illiteracy will be significantly reduced because of this phenomena resulting in a growth in the penetration rate of eServices.
07	As blockchain technology matures and governments realise its advantages, particularly in relation to security and transparency, its use will grow and expand to enable networked Public Services on a very large scale.
08	Government employees will be able to access their departmental systems and perform their daily work through their mobile.
09	Public service delivery to citizens, civil society and businesses will be dominated by mobile apps that specifically cater for a diverse range of the individuals' personal needs.
10	Public service entities will progressively embrace information resource management concepts, data warehousing and data mining techniques, by making use of an appropriate business intelligence engine for complex decision making.
11	Social media to be exploited for improving citizen's engagement for initiating, defining and formulating policies to encourage and improve participative government (citizens) and management (government employees) through collaborative governance.
12	The trend known as Future of Government Work is likely to increase the convergence of the government workforce and automation by changing government roles that give employees more time to focus on new complex tasks and advancing how, when and where work gets done.
13	The trend towards AI-augmented government in terms of spending is likely to be faster than spending in personal and consumer services (see also Prediction-03).
14	The trend towards improving end-to-end public service delivery via a unique digital identity has commenced and will continue to disperse in the public sector due to the maturity of digital authentication technologies in the private sector.
15	Using behavioural science ('nudging') to improve government outcomes is likely to expand in intensity and spread within governments at every level.
16	Governments individually and in a collaborative manner, will be establishing task forces and specialized ethics units to scrutinise algorithms for biases, and to make legislative proposals to control/regulate AI and Data exploitation (see Prediction-01 and 03).
17	Anticipatory government will grow as governments recognise and harness the power of information and find new innovative ways of applying it (see Prediction-09 and 12).
18	Cloud computing will expand in usage as governments recognise its full potential. Cloud computing has the potential to facilitate the Collaborative Governments concept.

(continued)

Table 12.1 (continued)

19	The trend towards having innovation accelerators to create safe spaces for government innovation is likely to escalate at a fast rate in the coming years.
20	The trend towards Smart government and smart city solutions for the Public Services landscape is likely to attract interest in the coming years, but general progress is likely to be slow due to the technical complexities, governance, substantial funding and lack of strong and visionary leadership.
21	The trend towards citizen experience in government is likely to grow and is likely to be narrowly deployed in government.

12.7   Conclusion

UNDP (2015) argues that most reforms in government are only partially successful not because, once implemented, they yield unsatisfactory outcomes, but because they never get past the implementation stage at all. They contend that learning lessons from experience, and applying them, is particularly essential. They provide some broad lessons from UNDP's experience, as they emerge from evaluations of past UNDP undertakings (UNDP, 2015, p.24):

(a) Keep the scope of change well-focussed and set realistic and well-defined targets. Avoid the temptation to address too many reform objectives simultaneously, since an incremental approach to reform, if sustained for long enough, also brings about radical transformations.

(b) Recognize that Public Administration Reform takes time. Governments need assistance in developing a long-term vision.

(c) Ensure there is full understanding of the reforms and support for them, not only at the level of leadership, but also at the level of line management and civil servants as a whole, and the public. Frank commitment or ownership of a project from its inception is essential.

(d) Publicizing good results and providing incentives and awards to successful implementers and users of the new systems, will encourage others to participate. This will also create a positive change in attitudes towards reform and mitigate resistance and fear of change.

(e) Ensure there is continued political will and support throughout all phases of public administration reform. Reform requires firm leadership and is a long-term process that requires commitment and sustained effort throughout the process. It is important that accountability mechanisms are in place before you consider mobilising pressure from below.

Thomas L. Friedman, author of 'The World Is Flat' used the book title as a metaphor for viewing the world as a level playing field in terms of conducting business and serving customers, wherein all competitors have an equal opportunity through the application of information technology, be they governments or private sector entities. Information technology has continued and will continue to provide opportunities for governments to initiate Public Service reforms, with the intention of improving the living standards of its citizens, in a variety of sectors be they general service, commerce, education, environment, health and safety, amongst so many others. Information technology has indeed paved the way to making the world flat in terms of creating a friendly and effective environment, where all the diverse stakeholders conduct their personal and business affairs. In such a scenario, governments are under unrelenting pressure to provide a much better service to their customers, be they the individual citizens, civil society and businesses, amongst others. Public service reforms and the systems they generate as a platform for service delivery are full of challenges and require sustained commitment from all levels of the Public Service. Public Service employees need to look for new ways of implementing change by taking advantage of the opportunities that technology provides in the day-to-day operations of government and its decision-making process. However, the most important factor for change to occur is to have strong, capable and above all visionary leadership. Visionary leaders see things and make sense of them and are not afraid to take the plunge.

References

Advisory Group on Reform of Australian Government Administration. (2010). *Ahead of the game: Blueprint for the reform of Australian government administration.* Australian Government Department of the Prime Minister and Cabinet.

Bouckaert, G., & Jann, W. (2017). Current and future trends in european public sector research. In S. Kuhlmann & O. Schwab (Eds.), *Starke Kommunen – wirksame Verwaltung.* Stadtforschung aktuell. Springer VS.

Building Bridges Initiative. (2020). *Advancing partnerships. Improving lives.* Available from: https://buildingbridges4youth.org/. Accessed on 10 July 2020.

Bush G. W. (2002). *The president's management agenda: fiscal year 2002.* Available from: https://georgewbush-whitehouse.archives.gov/omb/budget/fy2002/mgmt.pdf. Accessed on 11 July 2020.

Camilleri, E. (2011). *Project success: Critical factors and behaviours.* Gower.

Camilleri, E. (2019). *Information systems strategic planning for public service delivery in the digital era.* IGI Global.

Chew, B., Rae, J., Manstof, J., and Degnegaard, S. (2019). Citizen experience in government takes center stage: Treating citizens like customers to drive triple value impact. Deloitte Insights: A Report from the Deloitte Centre for Government Insights.

Cobert, B. F. (2017). U.S. Office of Personnel Management Cabinet Exit Memo. Available at: https://chcoc.gov/content/us-office-personnel-management-cabinet-exit-memo. Accessed on 11 July 2020.

Colgan, A., Rochford, S., & Burke, K. (2016). *Implementing public service reform – Messages from the literature.* Centre for Effective Services.

Dalmia, N., &Schatsky, D. (2019). *The rise of data and AI ethics: Managing the ethical complexities of the age of big data.* Deloitte Insights, A Report from the Deloitte Centre for Government Insights.

CEF Digital. (2020). *Once only principle: Reduce administrative burden for individuals and businesses.* https://ec.europa.eu/cefdigital/wiki/display/CEFDIGITAL/Once+Only+Principle. Accessed on 10 July 2020.

Eggers, W., & Beyer, T. (2019). *AI-augmented government: Climbing the AI maturity curve.* Deloitte Insights: A Report from the Deloitte Centre for Government Insights.

Eggers, W., & Turley, M. (2019). *What are the most transformational trends in government today?* Deloitte Insights: A Report from the Deloitte Centre for Government Insights.

European Commission. (2015). *Inside Look into Public Service Reform across Europe.* Published on Horizon 2020. Available at https://ec.europa.eu/programmes/horizon2020/en/news/inside-look-public-sector-reform-across-europe. Accessed on 13 July 2020.

Evens, Bill (2018). Ethics: Don't be derailed by the trolley problem. *IT Now, BCS, the Chartered Institute of IT.*

Flynn, N. (2001). Moving to outcome budgeting. Paper commissioned for the Finance Committee by the Scottish Parliament Research and Information Group. Available at: https://archive.parliament.scot/business/committees/historic/finance/reports-02/fir02-mob-02.htm. Accessed on 11 July 2020.

Friederich, C. J. (1940). Public administration and the nature of administrative responsibility. Public Policy: A Yearbook of the Graduate.

Ganapati, S. (2015). Using mobile apps in government. IBM Centre for the Business of Government.

Garvey, G. (1995). False promises: The NPR in historical perspective. In D. F. Kettl & J. J. DiIulio (Eds.), *Inside the reinvention machine: appraising governmental reform.* The Brookings Institution.

Gore A. (1997). *A brief history of the national performance review.* Available from: https://govinfo.library.unt.edu/npr/library/papers/bkgrd/brief.html. Accessed on 10 July 2020.

Government of Ireland. (2017). *Our public service 2020: Development and innovation december 2017.* Prepared by the Department of Public Expenditure and Reform. Available at: https://www.ops2020.gov.ie/app/themes/ops2020/dist/pdfs/Our-Public-Service-2020-WEB.pdf. Accessed on 13 July 2020.

Grzymala-Busse, A. (2017). *A tale of two illiberalisms: Why is poland failing where hungary succeeded?* Available at: https://theglobalobservatory.org/2017/08/poland-hungary-authoritarianism-fidesz-pis/. Accessed: 13 July 2020.

Guttal, S. (2010). Globalisation. *Journal Development in Practice, 17(4–5), 523–531.* Available from: https://www.tandfonline.com/doi/abs/10.1080/09614520701469492. Accessed on 9 July 2020.

Helfrich, D. (2019). *Five top trends for the public sector in 2019.* Available at: https://deloitte.wsj.com/cfo/2019/02/07/five-top-trends-for-the-public-sector-in-2019/. Accessed on 15 July 2020.

Henry, N., Holden, A., & Eggers, W. (2019). *Innovation accelerators: Creating safe spaces for government innovation.* Deloitte Insights: A Report from the Deloitte Centre for Government Insights.

Hutchinson, J., Bellman, J., & Hurst. S. (2019). *Digital citizen: Improving end-to-end public service delivery via a unique digital identity.* Deloitte Insights: A Report from the Deloitte Centre for Government Insights.

Jose, T. (2016). *What is outcome budgeting?* Available from: https://www.indianeconomy.net/splclassroom/what-is-outcome-budgeting/. Accessed on 10 July 2020.

Katz, E. (2016). *Major agency reforms in obama's budget.* Available from: https://www.govexec.com/management/2016/02/11-major-agency-reforms-obamas-budget/125894/. Accessed on 10 July 2020.

Katz, E. (2020). *11 major agency reforms in trump's 2021 budget.* Available from: https://www.govexec.com/management/2020/02/11-major-agency-reforms-trumps-2021-budget/163049/. Accessed on 13 July 2020.

Kettl, D. F. (2000). *The global public management revolution: A report on the transformation of governance.* The Brookings Institution.

Korte, K. (2019). *Hire the best and fire the worst': Trump proposes biggest civil service change in 40 years.* Available at: https://eu.usatoday.com/story/news/politics/2018/02/09/hire-best-and-fire-worst-trump-proposes-biggest-civil-service-change-40-years/315981002/. Accessed on 13 July 2020.

Light, P. C. (1997). *The tides of reform: Making government work, 1945–1995.* Yale University Press.

Lynch, M. (2014). *The geographer's craft project*. Department of Geography, University of Texas at Austin.

Lynn, L. E. (2003). *Recent trends in public management*. Conference paper delivered at the international seminar on public management organized by the centre for strategy and evaluation, Institute for Social Sciences, Faculty of Social Sciences, University of Ljubljana.

Mariani, J., Bourgeois, D., Taillon, J., & Appleton-Norman, K. (2019). Cloud as innovation driver: The foundation for employing emerging technologies in government. Deloitte Insights: A Report from the Deloitte Centre for Government Insights.

Martinho-Truswell, E. (2018). *How AI could help the public sector*. Harvard Business Review, January 2018.

Baker McKenzie. (2018). *New age consumerism and the consumer power-shift*. Available from: https://www.bakermckenzie.com/en/insight/publications/2018/12/new-age-consumerism-power-shift. Accessed on 8 July 2020.

Miller, B. (2017). *Automation beyond the physical: ai in the public sector*. Available at http://www.govtech.com/civic/GT-September-Automation-Beyond-the-Physical-AI-in-the-Public-Sector.html. Accessed on 18 July 2020.

Organization for Economic Cooperation and Development (OECD). (1995). *Governance in transition: Public management reform in OECD countries*. OECD.

Perricos, C., & Kapur, V. (2019). *Anticipatory government: Preempting problems through predictive analytics*. A Report from the Deloitte Centre for Government Insights.

Pollitt, C. (2000). Is the emperor in his underwear? An analysis of the impacts of public management reform. *Public Management, 2*(2), 181–199.

Price, N. (2017). *Public service in the age of trump*. Available at: https://democracyjournal.org/arguments/public-service-in-the-age-of-trump/. Accessed on 13 July 2020.

Robertson Foundation for Government. (2020). Government for the future: A view of things to come, drawing on perspectives of things past. IBM Center for the business of government website. Available at https://rfg.org/news/government-future-view-things-come-drawing-perspectives-things-past. Accessed on 12 July 2020.

Runciman, B. (2018). When ethics and IT collide. IT Now, BCS, the Chartered Institute of IT.

Sen, R., Antunes, M. E., & Kelkar, M. (2019). Smart government: Smart city solutions for the public services landscape. Deloitte Insights: A Report from the Deloitte Centre for Government Insights.

Shah, S., O'Leary, J., Guszcza, J., & Howe, J. (2019). Nudging for good: Using behavioral science to improve government outcomes. Deloitte Insights: A Report from the Deloitte Centre for Government Insights.

The Guardian. (2017). *The Guardian view on Poland and Hungary: heading the wrong way*. Available at https://www.theguardian.com/commentisfree/2017/jul/18/the-guardian-view-on-poland-and-hungary-heading-the-wrong-way. Accessed 13 July 2020.

The Independent. (2020). *Venice Commission: PM hails 'important step in evolution of Maltese democracy*. Available at https://www.independent.com.mt/articles/2020-06-19/local-news/Venice-Commission-PM-hails-important-step-in-evolution-of-Maltese-democracy-6736224354. Accessed on 13 July 2020.

Thompson, J. R. (2000). Reinventing as reform: Assessing the national performance review. *Public Administration Review, 60*(6), 508–521.

UNDP. (2015). Public administration reform: Practice note. Available at: https://www.undp.org/content/undp/en/home/librarypage/capacity-building/public-administration-reform-practice-note.html. Accessed on 14 July 2020.

WU GTPC (2017). *Blockchain 101 For Governments*. WU Global Tax Policy Center (WU GTPC) at the Institute for Austrian and International Tax Law of Vienna University of Business and Economics. WU, Wirtschaftsuniversität Wien.

Yochelson, J. (2017). *The future of public service under Trump*. Available at: https://www.sandiegouniontribune.com/opinion/commentary/sd-utbg-public-service-trump-20170126-story.html. Accessed on 13 July 2020.

Index

9 783030 743598